A Bibliography of Drug Abuse:
Supplement 1977-1980

A Bibliography of Drug Abuse

Supplement 1977-1980

by
Theodora Andrews
Professor of Library Science
Pharmacy, Nursing, and Health Science Librarian
Purdue University

Libraries Unlimited, Inc.   **Littleton, Colorado**

1981

LIBRARIES UNLIMITED, INC.
P.O. Box 263
Littleton, Colorado 80160

Library of Congress Cataloging in Publication Data

Andrews, Theodora.
    A bibliography of drug abuse. Supplement, 1977.

    Includes indexes.
    1. Drug abuse--Bibliography. 2. Alcoholism--
Bibliography. 3. Tobacco habit--Bibliography.
I. Andrews, Theodora. A bibliography of drug
abuse, including alcohol and tobacco. II. Title.
[DNLM: 1. Alcoholism--Abstracts. 2. Substance abuse
--Abstracts. 3. Substance dependence--Abstracts.
4. Tobacco use disorder--Abstracts. ZWM 270 A571b
1977 suppl. 1977-1980]
Z7164.N17A52 Suppl [HV5801] 016.3622'9 81-8194
ISBN 0-87287-252-1   AACR2

Libraries Unlimited books are bound with Type II nonwoven material that meets and
exceeds National Association of State Textbook Administrators' Type II nonwoven
material specifications Class A through E.

TABLE OF CONTENTS

Source Material by Subject Area (cont'd)

INTRODUCTION

The main volume of this publication, *Bibliography of Drug Abuse, Including Alcohol and Tobacco* (Libraries Unlimited, 1977), was well-received, not only in library-oriented review journals, but also in publications for the scientific and pharmaceutical professions. The interest those reviews reflect, coupled with the increasing number of publications appearing each year in the field of drug abuse (now frequently called "substance abuse"), has prompted the author to provide this supplement in order that bibliographic information in this culturally significant and controversial field remain up to date. The primary purpose of the new work is similar to that of the original bibliography—to provide guidance for reference services in all types of libraries, and to help researchers, practitioners, educators, and academic, public, and special librarians to select material from the large number of titles offered.

As compared to the 725 items annotated in the retrospective main bibliography, the supplement includes entries for 741 additional works, cutting across many subject areas. Most of these titles have been published since 1976, but a few older ones that were omitted from the main volume have also been listed here.

As in the original bibliography, each section of this volume is preceded by a few remarks that attempt to characterize the literature of that section. The supplement remains limited to English-language literature (although a few translations have been included). But, representative titles at all levels have been listed on virtually every aspect of this subject to ensure that the two volumes remain useful to many groups concerned with substance abuse—parents, community workers, teachers, treatment program directors, physicians and other health professionals, law enforcement officers, lawyers, social workers, researchers, and, of course, the victims themselves.

The nature of drug abuse literature has changed since the mid-1970s, reflecting recent trends—some for the better, some for the worse. For instance, more publications concerning alcohol and tobacco are listed here than in the earlier work, which is evidence of one shift of emphasis in drug abuse concerns. In addition, a new section on self-help materials has been added, because a number of new publications offer this kind of assistance in dealing with addiction and dependency. Growing emphasis is being placed on the problems of special groups other than young people, and a section has been added to treat works covering dependency problems of such groups as the elderly, women, writers, physicians, and minorities.

Reference works and treatises make up the bulk of the materials reviewed, although a section on periodicals has been provided and a few pamphlets and annuals are included. Indexing and abstracting tools, bibliographies, other reference works, and periodicals have been grouped in part I; the treatises, in part II. No audiovisual materials have been listed.

The drug scene has changed since the earlier bibliography was compiled, but it has not improved. The excesses of the late-1960s sparked an interest in drug use of all kinds, including abuse of such legal drugs as alcohol and the relatively harmless tobacco. More recently, a general decline in public concern with drug abuse has resulted in a decline in the number of sensational works. At the same time, recognition of the abuse of prescription drugs and solvents has steadily increased.

A point of view expressed by some is that we must learn to live with drug abuse and accept it, an attitude that indicates many have given up on solving the problem. On the other hand, enormous emphasis has been placed on treatment of substance abuse victims, as the number of publications in this area shows. Groups such as Alcoholics Anonymous take the view that abusers must be helped or they will perish, and the federal government has produced large amounts of material designed to assist in almost every phase of treatment and research efforts. A wide range of treatment methods *has* been applied, but unfortunately, results remain disappointing, although slow progress may be underway. The government also produces statistical publications reporting on such matters as incidence, prevalence, and epidemiology of drug use. Illicit drug use *is* growing, but the rate of growth has slowed.

Drug abuse education efforts aimed at the young have not been notably successful, and interest in the matter is waning. A prevailing view has been that one must not tell young people not to use drugs and alcohol because in their immaturity they will be more likely to do so. Comments are found in some works to the effect that one must deal with the drug matter in a "sane and workable way," (whatever that may imply). "Scare tactics" must not be employed. Publications do continue to appear emphasizing the undesirable physical and psychological effects of drugs, but neither approach has been found satisfactory.

There are also a great many new materials dealing with alcoholism — the foremost drug abuse problem. Several historical accounts of Prohibition have appeared, evidence of growing concern over how best to approach the drinking problem. In regard to control of other substances, particularly marijuana, there was an earlier trend toward lessening controls. However, as a result of growing evidence of the deleterious effects of this drug, that view has changed. There has been concern that harsh laws make matters worse, but in actuality, such laws have seldom been enforced. Emphasis has more often been on treatment and assistance to the abuser.

In the late 1960s, most books that reported on drug abuse studies ended with an appeal for "more research." Materials available in the late 1970s show that a great deal has been done in the past decade, much of it of significance. Findings indicate that most substances commonly abused are more harmful than was previously supposed, a natural consequence, probably, of the concentrated study of toxic substances' effects on the body. Possibly, further research in this area will reveal more about the addiction process and how it can be controlled.

A few new titles regarding the use of hallucinogenic substances in religious rites and rituals in other cultures have appeared in recent years. Quite a few books have also been published on growing hallucinogenic plants — mushroom species particularly. Further, several of the authors (and publishers) of these books are digressing into the "natural" foods and herbal medicine field, where considerable quackery abounds. In addition, while concern about amphetamine use of phencyclidine (angel dust), an extremely dangerous substance, is increasing.

Other trends of concern include polydrug use (the use of a variety of substances at the same time), drug use and driving, and the fact that street marijuana is increasing in potency. The physiological effects of marijuana are under intensive study, and the drug's therapeutic potential is being considered. From the user's perspective, several books on how to grow more potent varieties of the plant under varying conditions have been published recently. Finally, cocaine use is on the rise, particularly among the affluent user.

All of these trends are reflected in the literature represented in this volume. It is hoped that these comments and the reviews of the titles listed below will provide a view of the current substance abuse problems and assist the reader in understanding them.

Theodora Andrews

PART I

GENERAL REFERENCE SOURCES

1 _____

BIBLIOGRAPHIES, INDEXES, AND ABSTRACTS

There are a number of well-known index and/or abstract publications available that cover subject areas broader than drug abuse alone but that include references to such material. These are not listed in this bibliography because they are discussed in the main volume of this title *A Bibliography of Drug Abuse* (1977).

Listed here are several somewhat general bibliographies on drug abuse, such as Triche: *Drug Abuse Bibliography for 1976* (entry 14); Charles and Feldman: *Drugs: A Multimedia Source-Book for Children and Young Adults* (entry 5); and Fazey: *The Aetiology of Psychoactive Substance Use* (entry 7). Many other bibliographies listed, such as Barnes: *Drug Use and Driving* (entry 2); Busse, Mullog, and Weise: *Disulfiram in the Treatment of Alcoholism* (entry 4); and Chrusciel and Chrusciel: *Selected Bibliography on Detection of Dependence-Producing Drugs in Body Fluids* (entry 6), cover special aspects of drug abuse. In addition, many of the publications deal with the use of a particular drug, e.g., tobacco, cocaine, alcohol, and marijuana.

There are several titles that list audiovisual materials.

1.   Abel, Ernest L., comp. **A Comprehensive Guide to the Cannabis Literature**. Westport, CT: Greenwood Press, 1979. 699p. index. $37.50. LC 78-20014. ISBN 0-313-20721-6.

The literature covered in this bibliography was published before 1978 and deals with the plant *cannabis sativa L.* in virtually all of its aspects: psychotomimetic properties, industrial usage, cultivation, history, and legal status. The coverage is quite comprehensive, including materials from both popular and scholarly books and periodicals. In addition, some foreign language citations have been included, translated into English. No items from newspapers and newsletters have been listed.

The 8,177 entries are arranged alphabetically by senior author in one sequence, except for a supplementary addendum containing unintentionally omitted items and those published after the main bibliography was compiled. The latter is arranged in a separate alphabetical sequence. The compiler has supplied an introductory essay of about 20 pages which covers historical background, chemistry, analysis, pharmacology, physiological effects, therapeutic uses, prevalence, behavioral effects, and psychiatric considerations. A list of abbreviations of journals cited has been provided.

There are no annotations. Although there is a subject index, there is no access by author except through the senior author. A limited spot check of a few entries showed an unusually high number of errors in references.

2.   Barnes, T. H., comp.; assisted by S. F. Price. **Drug Use and Driving**. R. J. Hall, series editor. Toronto: Addiction Research Foundation, 1974. 106p. index. (Addiction Research Foundation Bibliographic Series, No. 7.) $4.50pa.

Subtitled "A bibliography of the scientific literature on the effects of drugs other than ethanol on driving or simulated driving of automobiles, piloting and motor performance," this book does not include alcohol literature, because it has been covered in other bibliographies. Experimental and clinical research studies, review articles, and general discussions of the topic have been included.

References are listed alphabetically by the name of the first author. Complete bibliographic information is provided, and the number of references cited is stated. Foreign-language titles are given in the original language followed by the English translation. Following each reference is a list of key word index terms that provide subject information. There are no annotations, however. Author, key word, and drug name indexes have been supplied.

The articles listed cover the period of the mid-1950s to 1973, although some older materials are included.

3.   **BioResearch Today: Addiction**. Philadelphia, PA: BioSciences Information Service, 1972- . Monthly.

This title is one of a group of 14 special abstract journals that cover specific research topics and that are subsets of *Biological Abstracts*. Each issue contains 100-250 abstracts. The scope of coverage includes studies on chemicals and medicinals that have addictive traits (e.g., alcohol, tobacco, opiates, hallucinogenic agents, etc.). Papers covering extraction, quantitation, metabolism, mechanisms of action, psycho- and neuropharmacologic aspects, psychiatric effects, toxicity, and other factors are abstracted.

The publication is of particular value for the researcher who is attempting to keep up.

4.   Busse, S., C. T. Mulloy, and C. E. Weise, comps. **Disulfiram in the Treatment of Alcoholism: An Annotated Bibliography**. Compiled at the Addiction Research Foundation Library with the assistance of C. M. Chamberlain and D. R. Tetera. Toronto: Addiction Research Foundation, 1978. 346p. index. (Addiction Research Foundation Bibliographic Series, No. 14.) $8.00pa. LC 79-670126. ISBN 0-88868-030-9.

In 1948 it was discovered that unpleasant symptoms were experienced by those who used alcohol and took the drug disulfiram. Since then it has been used in treatment of alcoholism. This bibliography is a compilation of 596 citations to research studies, clinical reports, case studies, review articles, and letters to the editor published between 1948 and 1977. About half the literature is in a language other than English, but English abstracts have been provided. The citations are arranged alphabetically by author. Included is a complete reference, with an abstract and index terms. Author and key word indexes are provided.

5.   Charles, Sharon Ashenbrenner, and Sari Feldman. **Drugs: A Multimedia Sourcebook for Children and Young Adults**. Santa Barbara, CA: ABC-Clio Press; New York: Neal-Schuman Publishers, 1980. 200p. index. (Selection Guide Series, No. 4.) $16.50. LC 79-13322. ISBN 0-87436-281-4.

The authors of this work, who are public librarians, say they wrote the guide for two reasons: there is no evaluative listing of drug education material for the young adult, and "works are often judgmental, inaccurate, and insensitive to the needs of young adults." It is presumed, evidently, that material made available to young people should be carefully screened, a viewpoint some would challenge, although most recognize that it is difficult to handle drug education for the young.

The material is presented in three sections. Part 1, which reviews print materials, is divided into general nonfiction, personal narratives, and fiction. Part 2, which covers nonprint material, is divided by type of material: 16mm films and videocassettes, audiocassettes and discs, filmstrips and sound/slide sets, and transparencies and slides. Parts 1 and 2 are of about equal length. Part 3, a short section, "Further Sources of Information," includes a list or agencies involved with drug abuse, a recommended reading list, and a directory of publishers and distributors.

The book is nicely produced and is useful to a limited extent. However, this reviewer has serious reservations about the evaluations of the material reviewed. There is a marked tendency to speak positively about works that accept, if not encourage, drug use. Works that bring out the seriousness of the drug problem and contain hard scientific evidence about deleterious effects of drug abuse are usually dismissed as not being suitable for young adults. Works by some of the most respected scientists in the field are negatively reviewed.

Attitudes about the use of drugs have changed a good deal since the 1960s as evidence of their harmful physiological effects has accumulated. The recent literature on drug abuse reflects this to a considerable extent. The authors of this book are more in tune with the earlier era.

6.   Chrusciel, T. L., and M. Chrusciel, comps. **Selected Bibliography on Detection of Dependence-Producing Drugs in Body Fluids**. Geneva: World Health Organization, 1975. 67p. (WHO Offset Publication, No. 17.) $6.00. ISBN 92-4-052004-X.

This comprehensive bibliography includes unannotated references to scientific literature and bibliographic compilations published or prepared from about 1969 to 1974. A few older works have been included if still relevant. Most of the materials referred to are periodical articles, but some books, conference proceedings, and reports have also been included. The references relate directly to the detection of dependence-producing drugs in body fluids or to technical problems connected with analytical methods employed.

Material is arranged alphabetically by author under the following headings: 1) Methods of detection, 2) Detection of opiates and synthetic narcotic drugs, 3) Detection of opiate antagonists, 4) Amphetamines and amphetamine-like substances, 5) Cocaine, 6) Ephedrine, 7) Barbiturates, 8) Other sedative and hypnotic drugs, 9) Cannabis, 10) Hallucinogens, and 11) Volatile substances.

7.   Fazey, C. **The Aetiology of Psychoactive Substance Use: A Report and Critically Annotated Bibliography on Research into the Aetiology of Alcohol, Nicotine, Opiate and Other Psychoactive Substance Use**. Paris: Unesco; distr., New York: Unipub, 1977. 226p. index. $15.75pa. ISBN 92-3-101508-7.

The bibliography section of this work appears to be the first published bibliography on the causes or motivation for psychoactive drug use. Forming the bulk of the publication, it is presented in two parts. The first is made up of critically annotated references; the second is an unannotated list. Preceding the bibliography is a review of the main trends in research and an appraisal of the problems of evaluating the material. Also included are recommendations, made by experts, on future research to be undertaken by Unesco or other organizations.

The references listed cover the anthropological, sociological, psychological, psychoanalytical, medical, and some biophysiological materials. Included are articles, books, reports, and monographs. Theses are not included. A list of the journals used in the citations has been provided. The journals are of research level for the most part. In all, over 2,000 references are provided, covering 1950 to the present.

The arrangement of the materials is unusual. The annotated material is by level of explanation (e.g., constitutional approaches, constitutional/individual approaches, individual approaches, individual/immediate environmental approaches, etc.). The material in the unannotated section is alphabetical by author.

Research is emphasized all throughout this high-quality work.

8.　　Frankel, B. Gail, Robert C. Brook, and Paul C. Whitehead. **Therapeutic Communities for the Management of Addictions; A Critically Annotated Bibliography**. With the assistance of Linda L. Adamtau and Carol M. Chamberlain. Toronto: Addiction Research Foundation, 1976. 204p. index. (Addiction Research Foundation Bibliographic Series, No. 12.) $7.00pa. LC 77-370091. ISBN 0-88868-921-X.

Widespread use of therapeutic communities for the treatment of addicts is a fairly new phenomenon. This bibliography covers the field up to June, 1976. The 305 citations are listed alphabetically by major author with an annotation and key words for indexing provided. In addition, the "highlights" and the "low lights" of the works are pointed out. A few unannotated references have been included in an appendix. Most of the materials listed are periodical articles, but there are some books, pamphlets, and brochures. Includes author, subject, and key word indexes.

9.　　Holleyhead, R., and Stuart S. Kind. **A Bibliography on Ethyl Alcohol for Forensic Science and Medicine and the Law**. North Yorkshire, England: Forensic Science Society; Edinburgh, Scotland: Scottish Academic Press; distr., New York: Columbia University Press, 1980. 444p. (Forensic Science Society Series of Monographs, Vol. 1.) $60.00. ISBN 0-9502425-6-X.

The intent of this computer-produced bibliography is to provide quick access to the literature relating to forensic aspects of ethyl alcohol. A few references involving methyl alcohol also have been included. Over 1,600 citations are provided, mostly to journal articles, but a few to books. Thousands of references were screened to prepare this bibliography. For the most part, only recent papers are listed, but a few definitive older ones are included. Some articles are major reviews in specific areas and contain many references.

The presentation is in five parts: 1) Subject index terms, 2) Subject index, 3) Authors, 4) Citations, and 5) Journal index. Complete citations are given in section 4 only.

The material cited should be of use to forensic scientists and others involved in legal matters, because the criterion for their selection was based on questions asked about alcohol by scientists, laymen, and the courts.

10.　　Joscelyn, Kent B., and Alan C. Donelson. **Drugs and Driving: A Selected Bibliography. Supplement One**. Prepared for the U.S. Department of Transportation, National Highway Traffic Safety Administration. Washington: The Administration; available through the National Technical Information Service, 1978, 279p. (various pagings). index.

The first supplement to the title listed below, this report updates the parent volume and expands coverage in some research areas, in particular, literature pertaining to drug usage patterns and drug analytical methodology. Like the parent volume, the supplement contains a short introductory section, then the topical, author, and titles indexes, and about 400 abstracts. The topical index contains cross-referenced lists of drugs by name and by usage.

11.   Joscelyn, Kent B., and Roger P. Maickel. **Drugs and Driving: A Selected Bibliography: Final Report**. Prepared for the U.S. Department of Transportation, National Highway Traffic Safety Administration. Washington: The Administration; available through the National Technical Information Service, 1977. 310p. (various pagings). index. LC 77-601392.

This report presents a selected, although rather comprehensive, bibliography of literature dealing with the relationship between drug use (other than alcohol alone) and highway safety. Abstracts of over 600 articles covering scientific, technical, and some general literature are included. Also included is literature that presents drug effects on behavior related to driving and materials that present legal constraints on drug/driving research and countermeasure programs.

After a brief introductory section, the bulk of the presentation is in four parts: a topical index, a title index, an author index, and the abstracts, the latter making up about half the volume.

12.   Lucia, Salvatore Pablo. **Wine and the Digestive System: The Effects of Wine and its Constituents on the Organs and Functions of the Gastrointestinal Tract. A Selected Annotated Bibliography**. San Francisco, CA: Fortune House, 1970. 157p. index. LC 74-12375-3.

According to the author, the purpose of this work is, in addition to providing the medical lore of wine, to acquaint the physician with the sociocultural literature on the subject since earliest times, to guide the reader through works that provide scientific proof of the value of wine, to permit an evaluation of its role as a nutrient and medicine, and to supply scientific evidence essential to move those whose bias rules their thinking on the subject.

There are seven sections as follows: 1) The effects of wine and its constituents in the overall functions of the gastrointestinal system, 2) The effects of wine and its constituents on the functions and disorders of the upper gastrointestinal tract, 3) Effects on the stomach, 4) Effects on the intestines, 5) Effects on the liver and gallbladder, 6) Effects on the pancreas, and 7) An epitome of the therapeutic uses of wine in disorders of the gastrointestinal system. Each section contains, in addition to the annotated bibliography, an essay on the effects of wine on normal functions, effects on abnormal functions, and contraindications. The references are in chronological order, covering very early classical literature to the present time.

While the author's enthusiasm for the use of wine may border on the sentimental, he does point out that large amounts are harmful and indicates disease conditions that contraindicate its use and cautions that it reacts synergistically with certain drugs. The book is interesting because of the references to early literature and the lore.

13.   Milgram, Gail Gleason. **Alcohol Education Materials: An Annotated Bibliography**. New Brunswick, NJ: Rutgers Center of Alcohol Studies, Publications Division, 1975. 304p. index. $15.00pa. LC 74-620158. ISBN 911290-44-3.

The laws of every state in the United States prescribe at least some teaching about alcohol in the schools, so this guide serves a real need. The coverage is quite comprehensive for the years covered, 1950 to May 1973. Listed alphabetically by author are 873 books, pamphlets, and periodicals. Annotations and a statement of audience level and main concepts have been provided. The items are indexed by title, audience level, type of publication, and subject.

The work is of high quality with good annotations. The materials listed are evaluated for content, readability, format, and attainment of stated objectives. Anyone concerned with alcohol education can profit by consulting the book.

14.   Triche, Charles W. III, and Diane Samson Triche, comps. **Drug Abuse Bibliography for 1976**. Troy, NY: Whitston Publishing Co., 1979. 372p. index. $22.50. LC 79-116588. ISBN 0-87875-127-0.

The seventh supplement to a list compiled by Joseph Menditto, *Drugs of Addiction and Non-Addiction, Their Use and Abuse: A Comprehensive Bibliography, 1960-1969*, this bibliography is a nearly complete listing of 1976 books and periodical articles pertaining to drug abuse. In addition, it contains some entries for earlier material that was overlooked in the 1975 volume.

The book is divided into three sections: 1) Monographs, books, and government publications, 2) Subject index to periodical literature, and 3) Author index. Material in the first section is arranged alphabetically by author, and the articles in the second section are arranged alphabetically by title under subject headings. A list of subject headings and cross-references has been supplied. In addition, a list of the bibliographies, indexes, and abstract publications searched in compiling the work has been included.

A limitation of the work is that only the senior authors of the publications are named in the entries and included in the author index. However, the series is a valuable listing of material.

15.   U.S. Alcohol, Drug Abuse, and Mental Health Administration. **Quality Assurance for Alcohol, Drug Abuse, and Mental Health Services: An Annotated Bibliography**. By O. B. Towery, Gordon R. Seidenberg, and Vittorio Santaro. Washington: GPO, 1979. 27p. [DHEW Publication No. (ADM) 79-796.]

This annotated bibliography gathers together a great deal of what has been written about quality assurance in alcohol, drug abuse, and mental health services. It is intended for those who are developing programs for assuring quality in their own services. This is important because the federal government, among others, seeks accountability from service providers.

A number of the entries cited concern the Professional Standards Review Organization (PSRO) Program, some deal with the experiences of model quality assurance programs, and a few general articles in such areas as program evaluation, medical records, and confidentiality have been listed.

The bibliography should give the reader an overview of current thought and activity in this field.

16.   U.S. National Audiovisual Center. **A List of Audiovisual Materials Produced by the United States Government for Alcohol and Drug Abuse Prevention**. Washington: NAC, 1978? 13p. index.

Though it is brief, this publication lists, by subject, slides, audiotapes, filmstrips, multimedia kits, videocassettes, and other audiovisuals available for purchase. In addition, 16mm films are included, some for rent and some for purchase.

Materials are arranged alphabetically by title under the following headings: 1) Alcohol and the body, 2) Alcohol and youth, 3) Alcohol—counseling and rehabilitation, 4) Drugs and the body, 5) Drugs and youth, 6) Drugs—counseling and rehabilitation, 7) Tobacco. Each entry includes such information as running time, producer, date, price, and an annotation. A title index is provided.

17.   U.S. National Clearinghouse for Alcohol Information. **In Focus: Alcohol and Alcoholism Media**. Washington: GPO, 1977; repr. 1980. 75p. index. [DHHS Publication No. (ADM) 80-32.]

This publication presents a selected list of currently available audiovisual materials on alcohol and alcoholism, produced since 1960. Also provided are two lists, publications relating to media resources and where to write or call for help regarding alcohol problems.

For films the following is given: title, year of release, medium, length, color or black and white, intended audience, television clearance, sale price, rental fee, distributor, and a synopsis of content.

18.   U.S. National Clearinghouse for Alcohol Information. **Selected Publications on Alcoholism Treatment Modalities**. Washington: GPO, 1977. 16p. (National Clearinghouse for Alcohol Information Grouped Interest Guide, No. 11-6.)

The entries in this bibliography of literature on the treatment of alcoholism are grouped under the following subject headings: Group and individual therapy, Behavior modification, Drug therapy, Aversive drugs, Electrotherapy, Other therapies, Detoxification modalities, Side effects and evaluation, and General readings. Short annotations have been provided. References to periodical articles, books, meeting papers, audiovisual materials, and documents have all been included.

A new issue of the guide is to appear every six months.

19.   U.S. National Clearinghouse for Alcohol Information. **Selected Publications on Animal Research on Alcohol Effects**. Washington: GPO, 1977. 45p. (National Clearinghouse for Alcohol Information Grouped Interest Guide, No. 4-6.)

The entries in this item in the Grouped Interest Guide series are arranged under the following subject headings: Dependence, tolerance and withdrawal; Stress and conflict; Strain differences; Drug interactions; Physiology and metabolism; Reinforcement and learning; Avoidance behavior; and Alcohol preference and consumption. Short annotations are included. Most of the references are to periodical literature, but some are to books, dissertations, and other materials.

A new issue of the guide is to be published every six months.

20.   U.S. National Clearinghouse for Alcohol Information. **Selected Publications on Drugs and Alcohol**. Washington: GPO, 1977. 15p. (National Clearinghouse for Alcohol Information Grouped Interest Guide, No. 12-6.)

The briefly annotated bibliographic references in this guide are to materials dealing with drugs and alcohol, particularly their combined use. The entries have been grouped under the following subject headings: Drug abuse, Pharmacology, and Drug interactions—animal studies. Most of the references are to journal articles.

A new issue of the guide is to be published every six months.

21.   U.S. National Clearinghouse for Alcohol Information. **Selected Publications on Heredity, Genetics, and Alcohol**. Washington: GPO, 1977. 3p. (National Clearinghouse for Alcohol Information Grouped Interest Guide, No. 6-6.)

This guide provides the user with briefly annotated bibliographic references to materials dealing with heredity, genetics, and alcohol. Most of the references are to journal articles.

A new issue of the guide is to be published every six months.

22.   U.S. National Clearinghouse for Alcohol Information. **Selected Publications on Psychological Studies of Alcohol and Alcoholism**. Washington: GPO, 1977. 29p. (National Clearinghouse for Alcohol Information Grouped Interest Guide, No. 14-6.)

The aim of this publication is to provide the reader with bibliographic references to literature on the psychological aspects of alcoholism. The entries are grouped under the followed subject headings: Sexuality; Alcoholic personality; Behavioral theories; Tests and testing; MMPI; Sensory perception; Vision; Temporal perception; Perceptual/motor skills; Stress, conflict and anxiety; Electrophysiology; Sleep studies; Memory; and Thought processes. Most of the references are to periodical literature. Short annotations are included.

A new issue of this guide is to be published every six months.

23.   U.S. National Clearinghouse for Alcohol Information. **Selected Publications on Sociocultural Aspects of Alcohol Use and Alcoholism**. Washington: GPO, 1977. 19p. (National Clearinghouse for Alcohol Information Grouped Interest Guide, No. 1-6.)

The annotated bibliographic references in this guide are to materials on the sociocultural aspects of alcohol use and alcoholism. The entries have been grouped under the following subject categories: Drinking habits—cultural, Socioeconomic status, Economically disadvantaged persons, Social forces, Alcoholic females, Elderly, Racial and ethnic groups, American Indians, Religious groups, Attitudes, History of alcohol use, and General readings. References to a wide range of materials are included: books, periodical articles, unpublished papers, documents, and others.

A new issue of the guide is to be published every six months.

In addition to this guide and the five others listed above, the Clearinghouse also issues similar bibliographies in nine other general subject areas as follows: *Occupational Alcoholism Programs*; *Legal Aspects of Alcohol Use and Abuse*; *Alcohol, Accidents, and Highway Safety*; *Education and Training About Alcohol*; *Teenagers and Alcohol*; *Physiologic Concomitants of Alcohol Use and Abuse*; *Rehabilitation Strategies for Alcohol Abusers*; *Alcohol and Mental Health*; and *Statistical and Demographic Research on Alcohol Use and Abuse*.

24.   U.S. National Institute on Drug Abuse. **Cocaine—Summaries of Psychosocial Research**. Prepared by Wynne Associates. Washington: GPO, 1977. 147p. index. [DHEW Publication No. (ADM) 77-391; NIDA Research Issues, No. 15.] $2.10pa. S/N 071-024-00564-9.

Abstracts of some 69 articles and books from both the scientific and popular literature on the psychosocial aspects of the use of cocaine are provided in this publication. The period covered is the turn-of-the-century to the present.

The abstracts have been grouped into five categories as follows: 1) Histories of cocaine use, 2) Overviews and perspectives, 3) Research and clinical observations, 4) Treatment studies, and 5) Incidence studies.

The purpose of the volume is to help stimulate further research on cocaine usage.

25.   U.S. National Institute on Drug Abuse. **Drug Abuse Prevention Films: A Multicultural Film Catalog**. Compiled by the Center for Multicultural Awareness. Washington: GPO, 1978. 52p. index. [DHEW Publication No. (ADM) 79-791.]

This catalog provides an annotated list of films suitable for drug programs, community centers, schools, libraries, and other groups concerned with the prevention of drug abuse within certain minority groups. The groups are Asian/Pacific

Islanders, blacks, Mexican Americans, Puerto Ricans, and Native Americans. The films were chosen for inclusion because they deal with primary drug abuse prevention with the multicultural context. In addition, each film has as its central character(s), members of one or more of the five minority groups, and must fit into one or more of four categories of prevention: information, education, alternatives, and intervention. Many of the films do not deal directly with drug use, but were selected because they deal with cultural and/or personal conflicts that can lead to drug problems.

The catalog contains the following sections: 1) Introduction, 2) Recommended films (list of 29 of the best), 3) Subject index of useful films (with brief descriptions), 4) Alphabetical index, 5) Other films reviewed (the list not recommended or appropriate), 6) Other sources of film reviews and evaluations, 7) Distributors and their addresses, and 8) Audience comments.

26.   U.S. National Institute on Drug Abuse. **Guide to the Drug Research Literature**. By Gregory A. Austin, Mary A. Macari, and Dan J. Lettieri. Washington: GPO, 1979. 397p. index. [DHEW Publication No. (ADM) 80-940; NIDA Research Issues, No. 27.] S/N 017-024-00980-6.

Material reporting research investigations in the field of psychosocial drug use and abuse has been brought together in this guide. It is designed to serve the needs of a diverse group of drug researchers. The publication provides a cumulative index to the first 27 volumes of the NIDA Research Issues Series and is a guide to other recent significant writings in the field. Over 1,300 indexed references are included.

The main listing, in addition to the standard literature reference, provides index fields such as the drug in question, the sample studied, subject headings, location of study, and methodology used. There are six indexes: author, drug, location, methodology, sample, and subject. A list of major journals is included.

27.   U.S. National Institute on Drug Abuse. **Primary Prevention in Drug Abuse: An Annotated Guide to the Literature**. Prepared by Louisa Messolonghites for the Prevention Branch, Division of Resource Development. Washington: GPO, 1977. 205p. index. [DHEW Publication No. (ADM) 76-350.] $2.60pa. S/N 017-024-00561-4.

In this attempt to canvas and organize the literature and other resources available to workers in the field of drug abuse prevention the annotated references are presented under the following headings: 1) Drug abuse prevention: history, strategies, and policies, 2) Education and training, 3) Community action, 4) Multimedia, 5) Information sources, 6) Evaluation, and 7) Additional readings. In addition, the following appendices are included: 1) State drug authorities and program contacts, 2) State drug education coordinators, and 3) Contacts in federal agencies with concerns for prevention.

28.   U.S. National Institute on Drug Abuse. **Where the Drug Films Are: A Guide to Evaluation Services and Distributors**. Washington: GPO, 1977. 19p. [DHEW Publication No. (ADM) 77-429.] $1.20pa. S/N 017-024-00607-6.

Films, slides, recordings, and other audiovisual materials are quite helpful in getting a message to an audience. There are many audiovisual materials on drug abuse, but their quality varies, and it has become evident that possibly they do more harm than good with youthful audiences. This valuable pamphlet is designed to help in the evaluation of these materials and tells where they are available.

The first section lists agencies and publications that conduct regular evaluations of drug abuse audiovisuals. The second section lists a few libraries that have films. The third section gives sources for federal materials, and the last section lists commercial and nonprofit distributors.

The publication does not include exhaustive lists, but it does give good, reliable sources.

29. U.S. National Institute on Drug Abuse. Office of Communications and Public Affairs. **Drug Abuse Films.** Compiled by Richard W. Sackett. Washington: GPO, 1980. 26p. index. [DHEW Publication No. (ADM) 80-914.]

This booklet lists about 50 films, both privately and federally produced, which deal with aspects of drug abuse frequently mentioned by requestors. All are available from their distributors for sale, rent, or, in a few cases, for free loan.

The list is arranged alphabetically by title of film. Information given about each includes the year of production, name and address of the distributor, the film's running time, sale price or rental fee, intended audience, and a brief synopsis. All the films are 16mm sound productions, and almost all are in color. An audience and a topical index are provided. No evaluative statements have been included about the films, and inclusion does not necessarily imply recommendation.

30. U.S. National Institutes of Health. **Smoking and Health: An Annotated Bibliography of Public and Professional Education Materials.** Prepared by Cancer Information Clearinghouse, Office of Cancer Communications, National Cancer Institute. Washington: GPO, 1978. 82p. index. [DHEW Publication No. (NIH) 78-1841.]

This bibliography of 290 items is intended for health care providers and educators. Both print and nonprint materials have been included. The arrangement is, for the most part, by subject topic, but there are special sections containing French- and Spanish-language materials. A great deal of the material included is popular in approach and is most suitable for young people.

31. Waller, Coy W., Jacqueline J. Johnson, Judy Buelke, and Carlton E. Turner. **Marihuana: An Annotated Bibliography.** New York: Macmillan Information, a Division of Macmillan Publishing Co., 1976. 560p. index. $14.95. LC 76-20635.

This extensive bibliography is intended for those interested in the technical literature on marijuana. There are 3,045 entries covering international scientific publications since 1964. The compilers state that by using this publication and an earlier one (*The Question of Cannabis, Cannabis Bibliography*, United Nations Commission on Narcotic Drugs, E/CN7/479, 1965, edited by Nathan B. Eddy), the literature through 1974 can be comprehensively surveyed.

In addition to the bibliography, the book contains introductory material on the chemical structure of the natural cannabinoids and on the metabolites, and a summary table of biological actions on marijuana in various laboratory animals.

The bibliography and the brief annotations make up the bulk of the work. Arrangement is alphabetical by senior author. This is an impressive work.

32. Weise, C. E. **Solvent Abuse: An Annotated Bibliography with Additional Related Citations.** Compiled at the Addiction Research Foundation Library, with assistance from S. Busse and edited by R. J. Hall. Toronto: Addiction Research Foundation, 1973. 231p. index. (Addiction Research Foundation Bibliographic Series.) $5.50pa. LC 74-180561.

The 273 articles described in this bibliography relate to the abuse of solvents (including gasoline and anesthetics) by inhalation. In addition, 237 additional references without annotations have been supplied. Research studies, clinical reports, review articles, and letters to the editor have been included. Arrangement is alphabetical by the senior author. There are key word, author, and subject indexes.

2

DICTIONARIES, ENCYCLOPEDIAS, AND DIRECTORIES

This short section lists one reference book of wide scope, Norback's *The Alcohol and Drug Abuse Yearbook/Directory* (entry 36). There are also a number of directories included that specifically offer help to the troubled addict, including one on treatment programs for women issued by the U.S. National Institute on Drug Abuse, *Directory, Women's Drug Abuse Treatment Programs* (entry 42).

There are three "encyclopedias" included, the *High Times Encyclopedia of Recreational Drugs* (entry 33), *Legal Highs: A Concise Encyclopedia of Legal Herbs and Chemicals with Psychoactive Properties* (entry 35), and Stafford's *Psychedelics Encyclopedia* (entry 37), which encourage the recreational use of drugs.

33.   **High Times Encyclopedia of Recreational Drugs.** New York: Stonehill Publishing Co., 1978. 417p. illus. bibliog. index. $12.95. LC 78-64633. ISBN 0-88373-082-0.

This publication is not really an encyclopedia, but a collection of articles taken from the periodical *High Times*, a highly successful magazine which encourages the use of "recreational drugs."

The chapter headings are as follows: 1) The dawn of drugs, 2) Drugs, religion and magic, 3) Psychoactive herbs and plants, 4) Household highs, 5) Aphrodisiacs, 6) Cannabis and its derivatives, 7) Marijuana growing, 8) Cocaine, 9) The psychedelic revolution, 10) Opiates, 11) Pharmaceuticals, 12) The black market economics, 13) Paraphernalia, and 14) John Law. In addition, appended materials include a collection of news items dealing with law, a collection of biographies of lawyers who handle drug cases, an interview with a former Bureau of Narcotics and Dangerous Drugs chief, news items dealing with health, two essays ("High Adventures"), and market quotations of street drug prices.

The book contains a great deal of controversial, if not sordid and depressing, material. The most noteworthy aspect of it is the historical outline of drug use through the ages, and the illustrations that accompany the text.

An exceptionally astute and amusing review of the book can be found in the February 1, 1979 issue of the *Journal of the Addiction Research Foundation*.

34.   Indiana. Department of Mental Health. Division of Addiction Services. **Indiana Substance Abuse Directory, 1978.** Indianapolis, IN: The Department, 1978. 185p. index.

Arranged alphabetically by city, this directory provides assistance in locating social service agencies that can help individuals who are at some degree of risk of substance abuse. Each agency listed is described, giving such information as program name, programmatic identification (e.g., treatment and/or rehabilitation), program setting (e.g., inpatient, outpatient, detoxification, etc.), services available, population served, hours, fees charged, service area, and certification renewal date. An appendix provides definitions of terms used.

35.   **Legal Highs: A Concise Encyclopedia of Legal Herbs and Chemicals with Psychoactive Properties**. New York: High Times; Hermosa Beach, CA: Golden State Publishing, 1973. 32p. illus. $2.00pa.

The purpose of this booklet is to provide the reader with brief information on various substances that are psychotropic but legal. These include plant materials in crude form and chemicals, either synthesized or extracted from natural materials. The entries are arranged alphabetically. For each the following is given: description, method of preparation, dosage and use, analysis of active constituents, effects, contraindications, and the name of a supplier in letter code. The code letters are identified at the end of the book with addresses given. Over 70 materials are listed, and include such familiar materials as nutmeg, catnip, dill, hops, and parsley, as well as some exotic and dangerous substances.

36.   Norback, Judith. **The Alcohol and Drug Abuse Yearbook/Directory 1979-80**. New York: Van Nostrand Reinhold, 1979. 649p. $39.50pa. ISBN 0-442-26110-1.

It is intended that future editions of this work appear biennially. The book has wide scope; it provides practical answers to a wide range of alcohol and drug related problems.

The first section contains general information about alcohol use and alcoholism with particular stress on prevention and treatment. Next follows a long section on alcohol treatment centers, which makes up the bulk of the book. The centers are arranged geographically by state and then by city. About each is given: address, contact person, type of program, services, and admission requirements. If the program is accredited by the Joint Commission on Accreditation of Hospitals, it is so indicated. Next there are short sections on Alcoholics Anonymous and Al-Anon Family Group Headquarters. The last section, on drug information, makes up about one-third of the book. There is brief general information about hallucinogens, marijuana, narcotics, sedatives, and stimulants. Then follows a listing of state drug abuse authorities, and a substantial listing of drug abuse treatment programs by state and city with information given similar to that given in the Alcoholism Treatment Center section.

The work should be quite useful to therapists, physicians, counselors, social workers, clergymen, law enforcement officers, and others who deal with drug and alcohol abusers. The sections that list the treatment programs are probably the most valuable parts of the book; the other material (which is brief anyway) may be difficult to locate because of the lack of an index.

37.   Stafford, Peter. **Psychedelics Encyclopedia**. Berkeley, CA: And/Or Press, 1977. 384p. illus. bibliog. index. $7.95pa. ISBN 0-915904-21-7.

This book reviews the literature on psychedelic substances, gives an account of their properties, traces the history of their use, and comments on social attitudes regarding them. It makes a strong plea for allowing their use legally to explore human consciousness and to bring about mystical experiences.

The views expressed are controversial and one-sided as little is said about the dangers inherent in the use of such substances. There seem to be some inaccuracies in the work, and most of the literature references are to secondary sources. However, the book with its many illustrations is interesting and the historical viewpoint good.

38.   U.S. Alcohol, Drug Abuse, and Mental Health Administration. Office of Program Planning and Coordination. **The Alcohol, Drug Abuse, and Mental Health National Data Book: A Reference Book of National Data on Incidence and Prevalence, Facilities, Services Utilization, Practitioners, Costs, and Financing.** By Thomas R. Vischi, Kenneth R. Jones, Ella L. Shank, and Lowell H. Lima. Washington: GPO, 1980. 149p. bibliog. [DHEW Publication No. (ADM) 80-938.] S/N 017-024-00983-1.

A great deal of information on the incidence and prevalence of alcohol, drug abuse, and mental disorders has been generated. This national data book facilitates access to it. Also covered are treatment facilities, services utilization, clinical manpower, and costs and financing of services. The compilation is not comprehensive, but should prove useful in helping users find their way through the data that currently exists. Coverage is not limited to federally funded programs. Most of the material is presented in condensed or tabular form. More data and analyses can be found in sources identified in the footnotes and bibliography.

39.   U.S. Bureau of Narcotics and Dangerous Drugs. Office of Scientific Support. Drug Control Division. **Drug Information Sources: A Survey of Selected Drug-Related Repositories and Information Services.** By Moshe Mangad, Elizabeth Fong, and Susan Reed. Washington: GPO, 1972. 101p. bibliog. (SCID-TR-6).

The brief descriptions in this publication are of information sources available to the Bureau of Narcotics and Dangerous Drugs that offer drug-related data. These sources are classified by type of organization and by type of service rendered. The former group is subdivided by government agencies, non-government information services, other information services, and libraries. The latter group includes publications and literature searching services such as computer data bases, indexing and abstracting services, card services, etc. Also included is a section entitled "Highlights and Evaluations of the Literature Searching Services." The information services are competently described.

The coverage of this publication is quite broad, including a listing of sources that give information about all drugs, not just those commonly abused. Although some of the material included in the document is out of date at this writing, it is still a valuable compilation.

40.   U.S. National Clearinghouse for Smoking and Health. **Directory of On-Going Research in Smoking and Health, 1976.** 6th ed. Compiled by Herner and Company. Washington: GPO, 1976. 397p. index. [DHEW Publication No. (CDC) 76-8320.]

An international source document for research on smoking and health, this edition contains research resumés from 37 countries, covering activities in the agricultural, biochemical, medical, behavioral, psychological, and related fields. The number of research reports included (869) has increased by more than 21% over the number in the 5th edition. Resumés are arranged in alphabetical order by country, and by state and/or city within the country. Includes indexes for principal investigator, organization, sponsor, and subject. Each description usually includes the following: name and address of the organization, project title, principal investigator, objective, methods or approach, results to date, project dates, source of financial support, and literature references.

41. U.S. National Institute on Drug Abuse. **Alternatives for Young Americans: A Catalog of Drug Abuse Prevention Programs.** Washington: GPO, 1979. 349p. [DHEW Publication No. (ADM) 78-691.] S/N 017-024-00855-9.

Generally, early efforts at preventing drug abuse among young people were unsuccessful. Neither the "scare tactics" nor the information campaigns were effective. It seems that meaningful "alternatives" to drug abuse, something to substitute for unfulfilled needs, might be more effective. Hence there is a need to identify programs and activities that give young people the opportunity to feel they have an active controlling part of their own lives.

This publication lists community-based programs that have helped. The entries are divided into five major categories: National Models, State selections, Honorable mentions, List of evaluated programs, and Descriptions of prevention programs. Complete descriptions of programs mentioned in any of the first four categories may be found in the last section. Each entry includes program name, address, contact person, phone number, hours available, and a program description. Any unique features are pointed out, and sources of income and annual budget figures are sometimes included.

42. U.S. National Institute on Drug Abuse. **Directory, Women's Drug Abuse Treatment Programs.** Washington: GPO, 1980. 95p. [DHHS Publication No. (ADM) 80-852; National Institute on Drug Abuse. Report Series. Series 44, No. 2.]

Until relatively recently treatment programs for drug abusers have not considered the special needs of women. Women have been reported to be harder to treat, probably because of such things as confusion over sex-role expectations and the need for supportive services such as child care. Services for women have been improving, however, on both the federal and state levels.

To reflect the changes in services for women, a directory of women's programs and program components was developed and published in 1979. This directory is an update of that listing. Programs are listed by state, alphabetically. About each is given: name, address, phone number, and a brief paragraph that describes the program.

The directory will be useful to persons in need of services, to providers of such services, and to professionals who may need to refer clients. The plan is to continue to revise and update it.

43. U.S. National Institute on Drug Abuse. **National Directory of Drug Abuse Treatment Programs.** Washington: GPO, 1976. 313p. [DHEW Publication No. (ADM) 76-321.]

A compilation of approximately 3,800 federal, state, local, and privately funded agencies that administer drug abuse treatment services in the United States and its territories, this work is an important source of information for those who seek treatment and referral agencies. It also serves as a resource tool for program managers, treatment personnel, clients, and those interested in the location and activities of treatment service units and their administrative agencies. Programs are listed if they were identified as a therapeutic community, halfway house, or free clinic, and if they were engaged in one or more of the following activities: administrative services, treatment and rehabilitation programs, central intake facilities, crisis intervention programs, and support services such as counseling.

The directory is arranged alphabetically by state, then alphabetically by city, and then program name within the city. Brief information about each program is given as follows: name, address, phone number, director's name, and a description of the program's activities. Most entries also include information on the services offered and the environment in which they are provided (such as "outpatient" or "residential" or "daycare").

A listing of state drug abuse authorities has also been provided.

44.   U.S. Office on Smoking and Health. **Directory of On-Going Research in Smoking and Health, 1978.** 7th ed. Compiled by Informatics, Inc. Washington: GPO, 1979. 433p. index. $6.25pa.

This edition of the directory presents summaries of 973 projects from 43 countries of the world, a larger number than in previous editions. Over half the studies (518) are U.S. projects. The most important research areas are cancer, cardiovascular diseases, pulmonary diseases, and pregnancy. In addition, interest in behavioral and educational research is growing.

The resumés are arranged in alphabetical order by country and within each country alphabetically by institution. Within the U.S. section, resumés are in alphabetical order by state, and within the U.K. section by country. The following information is given in most instances: project title, principal investigator, objective, method or approach, results to date, financial support, future plans, and project dates.

3

HANDBOOKS, MANUALS, AND GUIDES

This section contains material aimed at a variety of readers. The largest amount is for educators, counselors, and administrators of drug treatment programs. The U.S. government has produced many publications to assist these groups and to assist in training them. Other publications are for law enforcement officers, physicians, social workers, emergency room personnel, and drug users themselves. The revised edition of Bludworth's *300 Most Abused Drugs: An Identification Handbook* (entry 48) is a convenient guide for the law enforcement officer.

Several titles deal with hallucinogenic mushrooms, their identification, use, and toxicity. There is a guide to the recreational use of drugs, Dennis and Barry's *The Marijuana Catalog* (entry 54). A good deal of attention has been given of late to growing and gathering drug plants as the titles by Drake, Fleming, Frank, Lincoff, Menser, Oakum, Pollock, Mountain Girl, Stamets, and Starks indicate.

There are a number of important titles on treatment of drug abuse, both long term and emergency. There are those that deal with methods of detection and identification of drugs in the body, an important part of treatment programs. A unique title, issued by the National Institute on Drug Abuse, is *A Guide to the Investigation and Reporting of Drug-Abuse Deaths: Problems and Methods* (entry 99).

45.　Auvine, Brian, Betsy Densmore, Mary Extrom, Scott Poole, and Michel Shanklin. **A Manual for Group Facilitators**. A publication of the Center for Conflict Resolution. Madison, WI: Wisconsin Clearinghouse for Alcohol and Other Drug Information, 1978. 89p. illus. bibliog. $4.25pa.

The purpose of this manual is to provide an informal outline of useful and effective techniques that can assist in making group meetings go smoothly. The view is taken that a group is most effective when all its members can participate in the activities and decisions. The manual is not intended exclusively for those involved with alcohol or drug abuse programs or other crisis situations, but for anyone planning or presenting a workshop. A discussion of the values, dynamics, and common sense behind the group process is included as well as practical material. A glossary of specialized terms has been provided.

46.　Baselt, Randall C. **Disposition of Toxic Drugs and Chemicals in Man**. Vol. 1, *Centrally-Acting Drugs*. Canton, CT: Biomedical Publications, 1978. 306p. bibliog. index. $22.50. LC 77-93428. ISBN 0-931890-01-2.

This is volume 1 of a two volume set that is intended as a source of current essential information on the disposition of the chemicals and drugs frequently encountered in cases of human poisoning. This volume is devoted to licit and illicit drugs affecting the central nervous system, and the other volume deals with peripherally-acting drugs and common toxic chemicals, few of which are drugs of abuse. Classes of drugs of abuse considered in volume 1 are: 1) Analgesics (narcotics and non-narcotics), 2) Anesthetics, 3) Anticonvulsants, 4) Ataractics, 5) Hallucinogens, 6) Psychostimulants, and 7) Sedative-hypnotics.

Each substance is discussed separately with data included that relates to the body fluid concentration of substances in normal or therapeutic situations, concentration in fluids and tissues in instances of toxicity, and the known metabolic fate of those substances in man. In addition, brief mention is made of specific analytical procedures that may be used to determine each substance and its active metabolites in biological specimens.

The material presented is quite technical and is of special interest to toxicologists, pharmacologists, and clinical chemists who need to conduct analytical searches for these materials in human specimens or to interpret analytical data resulting from such a search.

47.   Berman, Eleanor. **Analysis of Drugs of Abuse**. New York; London; Rheine: Heyden and Son, 1977. 80p. bibliog. index. (Heyden International Topics in Science.) $11.00. ISBN 0-85501-226-9.

Though a small work, this book presents a "critical review of the analytical methods used in toxicological investigations" and gives applications of these methods to the analysis of various drugs of abuse. The author has had considerable experience in this area. The importance of clinical factors is stressed in reaching a decision as to whether a particular drug has been used and in assessing its significance.

The following chapters are presented: 1) What is drug abuse? 2) Classes of compounds called drugs, 3) Evolution of drug separation technology, 4) Development of methods of drug identification, 5) Techniques of drug identification, 6) Chromatography, 7) Immunochemical methods, 8) Do a toxicology! 9) Evaluation of drug analysis techniques, and 10) Therapeutic monitoring. An appendix contains absorption spectra of various drugs.

Analytical chemists have criticized the book on a number of counts: it is too brief; there are unnecessary errors (e.g., peyote is called a mushroom instead of a cactus); some methods are given too little attention; and it is difficult to see for whom the book is intended. On the positive side, the analysts consider the last three chapters to be well-done; many references to more comprehensive works have been included; and the book is a welcome addition to the limited literature of an important subject.

48.   Bludworth, Edward. **300 Most Abused Drugs: An Identification Handbook**. rev. ed. Tampa, FL: Trend House, 1976. 29p. illus. (col.) index. $2.95pa. ISBN 0-88251-070-3.

This publication is an updated edition of an earlier similar work. It contains color photographs of commonly abused drugs, many of them prescription tablets and capsules. Trade names, generic names, classification schedule numbers, ingredients, and amounts of each are indicated, with supplementary descriptions and a glossary of terms in separate sections. Publications such as this are very useful in helping laymen, physicians, and law enforcement officers identify abused drugs. A number of publications contain sections with similar photographs, but this compact booklet is as valuable as any.

49.   Bourne, Peter G., ed. **Acute Drug Abuse Emergencies: A Treatment Manual.**
New York: Academic Press, 1976. 361p. bibliog. index. $16.50. LC 76-28997. ISBN
0-12-119560-0.

Each chapter in this collection of preferred methods for treating drug abuse
emergencies was contributed by an individual recognized as an expert in treating the
condition described. The manual is primarily intended for the practicing physician
who sees only occasional drug problems, although others, such as emergency room
physicians and those in community mental health centers, free clinics, and drug treatment centers, will also find it valuable. No particular attention is given to the etiology
of drug abuse or rehabilitation of the patient.

The chapters are grouped under the following headings: 1) Differential
diagnosis, 2) Emergency treatment of opiate overdose, 3) Treatment of acute CNS
depressant emergencies, 4) Emergency treatment of adverse reactions to CNS stimulants, 5) Emergency treatment of adverse reactions to hallucinogenic drugs, 6) Emergency treatment of acute reactions to cannabis derivatives, 7) Emergency treatment
of inhalation psychosis and related states, 8) Emergency treatment of acute alcohol
intoxication, and 9) Special problems.

The book contains a great deal of useful information conveniently presented.
The index is quite detailed.

50.   Choulis, Nicholas H. **Identification Procedures of Drugs of Abuse.** Ghent,
Belgium: European Press, 1977. 454p. illus. bibliog. index. $79.00. ISBN 90-6295-
061-2.

The information presented in this book is basic to dealing with the analyses
of drugs commonly abused. The material has been organized into six sections. The
drugs are discussed under the following categories: stimulants, depressants, narcotics,
and hallucinogens. There is, in addition, a section on illicit street samples. Analytical
methods for each type of drug are examined. The emphasis is on instrumental methods
of analysis such as chromatography and spectroscopy.

Works of this kind are important because substances sold on the illicit drug
market contain a variety of adulterant materials in addition to the principal active
ingredient. There is no way to predict the make-up or potency of a given sample in
advance; each must be regarded as unique. The proper treatment of a victim of an
abused drug depends upon accurate analysis of the intake substance. As yet there
are no standard tests generally accepted for identifying all types of illicit drugs, but
books of this kind will assist analytical laboratories, industry, city and state police
departments, pre-employment screening facilities, heroin treatment centers, clinical
emergency rooms, and others in dealing with the drug problem. The book can also
be used by students in the health professions, particularly pharmacy, and in analytical
chemistry courses.

51.   Cox, Ann E. **The Management of Intoxicated and Disruptive Patients:
Emergency Department Training Manual.** Toronto: Addiction Research Foundation,
1979. 89p. illus. bibliog. $7.95pa. ISBN 0-88868-088-3.

This manual presents a training program that was found to be successful
in reducing violent incidents in hospitals and clinics that deal with disruptive patients.
The course was originally designed for hospital emergency room staff, but all those
who deal with disruptive patients should find it useful—police, ambulance attendants,
nursing home staff members, detoxification unit personnel, and general and psychiatric
hospital staffs.

The procedures discussed in the manual are based on the following assumptions: 1) Many patients behave in a disruptive manner because it is more effective in gaining attention, 2) Staff can contain disruptions and reduce the duration by altering their own responses to the patients, and 3) Intoxicated individuals should be held responsible for their behavior. They are not out-of-touch (unless they are unconscious), and they are responsive to their environment. Practical methods are stressed, and questions are provided at the end of each chapter to help focus on key aspects of the training.

52.   D'Andrea, Vincent J. **Psychoactive Drugs: A Guide for Public Safety and Social Service Professionals.** Menlo Park, CA: Cummings Publishing Co., 1977. 75p. bibliog. $3.75pa. LC 76-24507. ISBN 0-8465-1290-4.
    Dr. D'Andrea, a psychiatrist, intended this booklet to serve as a learning device and a reference work for students and professionals in such areas as public safety, law enforcement, youth counseling programs, correction and probation agencies, and paramedical programs such as emergency medical technology. No prior knowledge of chemistry, pharmacology or psychology is needed by the reader.
    The work is introduced by a short section on the brain and nervous system. The main section takes up psychoactive drugs under the following headings: 1) Downers (sedative-hypnotics), 2) Downers (narcotics), 3) Uppers (stimulants), 4) Highlighters (marijuana and methylenedioxyamphetamine), and 5) Scramblers (psychedelics). In addition, there are four appendices: 1) How law enforcement officials rank drug involvement in hazardous activity, 2) Regulations regarding drugs, 3) California Health and Safety Code regarding marijuana and other controlled drugs, and 4) Psychoactive drugs and transactional analysis. Also included is a glossary of drug-related terms.
    The material in this brief presentation is well-selected and successfully digested.

53.   DeAngelis, G. G. **Testing and Screening for Drugs of Abuse: Techniques, Issues, and Clinical Implications.** New York: Marcel Dekker, 1976. 140p. bibliog. index. $17.50. LC 75-40843. ISBN 0-8247-6417-X.
    The drug abuse epidemic has given rise to a number of new industries in the United States, among them the testing laboratories that provide testing to drug abuse treatment and rehabilitation enterprises. This testing has usually been analyzing urine for illicit drugs or licit drugs used illicitly.
    This book discusses analytical techniques descriptively and supplies references to more scientific works for those who desire them. The following matters are considered: cost, clinical implications, therapeutic usefulness or uselessness, certification, period of time testing should continue, trust, accuracy, validity, staff and client morale, false positives and negatives, and other human issues more difficult to define. A glossary of technical terms has been provided.

54.   Dennis, Paul, and Carolyn Barry. **The Marijuana Catalogue.** Chicago: Playboy Press, 1978. 314p. illus. bibliog. index. $1.95pa. LC 77-93132. ISBN 0-87216-457-9.
    This book, called "a comprehensive guide to grass, for the neophyte and veteran alike," covers a number of aspects of the subject. The authors' view, which permeates the whole presentation, is that marijuana use is good. They believe it is now acceptable to society, that it is harmless, and that the restrictive laws will soon be changed. Something similar to the interminable "Playboy Philosophy" applied to drugs is discernible throughout.

The following chapters are included: 1) The history of marijuana, 2) Scoring some grass, 3) Growing your own, 4) Cleaning, treating, rolling, and stashing, 5) Paraphernalia, 6) Getting stoned, 7) Cooking with grass, 8) The effects of marijuana, 9) Hashish, and 10) The pot-love connection. In addition, these appendices are provided: 1) The most frequently asked questions concerning marijuana, 2) The legislative history of marijuana, or how pot achieved its ill reputation, 3) Glossary, and 4) Bibliography.

A good many inaccuracies appear in the text, particularly in the historical material.

55.   Drake, Bill. **The Cultivator's Handbook of Marijuana.** rev. and expanded ed. Berkeley, CA: Wingbow Press; distr., Bookpeople (2940 Seventh St., Berkeley, CA 94710), 1979. 223p. illus. bibliog. index. $8.95. ISBN 914728-31-8.

Presented here, with photographs, charts, maps, and diagrams, is complete information on how to grow and cultivate the marijuana plant. Covered are such matters as the identification of male and female plants (females yield the more potent substances), choosing a site for planting, chemical makeup of the soil, pruning, grafting, light, seed selection, transplanting, and water and atmosphere requirements. In addition, harvesting and curing are covered. The book also contains a chapter on the history of the use of the marijuana plant with traditions and myths retold, and a discussion of legal problems.

Other material presented includes a chapter on the Cultivation of psychoactive tobacco. The author evidently believes that the tobacco used in commercial products is inferior to "true herbal tobacco."

Throughout the book, interspersed with practical advice, the author looks at what might be called the spiritual and psychic aspects of the subject. He calls marijuana a great force in the evolution of human consciousness, central to the liberation of feelings and ideas.

56.   Fleming, Dave. **The Complete Guide to Growing Marijuana.** San Diego, CA: Sundance Press, 1969. 45p. illus. $1.00pa.

This booklet contains instructions on how to grow your own marijuana plants. In addition to a small amount of background information, there are sections on the following: Selecting a site (indoor and outdoor), Intercropping, Obtaining seeds, Building a germinating box, Preparing the soil, Germinating, Planting the seeds, Transplanting, Artificial light, Care, and Harvesting, curing, and preserving the crop.

Probably one could grow marijuana following the instructions given, but certain suggestions appear impractical. For instance, in regard to indoor cultivation note the following passage, "If you have a large house, take an empty room and line the floor with tar paper or similar substance . . . . bring in the soil (each plant needs about a cubic foot of soil for root development), and you'll be in business."

57.   Frank, Mel, and Ed Rosenthal. **The Indoor/Outdoor Highest Quality Marijuana Grower's Guide.** San Francisco, CA: And/Or Press, 1974. 94p. illus. $3.50pa.

Detailed instructions on how to grow your own marijuana plants, particularly indoors, are provided in this small book; a shorter section on outdoor cultivation is also included. In addition, there is a section on an available commercial growing unit, and one on artificial lighting for the plants.

The authors claim that high quality, very potent plants can easily be grown using fluorescent lights, flower pots, and a good soil mixture.

58.   Frank, Mel, and Ed Rosenthal. **Marijuana Grower's Guide**. deluxe edition. Berkeley, CA: And/Or Press, 1978. 330p. illus. (part col.). bibliog. index. $8.95pa. LC 77-82452. ISBN 0-915904-26-8.

The Foreword in this book makes a plea for legalization of marijuana use, or at least a reform of the laws. Next there is a section entitled "General Information about *Cannabis*," which includes history, chemical composition, and information about the plant. The second section is on indoor growing of the plant; the third on outdoor cultivation; the fourth on flowering, breeding, and propagation; and the last section on harvesting, curing, and drying.

A very comprehensive treatment of the subject is presented, with many photographs of apparatus and equipment, colored micrographs of the plant, and lengthy bibliographic notes.

59.   **Getting the Word Out**. Edited by Mary Dee Tans. Madison, WI: Wisconsin Clearinghouse for Alcohol and Other Drug Information, University of Wisconsin Hospital and Clinics, 1979. 74p. (looseleaf). bibliog. $5.95.

Prepared to assist those who work in public information or health promotions, this is a manual for promoting a message, activities, or an organization. Matters such as planning campaigns, dealing with local media, targeting audiences, using resources and volunteers, and figuring cost benefits are dealt with. Those who will find the publication most valuable are community organizations, social service agencies, churches, schools, civic groups, and clubs.

In addition to basic information on planning and communicating, there are sections on newspapers, radio and TV, newsletters, brochures, and other media.

Several reading lists are provided, including one on alcohol and other drugs and a list of places to write for literature on the subject. Also, there are lists of materials on such matters as dealing with rural areas and low income and minority groups and on dealing with disabilities.

60.   Green, Helen I., and Michael H. Levy. **Drug Misuse . . . Human Abuse**. New York: Marcel Dekker, Inc., 1976. 566p. bibliog. $21.75. LC 76-1580. ISBN 0-8247-6273-8.

The authors speak of this work as a "handbook" designed to be read and referred to by parents, primarily, but also of interest to teachers, school administrators, health professionals, government officials, and anyone involved with the problems of drug misuse. It can be used as a guide for those who teach and counsel young people. It is fairly technical, although an attempt has been made to make it readable. Both history and matters of current concern are discussed. Included are procedures for dealing with specific problems of drug abuse and reliable information on particular drugs.

The 27 chapters are collected under three headings: 1) The problems of drug misuse, 2) Facts about the drugs of misuse, and 3) Miscellaneous facts, tables, and charts. Chapter headings are as follows: 1) Introduction, 2) There is a problem and a challenge, 3) The drugs of misuse, 4) A perspective, 5) Drugs in the society of the young, 6) Facts in drug misuse, 7) The case against cigarette smoking, 8) Drug misuse: symptoms and effects, 9) How to . . . , 10) Treating drug dependence, 11) There is a law, 12) The drugs of misuse: their history, 13) Facts about alcohol, 14) Facts about cannabis, 15) Facts about the hallucinogens, 16) Facts about narcotics and opiates, 17) Over the counter drugs: easy does it, 18) Facts about sedatives (hypnotics), 19) Facts about solvents (volatiles), 20) Facts about stimulants (amphetamines), 21) The "harmless" stimulants (tea, coffee, and cocoa), 22) Tobacco (nicotine), 23) Tranquilizers, 24) Symptoms to recognize, 25) A guide to diagnosis and emergency treatment, 26) Drugs can kill, and 27) A final word. Each chapter ends with a group of questions and answers related to the matters previously discussed. Also included are several appendices: 1) Drugs and chemicals currently being misused, 2) Sources of information, 3) Where to go for help (information or assistance), 4) Glossary of dependence-producing drugs, and 5) A recommended reading list.

The book contains a large amount of authentic useful information.

61.   Human Services Horizons, Inc. **Alcohol Abuse and Alcoholism Programs: A Technical Assistance Manual for Health Systems Agencies**. Prepared for the U.S. Department of Health, Education and Welfare, Bureau of Health Planning and Resources Development, and National Institute on Alcohol Abuse and Alcoholism. Springfield, VA: National Technical Information Service, 1978. 103p. bibliog. (Report No. HRP-0900411.) $6.50pa.

Intended for use by board members, planners, and project reviewers of health systems agencies, this manual makes use of interviews with health planning and alcohol abuse agencies. It was developed to provide information to assist in planning alcohol programs. Chapters presented are: 1) Introduction: the field of alcoholism, 2) Existing planning and review processes for alcoholism services, 3) Health systems agency interface with existing planning and review processes, and 4) Health systems agency implementation of planning and review processes for alcoholism services. Appended is a bibliography (annotated), other bibliographic resources, informational resources, state and territorial alcoholism authorities, and the Comprehensive Alcohol Abuse and Alcoholism Prevention, Treatment and Rehabilitation Act of 1970 (P. L. 91-616) as amended through 1976 (excerpts).

62.   Kinney, Jean, and Gwen Leaton. **Loosening the Grip: A Handbook of Alcohol Information**. Illustrated by Stuart Copans. St. Louis, MO: C. V. Mosby Co., 1978. 288p. illus. bibliog. index. $8.95pa. LC 78-2219. ISBN 0-8016-2673-0.

Intended as a handbook for an alcoholism counselor trainee or other professional worker who deals with alcohol problems, this work is particularly aimed at those who do not have an M.D. or Ph.D. degree. It presents a great deal of basic material and provides an overview of the issues involved in alcoholism treatment. In addition, it synthesizes information from the fields of medicine, psychology, psychiatry, sociology, anthropology, and counseling that applies to alcohol abuse and treatment.

A number of chapters in the book are based on lectures presented by the staff of the Alcohol Counselor Training Program conducted since 1972 by the Dartmouth Medical School, Department of Psychiatry, and the staff of the Dartmouth-Hitchcock Mental Health Center. As these lectures were presented by a number of different contributors, there is some repetition of material, and the amount of detail presented varies to a certain extent.

In addition to material on treatment, the following topics are considered: history of alcohol use; theories on drinking and the etiology of alcoholism; guidelines for diagnosis of alcoholism; effects of alcohol on the body and behavior; effects of alcoholism on the family; special populations such as women, adolescents and the aged; complications associated with alcoholism; and how to live as an alcohol professional. Scattered through the work in the margins are apt cartoons and quotations.

The book lumps all alcohol problems under the general heading of "alcoholism," and takes the view that abstinence is the only treatment goal. Other views that pervade the work are that Prohibition was an out and out failure and that all alcoholic

beverage control policies are doomed to failure. These views are somewhat contro-
controversial.

63.   Kinsolving, Janice, and Craig Wunderlich. **Projecting: A Facilitator's Guide to Alcohol and Other Drug Film Utilization**. Madison, WI: Wisconsin Clearinghouse for Alcohol and Other Drug Information, 1979. 56p. illus. bibliog. $2.50pa.

This manual was prepared cooperatively by the Wisconsin Clearinghouse for Alcohol and Other Drug Information and the Iowa Substance Abuse Information Center. Its aim is to assist those who wish to use films on alcohol or drug abuse for educational purposes, for instance, meeting coordinators, teachers, trainers, or community organizers.

The first chapter discusses film as a medium to achieve the intended goal. Chapter 2 lists common resources for obtaining films; chapter 3 presents guidelines for selection. The next three chapters deal with presentation of the film. Chapter 7 tells what can go wrong and offers remedies, and chapter 8 deals with evaluation. An appendix lists resources for evaluation, group facilitation, and operating AV equipment.

64.   Lincoff, Gary, and D. H. Mitchel. **Toxic and Hallucinogenic Mushroom Poisoning: A Handbook for Physicians and Mushroom Hunters**. Edited by Wilbur K. Williams; illustrations by Irene E. Liberman; with a foreword by Alexander H. Smith. New York: Van Nostrand Reinhold, 1977. 267p. illus. bibliog. index. $16.95. LC 77-24639. ISBN 0-442-24580-7.

The authors of this outstanding work, a mycologist and a physician who is also a mushroom specialist, have prepared an excellent compendium of useful materials as well as a readable book. They summarize the existing knowledge about the identity, biological characteristics, chemical composition, toxicology, and therapeutic management where toxic mushrooms are concerned. The book fills a considerable need as there has been an increase of recent years in the use of wild mushrooms as food, and some groups of people have begun consuming poisonous and hallucinogenic species for the "trip" that a light dose of the poison produces. Consequently there has been an increase in cases of mushroom poisoning.

The book is intended for mushroom hunters who may not be familiar with the specific symptoms of the various kinds of mushroom poisoning, and also for physicians and hospital emergency room personnel who are called upon to diagnose and treat poison cases.

The introductory chapter places the topic in perspective; the next six chapters take up types of poisoning most frequently encountered based on types of toxins involved; the next chapter covers a heterogeneous group of mushrooms containing many different poisons, only a few of which have been identified; and the final chapter provides a discussion of the best approaches to diagnosis and treatment of mushroom poisoning. There are also several rather technical appendices of chemical and mycological detail. The work is well-illustrated with line drawings and color plates.

Until fairly recently the matter of toxic mushrooms and mushroom toxins remained largely a mystery. Considerable light has been thrown on the subject in the past 20 years, and this book does much in communicating the information.

65.   Menser, Gary P. **Hallucinogenic and Poisonous Mushroom Field Guide**. Berkeley, CA: And/Or Press, 1977. 140p. illus. (part col.) bibliog. $5.95pa. ISBN 0-915904-28-4.

This book is intended as a field guide for the identification of the various genera and species of psychoactive and lethal wild mushrooms of the western half of North America, excluding Mexico. The reader is warned that some species share very similar characteristics and that some can only be identified through chemical analysis or expert microscopic evaluation. Confusing species may have lethal results.

The following sections are presented: 1) Introduction, 2) What are mushrooms? 3) How to collect, identify and dry, 4) Chemical qualities, 5) Key of macroscopic characteristics, 6) Genus and species information, with taxonomy and drawings, 7) Glossaries, and 8) Bibliography and selected readings.

The genus and species information section, which makes up about half the book, describes 24 species that are hallucinogenic. Eight species are also described which are lethal and which may be confused with the others.

66. Oakum, Peter. **Growing Marijuana in New England (and Other Cold Climates).** Ashville, ME: Cobblesmith, 1977. 44p. illus. bibliog. $2.95pa.

The author of this small book is a horticulturist who experimented with various techniques of cultivating marijuana in New England in order to improve the quality of the plant which ordinarily grows much larger (and with more potent resins) in a warm climate.

The first part of the presentation is a guide to field cultivation. The second is a more theoretical discussion of how to select strains of cannabis specially adapted to New England and how to distinguish low-yielding male from high-yielding female plants at the seedling stage by inducing precocious flowering. By making use of this technique the percentage of desirable female plants can be increased greatly in any given plot.

Although most books on the cultivation of marijuana for pleasurable use are of questionable quality, this one is scientifically accurate and probes some interesting and little-known aspects of the plant.

67. Poley, Wayne, Gary Lea, and Gail Vibe. **Alcoholism: A Treatment Manual.** New York: Gardner Press, Inc.; distr., Halsted Press, division of John Wiley and Sons, Inc., 1979. 159p. bibliog. index. $14.95. LC 78-13435. ISBN 0-470-26523-X.

This manual was designed primarily as a guide for alcoholism workers of various kinds, such as counsellors, therapists, educators, physicians, nurses, law enforcement officers, and social workers. In addition, the lay public may be interested in it as it outlines the present state of knowledge in many areas of the subject.

The authors do not consider any distinctions among the terms "alcoholism," "alcohol abuse," "alcohol-related problems," and "alcohol dependence."

The following are the section titles: 1) Alcohol in society, 2) Alcohol and its effects on the individual, 3) Causes of alcoholism, 4) Broad spectrum treatment programs, 5) Specific treatment interventions, 6) Day-to-day treatment of the alcoholic, and 7) Research and evaluation. There are also appendices on "How to get help" and "Where to find information."

The value of the work lies in the way questions are answered and the practical techniques outlined for the treatment of alcoholics.

68. Pollock, Steven H. **Magic Mushroom Cultivation.** San Antonio, TX: Herbal Medicine Research Foundation, 1977. 64p. illus. (part col.). bibliog. (Psychomycological Studies, No. 1.) $5.00pa. LC 77-82244. ISBN 0-930074-01-7.

The author of this small book states that interest in growing magic mushrooms (hallucinogenic psilocybin-containing types) at home has increased tremendously in recent times. A number of techniques for their cultivation are offered.

The following chapters are included: The magic mushroom life cycle, The simplest technique from scratch, Culture on agar media, Growing spawn on seed, Casing spawn to promote mushroom flushes, The rice-cake technique, Cultivation on compost, Storing the harvest, The magic mushroom agape.

It is of note that psilocybin is a controlled substance in the U.S., and unauthorized possession of the drug constitutes a violation of federal and most state regulations. However, there are evidently no laws in the U.S. prohibiting possession of the magic mushrooms *per se.*

69.   **The Primo Plant: Growing Sinsemilla Marijuana**. By Mountain Girl. Berkeley, CA: Leaves of Grass/Wingbow Press; distr., Bookpeople (2940 Seventh St., Berkeley, CA 94710), 1977. 96p. illus. bibliog. $4.50pa. ISBN 0-915070-04-9.

The purpose of this small book is said to be "to inform the public about growing marijuana, in all its diversity, to full perfection in America's different climate regions." Instructions are given especially for growing "sinesmilla" marijuana, the seedless variety, prized because it gives a superior "high." The reader is duly reminded that "growing marijuana is a natural act."

There are sections on: 1) Before planting, 2) Planting, 3) Growing, 4) Pruning and plant care, 5) Flowering, and 6) Harvest.

Should one wish to get involved in this illegal activity, the booklet should be of value as it offers practical tips and inspiration. Note the following passages: "Five or six big, healthy, female plants will supply a heavy smoker for a year with pure, organically-grown harmoniously attuned grass," and also: "Don't forget that this stuff *is* a weed and will grow under difficult conditions, depending on the soil and the sun, but the perfect plant requires loving attention."

70.   Reid, Eric, ed. **Assay of Drugs and other Trace Compounds in Biological Fluids**. Amsterdam: North-Holland Publishing Co., 1976. 253p. bibliog. index. (Methodological Developments in Biochemistry, Vol. 5.) $26.95. LC 76-22776. ISBN 0-7204-0584-X.

This book is not directly concerned with drug abuse, but it is of some interest in this area because the need for reliable micro-determinations of drugs of abuse in body-fluid samples is ever increasing.

The material presented is quite technical. The following is a list of section headings: 1) The end-step: advances in instrument techniques, 2) General analytical strategy, 3) Sample preparation, and 4) Tactical illustrations: analytical case histories.

71.   Schuckit, Marc A. **Drug and Alcohol Abuse: A Clinical Guide to Diagnosis and Treatment**. New York: Plenum Medical Book Co., 1979. 211p. bibliog. index. (Critical Issues in Psychiatry.) $16.95. LC 78-27854. ISBN 0-306-40215-7.

Intended for medical students, practicing physicians, psychologists, social workers, and other health professionals and paraprofessionals, this book can serve as a convenient guide, even as an emergency handbook, although the author has attempted to maintain a balance between the immediate needs of the physician and those of the student seeking an introduction to the subject. There are numerous bibliographical references with each chapter.

The chapter headings are as follows: 1) An overview, 2) The CNS depressants, 3) Alcoholism: an introduction, 4) The treatment of alcoholism, 5) Stimulants,

6) Opiates and other analgesics, 7) Cannabinols, 8) The hallucinogens, PCP, and related drugs, 9) Glues, solvents, and aerosols, 10) Over-the-counter drugs, 11) Multidrug misuse, 12) Emergency problems: a rapid overview, and 13) Rehabilitation. Each chapter is fairly self-sufficient. The largest amount of material is presented for alcohol. Alcohol and opiates, because there is more data available on them in regard to rehabilitation, are used as prototypes for the other discussions of rehabilitation.

The material is rather clearly and succinctly presented, and the book should serve its intended purposes reasonably well. It has, however, been criticized by at least one reviewer as being oversimplified to the extent that there is some distortion.

72.   Stamets, Paul. **Psilocybe Mushrooms and Their Allies.** Seattle, WA: Homestead Book Co.; distr., And/Or Press (Box 2246, Berkeley, CA 94702), 1978. 160p. illus. (part col.). bibliog. $9.95pa. LC 77-26546. ISBN 0-930180-03-8.

The primary purpose of this work is to identify the hallucinogenic and poisonous mushrooms of the United States and to separate them from those that are not. It can serve as a field guide. In addition, information is included on how to cultivate mushrooms.

There are five chapters as follows: 1) Mushrooms: habits and habitats, 2) Taxonomy, 3) The keys, 4) Species descriptions, and 5) Mushroom cultivation. Also included are two appendices, "The Mushroom Life Cycle" and "The Microscopic Dimension," and a glossary.

The book is well-illustrated with many color photographs, drawings, and diagrams. It is an accurate presentation.

73.   Starks, Michael. **Marijuana Potency.** Berkeley, CA: And/Or Press, 1977. 174p. illus. bibliog. $4.95pa. LC 77-82454. ISBN 0-915904-27-6.

Evidently it is a great problem for marijuana users that the effects of samples of the substance will vary because the chemical content varies. This book surveys the problem and gives technical information that may assist the user in this regard.

The following chapters are presented: 1) Marijuana constituents and their effects, 2) Growth conditions and potency, 3) Variations in the THC and CBD content, 4) Variations in content of noncannabinoids, 5) Harvesting and preparing marijuana and hashish, 6) Extraction of THC and preparation of hash oil, 7) Isomerization, and 8) Testing for THC and CBD content. In addition, appended materials include short sections on chemical hints, legality, structure-activity relationships, syntheses of THC and analogs, and precursors for THC synthesis.

The book contains a good deal of chemistry. The author informs the reader as follows: "Do not be put off by the chemical formulas and detailed tables in the book—they are absolutely necessary for an adequate understanding of marijuana potency and can be understood by anyone willing to spend a few hours reading. The rewards for making the effort are substantial—you will have a rational, scientific basis for buying, growing, harvesting, storing, preparing, testing and using marijuana and hashish."

74.   U.S. Alcohol, Drug Abuse, and Mental Health Administration. **Title XX Handbook for Alcohol, Drug Abuse, and Mental Health Treatment Programs.** Washington: GPO, 1978. 109p. [DHEW Publication No. (ADM) 78-739.] S/N 017-024-00787-1.

The Foreword of this publication explains that Title XX of the Social Security Act established a program of federal financial assistance to states to encourage them to furnish social services to individuals and families who meet certain eligibility criteria. The needs of those with alcohol, drug abuse, and mental health problems can be met through services offered through the Title XX Program. This handbook was prepared to assist those working in drug abuse programs on the state and local levels.

There are seven chapters as follows: 1) Introduction, 2) The Title XX planning process, 3) Provider status, 4) Client eligibility, 5) Service coverage, 6) Rates for reimbursement, and 7) Using Title XX for training purposes. In addition, a number of useful appendices have been included such as federal Title XX regulations taken from the *Federal Register* and sample copies of social service reporting requirements forms.

75.   U.S. Bureau of Health Planning and Resources Development, and the National Institute on Drug Abuse. **Drug Abuse: A Technical Assistance Manual for Health Systems Agencies.** Prepared by Marco Systems, Inc. Washington: GPO, 1978. 200p. (looseleaf). bibliog. (Health Planning Methods and Technology Series, No. 8.)

The purpose of this manual is to assist health systems agencies that receive certain federal funds in implementing their mandated responsibilities for the review of drug abuse projects under the Health Planning and Resources Development Act of 1974 (P.L. 93-641). The act requires the agencies to conduct reviews under several conditions, and the manual describes in detail each type of review. In addition to the descriptions, there are several appendices which include sections of the law, bibliographies, a glossary of drug abuse terms, and other useful material.

76.   U.S. Drug Enforcement Administration. **Drugs of Abuse.** 3rd ed. Washington: GPO, 1977? 33p. illus. (col.). bibliog.

This work is a valuable reference tool intended for the enforcement officer, other criminal justice personnel, health professionals, and educators. The material it contains is not especially technical, but it has little relevance for the lay audience.

There are sections on the following: narcotics, depressants, stimulants, hallucinogens, cannabis, product identification, the Controlled Substances Act, and slang terms; it also includes a bibliography. Information on the appearance and effects of abused drugs is given.

An outstanding feature is the inclusion of excellent color photographs of commonly abused drugs in crude and in tablet and capsule form. In addition, there are photographs of drug paraphernalia and drug plants such as the opium poppy, coca, marijuana, and the peyote cactus. These illustrations should be of considerable value in identifying abused substances.

The earlier editions of this work were special issues of *Drug Enforcement*.

77.   U.S. Federal Aviation Agency. Aviation Medicine Service. **Guide to Drug Hazards in Aviation Medicine.** Prepared by Windsor C. Cutting. Washington: GPO, 1962; repr. 1979. 97p. index. $2.75pa. S/N 050-009-00001-7.

Intended for aviaiton medical examiners, this manual is to help in determining whether the use of a particular drug should preclude flying or ground control work. The best policy, it says, is abstinence from all drugs, but illness sometimes makes the use of a drug necessary.

The drugs are listed by class and type. Some are drugs of abuse. The toxic effects relevant to aviation that they may produce are given with a conservative estimate of their allowable use. Time limits after use of a drug are also indicated.

78.   U.S. National Drug Abuse Center for Training and Resource Development. **Facts About Drug Abuse: Participant Manual.** William E. Link, Course Developer and Manager. Washington: GPO, 1978. 1 looseleaf v. (various paging). bibliog. [Publication No. (NDACTRD) 79-041P.]

This resource manual for the participant in a course of study on drug abuse is a companion volume to the one listed below, which is for the trainer. The publication is made up of excerpts or quotations from previously published material, original papers, and many bibliographic references.

The purposes of the course are said to be to identify the inaccurate images and unsound assumptions about substance abuse that can impede progress in dealing with the problem; to examine the phenomenon itself; to consider the social and historical development; to provide descriptions of drugs commonly abused and the possible hazards; to identify treatment methods; and to explore the role of family, school, community, and peer groups in prevention efforts.

79.   U.S. National Drug Abuse Center for Training and Resource Development. **Facts About Drug Abuse: Trainer Manual.** Washington, GPO, 1978. 1 looseleaf v. (various paging). [Publication No. (NDACTRD) 79-043T.] . $7.00. S/N 017-024-00803-6.

A companion to the volume listed above, this publication presents a course of study, a revision of *Drug Abuse: Fundamentals, Facts, and Insights*, which was produced by the National Drug Abuse Center. It is a basic course, designed primarily for those who work in drug abuse prevention, treatment, rehabilitation, and drug education efforts.

The material presented for the trainer is quite detailed. It includes nine "Modules," as follows: 1) Introduction and orientation, 2) The "problem" with "drugs" and "drug abuse," 3) The "problem" with "drug addiction," 4) A social and historical context for understanding substance use in the United States, 5) Substance actions and potential hazards, 6) Understanding and overcoming substance dependence, 7) Prevention and the community, school, family, peers, and youth, 8) Roles and strategies for prevention efforts, and 9) Closure and evaluation. The total training time for the course is about 28 hours, with approximately six hours of outside reading. If desired, the entire course can be presented in three and one-half days. Methods of presentation include lectures, mediated demonstrations, guided group discussions, task force exercises, and individual reading assignments. All of the course-specified information the trainer needs is in the manual. There is, in addition, an adjunct *Resource Manual* available which contains the basic information that the trainer and participant should master (*see* review above).

This course of study has been revised (*see* entry no. 90) with a new title, *Drugs in Perspective*.

80.   U.S. National Highway Traffic Safety Administration. **A Manual for Managing Community Alcohol Safety Education Campaigns.** Washington: GPO, 1978. 49p. illus. bibliog. DOT-HS-802-515.

The first point this booklet makes is that automobiles and alcohol are both national institutions, and that together they create disaster. There is a need for change, and although 85% of adults surveyed rated drunk driving as a serious social concern, there is usually an unwillingness to take personal action to prevent a drunk from driving. This publication outlines the steps to be taken to develop a community alcohol safety campaign, giving many practical suggestions.

The following chapters are presented: 1) The automobile and alcohol in daily life, 2) Developing a communications plan, 3) Defining objectives, 4) Identifying target audiences, 5) What every program needs: community support, 6) What does your community know about drunk driving? 7) Carrying out a campaign that works, 8) Working with the media/person-to-person presentations, 9) Managing the campaign. In addition there are two appendices: Capsule communications plans for target audiences, and a Sample survey questionnaire. A bibliography and other suggested resources have been included.

81.   U.S. National Institute on Alcohol Abuse and Alcoholism. **Counseling Alcoholic Clients: A Microcounseling Approach to Basic Communication Skills. Participant Handbook.** Developed by National Center for Alcohol Education. Washington: GPO, 1978. 43p. bibliog. [DHEW Publication No. (ADM) 78-710.] $2.30pa. S/N 017-024-00830-3.

This booklet is designed to help alcoholism counselors upgrade their abilities in using eight basic communication skills. The following fundamental core skills are treated: attending, paraphrasing, reflection of feeling, summarizing, probing, counselor self-disclosure, interpreting, and confrontation.

82.   U.S. National Institute on Alcohol Abuse and Alcoholism. **Programming Community Resources: A Training Program for Alcohol Program Administrators. Participant Workbook.** Developed by National Center for Alcohol Education. Washington: GPO, 1978. 68p. [DHEW Publication No. (ADM) 78-718.] $2.50pa. S/N 017-024-00835-4.

Designed to be used in conjunction with the *Trainer Manual* reviewed below, this publication contains the handouts participants will need for the sessions in section 3 of the manual.

83.   U.S. National Institute on Alcohol Abuse and Alcoholism. **Programming Community Resources: A Training for Alcohol Program Administrators. Trainer Manual.** Developed by National Center for Alcohol Education. Washington: GPO, 1978. 145p. [DHEW Publication No. (ADM) 78-717.] $3.25pa. S/N 017-204-00820-6.

The material presented in this manual is intended to help upgrade and develop the assessment and negotiation skills of management personnel involved in coordinating or developing resources among community agencies with the intent of providing services for individuals with alcohol problems.

There are five sections presented as follows: 1) What programming community resources is all about, 2) How to adapt PCR to meet particular requirements, 3) Session outlines, 4) Handouts and reference materials, and 5) Appendices. The Session Outlines section makes up more than half the book. The course has few lectures; it relies mainly on experimental activities, workshops, discussions, role plays, and the like.

84.   U.S. National Institute on Alcohol Abuse and Alcoholism. **Trainer Manual, Management Skills for Alcohol Program Administrators.** Developed by National Center for Alcohol Education. Washington: GPO, 1978. 224p. [DHEW Publication No. (ADM) 78-719.] $4.50pa. S/N 017-024-00819-2.

This manual is intended to refresh or upgrade managerial skills of managers, supervisors, and program directors in the alcohol field. Complete instructions on delivering a program are presented.

There are four sections as follows: 1) What management skills is all about, 2) How to adapt MS to meet particular requirements, 3) Session outlines, and 4) Appendices. The session outlines make up the largest part of the volume. There are few lectures included; experimental activities, workshops, discussion, and role plays are emphasized as methods.

85.   U.S. National Institute on Alcohol Abuse and Alcoholism. **Trainer Manual: Using Volunteers in Your Agency**. Developed by the National Center for Alcohol Education. Washington: GPO, 1978. 98p. illus. [DHEW Publication No. (ADM) 78-721.] $3.00. S/N 017-024-00897-4.
    A training model was developed to meet the needs of alcoholism service workers in planning, designing, and implementing volunteer programs in local agencies. This publication is part of a training package which is an eight-hour, four-session workshop. In addition to the manual there are available session outline cards, a "Volunteer Program Development Guide" for the trainee, and two sound filmstrips.
    Included in the manual are a session-by-session guide and five appendices as follows: 1) Training considerations and techniques: refresher material, 2) Managing a training event: planning and logistics review, 3) Participant handout masters, 4) Overhead transparency masters, and 5) Training evaluation: participant feedback instrument.

86.   U.S. National Institute on Drug Abuse. **Basic Management Skills: Participant Manual**. Developed by the National Drug Abuse Center for Training and Resource Development. Washington: GPO, 1979. 196p. bibliog. [Publication No. (NDACTRD) 79-BMS-141P.] S/N 017-024-00908-3.
    This publication contains material to be used in a course designed to assist managers at all levels of drug treatment and rehabilitation programs in analyzing their ability to manage and in improving their effectiveness as managers. Most of the content, however, focuses on middle and lower level management. There are 10 modules as follows: Orientation and overview, Management functions, Management theories, Management systems, Planning processes, Decision making, Management conflict, Personnel issues, Action plans, and Closing activities.
    Also available is a *Trainer Manual* (*see* below).

87.   U.S. National Institute on Drug Abuse. **Basic Management Skills: Trainer Manual**. Developed by the National Drug Abuse Center for Training and Resource Development. Washington: GPO, 1979. 142p. bibliog. [Publication No. (NDACTRD) 79-BMS-143-T.] S/N 017-042-00907-5.
    Trainer activities are outlined in this companion volume to the *Participant Manual* reviewed above.

88.   U.S. National Institute on Drug Abuse. **Diagnosis and Treatment of Adverse Reactions to Sedative-Hypnotics**. By David E. Smith and Donald R. Wesson. Washington: GPO, 1974. 68p. bibliog. index. [DHEW Publication No. (ADM) 75-144.] $1.15pa.
    Overuse of barbiturates is considered one of America's hidden drug problems. This manual has been prepared to assist physicians, nurses, and medical aides who must diagnose, detoxify, and treat people who have abused a variety of sedative-hypnotics.
    The first section is a quick "how to do it" resource; the second gives a psychopharmacological basis for the recommendations made in the first part. In addition, the manual presents an acute treatment plan for the management of overdose emergencies,

a matter of concern because many community-based drug programs are unfamiliar with this kind of overdose.

Section headings are as follows: 1) Definitions of barbiturate abuse, 2) Pharmacology of barbiturates, 3) Patterns of non-medical barbiturate use, 4) Assessment of the barbiturate abuser, 5) Approach to overdose, 6) Treatment of physical dependence of the barbiturate type, 7) Mixed opiate and sedative-hypnotic dependence, 8) Non-barbiturate sedative-hypnotics, 9) Other considerations, and 10) Glossary of drug terms relating to sedative-hypnotics.

89.   U.S. National Institute on Drug Abuse. **Drug Abuse Instrument Handbook: Selected Items for Psychosocial Drug Research.** Edited by Alexis Nehemkis, Mary A. Macari, and Dan J. Lettieri. Washington: GPO, 1977. 331p. index. [DHEW Publication No. (ADM) 77-394; NIDA Research Issues No. 12.] $4.65pa. S/N 017-024-00533-9.

The purpose of the work is to assist investigators in building upon previous research, and to facilitate contact between instrument developers and users. It is designed to help serve as a basic reference tool by identifying and reproducing over 2,000 representative items from 40 instruments used in drug abuse research. The items are categorized according to the areas they assess. Included are demographic, interpersonal, intrapersonal, and drug variables, plus detailed summaries describing the instruments utilized.

90.   U.S. National Institute on Drug Abuse. **Drugs in Perspective: Trainer Manual.** Course Development Team, William E. Link and others. Washington: GPO, 1979. 306p. (looseleaf). illus. [Publication No. (NDACTRD) 79-DIP-053T.] S/N 017-024-00905-9.

The course of study presented in this publication is a revision of two earlier ones, *Drug Abuse: Fundamental Facts and Insights* and *Facts About Drug Abuse* (entry 79). The authors wish to avoid the emotional overtomes and subjective interpretations that the term "drug abuse" elicits, hence the new title. The course is designed for drug abuse prevention and treatment workers, teachers, guidance counselors, community service workers, and others involved in like activities. The goal of the course is to assist participants in understanding the phenomenon of substance use and abuse by providing them with a framework that acknowledges differing perspectives. The focus is on the relative risks and social consequences of various patterns of behavior associated with drug use. In addition, it is hoped that a base of knowledge about drug abuse will be gained.

Detailed instructions are provided for the trainer. Training strategy combines didactic instruction with experimental learning.

The course is made up of eight modules as follows: 1) Introduction and orientation, 2) Perspectives on substance use and abuse, 3) A social and historical context for undertaking substance abuse in the United States, 4) Substance actions, 5) Understanding the phenomenon of substance abuse, 6) Approaches to the treatment of substance abuse, 7) Prevention approaches and strategies, and 8) Closure and evaluation. In addition, there are evaluation and test forms, questionnaires, and the like appended.

91.   U.S. National Institute on Drug Abuse. **Manual for Drug Abuse Treatment Program Self-Evaluation.** By Lynn Guess and Barry S. Tuchfeld, Research Triangle Institute. Washington: GPO, 1977. 60p. bibliog. [DHEW Publication No. (ADM) 77-421; Treatment Monograph Series.] $1.60pa. S/N 017-024-00572-0.

This manual was designed for program administrators, counselors, and others involved in learning how to examine the effectiveness of a drug treatment program. It is suitable for persons with elementary skills as well as for the sophisticated. There are three parts as follows: 1) Introduction and explanation of self-evaluation, 2) Suggested program measures and computational instructions, and 3) Comparison groups and procedures for self-evaluation.

There are two supplementary publications to this manual. *See* the following two entries.

92.   U.S. National Institute on Drug Abuse. **Manual for Drug Abuse Treatment Program Self-Evaluation, Supplement I: DARP Tables.** By L. Lynn Guess and Barry S. Tuchfeld, Research Triangle Institute. Washington: GPO, 1977. 12p. + appendices. [DHEW Publication No. (ADM) 77-450; Treatment Monograph Series.] $3.75pa. S/N 017-024-00580-1.

The first of two supplements to the manual listed above, this volume presents data based on treatment outcome information that agencies and clinics routinely collect and have available in files of individual clients.

In order to justify treatment strategies, overall treatment goals must be set and actual performance compared to these goals. Setting standards for success helps assess the effectiveness of treatment, identifies problems, and provides information for decisions about the allocation of resources. This volume presents figures that represent "normal" program performance. They are based on data collected on clients admitted between June 1, 1969, and March 31, 1973, to drug abuse treatment programs at 52 agencies receiving support from the National Institute of Mental Health. This data makes up the DARP (Drug Abuse Reporting Program) data base referred to in the title of the publication.

There are three chapters of text material included in the publication as follows: 1) Introduction and background, 2) Format of DARP tables, and 3) Comparison with DARP values. However, four appendices make up the bulk of the volume. These extensive tables present the following: 1) Values on selected treatment outcome measures from DARP methadone maintenance programs, 2) Values on selected treatment outcome measures from DARP therapeutic (residential) communities, 3) Values on selected treatment outcome measures from DARP drug-free outpatient programs, and 4) Values on selected treatment outcome measures from DARP outpatient detoxification programs.

93.   U.S. National Institute on Drug Abuse. **Manual for Drug Abuse Treatment Program Self-Evaluation, Supplement II: CODAP Tables.** By L. Lynn Guess and Barry S. Tuchfeld, Research Triangle Institute. Washington: GPO, 1977. 62p. [DHEW Publication No. (ADM) 77-489; Treatment Monograph Series.] S/N 017-024-00601-7.

This is the second of the two supplements to the title described in entry 91. Like the first supplement, it presents data based on treatment outcome information that agencies and clinics collect. Also like Supplement I, it presents figures that represent "normal" program performance, allowing self-evaluative comparisons to be made. The National Institute on Drug Abuse operates CODAP (Client Oriented Data Acquisition Process) as a data collection system to provide current information for planning, management, and evaluation purposes. Data are regularly collected on clients at admissions to and discharge from drug abuse treatment programs in about 1,800 clinics that receive federal funds.

The publication contains three chapters of text material: 1) Introduction and background, 2) Format of CODAP tables, and 3) Comparison with CODAP values. In addition, there are four appendices of tables as follows: 1) Values on selected treatment outcome measures from CODAP outpatient methadone maintenance programs, 2) Values on selected treatment outcome measures from CODAP drug-free residential (therapeutic) communities, 3) Values on selected treatment outcome measures from CODAP outpatient drug-free programs, and 4) Values on selected treatment outcome measures from CODAP outpatient detoxification programs.

94.   U.S. National Institute on Drug Abuse. **A Manual on Third-Party Reimbursement Strategy for States and Communities.** Washington: GPO, 1977. 71p. bibliog. [DHEW Publication No. (ADM) 78-499; Services Research Monograph Series.] $2.20pa. S/N 017-024-00617-3.

There are economic pressures in our society that require the search for new, alternative sources for support for drug abuse treatment programs. It is felt that third party support is an important alternate source. This manual was developed to assist in obtaining such support for drug abuse service delivery.

Text material covers such areas as the role of the single state agency or coordinating agency, understanding the problem, developing a strategy, and implementation. In addition, there are three important appendices, a glossary, a list of third party reimbursement sources, and a section on cost finding procedures.

95.   U.S. National Institute on Drug Abuse. **The Social Seminar: Drugs, Education and Society. A Resource Manual for the Group Facilitator.** Washington: GPO, 1975. 100p. bibliog. [DHEW Publication No. (ADM) 77-240, formerly 75-240. S/N 017-024-00469-3.

This manual was designed to provide guidance, assistance, and confidence for people who want to organize and lead a social seminar for drug education. Organized in two parts, the first is on understanding the social seminar; the second is the resource kit, made up of aids and activities to help one organize and lead the social seminar. The latter includes a list of films with synopses; sections on suggestions to assist a facilitator in values clarification, skill building, structured activities, how to plan a social seminar, and evaluation; and, last, a list of resources.

96.   U.S. National Institute on Drug Abuse. **Statewide Services Contract Policy and Practice Manual.** Washington: GPO, 1977. 1 v. (various paging). bibliog. index. [DHEW Publication No. (ADM) 77-519; Treatment Program Monograph Series, No. 3. S/N 017-024-00644-1.

Developed for use by treatment program managers at both the state and local level, this manual provides a framework to guide state agency management in administering treatment services contracts. The hope is that it will assist in maximizing the management of federally funded service delivery programs.

97.   U.S. National Institute on Drug Abuse. Division of Resource Development. Manpower and Training Branch. **Third Party Payments: Alternative Funding Sources for Drug Abuse Treatment Programs. Trainer's Manual.** By Ira Priesman. Washington: GPO, 1979. 330p. (looseleaf). [Publication No. (NDACTRD) 79-TPP-123T.]

This manual is intended for instructors of trainees who are administrators of drug abuse treatment projects. The course of study presented should give participants sufficient understanding of the third party payment system to enable them to determine whether it is feasible to obtain reimbursement for services provided to clients, to identify third party payers, to assess the implications of the third party payments system, and to develop a plan for obtaining such reimbursement.

Topics covered include background information, health service funding regulations, key issues, third party payers, confidentiality, administrative considerations, financial management, and project planning.

A *Trainee Handbook* is also available.

98.   U.S. National Institute on Drug Abuse. Division of Resource Development. Manpower and Training Branch. **Training of Trainers. Trainer's Manual.** rev. By Ann R. Bauman. Washington: GPO, 1977. 1 looseleaf v. (various paging) [Publication No. (NDACTRD) 79-TOT-023T.]

This manual presents a basic course designed for trainers in the drug abuse field who lack apprenticeship in training theory, design, and delivery. There are ten modules included, covering the following topics: 1) Introduction to learning theory: the learner, 2) Interpersonal communication and the group process, 3) From needs assessment to behavioral objectives, 4) Designing training activities, 5) Designing training activities (continued), 6) Small group presentations, 7) Individual presentations, 8) Evaluation, 9) Trainer interventions, and 10) Using training materials. Also included is an evaluation and test section.

99.   U.S. National Institute on Drug Abuse. Psychosocial Branch. Division of Research. **Guide to the Investigation and Reporting of Drug-Abuse Deaths: Problems and Methods.** Edited by Louis A. Gottschalk and others. Washington: GPO, 1977. 151p. bibliog. index. [DHEW Publication No. (ADM) 77-386.] $3.00. S/N 017-024-0059-6.

Although the subject matter is depressing, this guide makes an important contribution to an area of drug abuse that is probably inadequately studied. What can be learned from the dead can benefit the living. As one example, the ebb and flow of drug abuse epidemics can be better understood and trends charted.

The following chapters, each by a noted expert, are included: 1) Introduction and overview, 2) Onsite investigation, 3) Postmortem examination, 4) Treatment for survival prior to death and interpretation of postmortem toxicologic findings, 5) Forensic toxicology in death investigation, 6) The psychological autopsy, 7) Certification of death from narcotism and other psychoactive drugs of abuse, 8) Complication and analysis of mortality data, and 9) The medical examiner as an expert witness. Also, there are several useful appendices: 1) Reporting form of a drug-involved death: sample case file, sample copy of "Report of a drug-involved death," and code sheets, 2) Data on some potentially toxic chemicals in the postmortem, 3) Sample autopsy report forms from the Los Angeles County Medical Examiner-Coroner's Office, 4) Therapeutic and toxic concentrations of more than 100 toxicologically significant drugs in blood, plasma, or serum: a tabulation, 5) ICDA code categories most frequently equated with drug-induced deaths, 6) U.S. standard certificate of death, and 7) DAWN medical examiner form.

100.   U.S. National Institute on Drug Abuse, and National Institute on Alcohol Abuse and Alcoholism. **Substance Abuse Resource and Curriculum Guide for Physician Assistants and Nurse Practitioners.** Washington: GPO, 1979. 1 v. (various paging). bibliog. [DHEW Publication No. (ADM) 78-883.] $5.00pa. S/N 017-024-00948-2.

This guide was prepared by the Research Triangle Institute for federal agencies in the belief that nurse practitioners and physician assistants are valuable resource persons where drug abuse is concerned and that greater emphasis should be placed on their education in this field.

The following sections are provided, for the most part in outline form: 1) The drug and alcohol abuse problem, 2) Drug and alcohol abuse service settings and services, 3) Role of education in the recognition and management of substance abuse, 4) Substance abuse education for the nurse practitioner, and 5) Substance abuse education for physician assistants. In addition, there are three substantial appendices as follows: 1) Substance abuse curriculum for physician assistants and nurse practitioners, 2) Meharry Medical College, Department of Nursing Syllabus, and 3) Substance abuse training resources. The latter includes lists of federal agencies; components of the National Manpower and Training System; educational materials; single state agencies and other training and consultation resources; national resource agencies, foundations, and publication outlets; and persons who are experts in substance abuse and nurse practitioner/physician assistant practice.

101.   U.S. National Institute on Drug Abuse, and Office of Drug Abuse Policy, Executive Office office of the President. **Handbook on Drug Abuse.** Edited by Robert I. DuPont, Avram Goldstein, and John O'Donnell. Washington: GPO, 1979. 452p. bibliog.

The aim of this work is to make available to the drug abuse field a concise compilation of recent major developments in the area and their implications for treatment and research. A large number of respected authorities contributed to the work. Forty-two chapters are grouped under the following headings: 1) Overview of drug treatment, 2) Treatment modalities for narcotic addicts, 3) Treatment methods for specific needs 4) Drugs of recent public concern, 5) Drug problems in specific populations, 6) Psychosocial studies of drug users, 7) Epidemiological studies, 8) Special issues, and 9) Drug treatment in the future.

There may be some unevenness in the material in the various chapters of the handbook, but for the most part it is well done.

102.   U.S. Special Action Office for Drug Abuse Prevention. **A Guide to Urine Testing for Drugs of Abuse.** By Don H. Catlin. Washington: GPO, 1973. 24p. + appendix. bibliog. (Special Action Office Monograph, Series B, No. 2, November 1973.)

Programs for the detection and treatment of drug abuse have relied heavily on urine testing to measure objectively drug abuse and the effectiveness of the treatment programs. The purpose of this handbook is to provide the non-chemist an explanation of urine screening methodology. Emphasis is on the description and evaluation of individual tests, but some attention is given to the basic pharmacology of drugs, sources of error in drug testing, and the interpretation of test results. Definitions of terms are also included. In addition, a list of governmental agencies and individuals experienced in the development or evaluation of urine tests and a list of major manufacturers or distributors of urine-testing products have been included.

103.   U.S. Special Action Office for Drug Abuse Prevention. **Outpatient Methadone Treatment Manual.** Washington: GPO, 1974. 141p. bibliog. (Special Action Office Monograph. Series C, Number 2, August, 1974.)

This manual is intended to serve as a guide for drug treatment program administrators in both early planning and actual implementation of an outpatient methadone program. Essentially, a model outpatient methadone clinic is described.

104.   U.S. Special Action Office for Drug Abuse Prevention. **Residential Methadone Treatment Manual.** Washington: GPO, 1974. 141p. bibliog. (Special Action Office Monograph. Series C, No. 3.) $1.90pa. S/N 4110-00015.

This manual was prepared to serve as a guide for administrators of residential methadone treatment programs to assist them in early planning stages and in actual implementation of the treatment regimen. The object is to stabilize the patient on methadone or to detoxify the patient from heroin, using methadone, so that after a period of three to six weeks he or she can return to the community and continue in the program as an outpatient. Abstinence from drug use is the ultimate goal, of course.

105.   Vinson, Joe A., ed. **Cannabinoid Analysis in Physiological Fluids**. Based on a symposium sponsored by the Division of Analytical Chemistry at the 173rd Meeting of the American Chemical Society, 1979. 242p. bibliog. index. (ACS Symposium Series, 98.) $25.00. LC 79-10934. ISBN 0-8412-0488-8.

Cannabis preparations, especially marijuana and hashish, are the most widely used group of illicit drugs in the world. For this reason it is important that they can be detected in physiological fluids. Law enforcement officials and forensic scientists particularly have need for this information.

This publication contains 12 representative papers from a meeting at which experts presented different methods of analyzing for cannabinoids in body fluids such as blood plasma, urine, and breast milk. Methodologies using gas chromatography, mass spectrometry, radioimmunoassay, high pressure liquid chromatography, and thin-layer chromatography are presented.

106.   World Health Organization. **Detection of Dependence-Producing Drugs in Body Fluids**. Report of a WHO Meeting of Investigators. Geneva: WHO, 1974. 50p. bibliog. (WHO Technical Report Series, No. 556.) ISBN 92-4-120556-3.

The detection of drugs of abuse in body fluids is an important part of treatment programs, and many methods have been described in the recent past, but not all have been evaluated. In the field of public health there is a need for rapid, sensitive, simple, specific, and inexpensive tests.

This publication is a report of an international group meeting where comparative studies were discussed, research priorities and objectives reviewed, and public health requirements indicated. The matter of collaborating laboratories designated as reference centers where training and research facilities would be provided was also discussed.

The following are the section headings: 1) Introduction, 2) General considerations, 3) Methodology of detecting dependence-producing drugs in body fluids, 4) Prospects for meaningful detection of particular drugs, 5) The functions of national reference and other laboratories, 6) Quick diagnostic techniques applicable in acute intoxication, 7) Some important research areas, 8) International cooperation, and 9) Conclusions. In addition, appended materials include: 1) Haemagglutination-inhibition (HI) test, 2) Comparative studies of methods for detection of heroin use, 3) Methadone, 4) Barbiturates, and 5) Thin-layer chromatography of dependence-producing drugs.

4

PERIODICALS

This section lists recently initiated substance abuse periodicals and some older ones missed in the author's original *Bibliography*. Some new trends are discernible in periodical coverage of drug abuse. A number of titles that formerly covered alcoholism alone now cover drug abuse of all drugs. Likewise, those that originally focused on drug abuse now include alcoholism and perhaps tobacco use as well. This is probably a result of the realization that all substance abuse is similar.

A large number of the publications listed are of the newlsetter type, still a popular way of transmitting information on drug abuse. However, there are several substantial new scientific publications, such as *Alcoholism: Clinical and Experimental Research* (entry 112); *Chemical Dependencies: Behavioral and Biomedical Issues* (entry 118); *Drug Abuse and Alcoholism Review* (entry 123); *Research Communications in Substance Abuse* (entry 135); and *Substance and Alcohol Actions/Misuse* (entry 140).

There is a new scientific publication of unique type, the *Journal of Ethnopharmacology* (entry 129). It is concerned primarily with active plant substances used in medicines of past and present cultures.

The new scientific publications attest to the fact that there is currently much more active research in the substance abuse field than formerly, a long-felt need.

107.   **About A.A. . . . A Newsletter for Professional Men and Women.** New York: Alcoholics Anonymous, Inc. Biannually.

This newsletter contains information about the administration of the Alcoholics Anonymous organization and announcements of appointments, conferences, new A.A. publications, and like matters.

108.   **Addiction and Substance Abuse Report: The Continuing Story of Substance Abusive Behavior: Drugs, Alcohol, Tobacco, Medicines, Foods.** In two parts. New York: Grafton Publications, Inc. 1970- . Monthly.

The title of this newsletter was changed from *Addiction and Drug Abuse Report* with Volume 8, no. 9, 1977. Recent issues (since the title change particularly) have dealt more with the management of substance abusers than with cure. Trends in substance abuse are reported as well as what schools, plants, businesses, hospitals, or service agencies are doing about them. Also dealt with are such themes as how to spot substance abuse and how to handle it, treat it, or live with it.

The view of the editor seems to be that, more and more, society must learn to live with drug abusers.

109.   **Advances in Alcoholism.** Newport Beach, CA: Raleigh Hills Foundation.
1978- . Monthly.
        This 4-page newsletter is prepared and edited for the Raleigh Hills Foundation by the Alcohol and Drug Abuse Research Center of the Harvard Medical School—The McLean Hospital of Belmont, Massachusetts, through a grant provided by Raleigh Hills Hospitals, a division of Advanced Health Systems, Inc. Each issue contains an article on a subject of current interest in the field.

110.   **Alcohol, Tobacco and Firearms Bulletin.** Washington: Bureau of Alcohol, Tobacco and Firearms, Department of the Treasury. For sale by the Superintendent of Documents, GPO. $12.00 per year. Monthly.
        This publication is the authoritative instrument of the bureau for announcing its official rulings and procedures and for publishing Treasury decisions, legislation, administrative matters, and other items of general interest. The *Bulletin* incorporates all matters of the bureau that are of public record, and those contents of permanent value are consolidated each calendar year into cumulative issues, which are sold on a single-copy basis.
        The material in the *Bulletin* is presented in six parts as follows: 1) Treasury decisions, 2) Bureau rulings, 3) Bureau procedures, 4) Legislation, 5) Administrative matters, and 6) Announcements.

111.   **Alcoholism and Alcohol Education.** Washington: Resources News Service, Inc. 1971- . Monthly.
        This newsletter-type publication contains mainly information on federal programs and funding. The material is of particular value for researchers seeking sources of grant funds. Also included are some items reporting scientific findings.

112.   **Alcoholism: Clinical and Experimental Research.** New York: Grune and Stratton, Inc. 1977- . Quarterly.
        This is the official journal of the American Medical Society on Alcoholism and the Research Society on Alcoholism, component members of the National Council on Alcoholism. It publishes original refereed papers on specific laboratory and clinical problems and on the means available to the physician for treating alcoholism. It also includes items of interest to members of the societies, such as announcements of meetings, programs, and abstracts of papers.

113.   **American Council on Marijuana and Other Psychoactive Drugs, Inc.: Newsletter.** New York: American Council on Marijuana. 1979- . 2-3 times per year.
        The council, which is an incorporated nonprofit organization, has as its primary goal drug education. This newsletter prints news of current interest regarding marijuana and other psychoactive drugs and attempts to educate the public about the health hazards connected with their use.
        Included are editorials, meeting notices and conference programs, reports of research, notices of new books and other publications, and news about proposed legislation on drugs.
        The point of view taken is that abuse of these drugs is a serious problem.

114.   **Bottom Line on Alcohol in Society.** Lansing, MI: American Business Men's Research Foundation. 1978- . Quarterly.
        This journal publishes short reports dealing with research, issues, events, and opinions relating to public policy in the field of alcohol abuse. Special attention

is given to prevention of alcohol problems. Illustrations (cartoons especially) and charts and graphs are included.

The publisher sees man's use of beverage alcohol as having a net harmful effect on society.

115.   **Box 1980**. New York: Alcoholics Anonymous Grapevine, Inc. 1944- . Monthly. $5.00.

Formerly called *A.A. Grapevine*, this publication was initiated in 1944 as an eight-page newspaper, and was mailed free to all AAs in the World War II armed forces. It is now a 5½x7½-inch 48-page booklet somewhat akin to *Readers Digest* in style. The main articles present experiences and opinions of AAs and others interested in alcoholism. Also included are cartoons, jokes, letters to the editor, news, and a section "About Alcoholism," which contains notes, quotes, and reviews of material in other publications.

116.   **British Journal of Addiction to Alcohol and Other Drugs**. Edinburgh: Longman Group Ltd., Journals Division. 1903- . Quarterly.

This periodical has had a long history. It is sponsored by the Society for the Study of Addiction to Alcohol and Other Drugs, an organization founded in 1884, although called the Society for the Study and Cure of Inebriety at that time. "Proceedings" were published until 1903 when the *British Journal of Inebriety (Alcoholism and Drug Addiction)* was initiated. In 1947 the title was changed to *British Journal of Addiction (Alcohol and Other Drugs)*, essentially the present title.

The journal has been an important one. It has provided a forum for the exchange of information from all over the world; it has published contributions on the results of research, much of it from young British workers; and it has had a multi- and interdisciplinary flavor. In addition, it has published material on drug abuse in remote areas of the world. Another aim has been to publish material on all sides of controversial issues.

From 1962 through 1978 M. M. Glatt served as editor; the editor at this writing is Griffith Edwards. Both are authorities in the field.

117.   **British Journal on Alcohol and Alcoholism**. Journal of the Medical Council on Alcoholism. London: B. Edsall and Co. vol. 13, 1978- . Quarterly. $15.00.

Journal of Alcoholism and *Bulletin of Alcoholism* are former titles of this periodical. Each issue of the publication contains several special articles that report research results. In addition, there are editorials, notes, short reports, reviews of books, and reviews of articles from other periodical publications.

118.   **Chemical Dependencies: Behavioral and Biomedical Issues**. Jamaica, NY: SP Medical and Scientific Books. 1975- . Quarterly.

This publication, formerly called *Addictive Diseases*, deals with the broad scope of substance abuse throughout the world. Research papers are included of both the theoretical and the empirical type and from many socio-behavioral and biochemical-pharmacological disciplines. Contributions are invited from known authorities. Each issue ordinarily focuses on a particular aspect of addictive diseases, for example, female drug abusers, anthropological studies in addiction, or the abuse of legal drugs.

119.   **Concerns**. Don Mills. Ontario, Canada: Alcohol and Drug Concerns, Inc. 1902- . Quarterly.

Formerly called *Advocate*, this publication is the official publication of Alcohol and Drug Concerns, Inc. In format it is a 4-page newsletter that contains short news items (mostly of concern to Canadians), photographs, and editorials. As a subtitle the phrase "We encourage and promote a life-style that is independent of the use of alcohol and other harmful drugs" is used.

120.   **Critiques.** Madison, WI: Wisconsin Clearinghouse for Alcohol and Other Drug Information. 1979- . Bimonthly.

Written by the staff of the clearinghouse, this publication contains reviews and evaluations of current films, books, pamphlets, brochures, and newsletters concerned with alcohol and drug abuse. The emphasis is perhaps on film reviews.

Each review is about a page (typewritten) in length and includes, in addition to the usual bibliographic information, a synopsis, indication of the specific subject, intended audience, and an evaluation.

The intent of the publication is to assist those who are interested in utilizing alcohol and drug abuse materials in selection of suitable titles. Teachers, counselors, librarians, church groups, law enforcement officers, and those involved with community programs will find it of value.

Generally, the reviews are thoughtfully prepared; however, a criticism is that the viewpoint is more lenient toward drug and alcohol use than some would find desirable. Works are usually criticized if they stress undesirable effects of substance abuse.

121.   **DEA World.** Washington: U.S. Department of Justice, Drug Enforcement Administration, Office of Public Affairs. 1976- . Monthly.

For the most part, this publication contains news of the personnel of the Drug Enforcement Administration with many photographs included. Occasionally, articles appear regarding the work of the organization in dealing with drug enforcement. Sections on significant enforcement cases and significant compliance cases are included from time to time.

In February 1980 the Drug Enforcement Administration requested that the publication be discontinued as a U.S. Depository Library item because of the sensitivity of its contents, and the libraries were requested to discard the issues they had received. It is now an internal newsletter for DEA employees only.

122.   **Drug Abuse and Alcoholism Newsletter.** San Diego, CA: Vista Hill Foundation. 1972- . 10 times per year. Free.

Edited by Sidney Cohen, a noted authority on drug abuse, this 4-page newsletter is published by a nonprofit organization, the Vista Hill Foundation, as part of its continuing education and research program. It is distributed on a complimentary basis. Each issue contains a documented article on a problem of current interest in the drug abuse or alcoholism field.

123.   **Drug Abuse and Alcoholism Review.** New York: Haworth Press. 1978- . Quarterly.

Each issue of this publication contains one or two scholarly review articles on a special aspect of alcohol and/or drug abuse. In addition, there is a substantial section containing over 100 abstracts of journal articles taken from current literature pertinent to substance abuse, which are written on all aspects of the subject. Core journals in the field and a large number of peripheral journals of special interest are searched for material. An author and subject index to this section appears in each issue, and a cumulative one is planned for each year. The journal also includes a section entitled "The Fugitive Literature," which is made up of reviews of less widely distributed monographic publications than those issued by major publishing houses.

124.   **Druglink**. Information Letter. London: Institute for the Study of Drug Dependence. 1974- . Quarterly. Free.

This newsletter is intended primarily for social workers, physicians, teachers, and those who deal with drug abuse as part of their work. The publication contains information on significant developments in the United Kingdom and internationally, including articles on matters of current interest, assessments of media coverage of drug abuse, reviews of recent books and periodical articles, a calendar of conferences and meetings, reports from Parliament, and developments in United Kingdom law. Supplements are included occasionally which contain statistical data on drug use.

The publication should prove particularly valuable to those attempting to keep abreast of the drug scene in the United Kingdom.

125.   **Focus on Alcohol and Drug Issues.** Miami, FL: U.S. Journal of Drug and Alcohol Dependence, Inc. 1978- . Bimonthly.

The editorial objective of this publication is to reflect the state-of-the-art on specified aspects of drug abuse. The first issues have dealt with such subjects as the effect of alcoholism and drug use in the work place, marijuana update, teenage drinking, the use of alcohol and other drugs by women, alcoholism treatment, prevention of drug misuse, and drugs and driving.

126.   **Focus on Women: Journal of Addictions and Health.** Philadelphia: George F. Stickley Co. 1980- Quarterly.

This new journal focuses on the uniqueness of women and their special needs where problems of addiction or compulsive behavior are concerned. Interdisciplinary in scope, it accepts scholarly research articles in the fields of science, social policy, social action, psychology, drug abuse prevention and education, and related areas.

Each issue usually contains several articles, book reviews, and reports of research funding.

The editors feel, first, that the periodical is needed because so far studies done only on women have been limited, and second, that the publication can encourage such research and influence social policy.

127.   **International Drug Report.** Albany, NY: International Narcotic Law Enforcement Officers Association. vol. 20, 1979- . Monthly.

Though primarily a newsletter, this publication presents several review and/or reports in each issue as well as a section on legal decisions.

128.   **Japanese Journal of Studies on Alcohol/Arukoru Kenkyu.** Kyoto: Japanese Medical Society of Alcohol Studies. 1966- . Quarterly.

The text of this journal is in Japanese or English, and summaries for Japanese language articles are furnished in English.

Original papers or reviews dealing with aspects of alcohol's interactions with biological systems are particularly invited for publication, but articles on clinical and social aspects of alcohol are also occasionally published.

129.   **Journal of Ethnopharmacology: An Interdisciplinary Journal Devoted to Bioscientific Research on Indigenous Drugs**. Lausanne, Switzerland: Elsevier Sequoia S.A., 1979- . Quarterly.

This publication is primarily concerned with the investigation and description of the biological activities and the active substances of plants used in traditional medicines of past and present cultures. These are not all drugs of abuse, but many are, and a number of articles on such substances have been included in the journal.

Review articles, full-length papers describing original research, short communications describing limited investigations, and letters to the editor are published.

130.   **Labor-Management Alcoholism Journal**. New York: National Council on Alcoholism, Labor-Management Division. 1974- . Bimonthly. $24.00.

The title of this periodical has varied since its inception. It is perhaps the only publication currently available that deals exclusively with the problem of alcoholism among employees.

Included are studies on ongoing employee alcoholism programs and coverage of new developments in the field. Also, alcoholism arbitration cases are reported as are statistical results and other matters of concern to employees in industry. Special features include editorials, book reviews, and news items.

Workers in the occupational alcoholism field will find this publication of great interest.

131.   **Narcotics Law Bulletin**. Boston: Quinlan Publishing Co. 1974- . Monthly.

This brief publication in looseleaf format is punched to be filed in a 6x9-inch binder. Each issue contains short extracts of legal cases involving drug use. Decisions are indicated.

132.   **A New Day**. Jefferson City, MO: Division of Alcoholism and Drug Abuse/ Department of Mental Health. 1970- . Bimonthly. Free.

Until recently this publication was called *Drug Dependencies*. It is the official house organ of the division. The publication is of the newsletter type, each issue containing eight pages of news, photographs, book reviews, and official material such as information on statewide services, contracts management, and interagency programs.

133.   **News About Alcoholism in New York City**. New York: New York Affiliate of the National Council on Alcoholism, Inc. Four times per year.

The news printed in this publication appears under such headings as: The president's corner, What's new, Industrial news, Resources news, People, Public information news, Quotes, Training news, and Events. Also included are profiles of workers in the alcoholism field.

134.   **NIAAA Information and Feature Service**. Washington: U.S. National Clearinghouse for Alcohol Information of the National Institute on Alcohol Abuse and Alcoholism. 1974- . 10-14 times per year. Free.

The articles in this newsletter are designed to assist readers in keeping abreast of developments in the field of alcoholism and to help those who prepare local publications with their coverage of the subject. Included are articles on trends, opinions, and programs across the nation. Also, activities of the National Institute on Alcohol Abuse and Alcoholism and other alcoholism organizations are highlighted. The articles may be reproduced and used in other publications. In addition to the news items, there are letters to the editor, a column or recent publications, and a listing of meetings to be held.

This publication supersedes an earlier one called *Alcohol and Health Notes*.

135. **Research Communications in Substance Abuse**. Westbury, NJ: PJD Publications, Ltd. 1980- . Quarterly.

Both pure and impure substances and chemicals that are subject to abuse are treated in this journal. Natural and synthetic substances are both considered. The material is devoted to the physiology, toxicology, biochemistry, pathology, pharmacology, organic and medicinal chemistry, pharmacognosy, genetics, epidemiology, psychobiology, and related aspects of the substances. Original reviews, papers, research letters, and book reviews are published making use of direct photo-printing of typed manuscripts. The journal is intended to be of value to basic and clinical professionals as well as to research scientists and graduate students. The editorial board is made up of noted researchers in the field.

136. **Smoking and Health Bulletin**. Rockville, MD: Technical Information Center, U.S. Office on Smoking and Health. 1970- . Irregular.

This publication contains abstracts of articles on the health effects of smoking. The material in each issue is arranged under broad subject headings, and author, organizational, and subject indexes have been provided. At the end of a year cumulated indexes are issued. The material appearing in the bulletin is also available through an automated search and retrieval system. The articles indexed are from research or clinical journals for the most part.

137. **Sobering Thoughts**. Quakertown, PA: Women for Sobriety, Inc. 1976- . Monthly. $10.00.

For the most part, Dr. Jean Kirkpatrick provides the material for this four-page newsletter. Each issue ordinarily contains an article on a subject of current interest in the alcoholism field and a number of short news items and comments. The publication is intended primarily for the female audience to provide information, inspiration, and support.

Former titles were *Women for Sobriety Newsletter* and *Women Alcoholics*.

138. **Stone Age**. New York: Stone Age Corporation. 1978-1979. Quarterly. (Address: 116 East 27th St., New York, NY 10016.)

This "underground" publication is very similar to *High Times*, the widely distributed magazine that promotes drug use. The format, articles, features, and advertisements are much the same, but the general tone of *Stone Age* is perhaps a little less offensive. The editorial in the first issues says the periodical is "devoted exclusively to getting high." The intent is said to be to give the latest, most practical information a drug user needs about drugs, as well as the legal risks and defenses the user should know to stay "free as well as high."

Each issue contains featured articles; an interview; record and book reviews; sections on health, law, and paraphernalia; and many ads (some in full color) for products such as drug paraphernalia, books, jewelry, clothing, drug growers' plants and seeds, and art objects for the drug user.

Publication of the periodical was suspended after a few issues.

139. **Street Pharmacologist**. Coconut Grove, FL: Up Front, Inc. 1978- . Monthly. $20.00. (Address: P.O. Box 330589, Coconut Grove, FL 33133.)

The subtitle of this periodical is "Your Independent Drug Information Center." The publication contains news, comments, and articles related to drugs of abuse and their effects. In addition, analysis results of sample substances submitted to the journal are published. Each substance is described physically, with alleged contents, actual contents, and origin of the sample given in tabular form. The reader is advised that he or she may have a substance analyzed by wrapping a small sample of it and sending $5.00 to the address indicated. Later the reader may call anonymously and obtain the results.

The publication's aim is said to be to "collect and share information about drugs and health in ways designed to minimize problems people encounter in our chemically oriented society."

140.   **Substance and Alcohol Actions/Misuse: The International Research Journal for Rapid Communications in Basic and Clinical Science.** New York: Pergamon Press, 1980- . Bimonthly.

It is planned that this new rapid communication journal will focus on the basic mechanisms of actions and chronic effects of psychoactive agents having the potential for abuse. Clinical as well as basic sciences are to be covered. Articles published include original reports, mini- and state-of-the-art reviews, technical comments, short communications, and letters to the editor of a theoretical nature. Current information on research funding priorities is also included. Issues entirely devoted to a special topic will be published from time to time.

The journal is intended for biochemists, neurochemists, pharmacologists, anatomists, physiologists, endocrinologists, pathologists, toxicologists, behavioral scientists, and psychologists in government, industry, universities, hospitals, and clinics.

141.   **United Nations. Division of Narcotic Drugs. Information Letter.** United Nations, Division of Narcotic Drugs, Palais des Nations, CH-1211, Geneva 10, Switzerland. 1971- . Monthly.

These newsletters are not official documents, but are for information only. The publication is intended to disseminate useful new information that will help to improve understanding of the drug problem and the danger of its spreading. Foreign-language editions are available.

Among other newsworthy items, meetings are announced, publications listed, reports of research given, and approaches to drug control discussed.

142.   **U.S. Journal of Drug and Alcohol Dependence.** Miami, FL: U.S. Journal of Drug and Alcohol Dependence, Inc. 1977- . Monthly. $24.00.

The focus of this tabloid-sized publication is news and current concerns on all aspects of drug and alcohol abuse. Included are reports on federal legislative news as it relates to funding, regulations, and programming; advances in scientific research, treatment development, preventive education, enforcement policies, and social policy trends.

143.   **Washington Drug Review.** Washington: Resources News Service, Inc. 1970- . Monthly.

This newsletter merged with (as of October 1976) and now incorporates *Drugs and Drug Abuse Education News.* It provides key information from Washington on treatment and research phases of the drug abuse field. News of federal activities, trends, policies, and funding in the field is reported.

PART II

SOURCE MATERIAL BY SUBJECT AREA

5

GENERAL DISCUSSIONS, REVIEWS, HISTORIES, AND PERSONAL NARRATIVES

Most of the titles in this section provide general discussions of drugs and substance abuse problems. Several of these works deal with specific substances only, such as tranquilizers, sleeping pills, solvents, alcohol, and cocaine. There are about 15 titles of the personal narrative type, first hand accounts of experiences with drugs, and sometimes reports of treatment and cures. The latter often involve alcohol use. About 20 histories are listed, including accounts of the Prohibition era, works by Blocker, Coffey, Engelmann, Franklin, Kyvig, and Tyrrell.

Prohibition was a dead subject for many years, but the growing awareness of the current abuse problem has created new interest. Various viewpoints concerning the law are taken by the authors of these works. It has frequently been said that Prohibition did not prohibit. Per capita consumption of alcohol, however, did fall dramatically in the early years of Prohibition—as did alcohol related deaths. The books contain evidence, though, that some Americans went to absurd lengths to obtain illegal drink in the 1920s.

Also of historical value are reprinted editions of early works such as *The Narcotic Problem* by Ernest S. Bishop (entry 148), and Kane's *Opium Smoking in America and China* (entry 171). Books on psychoactive plants are growing in number, perhaps because of the current popular interest in herbs and herbal medicine, and several are listed here (*see* works by Emboden, Lehane, Ricciuti, Schleiffer, and Taylor). There are also some additional works on the subject listed in the section on hallucinogens.

Two titles listed here explore the use of drugs in classical literature: Tracy's *Subcutaneously, My Dear Watson* (entry 204), and Trawick's *Shakespeare and Alcohol* (entry 205).

144.   **Alcoholics Anonymous: The Story of How Many Thousands of Men and Women Have Recovered from Alcoholism**. 3rd ed. New York: Alcoholics Anonymous World Services, Inc. 1976. 575p. LC 76-4029. ISBN 0-916856-00-3.

The basic text for the Alcoholics Anonymous society, this book is now in its 3rd edition and has been very widely distributed since the 1st edition appeared in 1939. Called the "Big Book" by the A.A. members, its purpose has been to represent the membership of A.A. accurately, in the hope that many more would be led toward recovery by reading its explanation of the A.A. program and its evidence that the program works.

The first portion of the volume, which describes the A.A. recovery program, has been left unchanged through the course of revision. The second section, the

"Personal Stories," are divided into three groups. The first group, called "Pioneers of A.A.," has been preserved in full from the second edition. Thirteen new stories have been added in the 3rd edition to some older ones under the headings "They Stopped in Time" and "They Lost Nearly All." There are several appendices, notably a page on how to get in touch with A.A.

The personal stories are well-written, interesting, and representative of a variety of cases. Probably most alcoholics could identify with at least some of them.

145. Allen, Chaney. **I'm Black and I'm Sober.** Minneapolis, MN: CompCare Publications. 1978. 279p. illus. $6.95. LC 77-86454. ISBN 0-89638-008-4.

This book is an autobiographical account of a minister's daughter who is an alcoholic. She relates her experiences in fighting the disease and life in several places before she wins the battle and becomes an alcoholism lecturer and counsellor in San Diego. She gives credit to Alcoholics Anonymous, its principles, and fellowship, and includes other practical aids she has developed while working with alcoholics.

The same story was published in 1976 under the title: *I'm Black and I'm Drunk.*

146. Ausubel, David P. **What Every Well-Informed Person Should Know About Drug Addiction.** 2nd ed. Chicago: Nelson-Hall, 1980. 161p. bibliog. index. $12.95; $7.95pa. LC 79-16961. ISBN 0-88229-566-7; 0-88229-721-Xpa.

This is a revised and expanded edition of a 1958 work. The view of the physician author is that most persons, lay and professional, are poorly informed on drug addiction and that much misinformation is spread about. He attempts to set the record straight. Opiate addiction is stressed, but other drugs are also discussed.

The following are the chapter titles: 1) The problem of drug addiction, 2) Physiological and psychological effects of opiate drugs, 3) Psychological characteristics of opiate addiction, 4) Social characteristics of opiate addiciton, 5) Treatment and prognosis, 6) Addiction to nonopiate drugs, and 7) Prevention of drug addiction.

Ausubel's experience in working with addicted persons has led him to believe that a personality weakness predisposes some individuals toward addiction. As evidence of this he points to the motivational immaturity and feelings of inadequacy in those who turn to drugs to relieve their feelings and find hedonistic satisfaction. However, other factors are an influence, such as availability of drugs and social tolerance of their use.

It is made clear that the drug abuse problem is very complex, but the author believes that tough and honest enforcement of restrictive laws can perhaps eliminate much of the problem, but that strict enforcement is impossible when the population is apathetic or sympathetic toward drug use. Hospitalization is recommended for those already addicted, and harsher laws directed at pushers. Ausubel concludes that drug abuse will not be eliminated as long as related social problems such as unemployment, poor housing and nutrition, and discrimination exist. It is also important that more clinical and social research be carried out. He points to the adolescent and young male in urban slum areas abetted by adolescent stresses, gang influences, racial and social class tensions, social demoralization, availability of narcotics, and high community tolerance for the drug habit as making differential diagnosis difficult. There will be no dramatic breakthroughs in clinical drug addiction research soon.

147.   Bagshawe, A. F., G. Maina, and E. N. Mngola, eds. **The Use and Abuse of Drugs and Chemicals in Tropical Africa.** Proceedings of the 1973 Annual Scientific Conference of the East African Medical Research Council. Nairobi: East African Literature Bureau, 1974. 672p. bibliog. index.

The aim of this conference was to identify the medical, social, and environmental problems relating to the use and abuse of drugs and chemicals in the tropics, particularly in East Africa. The title of the book is somewhat misleading, as the papers do not deal with drug abuse in quite the usual sense of the term. The scope of the work is broader; it discusses overuse and irresponsible use of a very wide variety of medicines and chemicals. Antibiotics, antituberculosis drugs, pesticides, antidiabetic agents, corticosteroids, vaccines, diuretics, anesthetics, mercury-containing drugs, fungicides, and antihypertensives are discussed as well as some of the common drugs of abuse.

The subjects dealt with are timely because Africa has recently felt the full impact of the pharmaceutical revolution. Doctors leaving medical schools now have at their disposal a vast array of drugs. The conference participants hoped it would be possible to protect the physical and biological environment of Africa from the undesirable effects of drugs and chemicals and the young people from the "seductive ways of the new Western culture."

148.   Bishop, Ernest S. **The Narcotic Drug Problem.** New York: Macmillan, 1920; repr. New York: Arno Press, 1976. 165p. index. (Social Problems and Social Policy— the American Experience.) $10.00. LC 75-17204. ISBN 0-405-07476-X.

This work was reprinted because it was felt that there is a growing demand for material on the many aspects and phases of narcotic addiction and attempts at solution to the problem. The author was a medical practitioner who had had some experience with addicted patients and association with those who specialized in various aspects of the problem. His view was that two elements of the subject had received insufficient attention, one the suffering and struggles of the addict, and the other the nature of the physical disease with which the addict is afflicted. He attempts first to present the two elements, and secondly to make the reader aware of the importance of his own attitudes and activities in this regard for the benefit of humanity.

The following chapters are presented: 1) Introduction, 2) Fundamental considerations, 3) The nature of narcotic drug addiction-disease, 4) The mechanism of narcotic drug addiction disease, 5) Remarks on methods of treating narcotic drug addiction, 6) The rational handling of narcotic drug addiction-disease, 7) Relation of narcotic drug addiction to surgical cases and intercurrent diseases, 8) Laws, and their relations to narcotic drugs, 9) Some comments upon the legitimate use of narcotics in peace and war, 10) General survey of the situation and the need of the hour. A few case studies or personal statements have been appended. The addicted subjects for the most part became dependent on drugs because of some medical problem.

One gets the feeling while reading the book that the drug abuse problem has not changed a great deal since 1920. Presented are the familiar pleas for tolerance and understanding of the addict, more workable laws, better treatment modalities and facilities, and more research to reveal the mechanism of addiction.

149.   Blocker, Jack S., Jr., ed. **Alcohol, Reform and Society: The Liquor Issue in Social Context**. Westport, CT: Greenwood Press, 1979. 289p. bibliog. index. (Contributions in American History, No. 83.) $23.95. LC 78-73800. ISBN 0-313-20889-1.

The temperance movement in the U.S. has more often been studied for the insight it may provide into larger social processes than because of intrinsic interest in it. This book extends that tradition and, according to the editor, seeks two goals: 1) to explain the use of beverage alcohol and its response in terms of social structure, and 2) to identify and explain the effects of alcohol use and its response upon social structure.

Nine essays plus an introduction and a bibliography are presented reflecting the current state and suggest directions for further research. The chapters, by various authors who are either historians or sociologists, are as follows: 1) Introduction, 2) Sociological perspective on drinking and damage, 3) Temperance and economic change in the antebellum North, 4) "Water is indeed best": Temperance and the pre-Civil War New England college, 5) A social profile of the Women's Temperance Crusade: Hillsboro, Ohio, 6) Concerned citizens: The prohibitionists of 1883 Ohio, 7) The modernity of prohibitionists: An analysis of leadership structure and background, 8) Organized thirst: The story of repeal in Michigan, 9) Objection sustained: Prohibition repeal and the New Deal, 10) The Wet War: American liquor control, 1941-1945.

The focus of the book is on the northeastern U.S., where the organized temperance movement was strongest, and upon the years when the liquor issue was most prominent in American society and politics.

150.   Bryant, Lee. **The Magic Bottle**. Philadelphia and New York: A. J. Holman Co. Division of J. B. Lippincott Co., 1978. 253p. bibliog. $4.95pa. LC 78-16132. ISBN 0-87981-098-X.

An autobiographical account of Lee Bryant's successful battle with alcoholism, the work was undertaken because of the author's concern for the drinking women of today. Her view is that the plight of the woman alcoholic is usually ignored by society. The story of her own torment, the bizarre episodes of her life, and the details of her turn to sobriety with the help of spiritual guidance and religion are presented. It is a touching, moving story, probably typical in many aspects, and it should provide insights and offer support and inspiration to alcoholics and those concerned with them. There are strong religious overtones throughout the account.

151.   Burkett, Michael. **Tranquilizers: A Critical Look at America's Number One Drug Family**. Phoenix, AZ: Do It Now Foundation, 1975. 22p. bibliog. $0.40pa.

This short pamphlet discusses tranquilizers (defined broadly) for the layman, indicating their effects and the dangers inherent in their overuse. In conclusion, the author comments that like most drugs, tranquilizers can be beneficial in the hands of the right physician, but when any workable nondrug alternative can be employed, the benefits *always* exceed the risks.

The following drugs are discussed in some detail: Benzodiazapines (Valium, Librium), tri-cyclic anti-depressants, methaqualone, phenothiazines (Thorazine, et al.), phenobarbital, and meprobamate. Other sections are on the following topics: The prescribers; the prescribees; alcohol-tranquilizer combinations; tranquilizers, driving, and assorted safety tips; tranquilizers, pregnancy, and the nursing mother; shelf-life of prescription drugs in general; what to do if you are strung out; encountering overdoses and emergency situations.

Although brief, the booklet offers good practical advice and is well worth reading.

152.   Coffey, Thomas M. **The Long Thirst: Prohibition in America: 1920-1933**. New York: W. W. Norton, 1975. 346p. bibliog. index. $9.95. LC 75-17816. ISBN 0-393-05557-4.

The intent of this book is not to present a comprehensive history of the Prohibition Era but to focus on some of the events and careers of a selected group of individuals, and to "tell the story of Prohibition in human terms."

The author's view is that Prohibition was a mistake. His account emphasizes the growth of disrespect for law, the rise of organized crime, and the social strife unleashed by proponents and opponents of legal alcohol. The prohibitionists portrayed in the book make a poor showing, and proponents are pictured as more humane than their opponents.

The book does not directly suggest parallels between people portrayed in the book and specific people today, but there are implications of such.

153.   Donlan, Joan. **I Never Saw the Sun Rise**. Minneapolis, MN: CompCare Publications, 1977. 199p. illus. $5.95pa. LC 77-87738. ISBN 0-89638-007-6.

This book is a teenager's diary which covers a year and a half. During that time the writer became addicted to alcohol and drugs and went through treatment to become well again. It is a sensitive, very private account by a talented writer. Line drawings and poems by the author have been included.

Some insights into why teenagers use drugs can possibly be gained from the account, and it should interest parents, teachers, counselors, ministers, law enforcement officers, and physicians as well as young people.

154.   **Drugs and Drug Dependence**. Edited by Griffith Edwards, M. A. H. Russell, David Hawks, and Maxine MacCafferty on behalf of the Addiction Research Unit, Institute of Psychiatry, University of London. Farnborough, England, and Lexington, MA: Saxon House/Lexington Books, 1976. 252p. bibliog. index. (Saxon House Studies.) $18.00. LC 75-30136. ISBN 0-347-01126-8.

To present a view of how research methods have been applied to the socio-medical aspects of drug abuse, this work is in two sections: research studies and theoretical considerations. The research studies section is further divided into two parts. The first group of papers is concerned with epidemiological studies, and the second group with therapeutic aspects. Each section ends with a good editorial appraisal.

The book presents a realistic view of the drug abuse problem, with emphasis on the United Kingdom. Areas of ignorance are pointed out and important questions raised. Psychologists, psychiatrists, and social workers will be most interested in it. The theoretical chapters are especially noteworthy.

155.   Emboden, William. **Narcotic Plants**. rev. and enl. New York: Macmillian Publishing Co., 1979. 206p. illus. (part col.). bibliog. index. $15.95. LC 79-11758. ISBN 02-535480-9.

This is the 2nd edition of a successful 1972 publication that was perhaps the first comprehensive book of its kind on psychoactive plants. It presents an overview of the historical and contemporaneous use of psychoactive drugs throughout the world. The disciplines of botany, chemistry, anthropology, and archeology are integrated to explain the curious uses of the plants throughout history. The author, who is a Professor of Botany at California State University at Northridge and Research Associate in Botany at the Natural History Museum in Los Angeles, hopes the reader can learn something about narcotic plants and that the book will help clear up misconceptions, particularly so more informed decisions can be made by legislators, teachers, and the users of the plant drugs.

Emboden presents in narrative form how drugs have been used in almost every civilization of the ancient and modern world and how they have influenced the arts, religion, science, and medicine. Most ancient civilizations used them in magical and religious contexts, in foretelling the future, in communicating with the dead, and in withstanding the duress of harsh environments.

There are chapters on hypnotica (the sedatives and tranquilizers), tobacco (the enigmatic narcotic), hallucinogens, stimulants, and inebriants. In addition, two appendices cover a proposed structuring of some known mind-altering plant chemicals and a summation of the botany, geography, psychopharmacology and chemistry of narcotic plants. The latter is an abbreviated synopsis of the plants figured in the text. The following information is given about each: scientific name, common name(s), family, habitat, botanical description, primary narcotic effect, and active principle(s).

Emboden passes little judgment on the individuals who use psychoactive drugs today. He points out that every civilization has had to decide whether use of a certain drug constitutes a socially acceptable pastime or violates a legal or social sanction.

The work is well-done, and the illustrations, as in the original edition, are exceptionally fine.

It should be noted that the author has used the term "narcotic" in a very broad sense. A number of the substances discussed (e.g., coffee, tobacco, and Rauwolfia) are not ordinarily considered narcotics.

156.   Engelmann, Larry. **Intemperance: The Lost War Against Liquor.** New York: Free Press, 1979. 252p. bibliog. index. $10.95. LC 79-7103. ISBN 0-02-909520-4.

The story of prohibition in Michigan is told in this book by a journalist author. Michigan was considered a key state in the movement both by leaders of the temperance group and by law enforcement officials who were seeking a place for a controlled experiment. The aims of neither group were realized as much controversy, organized crime, and many confrontations developed there.

The book traces the beginnings of prohibition in the 1890s when there were great numbers of saloons in America, one for every 300 persons by 1907. It is presumed that the primary reason for the popularity of drinking places was a social one. They provided a variety of services for the working class, immigrants especially, and also acted as a safety valve for discontent. However, saloons came to be regarded as breeders of crime, violence, and prostitution, and large numbers joined the crusade against them by the mid 1910s. In 1916 a vote on the issue came up in Michigan, and eventually prohibition became law.

The state became the scene for many confrontations between law enforcement officers and rum-runners. In addition, temperance leaders, politicians, sociologists, the press, and others became involved in the controversy. Organized crime became established, and profits on rum-running and smuggling between Michigan and Canada were high. Unsuccessful attempts at enforcing prohibition and the depressed economy of the time turned the tide again, and Michigan was the first state to ratify the Twenty-first Amendment to the Constitution which repealed prohibition.

The subject has passed into obscurity for the most part, but since the rise of drug abuse of recent years and pressure to legalize the use of drugs such as marijuana, the history of the prohibition movement has been given more attention. The book is well-written and interesting and probably provides some insight into the social history of the time.

157.   Fleming, Alice. **Alcohol—the Delightful Poison: A History**. New York: Delacorte Press, 1975. 138p. illus. bibliog. index. $6.95. LC 74-22629. ISBN 0-440-01796-3.

This history of the use of alcohol begins with ancient Babylon and biblical times and ends with the current scene of increased drinking among American teenagers. It is well-done with interesting illustrations, a lively style, and a balanced view.

The presentation is in three parts: the history of alcohol, alcohol in America, and myth and truth. The chapter titles are as follows: 1) The discovery of alcohol, 2) Drinking in history, 3) Drinking customs and ceremonies, 4) Liquor in the language, 5) From colonial breweries to gin mills, 6) The teetotalers take over, 7) Prohibition: the noble experiment, 8) The mystery of alcoholism, 9) Myths and mistakes, and 10) The sober truth.

158.   Franklin, Jimmie Lewis. **Born Sober: Prohibition in Oklahoma, 1907-1959**. With a Foreword by J. Howard Edmondson. Norman, OK: University of Oklahoma Press, 1971. 212p. bibliog. index. LC 70-160492. ISBN 0-8061-0964-5.

An account of the political maneuvering surrounding Prohibition and repeal in Oklahoma, this book is suitable for both the general reader and the specialist in American social history.

Oklahoma passed a prohibition law in 1907. When it entered the Union it had prohibition written into its constitution. Continued pressure was applied to keep the state dry by such groups as the Anti-Saloon League and the Woman's Christian Temperance Union. In addition, the presence of Indians influenced prohibition legislation in the early years. It was felt that alcohol had to be kept from Indians for their own protection and that of society.

In 1933 the prohibition section of the Oklahoma constitution was altered to permit the sale of 3.2 percent beer. In 1959 a referendum was held in the state. Enforcement of the law had been difficult, and the voters ended prohibition in Oklahoma.

The author makes an attempt to integrate the Oklahoma story with that of the entire national experience.

159.   Girdano, Dorothy Dusek, and Daniel A. Girdano. **Drugs—A Factual Account**. 2nd ed. Reading, MA: Addison-Wesley Publishing Co., 1976. 232p. illus. bibliog. index. (Addison-Wesley Series in Health Education.) LC 75-18154.

The first edition of the work appeared in 1973. This edition, like the earlier, depicts the historical, social, and legal impact of drugs on society, and, in addition, provides information on the physiology of the nervous system and the pharmacology of drugs which will help the reader understand the drug problem, particularly behavior changes.

The following chapters are presented: 1) Why drugs? 2) Physiological basis of drug action on the central nervous system, 3) Alcohol, 4) Marijuana: the great debate, 5) LSD and other hallucinogens, 6) Amphetamines and other stimulants, 7) Smoking and health, 8) Barbiturates and nonbarbiturate sedatives, 9) The opiates, 10) Nonprescription drugs, 11) Drugs and the law, and 12) On being high. The chapters on smoking and on being high are new in this edition. Also, more complete information has been provided about the nervous system, and the counterculture is treated in more depth. The chapter "on being high" discusses non-drug highs such as meditation, biofeedback, yoga, and self-transcendence as well as drug highs. A glossary and special terminology sections have been provided.

The authors are professors of health education, and those involved in such pursuits particularly will find the book of interest.

160.   Glatt, M. M., ed. **Drug Dependence: Current Problems and Issues.** Baltimore, University Park Press, 1977. 332p. bibliog. index. $28.50. LC 77-2211. ISBN 0-8391-1101-0.

Each of the 12 chapters in this book is written by an internationally known authority, providing an in-depth study of the whole problem of drug dependence. The chapters are arranged under five headings as follows: 1) Nature, aetiology, epidemiology, 2) Medical complications, 3) Treatment, 4) Prevention, and 5) The laboratory's contribution.

The intent of the book is not to cover the whole   subject comprehensively and systematically; rather, it aims at discussing in greater depth than usual the aspects of the subject that are often not given the attention they deserve. The intended audience is professional readers with some postgraduate professional experience or interest in the subject matter. There is a great deal of material on the nature, causation, developmental process, physical complications, treatment, rehabilitation, and prevention of drug abuse.

161.   Goddard, Donald. **Easy Money.** New York: Farrar, Straus, and Giroux, 1978. 366p. $10.00. LC 77-29120.

This book is purported to be the true story of Frank Matthews, a black heroin and cocaine dealer who conspired with George Ramos to smuggle about $100 million worth of narcotics into the United States in 1972. The story was told to the author, a British journalist, by Ramos, who later gave testimony to the federal authorities which resulted in breaking the case (although Matthews escaped capture and presumably fled from the United States).

A revolting, although perhaps fascinating, picture is drawn of Frank Matthews who made $30 million by the time he was 29 years old. He wore pink leather jackets and floor-length white mink coats and drove luxurious Cadillacs and Mercedeses (he once mislaid a Mercedes altogether; narcotics officers found it months later in Harlem, covered with dust, but intact). It was said that Matthews tested whether he had cut his drugs with enough lactose by trying a dose on a local addict. If the unfortunate victim overdosed, Matthews knew he had to cut the drug more.

The author says he is concerned mainly with the nature of illegal drug traffic. His viewpoint is that the government is waging a futile war on human weakness. It would be preferable and as cheap, he thinks, to dispense drugs of abuse free to registered addicts at government clinics.

162.   Gottlieb, Adam. **Sex Drugs and Aphrodisiacs: Where to Obtain Them, How to Use Them, and Their Effects.** New York: San Francisco, CA: High Times/Level Press, 1974. 84p. $3.50pa.

The author of this small book states at the outset that many of the aphrodisiac materials offered for sale through advertisements in underground publications are of little value and outrageously overpriced. He sets about to tell the reader "what these aphrodisiac substances are, what effects they have, how they work, and how to use and not abuse them, and the names of legitimate suppliers." Included are discussions of some illegal drugs.

About 60 substances are discussed in alphabetical order. The entries include information on source of the substance, supposed effects, toxicity, ill effects, occasional historical and sociological comments, and perhaps methods of preparation for use.

The material presented seems to be reasonably accurate although no scientific documentation is included. It should be borne in mind that genuine aphrodisiacs have so far defied scientific detection; they exist mainly in folklore.

163.   Greene, Shep. **The Boy Who Drank Too Much**. New York: Viking Press, 1979. 149p. $8.95. LC 78-26370. ISBN 0-670-18381-4.

This book, aimed at the juvenile reader, is a fictional account of the life of a teenage alcoholic. The young victim's father is responsible for the death of the boy's mother who died in a car crash because of the father's drinking. The father relieves his tensions by beating the boy and relives his past achievements by pushing the son to excel on the school hockey team. The son is isolated and lonely and takes to drink. His condition deteriorates until he begins to accept help. The author gives a realistic description of the results of alcohol abuse, but shows how victims can be helped.

164.   Hafen, Brent Q., and Brenda Peterson. **Medicines and Drugs: Problems and Risks, Use and Abuse**. 2nd ed. Philadelphia, PA: Lea and Febiger, 1978. 429p. bibliog. index. $12.95pa. LC 78-5901. ISBN 0-8121-0637-7.

Prepared by two members of the Department of Health Sciences of Brigham Young University, this book is designed especially for use as a text in service courses on drugs and society or drug abuse in health education or psychology. It will also be of interest and value to those affected one way or another by a drug problem by helping them understand its nature. Material has been gleaned from many sources and compiled to provide the reader with understanding and insights into risks, benefits, and problems related to the therapeutic use of drugs and the abuse of these and illicit drugs. The subject has been treated comprehensively, sensibly, and well.

The authors' view is that too liberal use of over-the-counter products and liberal prescribing practices of some physicians have contributed to drug abuse. Although sincere efforts have been made to improve drug safety and advertising honesty, consumers cannot rely alone on these safeguards. The nature of the risks should be realized. The first chapters deal with the therapeutic use of drugs; the latter with abuse.

Chapter headings are as follows: 1) The health value of drugs, 2) Over-the-counter drugs, 3) Prescription drugs, 4) Drug development and safety, 5) Drug hazards and actions, 6) Drugs and pregnancy, 7) The problem and risk of drug abuse, 8) Motivational aspects of drug abuse, 9) The effect of mass media on drug abuse, 10) Drug dependence, 11) The social and psychological impact of drug abuse, 12) Legal control of drugs, 13) Alcohol and alcoholism, 14) Smoking, 15) Common stimulants, 16) Hypnosedatives and minor tranquilizers, 17) The narcotics, 18) Marihuana, 19) The hallucinogens, 20) Volatile substances, 21) Treatment and rehabilitation of the drug dependent, and 22) Preventing drug abuse. In addition, a glossary of technical terms has been provided.

165.   Hartmann, Ernest. **The Sleeping Pill**. New Haven, CT: Yale University Press, 1978. 313p. bibliog. index. $14.00. LC 78-6205. ISBN 0-300-02248-4.

The essays that compose this work are based upon research in the area of sleep. Since sleeping pills (or hypnotic medication) are frequently abused, the work is suitable for review here.

The contents are as follows: 1) Introduction, 2) Sleeping pills, past and present, 3) Who uses how much of what?, 4) Sleep, 5) The effect of sleeping pills on sleep, 6) Insomnia, 7) The psychodynamics of the sleeping pill, 8) The benefits and risks of sleeping pills, 9) Toward a safe and rational sleeping pill: three approaches, 10) L-tryptophan, and 11) The sleeping pill: conclusions. There are, in addition, two substantial appendices that directly report on research: 1) The effects of drugs on sleep: laboratory studies, and 2) The effects of drugs on sleep: a clinical study of sleeping medication.

Hartmann concludes that treatment for insomnia should be treatment for a specific illness or underlying cause whenever possible. There are times when the use of sleeping pills is appropriate, but they are overprescribed and overused, he says. They are dangerous, and the risks outweigh the benefits. Further, he believes that safer, more natural drugs may be developed, but thinks overall use will gradually decrease.

166.   Hyde, Margaret O. **Addictions: Gambling, Smoking, Cocaine Use, and Others.** New York: McGraw-Hill Book Co., 1978. 150p. bibliog. index. $7.95. LC 77-17024. ISBN 0-07-031645-7.

Written on the popular level, this book explores the roots of addiction in a nontechnical manner. The following are the chapter titles: 1) What is addiction?, 2) Cigarettes, 3) Compulsive gambling, 4) Addiction to food, 5) Coffee, tea, and colas, 6) Cocaine and other stimulants, 7) Alcohol, barbiturates, and tranquilizers, 8) The marijuana controversy, 9) Heroin and other opiates, and 10) Jogging and other addictions. As can be seen, some unusual "addictions" are discussed, such as gambling, overeating, and jogging. The author compares these with drug use, although addiction to jogging is called "positive addiction."

The book is interesting to read and is somewhat instructive, but it really answers few questions about the complex nature of addiction.

167.   Inglis, Brian. **The Forbidden Game: A Social History of Drugs.** New York: Charles Scribner's Sons, 1975. 256p. bibliog. index. $8.95. LC 75-12382. ISBN 0-684-14428-X.

This book was written by a British journalist, not a scientist or a historian. Emphasis is on the social aspects of drug use throughout history. The following are the chapter titles: 1) Drugs and shamanism, 2) Drugs and the priesthood, 3) The impact of drugs on civilisation, 4) The impact of civilisation, 5) Spirits, 6) The Opium Wars, 7) Indian hemp, 8) The poet's eye, 9) Science, 10) Prohibition, 11) The international anti-drug campaign, 12) Heroin and cannabis, 13) The collapse of control, and 14) Psychopharmacology.

The author's views range widely. One expressed opinion is that society should decide how to legalize a "social" drug rather than whether or not it should be legalized. To prohibit it has historically been shown to be futile, he says, and a person may be driven from a minor to a major drug by prohibition. Further, he thinks that governments are not honest about why they attack drug habits. He believes they do so because they fear drugs will make people, particularly the young, less amenable to discipline, and are not primarily concerned about the health, morals, and welfare of their subjects. He recognizes that all drugs can have adverse effects, but feels that their use with discrimination is acceptable and sees value in the drug-induced vision of a wider existence brought on by hallucinogens.

Whatever the merit of the author's many views, he lacks understanding of psychopharmacology and the nature of addiction. He sees addiction as a psychological disorder—an oversimplification of a complex condition. The book is probably of most value for the history it contains.

168.   International Action Conference on Substance Abuse, First, November 9-13, 1977. **Proceedings.** Vol. 1, *Alcohol: Use and Abuse.* Vol. 2, *Education and Health.* Vol. 3, *Intervention and Prevention.* Vol. 4, *Treatment and Therapeutic Communities.* Phoenix, AZ: Do It Now Foundation, 1979. 4 v. bibliog. $35.00pa. set; $10.00 each.

These volumes contain the proceedings of a conference sponsored by the Do It Now Foundation and the International Council on Alcohol and Addictions. Also cosponsoring were a number of other organizations concerned with drug abuse. The proceedings have been transcribed from tapes; no formal papers were presented, although some follow-up documents are included. The participants are not for the most part well-known experts in the field, but are individuals who have been in close contact with substance abuse and/or abusers in one way or another. Many are involved with treatment centers, hospitals, local community programs, and educational institutions. Over 125 sessions were offered at the conference, and these volumes present the best of them.

169.   Jones, Hardin B., and Helen C. Jones. **Sensual Drugs: Deprivation and Rehabilitation of the Mind.** New York: Cambridge University Press, 1977. 373p. bibliog. index. $15.95; $3.95pa. LC 76-8154. ISBN 0-521-21247-2; 0-521-29077-5pa.

The senior author of this work is a professor of medical physics and physiology and has served as a consultant to the U.S. Department of Defense on the drug abuse problems of servicemen. Much of the material presented was used in a course on drug abuse for students who had no background in physiology. For this reason the book is quite readable, although perhaps a bit oversimplified in the pharmacological area.

Chapter headings are as follows: 1) Introduction: sensual drug abuse, 2) The brain, the senses, and pleasure, 3) Action of sensual drugs, 4) Hazards of sensual drugs, 5) Addiction and dependency, 6) Sexual deprivation, 7) Drug abuse among American soldiers in Southeast Asia, 8) Rehabilitation, 9) Mind expansion, and 10) Marijuana.

The material presented is controversial to some degree because the viewpoint taken is that the health hazards of drug use, particularly marijuana, are much more serious than many believe. Documentation for this view is included. A good deal of emphasis has been put on the effects of drugs on the sexual processes, and evidence is given to show that sexual responses are altered and functions impaired by drugs, a powerful influence, the authors feel, in getting addicts to give up drugs.

The book is intended for the drug user and for those who deal with problems arising from drug use. The advice offered to the drug abuser, said to be old fashioned, is as follows: resolve to give up drugs; improve general health; develop the capacity for enjoyment; give support and affection; reestablish self-confidence; and attend to spiritual needs.

The noted pharmacologist, W. D. M. Paton, says in the conclusion of his Foreword to the book: "To my mind, one of the deepest indictments of Western culture is, not the existence of a drug "problem" (that is an ancient phenomenon), but the fact that for many, their use of drugs has been the most interesting thing they have yet met in life. It is because the book takes things seriously at this level that I so willingly write this foreword."

170.   Jones, Kenneth L., Louis W. Shainberg, and Curtis O. Byer. **Drugs and Alcohol**. 3rd ed. New York: Harper and Row, 1979. 214p. illus. bibliog. index. $6.50pa. LC 78-15391. ISBN 0-06-043436-8.

This book is a current text and reference work on drug types and actions, drug laws, treatment, and psychological implications of drug use. The authors take the view that each person must make decisions regarding the use of drugs and alcohol, and must act as an informed member of society where voting or expressing opinions on the legality of drugs is concerned. The readers of the book are provided with facts about drugs to enable them to make better decisions. The authors are college faculty members who have had many years of communication with young people, and the book is suitable for textbook use. A glossary has been provided, and each chapter closes with a summary in outline form.

The chapter headings are: 1) Proper use of drugs, 2) Neurological aspects of abusible drugs, 3) Drugs commonly abused, 4) Psychological and sociological factors in drug abuse, 5) Enforcement and/or treatment?, 6) Alcoholic beverages: use and abuse, and 7) Alcoholism (alcohol dependence).

The book contains much practical material. For instance, there is a 10-page table of drug interactions, a table of physiological effects of alcoholic beverages, a diagram of the legal process for commitment for drug abuse in California, a diagram of overlapping effects of abused drug groups, and a chart of the spectrum and continuum of drug actions.

The section on alcohol abuse addresses special problems, such as the young problem drinker and alcoholism in women and the elderly. Good material is included to assist individuals in recognizing an alcohol problem in themselves as well as in others.

171.   Kane, Harry Hubbell. **Opium-Smoking in America and China**. New York: Arno Press, 1976. (Reprint of the edition published by Putnam in 1882). 156p. bibliog. (Social Problems and Social Policy: The American Experience.) $10.00. LC 75-17227. ISBN 0-405-07497-2.

The 1882 edition of this work carried the subtitle: "A Study of Its Prevalence, and Effects, Immediate and Remote, on the Individual and the Nation." The author was a physician who believed that descriptions in travel books of the practice of opium use available in the 1880s were either very meagre or positively untruthful. He regretted that "some six thousand of our countrymen, male and female, whose ranks are being daily recruited from the over-curious, foolish, indolent, or wilfully vicious . . . abound in places where this drug is sold and smoked."

The following topics are discussed: origin and spread of opium use; early history of opium growth in India; description of the manner of smoking; effects upon the novice; general effects of the practice; effects on the different systems, organs, etc.; cures, relapses and mode of treatment; and the opium trade.

The author felt that the opium habit could be cured although he allowed he had not treated enough cases nor had enough time elapsed to speak definitely about relapses.

The book is interesting particularly for the history included. Sadly, it reminds one that things have not progressed very far in drug abuse prevention and treatment in the past 100 years. The author's "Measures for Reform" sound very familiar.

172.   Kirkpatrick, Jean. **Turnabout: Help for a New Life.** Garden City, NY: Doubleday, 1978. 183p. index. $6.95. LC 77-79558. ISBN 0-385-12513-5.

This work is an autobiographical account of the last years of Jean Kirkpatrick's problem drinking and subsequent recovery. The author, who has a Ph.D. degree in sociology, aims the work at the woman who is worried about her drinking. She describes her thoughts and feelings, the loss of control over alcohol, and the subsequent feelings of being sick, remorseful, and guilty.

Most of the book is the author's personal account of her struggle. The last chapters, however, discuss the self-help program of treatment, "Women for Sobriety," which was founded in 1975 by Dr. Kirkpatrick to help women overcome problem drinking. The organization is similar to Alcoholics Anonymous. However, members need not say that they are "alcoholic," only that they have a "drinking problem." There are "13 Statements of Acceptance" (similar to A.A.'s 12 Steps). The difference lies in W.F.S.'s emphasis on overcoming self-defeating guilt and building strengths rather than admitting to weaknesses. In addition, it is felt that many women require the all-female corrective experience. If there are no males present there can be no relying on a male for direction and approval, and productive models of behavior can be substituted.

The concluding chapter tells the reader how to go about obtaining information on how to join or start a Women for Sobriety group.

173.   Kurtz, Ernest. **Not-God: A History of Alcoholics Anonymous.** Center City, MN: Hazelden Educational Services, 1979. 363p. bibliog. index. $12.95. LC 79-88264. ISBN 0-89486-065-8.

The author of this work, a historian, was given access to the archival files of Alcoholics Anonymous in order to produce this account of the discovery and development of the program and fellowship of A.A. The title refers to the message of A.A. to its members that they are not infinite, not absolute, *Not-God*. The message insists that alcoholics are not in control of themselves; they are powerless over alcohol.

The book contains a great many anecdotes and excerpts from the diaries, correspondence, and memoirs of A.A.'s early figures. The author points out the debts that A.A. owes to such persons and groups as the psychiatrist Carl Jung, the philosopher William James, the Akron social matron Henrietta Seiberling, John D. Rockefeller, Jr., the Oxford Group of Frank Buchman (who attempted to recapture primitive Christianity), some Irish-American Catholic priests, and fundamental religion.

The presentation is in two parts, the history and the interpretation. Chapter headings are as follows: 1) Beginnings: November 1934-June 1935. The limitations of the drinking alcoholic, 2) First growth: June 1935-November 1937. The limitations of the sober alcoholic, 3) Independent existence: November 1937-October 1939. Finding wholeness in limitation, 4) Prelude to maturity: October 1939-March 1941. Needing others—the era of publicity, 5) Attaining maturity: 1941-1955. The limitations of Alcoholics Anonymous, 6) Responsibilities of maturity: 1955-1971. Alcoholics Anonymous and the wholeness of limitation, 7) The larger context of American history, 8) The context of the history of religious ideas, and 9) The meaning and significance of Alcoholics Anonymous.

The book is outstanding in a number of respects. It is very readable and interesting; it places the psychological and religious underpinnings of the organization in perspective; and it should provide support to anyone undergoing the experience of alcoholism or other dependency treatment.

174.   Kyvig, David E. **Repealing National Prohibition.** Chicago: University of Chicago Press, 1979. 274p. illus. bibliog. index. $21.00. LC 79-13516. ISBN 0-226-46641-8.

The author of this well-documented work is a historian who has presented a thoughtful account of the adopting of national prohibition in the U.S. and its subsequent repeal. The emphasis is not on the sensational aspect of the era—gang wars and bathtub gin—but rather upon the organizations, individuals, and social, economic, and political influences that shaped the sequence of events. The author's view is that historians have never adequately explored the reasons of the Eighteenth Amendment's reversal, the process by which it occurred, or why it occurred so soon after the adoption of the amendment. He has attempted to throw light on the shifts in political attitudes of the time and upon the processes involved. The story is told of the resourcefulness of the prohibitionists in getting the prohibition amendment passed, and then the equal resourcefulness of the repealists in getting it repealed, both unexpected political events.

In conclusion, Kyvig points out that the problem of alcohol remains unsolved. Of many approaches to liquor regulation tried by states since 1933, not one has been a success at producing temperate drinking. No balance has been reached between helping alcohol abusers and respecting the desires of those who use it sensibly. However, it seems unlikely that national prohibition will ever again be tried.

175.   Lehane, Brendan. **The Power of Plants.** Designed by Emil Bührer and Robert Tobler. New York: McGraw-Hill Book Co., 1977. 288p. illus. (part col.). bibliog. index. $39.95. LC 77-7551. ISBN 0-07-037055-9.

This fine book, with more than 800 beautiful illustrations, is based on the view that plants are the foundation of all existence. "They are the source of our nourishment and health, pleasures and ecstasies; they sustain religions, cultures, civilizations."

Of the five chapters, on various aspects of plants, there is one of about 50 pages on the "Power to Alter Consciousness." Subheadings used are: 1) Doors of perception, 2) Philters—potions for lovers, 3) Journeys of the mind, 4) Peyote, ololiuqui, mandragora, 5) Tobacco, coca, betel nut, 6) Ayahuasca, kava-kava, coffee, 7) Khat, magic mushroom, fly agaric, 8) Iboga, chocolate, cola, 9) Tempest in a teapot, 10) Wine—the red and the white, 11) Beer—the celestial gargle, 12) Cannabis—hemp, hash, pot, bhang, 13) Opium—somber and seductive splendors, 14) LSD and the Fire of St. Anthony, and 15) Art and drugs.

A fascinating account is presented with emphasis on history, art, legend, and lore.

176.   Leite, Evelyn. **To Be Somebody.** Center City, MN: Hazelden Literature, 1979. 146p. $3.95pa. LC 78-060063. ISBN 0-89486-060-7.

A personal account of a woman's life whose husband is an alcoholic, this book portrays how the wife gains a hold on her life with the help of Al-anon. The author shows the truth of Al-anon's viewpoint that those who live with an alcoholic become victims as much as the alcoholic is.

Possibly, the story is typical of those who are victimized by alcoholism, and perhaps those in similar circumstances who read the book will be able to benefit from it and shortcut their own road to recovery.

177.   Luks, Allan, comp. and ed. **Having Been There**. Introduction by Ring Lardner, Jr. New York: Charles Scribner's Sons, 1979. (Available from the National Council on Alcoholism, Inc., New York City Affiliate, 133 East 62nd St., New York, NY 10021.) 189p. $8.95. LC 79-84843. ISBN 0-684-16170-2.

The short stories in this collection portray the struggles of alcoholics and those who have been affected by alcoholism in others. There are 18 stories, chosen from over 500 entries in a national competition sponsored by the National Council on Alcoholism, New York City Affiliate. The stories are excellent; a remarkable perspective on the alcoholic condition has been achieved. The rationalizations, the denials, the tricks, the games, and the nightmares of the alcoholic are all revealed in the stories. The highly personal narratives cover the complete range of the alcoholic problem: the beginning stages, habitual drunkenness, the call for help, and eventually the steps to giving up drinking.

The stories are grouped in three sections: 1) Their children, spouses, lovers, brothers . . . , 2) Drinkers and their stories, and 3) Tomorrow will (not) begin a new life.

The plots of the tales are different. Included are stories about a boy scheming to have his alcoholic father beaten, a physician diagnosing the irreversible deterioration of an alcoholic who has refused treatment, a talented entertainer sacrificing her career to assist a quarrelsome alcoholic lover, and a recovered woman nervously attending a cocktail party but having the courage to drink coffee.

Everyone should read the book. It is deeply touching as well as enlightening. Both alcoholics and others will gain a better understanding of the addiction.

178.   Madden, J. S. **A Guide to Alcohol and Drug Dependence**. Bristol, England: John Wright and Sons, 1979. 248p. illus. bibliog. index. £8.50. ISBN 0-7236-0504-1.

This is an introductory text most suitable for medical students, but physicians, health professionals, social workers, and law enforcement officers can also benefit by reading it. Clinical features and treatment of dependence are stressed.

An introductory chapter covers the definitions, incidence, and causes of alcohol and drug dependence; following are chapters on alcohol and other drugs. Disabilities, social features, and the psychological aspects of treatment are considered. For each group of substances discussed the following is given: chemistry, pharmacology, and acute and chronic toxicity; potential for physical dependence; treatment of acute intoxication and withdrawal; long-term management; and prognosis. Covered are barbiturates, opioids, amphetamines, hallucinogens, cannabis, benzodiazepines, solvent inhalation, and obsolete drugs such as methaqualone and phenacetin. The last chapter is on prevention of drug dependence.

For added interest the author has made references from time to time of drug use by literary figures such as De Quincey, Coleridge, and Baudelaire. The book is very well documented with extensive literature references with each chapter.

179.   Madden, J. S., Robin Walker, and W. H. Kenyon, eds. **Alcoholism and Drug Dependence: A Multidisciplinary Approach**. Proceedings of the Third International Congress on Alcoholism and Drug Dependence held in Liverpool, England, April 4-9, 1976. New York: Plenum Press, 1977. 479p. bibliog. index. $39.50. LC 76-30574. ISBN 0-306-31019-8.

The papers reprinted here survey recent advances in the knowledge of the aetiology, epidemiology, early recognition, management, and the social and industrial implications of drug and alcohol abuse. Experts from 18 countries presented the papers, which are grouped under these five headings: 1) General, 2) Aetiology and epidemiology, 3) Treatment, 4) Rehabilitation, and 5) Prevention and education.

A few of the findings as reported follow. The per capita rate of alcohol consumption of a nation intimately affects its incidence of alcohol problems. However, the amount of alcohol consumed within a state is usually amenable to government intervention by legal and fiscal measures. Different attitudes and culturally determined reactions to alcohol use contribute to the differing incidences of alcoholism among communities. The surge of drug abuse had lost impetus at the time of the conference, but the alcoholism problem was growing.

180.   Marks, John. **The Benzodiazepines: Use, Overuse, Misuse, Abuse.** Baltimore, MD: University Park Press, 1978. 111p. bibliog. index. $15.00. LC 78-54673. ISBN 0-8391-1266-1.

The author in his Foreword tells briefly about how the benzodiazepine drug with the trade name Librium was discovered when a laboratory was being cleaned out because a project was being abandoned. The drug was found to be a sedative and muscle relaxant of considerable value. Other drugs of this chemical group were developed subsequently. However, as is so often the case, there has been concern about whether dependence results from continued use. This book contains the author's independent analysis of the problem.

The work is in four parts: 1) The general problem of dependence, 2) Benzodiazepine dependence, 3) Significance of benzodiazepine dependence within the community, and 4) Conclusions.

In the second part the evidence concerning the benzodiazepines is analyzed critically. Details of animal studies, human experiments, reports, anecdotes, and surveys are considered. The dependency syndrome is described. The role of these compounds in mixed drug abuse is considered, as is the risk of dependence when they are used therapeutically. Medical, social, and legal aspects are considered in the third section.

The author's conclusions are that there are too many protests from the would-be drug controllers, although it is obvious that this group of drugs produces withdrawal symptoms similar to those produced by barbiturates, but not so severe. Patients become anxious when they learn of this. However, one should see the problem in social perspective. People have always sought sedatives or stimulants to ease their lot in life, and always will. If every addictive drug were banned, we would force everyone back to alcohol (which, of course, is already the case to a certain extent). Dr. Marks feels that benzodiazepines are the least addictive and aggression-producing drugs of our presently known tranquilizers.

181.   Marr, Dean. **From Liquor to Loneliness to Love and Laughter.** Kansas City, MO: Sheed Andrews and McMeel, Inc., 1978. 175p. LC 78-59657. ISBN 0-8362-6502-5.

In this personal narrative of a recovered alcoholic, the author tells of his own experiences with alcohol and recovery and, in addition, tells of acquaintances, some of whom recovered.

The presentation is in parts, showing the progression of alcoholism and recovery in the titles: 1) Social drinking, 2) Submerging, 3) Drowning, 4) Infancy, and 5) Adolescence, or the return of self-esteem.

The work is clever, effective, interesting, and insightful.

182.   Marshall, Shelly. **Young, Sober, and Free**. Center City, MN: Hazelden, 1978. 137p. $4.95pa. LC 78-060061. ISBN 0-89486-055-0.

This book consists mainly of stories of personal experiences of young people who have been addicted to drugs or alcohol. It was written to reach out to other young sufferers in the hope that they might accept help and thereby avoid years of trouble and premature death. No new program of treatment is presented. Those of Alcoholics Anonymous, Narcotics Anonymous, and the Palmer Drug Abuse Program are merely supplemented with the message in the book.

While the book is directed to young persons, there is material for all who are concerned with the drug abuse problem. A strain of spirituality runs throughout the work.

183.   Mendelson, Wallace B. **The Use and Misuse of Sleeping Pills: A Clinical Guide**. New York and London: Plenum Medical Book Co., 1980. 220p. illus. bibliog. index. $22.50. LC 79-21856. ISBN 0-306-40370-6.

Intended to be useful to the physician, scientist, and the student, this book covers the major areas of sleeping pill (hypnotics) use.

There are many ramifications of the use of the drugs: hazards of abuse; potential suicide; influence on daytime performance; interaction with alcohol and other drugs; and special problems when used by the elderly, the pregnant, or those with liver or kidney dysfunction. In addition, there is controversy over their long term effectiveness.

There are 12 chapters as follows: 1) Basic concepts about sleep and insomnia, 2) Prevalence of sleep disturbance and hypnotic use, 3) Pharmacology of prescription hypnotics, 4) The efficacy of hypnotics, 5) Suicide and hypnotics, 6) Residual daytime effects of hypnotics, 7) Interactions with ethanol, 8) Hypnotic dependence, 9) Hypnotics and the elderly, 10) Other pharmacologic approaches, 11) Nonpharmacologic treatment of insomnia, and 12) Conclusion: implications for medical practice. Each chapter begins with an introductory section particularly designed to assist the student, and ends with a summary and conclusions section. Numerous tables of research data are included with the text material.

The author concludes that large numbers of Americans seek help for insomnia, but that the drugs available (although varied and widely used) have little scientific support. When they are prescribed, it should be in small quantities, without automatic refills, and the patient should be conditioned to the notion that they will only be used briefly and are not a panacea.

184.   Michaux, Henri. **Miserable Miracle (Mescaline)**. With eight drawings by the author. Translated by Louise Varèse; American edition arranged by Anaïs Nin. San Francisco, CA: City Lights Books, 1963. 89p. illus. $1.95pa.

The French poet and painter, Henri Michaux, had this work published in French in 1956, and parts of it have appeared translated in *Evergreen Review* and *Paris Review*. The work records in words and drawings the experience the author had with mescaline. The Foreword says the original manuscript, produced with the author under the influence of the drug, was drawn rather than written, and was prepared hastily and in jerks, with interrupted sentences and with syllables flying off and words fused together. The translation evidently preserves some of the atmosphere of the original. There is an overlapping of visual imagery and written language apparent in the descriptions.

The experience was not altogether pleasant. It was described many times in the text as intolerable and unbearable, but that such was the price of paradise.

After the experience Michaux thinks he can recreate a mescaline trip without mescaline. In addition, he says in conclusion that he is not a drug user; he is more the water-drinking type.

185.   National Drug Abuse Conference. 3rd, New York, 1976. **Critical Concerns in the Field of Drug Abuse**. Proceedings of the Third National Drug Abuse Conference, Inc. Conference chairperson, Joyce H. Lowinson; conference co-chairpersons, Beny J. Primm, Shirley D. Coletti; conference coordinator, Ira J. Marion; editorial compilers, Arnold Schecter, Harold Alksne, Edward Kaufman. New York: Marcel Dekker, 1978. 1426p. bibliog. index. $45.00. LC 78-12871. ISBN 0-8247-6483-8.

This large volume contains the papers of a conference presented by social scientists, epidemiologists, researchers, physicians, program administrators, criminal justice representatives, lawyers, government officials, and others. The material is intended to define significant areas for new research and to help workers in the field keep abreast of recent developments. Two particularly valuable presentations deal with federal strategies in the area of substance abuse and with the international nature of the problem.

The many papers are grouped under the following headings: 1) Public policy, 2) Epidemiology, 3) Prevention, 4) Evaluation, 5) Treatment (including sections on detoxification, drug free, methadone maintenance, and general), 6) Issues (including sections on legal, criminal justice, minority issues, women's issues, pregnancy and neonatality, parenting and child abuse, and vocational issues), 7) Alcohol abuse, 8) Drugs and alcohol, 9) Polydrug abuse, 10) Family therapy, 11) Administration and management (including general aspects, funding, and issues and problems of staff development, 12) Research (including basic pharmacology and clinical pharmacology), and 13) Other issues.

186.   National Drug Abuse Conference, 4th, San Francisco, 1977. **A Multicultural View of Drug Abuse**. Edited by David E. Smith, Steven M. Anderson, Millicent Buxton, Nancy Gottlieb, William Harvey, and Tommy Chung. Cambridge, MA: G. K. Hall and Co./Schenkman Publishing Co., 1978. 616p. bibliog. $37.50. LC 78-17971. ISBN 0-8161-2127-3.

About 70 papers of the total of 280 presented at the Fourth National Drug Abuse Conference are reprinted in this volume. The authors were scientists, administrators, public policy makers, educators, labor and management representatives, and those involved with all aspects of treatment and prevention of drug abuse.

The papers are divided into sections and subsections as follows: 1) Drug abuse policy, regulatory and law enforcement issues. Public policy; regulatory and criminal justice; 2) Drug and typology issues: Heroin; polydrug; cocaine; marijuana issues; typology of drug abuse; health professionals; 3) Issues in combined alcohol and drug abuse treatment; Prevention and training issues; 5) Treatment and evaluation issues: Crisis intervention and counseling; narcotic antagonists; methadone; detoxification; therapeutic communities; family therapy; innovative, alternative treatment approaches; evaluation; 6) Vocational rehabilitation and industrial issues; and 7) Age, sexual and multicultural issues: Youth issues in alcohol and drug abuse; drug abuse in the elderly; women's issues in drug abuse, gay issues in drug abuse; black issues in drug abuse; Puerto Rican, Cuban, and Latino issues in drug abuse; Chicano and Chicana issues in drug abuse; American Indian issues in drug abuse; Asian issues in drug abuse; and multicultural issues and drug abuse policy.

The last mentioned paper, a summary, presents the viewpoint and recommendations of a minority group member who feels that minorities are more victimized than others by drug-related problems and issues.

187.   Nero, Jack. **Drink Like a Lady, Cry Like a Man: The Love Story of a Man and His Recovering Alcoholic Wife.** Minneapolis, MN: CompCare Publications, 1977. 285p. bibliog. $6.95pa. LC 77-86453. ISBN 0-89638-006-8.

This book is the account of a marriage that survives in spite of the wife's alcoholism and a husband who at first does not know how to deal with the problem. The husband watches the wife change from a social "life of the party" drinker to a depressed, unreasonable alcoholic. He tries to help by supervising her "cutting down," providing psychiatric help, hospital care, and a "controlled" vacation. Recovery does not come until she enters a residential treatment center, and he deals with his problem through Al-Anon.

Emphasis throughout the book is on alcoholism as a family illness. The reader can learn a great deal about symptoms, treatment, and psychological aspects of alcoholism.

188.   Newland, Constance A. **My Self and I.** New York: Signet Books, 1962. 256p. bibliog. $0.75pa.

This personal account of the use of LSD in psychotherapy was written by the patient. The author had had orthodox Freudian psychoanalysis, presumably without benefit, before entering into the LSD sessions. At the time of the writing of the book, LSD was considered "mind-loosening," and the belief was held that the drug results in a selective undoing of the ego functions, each process uncovering and bringing into consciousness earlier ego images. It is of note that since LSD is no longer used for legitimate treatment of any kind (because of the dangers perceived in its use), and never was used very much, it is not possible to assess its true value.

The author explores her own psyche and takes the reader into her incredible hallucinations. Although the experiences related are frightening and bizarre, the author writes well and the ending is satisfactory. She feels she is better off for having had the LSD experience/treatment. The title of the work refers to the relationship between the totality of the psychic self and the "I"; formerly one part of the patient rejected the other, but after therapy they were united as one.

189.   Newman, Joseph, ed. **What Everyone Needs to Know About Drugs.** Washington: U.S. News and World Report, 1970. 239p. illus. index. $2.95pa. LC 76-134994.

The material included in this book is well-selected and well-written, and although it is older, it is still of interest and value.

The work is in three parts as follows: part 1, The facts about drugs; part 2, What young people say; and part 3, What the experts say. The young people's section includes How a high school senior sees drugs, Drugs on a college campus, A student smoker speaks out, and A young woman tells her story.

The section by the experts contains the following: 1) A judge's view of marihuana, by Chief Justice G. Joseph Tauro, 2) Speed: the risk you run, by Dr. Sidney Cohen, 3) A psychiatrist looks at LSD, by Daniel X. Freedman, 4) Youth and family, by Arthur Mandelbaum, 5) Youth and drugs, by Dr. Cecil Chamberlin, 6) If your child takes drugs . . . , by Dr. Richard H. Blum, 7) Drug use and student values, by Dr. Kenneth Keniston, and 8) Drugs: do they produce open or closed minds?, by Dr. Dana L. Farnsworth.

190.   **The Opium Trade, 1910-1941**. Wilmington, DE: SR Scholarly Resources, Inc., 1974. 6v. $215.00. LC 74-19745. ISBN 0-8420-1795-X.

This publication is a reprinted (facsimile) edition of a collection of documents and correspondence known as the Foreign Office Collection (F.C. 415) in the Public Record Office, London. Well-known to scholars all over the world, it is a valuable source for research on the drug trade, including its social and political implications. The work deals with the narcotics trade on an international level, especially with Asia during the decades of upheaval. The papers and reports included were formerly confidential documents of the British Foreign Office.

The complexity and difficulties involved in controlling illegal drug trade and the smuggling of opium and other narcotics are clearly shown. For many decades prior to 1909, England was a great beneficiary of the opium trade. About 1910 the government decided that efforts should be made to curtail or suppress illegal trading in narcotics. The response of a number of nations was negative. For example, Germany threw obstacles in the way (evidently because of pressure by the powerful Merck Chemical Company), and Japan and China were deeply involved. Papers of several conferences are included, such as the Shanghai in 1909, and the Hague in 1912, and the various meetings sponsored by the League of Nations.

191.   **Our Chemical Culture: Drug Use and Misuse**. By Marcia Summers, James G. Trost, E. Leif Zerkin, Dinah Prentice, Dorothy Feeley, and James R. Gamage. Madison, WI: STASH Press, 1975. 116p. illus. bibliog. $5.00pa. LC 75-15090. ISBN 0-915818-07-8.

This basic book on drugs of abuse is intended mainly for high school and college age students. The currently abused drugs are discussed, including historical background, uses and misuses, physiological and psychological effects, potentials for dependence, and treatment.

The following are the chapter headings: 1) Some basics, 2) Alcohol, 3) Cannabis, 4) Hallucinogens, 5) Inhalants, 6) Narcotics, 7) Depressants, 8) Stimulants, 9) Tobacco, and 10) Some important issues. A bibliography of additional readings and a glossary have also been included.

The point of view of the book is unbiased. Little attempt is made to influence the reader one way or another about drugs, an attitude many feel is necessary in dealing with young people.

192.   Pradhan, Sachindra N., and Samarendra N. Dutta, eds. **Drug Abuse: Clinical and Basic Aspects**. St. Louis, MO: C. V. Mosby Co., 1977. 598p. illus. bibliog. index. $23.00. LC 77-1472. ISBN 0-8016-4037-7.

This work is intended primarily for those in the medical community: physicians, dentists, nurses, pharmacists, physician assistants, and students in these professions. In addition, much of it is of interest and value to others such as psychologists, social workers, drug treatment center personnel, and basic and clinical researchers in the field. A great deal of basic information and material on clinical aspects of drug abuse has been brought together. The contributors, who are noted professionals in drug abuse work, attempt to give perspectives and interpretations of research and clinical findings.

The book is made up of 37 chapters grouped in six sections as follows: 1) General aspects of drug abuse, 2) Psychopharmacology of commonly abused drugs, 3) Clinical aspects of drug abuse: manifestations, management, and aftercare, 4) Special clinical problems in drug abuse, 5) Sociolegal-educational aspects, and 6) Research.

In addition, there are two appendices, a useful article on adulterants of street drugs, and a glossary of street slang terms used by addicts.

This is an impressive, comprehensive book which should prove quite useful and enlightening.

193.   Rettig, Richard P., Manuel J. Torres, and Gerald R. Garrett. **Manny: A Criminal-Addict's Story**. Boston: Houghton Mifflin Co., 1977. 264p. bibliog. $7.25pa. LC 76-14654. ISBN 0-395-24838-8.

The personal account of the life of Manny Torres, a Puerto Rican boy in New York City, begins with the death of Manny's father, a middle-class shopkeeper. The remaining family moves to a poor neighborhood and Manny and his brother begin experiences with gang life. Manny then passes through encounters with gambling, marijuana, heroin, street hustling, and crime. He is sent to Sing Sing Prison in New York State. After prison he goes back to drugs and hustling and spends time in Synanon, the rehabilitation center. This part of the account is especially interesting because the sense of the smothering comfort of total commitment to Synanon and the submission to absolute rule come through. Manny's comment is that "You never use dope if you never leave, but who wants to stay in prison forever?"

Manny goes back to his old life and is again arrested and sent to a California prison for a long sentence.

The concluding chapter shows Manny in the California Rehabilitation Center where the possibility of a turnaround is in evidence. His energies are channeled into education (at Humboldt State University) which seems to offer a chance for reconstituting his personal life.

The hope of the authors is that readers may contemplate the types of social change that might ultimately minimize the recurring story of people like Manny in our society.

194.   Ricciuti, Edward R. **The Devil's Garden: Facts and Folklore of Perilous Plants**. New York: Walker and Co., 1978. 172p. illus. index. $9.95. LC 77-79624. ISBN 0-8027-0581-2.

The author of this work, who has written a number of natural history books for children, has produced here a nontechnical, interesting, and attractive publication on intoxicating and harmful plants. He takes the view that the need many people feel to get back to nature has inspired a new interest in gardening, house plants, and wild foods. While this is good in that it encourages appreciation of nature, many individuals believe that "natural" means "beneficial" which is an unwarranted and dangerous assumption where plants are concerned.

The book begins with a historical look at how certain plants have been associated with death and the occult arts. The abuse of intoxicating and hallucinogenic plants is then discussed from the point of view of the present time. The common drugs of abuse are covered as well as many other substances. The harmful and dangerous effects of drug plants are stressed.

The book has a dual aim. It warns the reader of the dangers of common toxic plants such as yews, castor beans, oleander, and the nightshade, and it also points out the dangers of the common drugs of abuse such as cocaine, opiates, marijuana, and hallucinogenic mushrooms.

While there are many references in the text to various historical events and scientific studies concerning dangerous plants (which seem to be authentic), no formal bibliography has been included.

195.   Saltman, Jules. **What You Should Know About Drug Abuse.** New York: Public Affairs Committee, 1977. 28p. illus. (Public Affairs Pamphlet No. 550.) $0.50pa.

This well-written pamphlet provides reliable information on the drug abuse problem. It is part of a series that provides information to the American public on vital economic and social problems.

Background information and general statistics are first presented. Next, there is a section on the drugs of abuse which takes up each type separately. Other sections are headed as follows: 1) What is being done, 2) Controlling the drug traffic, 3) Legal efforts to control addiction, 4) The move to treatment, 5) Techniques of treatment, and 6) What are the answers?

In reply to the last question, the author sees no easy solutions, but points out that treatment clinics, methadone maintenance programs, and government and various service agencies provide assistance to those who want to make use of them.

196.   Schecter, Arnold, Harold Alksne, and Edward Kaufman, eds. **Drug Abuse: Modern Trends, Issues, and Perspectives.** Proceedings of the Second National Drug Abuse Conference, Inc., New Orleans, 1975. New York: Marcel Dekker, 1978. 1219p. bibliog. index. $45.00. LC 78-4091. ISBN 0-8247-6475-7.

The 177 conference papers collected here present a diverse view of the drug abuse problem. The coverage is quite comprehensive, including medical, pharmacological, psychological, sociological, and legislative areas. The intent of the conference was to present a single, comprehensive program of sharing information, acquiring skills, and modifying attitudes about the drug dependence field.

The papers are presented under the following headings: 1) Epidemiology of drug abuse, 2) Treatment (therapeutic communities, methadone maintenance, detoxification, and other approaches), 3) Drug abuse treatment personnel, 4) Clinical pharmacology (narcotic antagonists, LAAM), 5) Drug-dependent mothers and infants, 6) Evaluation of drug abuse treatment, 7) Minority issues, 8) Women's issues, 9) Legislative issues, 10) Vocational issues, 11) Alcohol abuse, 12) Training and education, 13) Community issues, 14) Psychological issues in drug abuse, 15) Legal issues, 16) Cocaine, 17) Basic pharmacology: marijuana, and 18) Miscellaneous.

The work is notable for the information it contains about specific treatment methods, the design and evaluation of rehabilitation programs, and matters of social import. Physicians, other health professionals, psychologists, social workers, law enforcement officers, and all those concerned with drug abuse problems will find the work of considerable value.

197.   Schleiffer, Hedwig. **Narcotic Plants of the Old World Used in Everyday Life: An Anthology of Texts from Ancient Times to the Present.** Introduction by Richard Evans Schultes. Monticello, NY: Lubrecht and Cramer, 1979. 193p. illus. index. $12.50; $7.95pa. LC 79-66004. ISBN 0-934454-01-9; 0-934454-00-0pa.

This is a companion volume to the author's earlier work, *Sacred Narcotic Plants of the New World Indians: An Anthology* (*see* Andrews: *A Bibliography of Drug Abuse,* 1977, entry 572). The term "narcotic" in the title of the book is used in a broad, classical sense; many of the substances discussed are not usually considered narcotics. A great many are hallucinogens.

The book contains texts from classical literature that describe or refer to "narcotic" plants even though the author may have been unaware of the properties of the plant under discussion. Meaningful quotations have been culled from a wide range of literature—historical, anthropological, medical, botanical, and other.

The following plants are discussed: mushrooms, canna, amaryllis, dogbane, hemp, heath, beach, mint, logania, nutmeg, poppy, pepper, nightshade, caltrop, and some unidentified ones. There is an index of authors quoted, as well as one of vernacular names of plants and plant products, and one of Latin names of genera and species.

The book is quite well-done and provides an interesting glimpse of the history of some of the most important medicinal and toxic plants.

198.   Sloman, Larry. **Reefer Madness: The History of Marijuana in America**. Indianapolis, IN; New York: Bobbs-Merrill Co., 1979. 404p. illus. index. $12.95. LC 78-55646. ISBN 0-672-52423-6.

Written by a journalist who has contributed to such periodicals as *Rolling Stone* and *Penthouse*, this book is a popular social history of marijuana and the "marijuana culture." It begins with the early use of the plant as a source of clothing and rope, then takes up early medicinal uses, and moves on to the use of marijuana as a "recreational" drug. The subculture of the drug is traced from the 1930s when it had its own language, music, and literature, and was particularly used by jazz musicians, to the more recent use by hippies and others in the counterculture of the 1960s.

The author's viewpoint is sympathetic to use of the drug, although an attempt was made to interview those on both sides of the controversy, including law-enforcement officials, dealers, and pot smokers of all socioeconomic levels. The "U.S. Bureaucracy," the Bureau of Narcotics and Dangerous Drugs, and a number of individuals who are known to be anti-marijuana are placed in an unfavorable light, while pot users are protrayed as harmless fun-loving victims who are steadily outwitting the adversary in spite of everything.

The book is not entirely understandable to one who is uninitiated in the drug culture of the day. However, it is obvious that Sloman believes marijuana is here to stay and that it has become respectable.

199.   **Solvents, Adhesives, and Aerosols**. Proceedings of a Seminar Held in Toronto in May, 1977 by the Ontario Ministry of Industry and Tourism in cooperation with the Addiction Research Foundation. Toronto: Addiction Research Foundation, 1978. 92p. bibliog. $4.95pa. ISBN 0-88868-023-6.

The eight papers presented in this work review the various factors involved in solvent and aerosol abuse. Suggestions are made in terms of coordinated and comprehensive treatment approaches. Participants in the seminar include representatives of regulatory agencies, community associations, industry, and others.

The following papers make up the publication: 1) Solvents—an industrial perspective, 2) Aerosol product safety, 3) Inhaling intoxicants: historical, biological, and social perspectives, 4) The community drop-in centre, 5) Solvents and vandalism, 6) Solvent inhalation—legislative controls, 7) An international perspective on solvents and aerosols, 8) Community approaches to the control of solvent and aerosol sniffing.

200.   Strasser, Todd. **Angel Dust Blues**. New York: Coward, McCann and Geoghegan, Inc., 1979. 203p. $8.95. LC 78-31735. ISBN 0-698-20485-9.

This is a novel, the story of a high school student, Alex, who becomes increasingly alienated from his successful parents. They spend the winter in Florida while their son remains in the family home near New York with a housekeeper. Alex becomes involved with drug dealing through friends. The trouble gets deeper and deeper, and the only bright spot in Alex's life is a new girl friend who helps him to see he must accept responsibilities.

Eventually, Alex is faced with a hard decision where a fugitive drug dealing friend is concerned. Alex decides to turn him in because he feels the friend must have medical assistance. It was the right choice, although the friend will perhaps die of an overdose of drugs anyway. Alex realizes at last that he will be able to act on his own and make the correct decisions no matter what the relationship with his parents and others.

It is a touching story, well-told, and with a viewpoint that may help young people.

201.   Swinson, Richard P., and Derek Eaves. **Alcoholism and Addiction.** London; Totowa, NJ: Woburn Press, 1978. 346p. bibliog. index. $14.00. LC 79-311090. ISBN 0-7130-0167-4.

The overview of the drug abuse and alcoholism problem this work provides is written in simple terms suitable for those without medical background or much knowledge of the health professions. In general, the subject is covered from the British point of view, although reference is made from time to time to like or contrasting situations in the United States and Canada. Particularly, the statistical data refer to the United States.

The material is of good quality, but the literature references are mostly to earlier publications.

202.   Tan, Chung. **China and the Brave New World: A Study of the Origins of the Opium War (1840-42).** Durham, NC: Carolina Academic Press, 1978. 271p. bibliog. index. $12.95. LC 78-50590. ISBN 0-89089-086-2.

The Opium War of 1840-1842 has been a topic of much academic debate. The controversy about the Sino-British War centers around whether or not the war really was an "opium war." Some scholars believe the British expeditionary force was sent to China to fight for the interest of the opium trade. Other viewpoints have been offered, more complicated ones, such as the theory that it was a cultural conflict, on one side agricultural and dynastic interests, on the other the industrial and capitalistic. The author says his book is an attempt to revitalize the opium-war perspective. He presents a well-documented account.

Chapter headings are: 1) Academic controversy, 2) Historical reality and baseless theory, 3) Manchu policy vis-à-vis Sino-British trade, 4) Britain's interest in China trade, 5) Sino-British tension and tensile strength, 6) British offensive and Chinese victim, 7) The anti-opium and anti-anti-opium wars, and 8) Conclusion.

The ultimate aim of the book is to interpret the causes of the war as a framework for understanding China's interactions with the modern West.

203.   Taylor, Norman. **Narcotics, Nature's Dangerous Gifts.** rev. ed. of *Flight from Reality.* New York: Dell Publishing Co., 1966. 222p. bibliog. index.

The author of this work, who is known for his classic works in botany, in 1949 published an earlier edition of this book under the title *Flight from Reality.* The following chapters are presented: 1) The pleasant assassin: the story of marihuana, 2) The abyss of divine enjoyment: the story of opium, morphine and heroin, 3) The divine plant of the Incas: the story of coca and cocaine, 4) The accident of alcohol, 5) The lively image and pattern of hell: the story of tobacco, 6) Come and expel the green pain: the story of ololiuqui and peyotl (mescaline), 7) Five exotic plants: the stories of pituri, fly agaric, caapi, kava, and betel, 8) Three habit-forming beverages: the stories of coffee, chocolate, and tea, and 9) A boon or a curse? The story of LSD.

The viewpoint of the more recent work is a bit different from that of the earlier, which stressed that people never cease to look for things that offer respite from reality. This edition, as the title suggests, stresses that drugs are both a boon and a curse. The author is sympathetic to the plight of addicts and feels that they need medical care. However, he labels as bizarre nonsense a statement one habitual amateur user of LSD wrote, "What's a few suicides compared to the good LSD does?"

204.   Tracy, Jack. **Subcutaneously, My Dear Watson: Sherlock Holmes and the Cocaine Habit**. With Jim Berkey. Illustrated by Paul M. McCall with Sidney Paget's original representations of Sherlock Holmes and other turn-of-the-century illustrations. Bloomington, IN: James A. Rock and Co., 1978. 91p. illus. bibliog. $6.95; $3.95pa. ISBN 0-918736-02-1; 0-918736-03-Xpa.

The matter of Sherlock Holmes' use of addicting drugs has long been a point of controversy among fans of A. Conan Doyle's great detective of fiction. Tracy is a member of the Baker Street Irregulars, the national society of Holmes enthusiasts. The recent renewed interest in cocaine use has sparked further debate on the matter, and this book is a contribution which studies Holmes' use of the drug as outlined in the stories. The author says that "In among the conflicting biases of the moralists, the apologists, and the revisionists is to be found the real story of Sherlock Holmes and cocaine."

It is of note that the use of cocaine and of the other drugs Holmes used was not illegal in Victorian England. Holmes says in *The Sign of the Four*: "I suppose that its (cocaine's) influence is physically a bad one. I find it, however, so transcendently stimulating and clarifying to the mind that its secondary action is a matter of small moment." Tracy believes the drug freed Holmes from paralyzing attacks of melancholia, and points to the evidence of this in the stories. Also, the suggestion is made that it may have accounted for the detective's vigor and phenomenal success. The tone of the book is whimsical, in keeping with the spirit of all Sherlock Holmes buffs.

The book is of interest to those concerned with the attitudes prevalent in the late nineteenth century on the use and effects of cocaine as well as to Holmes fans.

205.   Trawick, Buckner B. **Shakespeare and Alcohol**. Amsterdam: Rodopi, 1978. 100p. ISBN 90-6203-448-9.

This monograph is a study of the frequency and significance of Shakespeare's references to alcoholic beverages, of which there were found to be 360, and in addition, 196 figures of speech in the 38 plays. The work is in four parts. The first deals with the plays in an attempt to show how the references or figures of speech further the dramatic action, contribute to character portrayal, aid in revealing the underlying thought, and help establish the mood or tone. The second section presents generalizations about the use and abuse of alcohol by the characters; the third consists of the analysis of statistics on the references and figures of speech; and the fourth section suggests certain attitudes in the plays that may be a reflection of Shakespeare's own views.

The conclusion is drawn that the plays reflect Shakespeare's own temperance as a person.

206.   Tyrrell, Ian R. **Sobering Up: From Temperance to Prohibition in Antebellum America, 1800-1860**. Westport, CT: Greenwood Press, 1979. 350p. bibliog. index. (Contributions in American History, No. 82.) LC 78-22132. ISBN 0-313-20822-0.

The author of this historical work on temperance and the prohibition movement points out that until the nineteenth century, few Americans dreamed of excori-
ating liquor, which had been widely accepted and deeply engrained in their social
habits. However, during the twentieth century, the temperance movement produced
political upheaval and helped shape cultural and moral standards of the country. The
hope was to eradicate not only liquor but concurrently crime, immorality, poverty,
and insanity.

The following are the chapter headings: 1) Liquor in colonial and early
republican America, 2) Men of moderation, 3) The apostles of abstinence, 4) The
sources of temperance support in the 1830s, 5) The ideology and social outlook of
mainstream temperance, 6) The origins of teetotalism, 7) The Washingtonians: artisans
and alcohol, 8) Cooperation and conflict in temperance agitation, 1840-1850, 9) The
local origins of prohibition, 10) The politics of Maine law prohibition, and 11) The
decline of prohibition.

The author concludes that prohibition was easier to win than to maintain.
However, the impact of antebellum temperance on American politics and society
was felt for several generations.

207.   U.S. Bureau of Narcotics and Dangerous Drugs. **Amphetamines, Barbiturates
and Hallucinogens: An Analysis of Use, Distribution and Control.** By William H.
McGlothlin. Washington: GPO, 1973. 101p. + appendices. bibliog. (SCID-TR-9.)
    This study represents a summarization of data to which the author has
added deduction and interpretation. Much of the information utilized came from
unpublished sources and interviews.

The first part covers amphetamines and barbiturates, and includes an overview, production figures, retail sales, amounts available for illicit use, surveys of use,
the illicit market, and control measures. The second section, on hallucinogens, covers
early history, patterns of use (prevalence, frequency and amount), the illicit market,
the role of LSD in the new drug subculture, and control measures. In addition, there
are four appendices as follows: 1) Diversion from licit manufacturing and distribution channels, 2) Observations on the illicit marketplace of psychedelics, amphetamines, and barbiturates–1972, 3) An economic analysis of amphetamine controls,
and 4) An analysis of the frequency and content of drug-related material published
in the underground press.

Material of the kind presented becomes dated very rapidly, so it should be
borne in mind that the data is probably reliable for a limited period in time only.
However, it is quite interesting from the historical viewpoint, and it contains information not readily available elsewhere. Of particular note is the last appendix, on the
underground press. It is somewhat unrelated to the rest of the report, but was
included in fulfillment of one of the contract requirements. It is one of the few
reports of this kind.

208.   U.S. Drug Enforcement Administration. **Drug Abuse and Misuse.** Prepared
by H. E. Tebrock. Washington: GPO, 1978. 21p.
    The aim of this booklet, which contains in digested form a great deal of
information about drugs of abuse, is to make the reader aware of signs and symptoms
of drug misuse and thus know when to seek help for the victims. The following sections are presented: Definitions of terms used, How to identify the drug user, Common
signs of drug misuse, Indications of possible misuse by type of drug, and A list of
commonly abused drugs. The latter section includes a general description of the drugs,

how to identify the substances, methods of use, specific signs and symptoms of use, and slang and street terms for the drugs.

209.   U.S. Drug Enforcement Administration. **Erythroxylon Coca: A Lecture.** By John T. Maher. revised. Washington: GPO, 1976. 63p. illus. bibliog.

The focus of this presentation is on coca and its principal derivative, cocaine. Until relatively recently cocaine usage was not considered a problem in the United States, although European countries have traditionally experienced a high rate of its use, and its consumption has been a problem in South America. It is now becoming a drug of choice among more affluent drug users in the United States.

The lecture includes sections on background, history, botany, harvesting, chemical analysis, ecology, biosynthesis, routes of administration, illicit extraction procedures, and illicit traffic.

210.   U.S. Drug Enforcement Administration. **Opium and Its Derivatives: A Lecture.** By John T. Maher. revised. Washington: GPO, 1976. 46p. illus. bibliog.

This is a good, compact presentation on opium and its derivatives. First, the history and development of the opium problem are presented in some detail. Then, the medicinal value of the products is emphasized along with the problem of abuse. The opium plant and its cultivation is described, and opium and its derivatives are discussed. There is a section on each of the drugs: opium, morphine, heroin, codeine, dilaudid, oxycodone, omymorphone, and opium preparations.

211.   U.S. National Institute on Drug Abuse. **Let's Talk About Drug Abuse: Some Questions and Answers.** Washington: GPO, 1979. 40p. illus. bibliog. [DHEW Publication No. (ADM) 78-706.] $2.75pa. S/N 041-010-00033-9.

A revision of a 1975 publication called *Questions and Answers About Drug Abuse*, the booklet begins with a "Drug Quiz" to test knowledge about drug abuse. The rest of the publication presents questions and answers about varied aspects of drug abuse. Most abused substances are discussed. The publication would prove useful as a basis for a discussion of drug abuse education and prevention in the community, school, or home. A list of information clearinghouses, resource organizations, and single state agencies has been included.

212.   U.S. National Institute on Drug Abuse. **Perspectives on the History of Psychoactive Substance Use.** By Gregory A. Austin. Washington: GPO, 1978. 280p. bibliog. index. [DHEW Publication No. (ADM) 79-810; NIDA Research Issues 24.] S/N 017-024-00879-6.

The 34 studies ("perspectives") in this document individually summarize significant developments in the history of psychoactive substance use in developed countries of the world since the sixteenth century. The intent of the work is to show the ubiquity of drug use in the past and the complex and varied factors that have influenced its spread, society's response, and the effects of that response. Tobacco, coffee, alcohol, cannabis, cocaine, opium, and the opiates are discussed.

In addition to the perspectives, the volume contains a summary chart and a synoptic chronology of drug usage in various countries. Each perspective itself contains an introductory review, chronology, and summaries of previous research.

213.   U.S. National Institute on Drug Abuse. **Sedative-Hypnotic Drugs: Risks and Benefits**. Edited by James R. Cooper. Washington: GPO, 1977. 112p. bibliog. [DHEW Publication No. (ADM) 78-592.] $3.00pa. LC 78-601143. S/N 017-024-00812-5.

Recently, concern has developed over the risks associated with the use of sedative-hypnotics, particularly the barbiturates. Consequently an assessment was made by intergovernmental agencies on the risks and benefits associated with these drugs, both individually and by pharmacologic class. This report presents the findings. It contains a survey and review of the available literature, an epidemiological report, and a summary of an expert panel's discussion of the relative safety and efficacy of the sedative-hypnotics.

In summary, the opinion is expressed that most barbiturates could be replaced with benzodiazepines. However, more research on the latter is required in regard to efficacy and safety before any regulatory action should be taken to proscribe the barbiturate class of drugs. Also, physician and patient education should occur first.

214.   U.S. National Institute on Drug Abuse. **Voluntary Inhalation of Industrial Solvents**. Edited by Charles Wm. Sharp, and L. Thomas Carroll. Washington: GPO, 1978. 404p. illus. bibliog. [DHEW Publication No. (ADM) 79-770.]

The material in this publication is based on scientific papers presented at an international conference held in Mexico City in 1976. The intent of the conference, which was sponsored by the governments of the U.S. and Mexico, was to contribute to a multidisciplinary approach to understanding and responding to the problem of inhalant abuse. Thirty papers are presented by authorities in a wide range of health and social disciplines. They are grouped under the following headings: 1) Epidemiology, 2) Sociocultural studies, 3) Psychosocial studies, 4) Clinical studies, 5) Neurophysiology, 6) Pharmacology and toxicology, 7) Behavioral studies, and 8) Treatment and rehabilitation.

The problem of inhalant abuse is a serious one because it is widespread. Volatile solvents are readily available in the home and at work; they are inexpensive; and they are legal. For these reasons young people, often preteens of lower socioeconomic status who cannot afford other intoxicants, experiment with inhalants and use them as recreational drugs, thus contributing to negative effects on physical and emotional maturity and the evolution of drug abuse behaviors.

215.   Wesson, Donald R., Albert S. Carlin, Kenneth M. Adams, and George Beschner, eds. **Polydrug Abuse: The Results of a National Collaborative Study**. New York: Academic Press, 1978. 395p. illus. bibliog. index. $24.50. LC 78-12620. ISBN 0-12-745250-8.

This book summarizes the results of a study initiated in 1973 by the Special Action Office of Drug Abuse Prevention to reach, treat, and study a large sample of polydrug users. Polydrug use is defined as the abuse of a psychoactive drug singly, in combination, or sequentially that does not include heroin or alcohol as the primary drug. Included are prescription drugs obtained illegally, prescription drugs used in dosages beyond those prescribed medically, and over-the-counter drugs used in amounts over what is recommended on the package.

The book presents 17 chapters by various authors. It describes the demographic, psychological, and physiological characteristics of individuals in treatment and a sample of users not in treatment. Techniques are examined that have brought polydrug users into clinical settings. Physician attitudes concerning drug abuse treatment and the response of traditional health-care agencies to non-opiate abusers are discussed. Information is provided on managing a collaborative research effort, and recommendations for future research in the area of polydrug use are offered.

The work is of particular value to professionals in medicine, psychology, and drug abuse treatment efforts as it should help them understand more fully the polydrug problem and lead to the development of better intervention strategies.

216.   Wesson, Donald R., and David E. Smith. **Barbiturates: Their Use, Misuse and Abuse.** New York: Human Sciences Press, 1977. 144p. bibliog. index. $14.95; $4.95pa. LC 76-41079. ISBN 0-87705-249-2; 0-87705-314-6pa.

The drugs treated in this small book are frequently abused, although not as much attention has been given to this problem as to the abuse of other classes of drugs. The following chapters are included: 1) Introduction, 2) Pharmacological characteristics of the barbiturates, 3) Medical uses, 4) Misuse and abuse, 5) Complications of abuse, 6) Physical dependency, 7) Nonmedical aspects of barbiturates. Also, there are two appendices: 1) Generic, chemical, and trade names of the barbiturates, and 2) Street terms for barbiturates and other drugs.

The authors are physicians who have had considerable experience and success in treating barbiturate abusers, and they discuss various treatment techniques. The authors conclude that the barbiturates most often abused currently are the most expendable medically. The number of prescriptions written for the barbiturates is declining. Other drugs are used in their place (although they cost more). Although barbiturate abuse is a considerable problem, it would not cease if the drugs were suddenly removed from the American market. Most abused barbiturates are brought into the country illicitly. Knowledge about the treatment of barbiturate abusers is still in its infancy. And finally, the authors say that "teaching drug abusers how to cope with everyday anxieties without resorting to pharmacological oblivion is a long arduous process."

This valuable book is of particular interest to physicians, although others involved with or interested in drug abuse may profit from reading it.

217.   West, Elliott. **The Saloon on the Rocky Mountain Mining Frontier.** Lincoln, NE; London: University of Nebraska Press, 1979. 197p. illus. bibliog. index. $14.50. LC 78-24090. ISBN 0-8032-4704-4.

This study is an attempt to examine the saloon on the Western frontier in the mining towns of the Rocky Mountains, a subject that has been neglected, according to the author, except for sensational and anecdotal accounts. The region under consideration was settled by prospectors seeking precious metals during the years 1858 to the early 1890s. The high point of national alcohol consumption came during the two or three generations preceding the mining booms of the far West, but it declined somewhat and stabilized   after 1860. It was much less than that of European countries. Even so, drinking places in the old West usually outnumbered all other retail establishments combined, and saloons were significant institutions because of their social impact upon a mining town.

The book describes in detail various aspects of saloons and the liquor trade on the mining frontier. The saloon is placed in the context of the towns' physical growth, social composition, and prevailing attitudes. The author has relied heavily for his well-documented account on contemporary reports, reminiscences, censuses, local town records, and mining town newspapers.

The first chapter examines the popular image of the hard-drinking mining frontier and discusses ill effects of mass drinking on the society of the camps. Following chapters describe the saloon and its development, the owners, and social roles of the drinking places. Economic aspects are then considered, and the last chapter remarks on the changing role of the tavern in towns that survived. The book concludes with an evaluation of the saloon's significance to the frontier. Two appendices are included: 1) A census profile of saloon owners and the adult mining town population, and 2) A biographical profile of saloon owners.

The author sees the old saloon as a breeding place for trouble and mischief. But it was also a public place available for common needs, a gathering for human contact in a solitary and trying land. It was the most complex and versatile retail business of the Rockies, and a natural outgrowth of the social environment.

218.   Westermeyer, Joseph. **A Primer on Chemical Dependency: A Clinical Guide to Alcohol and Drug Problems**. Baltimore, MD: Williams and Wilkins, 1976. 231p. bibliog. index. $11.95. LC 76-13192. ISBN 0-683-08943-9.

Alcohol dependence is the major emphasis of the work, which was prepared primarily for physicians with limited knowledge or experience in dealing with chemical dependency. Other health science workers, such as nurses, clinical psychologists, social workers, and medical students, will also find it useful. In addition, law enforcement officers may find it contributes to an understanding of the drug abuse problem. The terminology used is not overly technical, and jargon has been kept to a minimum.

The following are the chapter titles: 1) Models for chemical dependency, 2) Predisposing factors, 3) The chemical dependency syndrome, 4) Subgroups of chemical dependency, 5) Medical epidemiology, 6) Clinical diagnosis, 7) Treatment modalities I: Somatotherapies, 8) Treatment modalities II: Psychotherapies and sociotherapies, 9) Treatment outcome, 10) Public health planning, and 11) The physician and chemical dependence. Case examples are included throughout the work.

The author points out that chemical dependency is the most common mental health disorder, far exceeding others. For this reason physicians should expand their fund of knowledge and skills on this topic.

219.   Woods, Geraldine. **Drug Use and Drug Abuse**. New York: Franklin Watts, 1979. 65p. illus. bibliog. index. (A First Book.) $5.90. LC 79-11739. ISBN 0-531-02941-7.

This small book, intended for juveniles, outlines the medicinal uses of drugs, but emphasizes problems involving the "recreational" use of substances such as narcotics, amphetamines, tobacco, alcohol, and LSD. In addition, abuse of such over-the-counter drugs as aspirin and cough syrup is discussed. There is a short glossary and a short list of agencies that provide help for the addicted.

The author, who is a professional writer, has done a commendable job with this factual, dispassionate presentation.

220.   Worick, W. Wayne, and Warren E. Schaller. **Alcohol, Tobacco and Drugs: Their Use and Abuse**. Englewood Cliffs, NJ: Prentice-Hall, Inc., 1977. 170p. illus. bibliog. index. $7.95; $4.95pa. LC 76-30295. ISBN 0-13-021444-2; 0-13-021436-1pa.

Designed primarily as a text for college-level courses, this book discusses social and individual implications of the use of alcohol, tobacco, and drugs. There are also chapters on the theories of dependence and countermeasures against abuse of various substances. The theme of the presentation is that alcohol, tobacco, and drugs are part of our society and must be dealt with.

Each chapter is followed by a summary. The final summary points out that while much has been done in the fields of law, medicine, and education to counter the substance abuse problem, efforts have generally failed and the problem still remains. However, the efforts have often been haphazard and uncoordinated. The authors' view is that the approaches should be revised, reevaluated and continued. Emphasis should be placed in the following order: on prevention through education, on treatment and rehabilitation, and on deterrence through the use of existing laws.

221.   Young, Lawrence A., and others. **Recreational Drugs.** New York: Collier Books, a division of Macmillan Publishing Co., 1977. 216p. index. $5.95. LC 77-11866. ISBN 0-02-059900-5.

The authors of this work, who seem to be professional writers, journalists, and attorneys, take the view that since more people are using drugs "recreationally" than ever before, it is important   that they understand as much as possible about them in order to minimize the dangers. The book is intended to provide nontechnical information needed by users, abusers, experimentors, and nonusers alike. The authors say the information contained is based on research, not experience. However, the style of expression and the viewpoint is perhaps more akin to that of the drug culture and the press than that of the laboratory.

About 90 substances are discussed, arranged in alphabetical order, and some unusual substances have been included. For the most part the information given is accurate, though perhaps oversimplified, and many may not agree with the emphasis and the views expressed on the comparative dangers of the substances.

The most unlikely substance included is sugar (sucrose), digressing into the "health food" area. And, incidentally, if this entry does not contain misinformation it at least misleads. The reader is advised not to use "raw" sugar because it is just as worthless in terms of nutritional value as white, but to substitute "natural" sugar instead.

6

INCIDENCE AND PREVALENCE

Most of the publications in this section are U.S. government documents. The past few years the federal government has made considerable effort to report on virtually all aspects of illegal (and occasionally legal) substance abuse. Many of the publications report statistics, notably those in the *Statistical Series* of the National Institute on Drug Abuse, Division of Scientific and Program Information. Hughes's and Brewin's *The Tranquilizing of America* (entry 223) emphasizes the current overuse of prescription drugs. *Longitudinal Research on Drug Use* (entry 224), edited by Kandel, reports on activities of drug abusers over a relatively long period of time.

Statistics show that there has been no decrease in over-all drug use, but there has been a decline or leveling off from the highest rates of increase in the 1960s. Also, there has been a reduction in the acute emergencies that flooded hospitals in the late 1960s.

222.   Alcoholism Research Foundation. **Statistics of Alcoholism in Canada, 1871-1956. First Report.** Compiled by Robert E. Popham and Wolfgang Schmidt with the assistance of R. G. Williams, Jean Bronetto, and C. P. Cooper. Foreword by John R. Seeley. Toronto: University of Toronto Press, 1958. 155p. $6.00.

Prepared as the first of a series reporting Canadian alcohol statistics, this compilation is made up almost entirely of tables of data, which are arranged in five parts as follows: 1) The size and characteristics of the drinking population, 2) The apparent consumption of alcoholic beverages, 3) Convictions for offenses involving alcohol, 4) Statistics relating to the prevalence of alcoholism, and 5) Census population and intercensal population estimates.

223.   Hughes, Richard, and Robert Brewin. **The Tranquilizing of America: Pill Popping and the American Way of Life.** New York: Harcourt Brace Jovanovich, 1979. 326p. bibliog. index. $11.95. LC 79-1830. ISBN 0-15-191072-3.

The authors of this "exposé" are journalists. Their viewpoint is that Americans are living in an age of chemical escape, are overmedicated, and have become "prescription junkies" who use dangerous drugs with the blessings of the law. Particular emphasis is given to use of drugs to control unruly children and adolescents, helpless geriatric patients, and unhappy women. The drug industry is blamed for this situation, but physicians, the Congress, and the Food and Drug Administration are also criticized (the latter groups, however, are said to be controlled by the industry).

Chapter headings are: 1) What price tranquillity?, 2) Sedativism: the now health crisis, 3) Women as victims, 4) Poisoning our future, 5) Chemically controlling children, 6) Chemical solitary confinement, 7) The pacification of the elderly, 8) Selling the chemical solution, 9) The FDA: your friend or the drug industry's?, 10) Over-the-counter relief, and 11) Beyond *Brave New World*. In addition, there are three appendices: a prescription drug chart with uses and ill effects, a list of agencies that offer help to the addicted and troubled, and selected readings.

The book is reasonably well-written and documented. Many, however, will feel that the case presented is overdrawn. The use of legal drugs may be somewhat out of hand currently, but there is a positive side to the matter. In the U.S. there are relatively few in mental institutions; women probably cope better with stress than formerly; and hyperactive children are perhaps better managed. The use of prescribed drugs is far better controlled than that of the illicit variety.

224. Kandel, Denise B., ed. **Longitudinal Research on Drug Use: Empirical Findings and Methodological Issues.** Washington: Hemisphere Publishing Corp.; distr., Halsted Press, a division of John Wiley and Sons, Inc., 1978. 314p. bibliog. index. $22.50. LC 78-6093. ISBN 0-470-26287-7.

In the past, knowledge of drug users was based primarily on studies that were done retrospectively. Many beliefs based on these studies were found to be wrong, and a need was felt for longitudinal studies, prospective studies in which respondents were followed over time. Such studies were started early as surveys, but, of course, have been rather long in completion. The results of some are now available, and this work reports on a number of them. Correlations are reported between drug use and parental influence, deviant behavior, sexual behavior, drug use by friends, personality, parental drug use, alcohol use, and the like.

Most of the chapters of the book are revisions of papers presented at a Conference on Strategies of Longitudinal Research on Drug Use, held in 1976 in San Juan, Puerto Rico. A few have been presented in similar form in the National Institute on Drug Abuse monograph "Predicting Adolescent Drug Use" (*see* Andrews, *A Bibliography of Drug Abuse*, 1977, entry 378).

There are problems involved in longitudinal studies. One in particular is pointed out in the paper "Panel Loss in a High School Drug Study" by Josephson and Rosen. Briefly, what happens is that a certain percentage of the original sample in a study cannot be located for follow-up studies, and the generalization of the conclusions becomes questionable.

The papers are divided into four sections: 1) An overview, 2) The high school years, 3) After school: college students and adults, and 4) Commentaries. In the last section theoretical and methodological issues are discussed and a historical overview of the various approaches to the study of change is presented.

This book is not for the general reader, but should be of interest to sociologists, to those who work with drug abusers, and to researchers in the field.

225. Smart, R. G., and others. **A Methodology for Student Drug-use Surveys.** Geneva: World Health Organization, 1980. 55p. bibliog. (WHO Offset Publication No. 50.) S Fr 7.- . ISBN 92-4-170050-5.

Many surveys on drug abuse by young people have been conducted, but it has been difficult to compare findings because investigators have used different methods and instruments. This report describes a World Health Organization study that brought together experts from various countries to agree on a set of core data items for a standard student drug-use questionnaire for self-administration. The questionnaire was tested on more than 1,600 students in Burma, India, Malaysia,

Mexico, Nigeria, Pakistan, and Thailand, and was found to be reasonably reliable and valid.

The report is in four parts: 1) Introduction, 2) Development of the questionnaire and plan for its testing, 3) Results of testing the questionnaire in seven countries, and 4) Application and further development of the final questionnaire. In addition, there are these appendices: Methodological guidelines for self-administered surveys of youth, Student drug-use questionnaire, Instructions to investigators for use of the questionnaire, and Optional questions.

In light of some of the experience gained in the test, some revisions were made in the questionnaire, and the revision is included. It contains questions on demographic characteristics, drug use frequency, and age of first use for 13 types of drugs including alcohol and tobacco. Information on honesty in answering the questions was gathered and reported.

226.   U.S. National Center for Health Statistics. **Use Habits of Cigarettes, Coffee, Aspirin, and Sleeping Pills, United States, 1976.** By Gordon Scott Bonham, and Paul E. Leaverton. Washington: GPO, 1979. 48p. bibliog. [DHEW Publication No. (PHS) 79-1559; Vital and Health Statistics: Series 10; Data from the National Health Survey, No. 131.] $2.25pa. LC 79-17793. ISBN 0-8406-0163-8. S/N 017-022-00678-2.

The statistical material presented in this survey was obtained by making use of health interviews of a representative sample of the noninstitutionalized population of the U.S. regarding their use of the four drugs or habit-forming substances. Indicators of health are presented for persons over 20 years of age who used them and those who did not.

The publication contains about 18 pages of text material with graphs and tables included. Detailed tables cover about 13 more pages. In addition, there are three appendices: 1) Technical notes on methods, 2) Definition of terms, and 3) Health habits pages from the questionnaire.

Among other findings, the survey showed that persons who had never smoked were healthier than smokers; and smokers, healthier than former smokers. There was no evidence that heavy coffee drinking is related to poor health. Persons who regularly used aspirin were less healthy than those who used it less often. The use of sleeping pills was related to almost all measures of poor health.

227.   U.S. National Institute on Drug Abuse. **DAWN City Summaries: A Report of Emergency Room Data from the Drug Abuse Warning Network.** Washington: GPO, 1976. 26p. [DHEW Publication No. (ADM) 76-235.]

This report is based on data from a survey conducted by IMS America, Ltd., which has been supported by the National Institute on Drug Abuse and the Drug Enforcement Administration. Called the Drug Abuse Warning Network (Project DAWN), the contractor has collected representative information concerning drug abuse incidence by utilizing a nationwide network of reporting units. The report under consideration presents only part of the information collected by DAWN, namely the basic statistic identified as "drug mention" (an entry that includes the number of times use of a drug is mentioned on a facility report). The publication contains graphic reports on 23 representative cities (standard metropolitan statistical areas) and brief explanatory material.

228.   U.S. National Institute on Drug Abuse. **Drug Abuse Deaths in Nine Cities: A Survey Report.** By Louis A. Gottschalk, Frederick L. McGuire, Jon F. Heiser, Eugene C. Dinovo, and Herman Birch. Washington: GPO, 1979. 176p. [DHEW

Publication No. (ADM) 80-840; NIDA Research Monograph 29.] LC 80-600013.
S/N 017-024-00982-2.

It is felt that drug related deaths can serve as a barometer of sorts of the
extent and seriousness of the drug abuse problem. This study looks at the characteristics of the decedents, the system of data collection, and the activities involved
in certifying a death. There has, in the past, been inconsistencies in data collected
from medical examiners' and coroners' offices which this study may help correct
in the future. The nine cities surveyed were: Chicago, Cleveland, Dallas, Los Angeles,
Miami, New York, Philadelphia, San Francisco, and Washington. Much of the material
presented is in tabular format.

The following are the chapter headings: 1) Introduction and overview, 2)
Methods of study, 3) General description of cases, 4) Role of drugs in death, 5) Treatment of victim prior to death, 6) On-site investigations, 7) Postmortem findings,
8) Details of the toxicological examinations, 9) Sociodemographic characteristics
of cases, 10) Accidental deaths, 11) Suicides and homicides, and 12) Discussion and
conclusions. Two substantial appendices have been included: 1) Reporting forms and
code sheets, and 2) Specific psychoactive drugs and/or the classes of such drugs associated with 3004 drug-involved deaths.

Conclusions indicate the two classes of drugs responsible for most deaths
were opiates and barbiturates, with opiates responsible for twice as many as barbiturates. Some of the most poignant findings were the relative youth of the victims and
the fact that postmortem findings were for the most part normal, suggesting how
unnecessary is the tragedy of drug abuse deaths.

229.   U.S. National Institute on Drug Abuse. **Drug Abuse Epidemiology Data
Center (DAEDAC) General Information, October 1979.** Washington: GPO, 1979.
69p.

The Drug Abuse Epidemiology Data Center is a federally funded, nonprofit
research archive operated by the Institute of Behavioral Research at Texas Christian
University for the National Institute on Drug Abuse. It maintains a large file of
coded raw data from original drug surveys on computer tapes and punched cards.
These files are available for research and analysis. In addition, DAEDAC also maintains a file of statistical data and research results from reports and other documents,
called the Aggregate File. Literature searches and searches for actual data can be
made by computer for the scientific community.

The booklet provides detailed information about the Center's policies, cost
schedule, and staff, as well as its services.

230.   U.S. National Institute on Drug Abuse. **The Epidemiology of Drug Abuse:
Current Issues.** Edited by Louise G. Richards and Louise B. Blevens. Washington:
GPO, 1977. 259p. bibliog. [DHEW Publication No. (ADM) 77-432; NIDA Research
Monograph 10.] $2.60pa. LC 77-70239. S/N 017-024-00571-1.

The papers presented in this monograph are edited transcripts from a conference held in Miami Beach on November 18-19, 1974. The presentations and discussions are a reflection of the state of the art in 1975. It was hoped that they would
provide a foundation for future improved research in the area. Few were satisfied
with the technique at hand, and there has been much searching, examining, and
speculation about better ways of comprehending the extent and nature of drug
abuse.

Eight questions were offered to conference participants upon which to
build their presentations: 1) What is the extent of opiate addiction in the U.S.?,

2) How accurate are the sample survey data now abundant?, 3) How can the adverse consequences of drugs be measured as they occur among users?, 4) How accurate are data on clients in treatment?, 5) Is it possible to predict drug abuse epidemics? Further, can the next new fad be predicted?, 6) Can states and cities assess their own drug abuse problems accurately, at a reasonable cost?, 7) Are there indicators of drug abuse accurate enough to assess incidence or prevalence?, and 8) How can one resolve conflicting estimates of the same phenomenon? The participants addressed these questions as best they could and, in addition, commented on other developments of a conceptual or philosophic nature.

The papers are grouped under the following headings: 1) Issues underlying incidence and prevalence, 2) Problems in data acquisition, 3) Problems related to applying and extrapolating data, 4) Current estimates, ranges, and trends, and 5) Current epidemiology program and recommendations.

231.   U.S. National Institute on Drug Abuse. **The Epidemiology of Heroin and Other Narcotics.** Edited by Joan Dunne Rittenhouse. Washington: GPO, 1977. 249p. bibliog. [DHEW Publication No. (ADM) 77-559; NIDA Research Monograph 16.] $3.50pa. LC 77-88154. S/N 017-024-00690-4.

This publication contains the report of the work of a Task Force on the Epidemiology of Heroin and Other Narcotics. The contributors were asked to discuss the state of the art of heroin epidemiology, identify any gaps in knowledge, suggest to the National Institute on Drug Abuse how such gaps might be addressed through research, and identify any apparent policy implications. The papers are arranged under the following headings: 1) Spectrum of use: heroin and other narcotics, 2) Estimates of user populations for heroin and other narcotics: available methodologies and their limitations, 3) Treated prevalence, and 4) Consequences of use: heroin and other narcotics.

One fact is very evident from the material presented in this volume: there is a need to *define* and *measure* the prevalence of the disease, social problem, or undesirable condition we are trying to understand, prevent, stamp out, or at least mitigate.

232.   U.S. National Institute on Drug Abuse. **Highlights from the National Survey on Drug Abuse: 1977.** By Ira Cisin, Judith D. Miller, and Adele V. Harrell, Social Research Group, The George Washington University. Washington: GPO, 1978. 36p. bibliog. [DHEW Publication No. (ADM) 78-620.] S/N 017-024-00725-1.

Intended primarily to provide estimates of levels of illicit drug use in the United States, this report expresses the survey's findings in statistical terms, which can form an empirical basis for program and policy formulation on the federal level and provide data for use by professional workers in the drug abuse field. The 1977 study referred to in the title is the fifth of such studies, but this publication is the first to summarize highlights. (*See* entry 234.)

Five major drugs or classes of drugs are considered: marihuana/hashish, cocaine, hallucinogens, heroin, and other opiates. The publication presents text material and a large number of graphs to illustrate findings.

In conclusion, the publication states that it is risky to speculate on future patterns of drug use, because social, economic, and political factors can influence trends. However, the surmise is made that the chain of events described in the publication could cause not only an increase in the prevalence of illicit drug use but also change the patterns that now characterize this behavior. Illicit drug use is now associated with a specific time of life and the youth culture, and many discontinue drug use as they assume adult roles. However, if the social barrier to drug taking (particularly marijuana) is down, users may be less inclined to discontinue use, and occasional users may increase their frequency of use. If such modifications occur, the magnitude of change in the drug use picture could dwarf the trends set in the late sixties.

233.   U.S. National Institute on Drug Abuse. **Inhalant Use and Treatment.** By Terry Mason. Washington: GPO, 1979. 62p. bibliog. [DHEW Publication No. (ADM) 79-783; Services Research Monograph Series.] S/N 017-024-00904-1.

This report presents findings from a study that attempted to assess patterns of inhalant use in six communities, the problems and treatment needs of users, services sought and provided, and the general response to the health delivery systems available.

The following are the section headings: 1) Literature review, 2) Pilot study methodology, 3) Description of treatment programs visited, 4) Background data on inhalant abusers in treatment, 5) Drug use patterns, 6) Response of inhalant users to treatment, 7) Response of the health care delivery system, and 8) General discussion and conclusions.

Inhalant abusers were seen as different from other drug abuse populations. They were found to be younger, more delinquent and disruptive, and suffering from low self-esteem and lack of motivation. Most would prefer some other drug of abuse (particularly marijuana), but inhalants were more available. Most have attempted to stop using the drugs, but have had little success. Treatment programs have not been very helpful. It is concluded that treatment in the community context will be most successful.

234.   U.S. National Institute on Drug Abuse. **National Survey on Drug Abuse: 1977. A Nationwide Study—Youth, Young Adults, and Older People.** Volume 1, Main Findings. By Herbert I. Abelson, Patricia M. Fishburne, and Ira Cisin. Washington: GPO, 1977. 159p. + appendices. [DHEW Publication No. (ADM) 78-618.] S/N 017-024-00707-2.

This publication is the fifth in a series of reports on the extent of drug abuse in the United States. The other reports have various titles. This one is in two volumes; the second volume is on methodology. Volume 1 provides the reader with statistical information on prevalence, incidence, and correlates. A great proportion of the volume is made up of statistical graphs and tables, but text material is also included to put the results in perspective.

Findings show an increase in use of PCP, marijuana, cocaine, stimulants, sedatives, and tranquilizers, especially among young adults. The percentage of youths using marijuana is higher than before.

Highlights of the survey are reported in another publication. (*See* entry 232.)

235.   U.S. National Institute on Drug Abuse. **A Strategy for Local Drug Abuse Assessment.** Washington: GPO, 1980. 27p. bibliog. [DHEW Publication No. (ADM) 80-966; NIDA Technical Paper.]

It is felt that in the field of drug abuse treatment and prevention, there has been a lack of coordinated and systematic assessment of the drug abuse problem. The purpose of this short technical paper is to provide local program planners, administrators, and other decisionmakers with basic tools to assess local drug abuse conditions. A strategy is described that should provide users with data on which to base judgments. Utilization of "indicators" is stressed. These include: drug abuse treatment admissions, hepatitis cases, drug-related deaths, nonfatal emergency room episodes involving drug abuse, drug law violation arrests, and drug retail price and purity levels.

236.   U.S. National Institute on Drug Abuse. **Synthetic Estimates for Small Areas: Statistical Workshop Papers and Discussions.** Edited by Joseph Steinberg. Washington: GPO, 1979. 282p. bibliog. [DHEW Publication No. (ADM) 79-801; NIDA Research Monograph Series, No. 24.] $5.00. LC 79-600067. S/N 017-024-00911-3.

The "synthetic estimates" mentioned in the title of this monograph are methods of using national survey data and census data to produce estimates of incidence or prevalence of drug abuse in states and local areas. This publication contains workshop papers by statisticians and scientists that air the strengths and weaknesses of the known methods.

The papers are grouped in four parts. Part I is a historical overview, part II consists of papers on methodological contributions, and parts III and IV contain groupings of applications. In addition to the technical papers, each section contains discussions and comments.

The participants in the workshop gave the existing techniques of synthetic estimates for small areas a mixed review. They were said to be useful in some situations where small area data are not available. There are other situations where such estimates are not useful, and in some cases they may be worse than no data at all. Professional statistical judgment needs to be exercised before synthetic estimation use is recommended.

237.   U.S. National Institute on Drug Abuse. **Toward a Heroin Problem Index— An Analytical Model for Drug Abuse Indicators.** By Philip H. Person, Robert L. Retka, and J. Arthur Woodward. Washington: GPO, 1976. 33p. bibliog. [DHEW Publication No. (ADM) 76-367; National Institute on Drug Abuse Technical Paper.] $0.85pa. S/N 017-024-00522-3.

Although admitting that the "Drug Abuse Problem" is difficult to define precisely, the authors of this paper hypothesize that there exists a rational way of combining the drug abuse indicators usually considered which would give a better, stronger, more defensible impression as to what is happening in drug abuse prevalence. They also examine the nature of some of the indicators and develop an indicator combining methodology. Lastly, they apply the method to real data sets generally considered to be drug abuse indicators.

The material is presented under the following headings: 1) Indicators and measurements, 2) Assumptions for an analytical model for deriving a drug abuse prevalence index, 3) A methodology for combining drug abuse indicators, 4) Demonstration of drug abuse indicator analysis, and 5) The heroin problem index.

238.   U.S. National Institute on Drug Abuse. Division of Scientific and Program Information. **Statistical Series E.**
See reports below.

238a.   **Annual Data, 1977, Data from the Client Oriented Data Acquisitions Process (CODAP).** Washington: GPO, 1978. 309p. [National Institute on Drug Abuse, Statistical Series: Series E, Number 7; DHEW Publication No. (ADM) 79-736.]

This report focuses on displaying relationships among the variables classified in CODAP data. All material is presented in tabular form. The variables are shown in relation to selected primary drugs simultaneously. Also, the variables are presented as they are related to each other in different combinations for all clients, regardless of the drug use. In addition, there are tables that present data on clients who have a particular primary drug of abuse.

238b.   **Annual Summary Report, Data from the Client Oriented Data Acquisition Process (CODAP).** Washington: GPO, 1975- . Annual. [National Institute on Drug Abuse, Statistical Series; DHEW Publication (ADM).]

These annual reports present statistics on client characteristics, drug abuse patterns, and treatment based on CODAP data aggregated at national, state, and Standard Metropolitan Statistical Area levels. Most of the information is presented in tabular or graphic form.

238c.   **Quarterly Report Provisional Data, Data from the Client Oriented Data Acquisition Process (CODAP).** Washington: GPO, 1977- . Quarterly. [National Institute on Drug Abuse, Statistical Series; DHEW Publication (ADM).]

This publication continues earlier series with variant titles. The quarterly reports present statistics on client characteristics, drug abuse patterns, and treatment experience based on national data collected from federally funded treatment facilities.

A 1979 report showed, among other findings, that opiates were the primary drug of abuse at admission by 49% of the clients, with heroin reported by 42%. Forty-one percent of all clients were self referrals.

238d.   **SMSA (Standard Metropolitan Statistical Areas) Statistics, 1978, Data from the Client Oriented Data Acquisition Process (CODAP).** Washington: GPO, 1979. 318p. [National Institute on Drug Abuse, Statistical Series: Series E, Number 14; DHEW Publication No. (ADM) 80-868.]

The material in this publication is presented in nine tables. These tables contain percent distributions describing client admission and discharge activities which can be defined as client characteristics and treatment activity. The nine tables are repeated for each of 50 standard metropolitan statistical areas. There is a short narrative summary of findings.

238e.   **State Statistics, 1977, Data from the Client Oriented Data Acquisition Process (CODAP).** Washington: GPO, 1978. 315p. [National Institute on Drug Abuse, Statistical Series: Series E, Number 8; DHEW Publication No. (ADM) 78-755.]

This report provides tables showing client characteristics, patterns of drug abuse, and treatment activity for the individual states, the District of Columbia, Puerto Rico, and the Virgin Islands. Tables showing national client characteristics are also included.

238f.   **Trend Report, January 1975-September 1977, Data from the Client Oriented Data Acquisition Process (CODAP).** Washington: GPO, 1978. 154p. [National Institute on Drug Abuse, Statistical Series: Series E, Number 5; DHEW Publication No. (ADM) 78-733.]

This report illustrates in tabular and graphic form the characteristics of clients admitted to treatment of drug abuse in federally funded programs. Trends across the period were relatively stable for all drugs, except for a rise in heroin abuse (11%) followed by a 10% decrease. Marijuana abuse had an opposite trend from heroin and leveled off in 1977. There was a slight increase in percentage of clients over age 26 when admitted to treatment.

239.   U.S. National Institute on Drug Abuse. Heroin Indicators Task Force. **Heroin Indicators Trend Report—An Update, 1976-1978.** Washington: GPO, 1979. 19p. bibliog. [DHEW Publication No. (ADM) 79-892.] $1.50pa. S/N 017-024-00950-4.

One of a series of publications that provide information on the current status of the heroin problem in the U.S., this report contains comments concerning the rationale for selection of indicators. Then graphs, tables, and comments on the following national indicators are provided: heroin-related deaths, heroin-related emergency room visits, heroin average price and purity, heroin treatment admissions, household and high school surveys, and estimated number of heroin users. In addition, data based on Standard Metropolitan Statistical Area Indicators is given.

All indicators uniformly showed declining trends for 1976 through 1978, on the average. In a few areas, however, the number of emergency room visits or deaths increased; San Francisco, Miami, and Philadelphia showed sharply increasing trends.

The indicators provided in the publication will give drug abuse treatment planners and practitioners, law enforcement officers, health professionals, and funding agencies information upon which to base policy and planning strategies.

240.   U.S. Special Action Office for Drug Abuse Prevention. **Drug Incidence Analysis.** By Leon Gibson Hunt. Washington: GPO, 1974. 36p. (Special Action Office Monograph, Series A, No. 3, August 1974.)

This monograph brings together some techniques to help communities understand their changing drug abuse problems. The study of trends in drug abuse incidence gives a picture of the changing nature of the problem and aids in prediction of future dimensions. In addition, an analysis of the trends can help put theories of causes of drug abuse into perspective.

The presentation is in two parts as follows: 1) Drug incidence data: its meaning and uses in planning, and 2) Analysis of incidence data. Many graphs accompany the text.

241.   U.S. Special Action Office for Drug Abuse Prevention. **The Vietnam Drug User Returns.** Final Report, September 1973. Principal investigator, Lee N. Robins. Washington: GPO, 1974. 95p. + appendices. bibliog. (Special Action Office Monograph, Series A, No. 2.) $2.10pa. LC 74-600015.

This report puts in perspective the problem of the Vietnam drug user and makes a contribution toward understanding the natural history of drug abuse as well. The following chapters are included: 1) Introduction, 2) Study design, 3) Obtaining interviews, urines, and records, 4) Validity of interviews, 5) Portrait of the Vietnam soldier, 6) Drug use in Vietnam, 7) Return to the United States, 8) After discharge, 9) Drug use after Vietnam, 10) The association of drug use with post-Vietnam adjustment, 11) Shifts in drug use over time, and 12) Returnees' opinions about army and Veterans Administration policies.

The results may be summarized as follows: 1) half the men came to Vietnam without drug experience (other than marijuana) and were still nonusers 8-12 months after their return; 2) 6% were using the same drugs they used before Vietnam 8-12 months after return; 3) 20% had become users or had increased the variety of drugs used as compared with before Vietnam; 4) 25% had stopped using drugs they used before Vietnam or decreased the variety used; and 5) 2% had exchanged the type of drugs they used before Vietnam for others. In general the results showed that a change of environment brought about a great decrease in addiction.

242.   U.S. Veterans Administration. Office of Controller. Reports and Statistics Service. **Alcoholism and Problem Drinking: 1970-1975: A Statistical Analysis of VA Hospital Patients.** By Alice P. Carmody, Louis Mesard, and William F. Page. Washington: GPO, 1977. 161p. (Controller Monograph No. 5, Patient Census Data.)

The purpose of this report is to present statistical data about VA hospital patients who were classified as alcoholics or problem drinkers from 1970-1975. Trends in the size and composition of the group are identified, and such variables as age, period of service, marital status, compensation and pension status, and attained stay were analyzed. Most of the material is presented in tables and graphs.

Among other findings: hospital discharges for alcoholism increased steadily; there was a trend toward increased proportions of patients under 35 years of age defined as alcoholics and problem drinkers; and differences in black and white patients were very slight.

7

PREVENTION, TREATMENT, REHABILITATION, AND COMMUNITY ACTION PROGRAMS

This section lists publications that deal in general with prevention and treatment of drug and alcohol abuse. Those covering the more strictly medical aspects of treatment and research on the subject are included in section 14. Of the books listed in this section, about 20 deal with alcoholism alone.

Drug abuse and alcoholism treatment approaches have not changed very much over the past decade. A variety are still used since it is evident that some patients respond to certain methods better than others. There has been a tendency toward more rigid evaluation of programs, but success rates are still rather poor. A great deal of pessimism has been expressed in recent publications in contrast to earlier optimism. Therapists in the field say their perspective has been clouded; progress seems at a standstill; rehabilitation centers have been hit by scandal; and dedicated people are burning out. The earlier optimism was perhaps unrealistic, though, and there is still emphasis on therapeutic communities, alternatives to drug use, and professional psychiatric help. Increasing numbers of self-help publications are becoming available, enough that a separate section has been included in this bibliography.

The U.S. government has provided a number of publications on treatment and prevention, covering such areas as alternatives, therapeutic communities, financing and management of programs, followup studies, and program evaluation.

243.   Adams, J. Winstead. **Psychoanalysis of Drug Dependence: The Understanding and Treatment of a Particular Form of Pathological Narcissism.** New York: Grune and Stratton, 1978. 329p. bibliog. index. $23.50. LC 78-71183. ISBN 0-8089-1148-1.

Written by a psychoanalyst, this work outlines a process of treating drug abuse patients, an adaptation and expansion of "Modern Psychoanalysis," a system of ideas and tactics elaborated in the 1950s by Dr. Hyman Spotnitz, who was a pioneer in the psychotherapy of schizophrenia.

The author of the Foreword remarks that therapists in the field of drug abuse and addiction are currently very pessimistic. Treatment seems at a standstill; rehabilitation centers are spotted by scandal; and dedicated people are demoralized. Brilliant hopes so often have ended in disappointment. However, he believes that Adams' book brings a ray of light to the scene by making a noteworthy and practical contribution to the problem of drug abuse psychotherapy.

The first part of the book defines the problem under consideration, and the second part is a survey of current approaches in the treatment of drug dependence. The following are the chapter headings: 1) Introduction, 2) Review of the literature, 3) Treatment methodology, 4) Clinical case studies, 5) Introduction to treatment,

6) Group treatment and the "street addict": a preanalytic method, 7) The therapeutic community, and 8) Summary.

244.   Addiction Research Foundation of Ontario. **In Perspective: A Review of the Current Status of Projects and Programs.** Toronto: Addiction Research Foundation, 1978. 23p.

Four sections compose this summary of the foundation's activities: 1) Particular concerns, 2) Extent and use of health-related issues, 3) Treatment resources, and 4) Education and prevention. The first section covers alcohol-related problems of young people, the drinking-driving program, alcohol in the workplace, the management and rehabilitation of the chronic inebriate, and work with native people. The second section outlines some of the foundation's research activities, such as the impact of alcohol consumption on public health, disease related to the consumption of alcohol and other drugs, drug identification and overdose, and dependence on narcotics and analgesics. The third part deals with better methods and delivery of treatment services. The final section covers the development of manpower for education and public education and information.

245.   Anderson, Daniel J., Sister Mary Leo Kammeier, and Helen L. Holmes. **Applied Research: Impact on Decision Making.** Center City, MN: Hazelden, 1978. 31p. $3.95pa. ISBN 0-89486-043-7.

This booklet reports on a 1970-1971 research project that was initiated at the Hazelden Treatment Center to investigate a wide range of issues and problems concerning chemical dependency. Primarily, the publication deals with how the findings affected policies and programming at Hazelden, a residential facility for chemically dependent persons.

The following are the chapter headings: 1) Project planning and implementation, 2) Formulation of major concepts, 3) Application to treatment, 4) Application to training and education, and 5) Summary.

Major findings of the project included: 1) support for the concepts of chemical dependency as a treatable primary illness; 2) an indication that treatment programs that incorporated individualized planning could effectively serve the needs of different categories of patients; 3) Demonstration of the effectiveness of rehabilitation with patients legally committed to a treatment facility; 4) support for abstinence as an appropriate goal; 5) support for a multidisciplinary approach to treatment in an environment with peer group involvement in mutual problem solving; and 6) an awareness of the effectiveness of evaluation as a follow-up support for patients.

In addition, post-treatment data have been supplied in an appendix. Notably, it was found that there was a strong positive correlation between Alcoholics Anonymous attendance and abstinence or improvement in drinking behavior.

246.   Boström, Harry, Tage Larsson, and Nils Ljungstedt, eds. **Drug Dependence: Treatment and Treatment Evaluation.** Symposium, October 15-17, 1974. Stockholm: Almqvist and Wiksell International, 1975. 312p. bibliog. (Skandia International Symposium.) Kr. 98.00. LC 75-595993. ISBN 91-2200017-8.

Eighteen symposium papers and the discussions that followed them are presented in this volume. Some of the topics covered are: Amphetamine abuse in Japan, The Daytop Village treatment center in New York, Psychotherapy in treatment, Coercion in treatment, Adolescent drug dependents in psychiatric hospitals, Facilities for addicts in Gothenburg (Sweden), The Oslo Half-Way-House, Methadone maintenance, Opioid antagonists, Propranolol in heroin dependence, Methods of treatment evaluation, Follow-up studies, and Evaluations of various treatment techniques.

The symposium participants are experts from all parts of the world, but particularly the Scandinavian countries.

247.   Bourne, Peter G. **Methadone: Benefits and Shortcomings.** Washington: Drug Abuse Council, Inc., 1975. 26p. bibliog. $1.25pa. LC 75-35491.

This publication presents a concise review of the use of methadone for maintenance purposes as a treatment for heroin addiction. The literature of the subject is thoroughly covered. The goals of the treatment are explored, the objectives pointed out, and the accomplishments and failures discussed. The conclusion drawn is that possibly the benefits of methadone maintenance are slight in comparison to those that were originally expected. However, they are still substantial when compared with the life to which the addict is otherwise doomed.

248.   Brandsman, Jeffrey M. **Outpatient Treatment of Alcoholism: A Review and Comparative Study.** In collaboration with Maxie C. Maultsby, Jr., and Richard J. Welsh. Baltimore, MD: University Park Press, 1980. 213p. bibliog. index. $16.95. LC 79-9541. ISBN 0-8391-1393-5.

The intent of this book is to explore the possibilities of outpatient treatment for alcoholics. The results of a five-year study are reported. It evaluated four different kinds of psychotherapeutic treatment. These included Alcoholics Anonymous, traditional insight therapy, and rational behavior therapy (both professionally delivered and self-help). A no-treatment control was also studied.

Chapters presented are: 1) Review of the literature, 2) Methodology, 3) Instrumentation, 4) Results, 5) Imported therapists: a strategy for expanding efficient alcoholism services, 6) The efficacy of coercion, 7) Self-help methods, 8) Professional vs. nonprofessional treatment, and 9) Summary and conclusions. In addition, a large section of the book is made up of appendices, which include forms, interviews, questionnaires, rating scales, and statistical tables.

Results and conclusions follow. On an absolute scale the outcomes were not outstanding, although comparable with other studies. Treatment will help a patient with alcohol problems including his or her legal, behavioral, and general maladjustment. Alcoholics Anonymous had the most dropouts. For legal problems insight therapy seemed best. For total dry days, professional help was superior. And finally, treatment of any kind was superior to no treatment. It was also found that the use of coercive pressures seem warranted and should be explored further legally and therapeutically.

The book provides important empirical evidence.

249.   Brook, Robert C., and Paul C. Whitehead. **Drug-Free Therapeutic Community: An Evaluation.** New York: Human Sciences Press, 1980. 158p. bibliog. index. $12.95. LC 79-20477. ISBN 0-87705-383-9.

In this publication the philosophy and use of the therapeutic community in the treatment of drug abusers is explored. Significant research is evaluated as are historical and contemporary studies on the effectiveness and successes of this modality of treatment.

A major section of the book is concerned with a treatment program for amphetamine abusers. Follow-up studies were done and reported on to provide assistance in future programs.

It is concluded that therapeutic communities are effective in a great number of drug dependency cases. Professional supervision is a factor in success as is the empathy among the patients.

250.   Brown, Barry S., ed. **Addicts and Aftercare: Community Integration of the Former Drug User**. Beverly Hills, CA; London: Sage Publications, 1979. 294p. bibliog. (Sage Annual Reviews of Drug and Alcohol Abuse. Vol. 3.) $18.50; $8.95pa. LC 79-18156. ISBN 0-8039-1148-3; 0-8039-1149-1pa.

This volume provides a theoretical basis for providing community integration services for former drug users, and also presents practical suggestions for providing them. Most of the chapters deal with problems of individuals who have spent time in a mental or a correctional institution and have been separated physically from a community. The contributions included are drawn from a variety of other fields, although all deal with community integration activities: family activities, work activities, efforts of self-help groups, the use of volunteers, assistance of advocacy groups, and the use of litigation to enforce community rights and responsibilities. Some suggestions and many implications for further research appear in the text.

After a general introduction, the book is presented in these parts: 1) The client in the community, 2) Self-help models for continuing care, 3) Models for continuing care using community organizations, 4) Human resource organizations in continuing care, and 5) Client advocacy.

The book will interest those involved in drug abuse services and those in various aspects of community integration.

251.   Collier, D. F., and S. A. Somfay. **Ascent from Skid Row: The Bon Accord Community 1967-1973**. Researcher and Program Consultant: Gustave Oki. Toronto: Addiction Research Foundation of Ontario, 1974. 108p. illus. (Program Report Series No. 2.) $3.50pa. ISBN 0-88868-004-X.

The Bon Accord Community was established in 1967 for homeless alcoholics, a pilot project of the Addiction Research Foundation. The book describes Bon Accord's history, present status, and future direction. The rural rehabilitation unit emphasizes the autonomy of the individual in that it provides a community government structure. There is a furniture-making industry through which residents can pay their way and learn skills.

The treatment technique used with patients is behavior modification in social, political, economic, and drinking areas.

Contents of the book are as follows: 1) Introduction, 2) The applicants, 3) The community, 4) Admission procedures, 5) Changing behavior, 6) Social behavior, 7) Political behavior, 8) Economic behavior, 9) Drinking behavior, 10) Physical health, 11) Results, and 12) Conclusions and projections. In addition, these appendices have been provided: Bon Accord admission criteria, the community government-structure and function, Elora survey on Bon Accord, and glossary of skid row argot.

252.   Cook, Tim. **Vagrant Alcoholics**. London and Boston: Routledge & Kegan Paul, 1975. 189p. bibliog. index. $15.50. ISBN 0-7100-8118-9.

This book is an account of the development of the Alcoholics Recovery Project, a small voluntary organization in Great Britain concerned with the problems of vagrant alcoholics. The author believes that the project has made some progress in dealing with the problems of the homeless alcoholic. The objective of the project was to try to discern more clearly the real nature faced by the vagrant and to bear in mind the historical legacies we all share with him—the female alcoholic was not considered.

The chapter titles are as follows: 1) Introduction, 2) The beginning, 3) The first phase, 4) Shop fronts, 5) Other work of the project, 6) Detoxification centres, 7) Views from the other side, 8) Assessment and evaluation, and 9) Concluding considerations.

In conclusion, the author makes a number of recommendations. Particularly, he believes there is a desperate need of a concerted attack on the problem, and feels this can only come about from the establishment of a commission or council with authority. He further believes that resolving any part of the skid row problem is a full-time job, not something to be left to volunteers involved elsewhere, and put at the tail end of a busy week.

253.   Davis, Carl S., and Marlin Ruth Schmidt, eds. **Differential Treatment of Drug and Alcohol Abusers.** Palm Springs, CA: ETC Publications, 1977. 124p. bibliog. index. $8.50. LC 76-54203. ISBN 0-88280-048-5.

The material presented in this publication is an extension of the papers presented at a conference on Differential Treatment in Drug Counseling Programs, held at the University of Iowa in 1974. The papers represent a balance between the general theory of differential treatment models and some exploration in the field of drug/alcohol treatment and programming. Generally, the current state of drug abuse treatment is still sadly wanting despite the money, politics, and professional activity expended in the development of treatment approaches. The view taken in this book is that all techniques are probably effective to some degree, but effective in a differential manner depending upon types of clients and objectives. The intent of the book is to stimulate professionals working in the area of drug abuse treatment to explore a new approach to the design and development of drug counseling procedures and programs, the differential treatment approach.

The following are the titles of the papers: 1) Therapeutic outcomes of drug treatment: the state of the art, 2) Paradigm for developing and analyzing the differential treatment programs, 3) Some applications of the Lewinian model to community mental health: a program of differential treatment and research, 4) Differential treatment in a high-risk urban area, 5) Theoretical speculations about marijuana and drug issues, 6) Using a differential treatment approach with high-risk high school students, 7) Cost benefit analysis as applied to differential treatment models, and 8) The differential treatment model and drug counseling: an epilogue.

254.   **Diagnosis and Treatment of Alcoholism for Primary Care Physicians.** Toronto: Addiction Research Foundation, 1978. 39p. $1.95pa.

The Ontario Medical Association and the Addiction Research Foundation have collaborated to prepare this valuable handbook, which is a practical guide for physicians in dealing with the victims of alcohol.

In three parts, the booklet discusses in outline form the dilemma, the diagnosis, and the treatment of alcoholism. Both physical and psychological aspects are considered. Appended are a list of agencies in Ontario that offer information and assistance with alcohol problems, and a list of Ontario Detox Centres.

255.   Einstein, Stanley, ed. **The Community's Response to Drug Use.** New York: Pergamon Press, 1980. 369p. illus. bibliog. index. $45.00. LC 79-16278. ISBN 0-08-019597-0.

Thirteen individuals well-known in the field of drug abuse and/or community health contributed the twelve chapters that make up this book. The material is presented under three headings: Drug Use and Its Control, Drug Education, and Research.

The first part begins with historical and theoretical considerations. Then several chapters follow that discuss drug use and control in these countries: Australia and New Zealand, Singapore and the Southeast Asian region, Canada, the United States, the United Kingdom, and Israel. The second part contains only one chapter, "Drug Abuse Prevention: Issues, Problems, and Alternatives." The following papers make up the last section: Methodology in community research; Addiction as a community disorder; The pharmaceutical industry and drug use and misuse; and Alternatives to drugs: new visions for society.

In general, the material in the book is well-prepared and on a high level. There are many references to the literature. A number of sections are perhaps discouraging since many problems are pointed out but few solutions provided. There is no overall summary pulling the ideas presented together.

256.   Forrest, Gary G. **The Diagnosis and Treatment of Alcoholism**. 2nd ed. Springfield, IL: Charles C. Thomas, 1978. 348p. bibliog. index. $17.50; $12.95pa. LC 27117. ISBN 0-398-03779-5; 0-398-03780-9pa.

The author of this work attempts to communicate to alcohol rehabilitation personnel a global treatment approach that he has found successful as a licensed clinical psychologist and Executive Director of Psychotherapy Associates and The Institute for Addictive Behavioral Change, Colorado Springs, Colorado.

This second edition includes some material not covered in the first, particularly a chapter on "Marital and Family Therapy." In addition, new material is included in the "Behavior Therapy" chapter and in the chapter on sexual issues. Five-year follow-up data also has been included in the final chapter.

The author makes it clear that no new or significant "breakthroughs" have emerged in the field of alcoholic treatment and rehabilitation, and that efforts at prevention and education have not been particularly successful. He believes the problems associated with chemical dependency and addiction have only begun to be felt in Western culture.

The following are the chapter titles: 1) What is an alcoholic?, 2) Developmental stages of alcoholism, 3) Sociological and physiological considerations related to alcoholism, 4) Personality characteristics of the alcoholic, 5) The relevance of diagnosis in the treatment of alcoholism, 6) Treatment I: individual psychotherapy, 7) Treatment II: group psychotherapy, 8) Treatment III: Alcoholics Anonymous, 9) Treatment IV: residential treatment, 10) Treatment V: behavior therapy, 11) Treatment VI: marital and family therapy, 12) Treatment VII: the recovery issue, 13) Treatment VIII: toward a causitive theory of alcohol addiction, 14) Alcoholism and self-disclosure, 15) Alcoholism, death and birth, 16) Alcoholism: the emotional plague revisited, 17) Hidden alcoholics in the military, 18) Resolution of the alcoholic power fantasy, 19) Alcoholism: an erotic experience, 20) Successful rehabilitation of the alcoholic patient: a case history, 21) Clinical impressions of the unsuccessfully rehabilitated alcoholic patient, 22) Self-disclosure and sobriety, 23) The effect of group psychotherapy upon levels of anxiety, depression and hostility within an alcoholic population, and 24) Alcoholic rehabilitation: for better or for worse? The first five chapters are background information, the second section contains the strategies of treatment, and the third is made up of clinical readings.

257.   Gideon, William L., ed. **Alcoholism Counseling**. Matteson, IL: Good and Golden, 1976. 3v. bibliog. V. 1, $12.50; V. 2, $27.50; V. 3, $35.00.

This work is made up of a series of lectures developed and presented for the Alcoholism Counselors Program at the University of Houston. The major objective of the course of study is to generate and produce more effective, mature alcoholism counselors. Fifty-nine persons contributed to the 3-volume work. They were instructed to retain the quality of oral presentation rather than that of writing in the hope that this would make the curriculum more easily utilized by those training for counseling.

The material is presented in six parts as follows: 1) Alcohol problems in a drinking society, 2) Individual and group involvement: a recovery process for the alcoholic, 3) Practical training for the alcoholism counselor, 4) Therapeutic approaches and techniques for the alcoholism counselor, 5) Human behavior and the use and abuse of alcohol, and 6) Counseling approaches in various settings.

A great deal of practical, readable material is contained in the work. The editor, a recovered alcoholic himself, presents his own philosophy of alcoholism counseling in the last chapter. He likes to think of counselors as a group of community care-givers. They have been given the available knowledge relative to the field of alcoholism, an appreciation of the recovery process, an understanding of specific techniques and skills, diagnostic capability regarding human behavior, and experience with a variety of approaches used in different settings. In addition, the hope is expressed that the therapeutic group involvement has enhanced the counselor's own life experience. Ethical considerations and a professional code for counselors are given attention, and lastly the editor's own credo is outlined.

258.   Glaser, Frederick B. **The Phase Zero Report of the Core-Shell Treatment System Project: Early Working Papers.** Toronto: Addiction Research Foundation, 1978. 172p. bibliog. $4.95pa. ISBN 0-88868-032-5.

The eight papers in this volume offer a comprehensive statement of the theoretical basis of a system that evolved out of direct observations of a large number of drug abuse treatment programs. Paper titles are as follows: 1) Testimony before the United States Senate Subcommittee on Alcoholism and Narcotics, 2) Assumptions and counter assumptions in treatment and treatment research, 3) Selecting patients for treatment: an heuristic model, 4) The treatment of persons dependent on psycho-active drugs (The Science Centre Presentation), 5) The primary care module, 6) The assessment module, 7) Problem-Indicator Intervention matrix: an attempt, and 8) Specifying the shell. The first four papers present a perspective of the system; the last four touch upon particular details of primary care, assessment and assignment, research, and treatment.

259.   Glaser, Frederick B., Stephanie W. Greenberg, and Morris Barrett. **A Systems Approach to Alcohol Treatment.** Toronto: Addiction Research Foundation, 1978. 303p. bibliog. $14.95pa. ISBN 0-88868-025-2.

This publication reports on alcoholism treatment programs in Pennsylvania around the year 1973. The picture presented is not reassuring, but is probably typical. Also presented in detail is the development of the basic methodology of the study and its application to a cognate treatment system.

The work is divided into sections as follows: 1) The plan, 2) The treatment programs, 3) Intervention efforts other than treatment programs, and 4) Conclusions (including findings and recommendations). In addition, there are four appendices: 1) Tables, 2) Program Directory, 3) Relevant legislation, and 4) Government policy and the problem of alcoholism.

The aim of the work is to ask that new commitments be made to helping alcoholic people and to present a factual base from which a systematic alcoholism service delivery program can be developed.

260.   Groupé, Vincent, ed. **Alcoholism Rehabilitation: Methods and Experiences of Private Rehabilitation Centers.** New Brunswick, NJ: Publications Division, Rutgers Center of Alcohol Studies, 1978. 138p. bibliog. index. (NIAAA-RUCAS Alcoholism Treatment Series, No. 3.) $6.00pa. LC 78-620026. ISBN 911290-49-4.

The material presented in this book is an outgrowth of a Conference on Experiences of Private Alcoholism Rehabilitation Centers held in Palm Beach, Florida, in 1975. Representatives of centers in most parts of the country participated. Thirteen different centers that treat mainly middle-class alcoholics are described in the book, giving history, philosophy, and treatment methods.

The following facilities are treated: The Alcoholic Clinic of Youngstown, Carrier Clinic, Chit Chat Farms, Cumberland Heights, Gateway Rehabilitation Center, Hazelden Foundation, Little Company of Mary Hospital (Evergreen Park, IL), Little Hill-Alina Lodge, Livengrin Foundation, Lutheran General Hospital (Park Ridge, IL), Smithers Alcoholism Treatment and Training Center, Starlite Village Hospital, and Willingway Hospital. In addition, a chapter on Alcoholics Anonymous has been included which outlines its history, principles, and techniques of treatment. All of the centers stress the importance of AA in recovery and aftercare.

Details of follow-up studies of patients after discharge have been omitted. It is presumed that they will be published elsewhere.

261.   Gust, Dodie. **Face to Face with Alcoholism.** Center City, MN: Hazelden, 1979. 52p. $3.95pa. LC 78-60065. ISBN 0-89486-064-X.

The author of this booklet takes the view that the alcoholic's tendency to deny the problem and rationalize his or her behavior must be confronted. "Confrontation" is a nonjudgmental presentation of definite statements regarding drinking behavior, and it should be linked with concern, the offer of help, and positive alternatives. The publication presents guidelines for using the technique, specifically for the family, the physician, the law enforcement officer, and the attorney. These individuals are believed to play a vital role in the intervention process, but others also may adapt the technique for their own situation.

262.   Hinshelwood, R. D., and Nick Manning, eds. **Therapeutic Communities: Reflections and Progress.** London: Routledge and Kegan Paul, 1979. 336p. bibliog. index. £9.50; £5.50pa. LC 79-308718. ISBN 0-7100-0109-6.

The 29 papers in this collection were originally presented at meetings of the Association of Therapeutic Communities. The volume's seven sections cover history, current status, the basic ideas of the community, their theory and practice, staff support and training, clinical case studies, and research. The contributions vary in quality and come from a variety of disciplines, such as psychiatry, sociology, psychology, psychiatric nursing, and social work, as well as from former patients.

The work expresses considerable anxiety about the future of therapeutic communities. Their existence was always precarious because they were often regarded as anti-authoritarian in attitude and unconventional. Patients rather than physicians seemed to be in charge. The communities have lost much of their earlier momentum, and assessment of success has been difficult.

This book makes a contribution toward understanding the problems, failures, and successes of the movement.

263.   Hughes, Patrick H. **Behind the Wall of Respect: Community Experiments in Heroin Addiction Control.** With a Foreword by Daniel X. Freedman. Chicago: University of Chicago Press, 1977. 162p. illus. bibliog. index. LC 25640. ISBN 0-226-35930-1.

This book was written by a psychiatrist who has had a strong interest in public health methodologies and who helped start drug treatment programs in Illinois. The "wall of respect" mentioned in the book title refers to a location in Chicago, the corner of 43rd Street and Langley Avenue on the South Side, which has two brick walls facing each other. Local artists had transformed them into brightly colored murals of rising black pride and militancy. Addicts frequented the buildings behind the walls. In these buildings the author and his colleagues developed notions of the dynamics of heroin spread and of how treatment programs might halt that process. A community treatment project was designed for that locale, and similar approaches were later used in other Chicago neighborhoods, each with increasing effectiveness. The book tells the story of these projects.

Following are the chapter headings: 1) Behind the wall of respect, 2) Developing a mobile epidemiological team, 3) Penetrating Chicago's heroin subculture, 4) Reducing the number of addicts at neighborhood copping areas, 5) Reducing incidence of new cases: Chicago's post-World War II heroin epidemic, 6) A model for researching and intervening in heroin epidemics, 7) Containing a heroin epidemic in Altgeld Gardens, 8) Epidemiological elements in other drug programs, and 9) Toward the heroin-free community.

In summary, the author makes a case for the application of epidemiological principles and techniques in setting up drug treatment programs. He believes that community involvement is necessary with the establishment of neighborhood-based facilities. He warns against the tendency toward becoming entrenched in rigid bureaucracies.

264.   Jones, Maxwell. **Maturation of the Therapeutic Community: An Organic Approach to Health and Mental Health**. New York: Human Sciences Press, 1976. 169p. bibliog. index. (Community Mental Health Series.) $14.25. LC 75-11002. ISBN 0-87705-264-6.

Although this book does not deal directly with drug abuse, it is of interest because the therapeutic community has frequently been used in the treatment of addicts. The book deals primarily with the concept of the therapeutic community or community psychiatry as an "open system" as it applies to health. Open systems present opportunities for interaction between pupil and teacher, and pupil and pupil, as well as within groups spontaneously formed around a common interest. Such a system calls for shared decision making and a feeling of shared responsibility, according to the author. Is is presumed that this fosters a positive effect on health and self-fulfillment and helps people help themselves.

In two parts, the heading of the sections are: 1) Social systems, and 2) A systems approach to health and mental health institutions.

265.   Kammeier, Sister Mary Leo, and J. Clark Laundergan. **The Outcome of Treatment: Patients Admitted to Hazelden in 1975**. Center City, MN: Hazelden, 1977. 57p. $4.95. LC 78-102232. ISBN 0-89486-045-3.

This publication reports on a follow-up study of patients admitted to the Hazelden Rehabilitation Center for chemical dependency during 1975. Data was gathered from intake interviews and treatment records of about 1,500 patients. In the matter of treatment, the importance of Alcoholics Anonymous was emphasized, but the study was multidisciplinary in scope.

Outcomes showed that patients who stopped drinking entirely reported the most improvement; for example, they had the lowest level of personal problems, received more job promotions, etc. Those who reduced drinking showed more improvement than was anticipated, and even patients who used alcohol frequently showed more positive changes than expected. In a general way similarities between the outcomes of male and female patients existed, but more variance than was anticipated was indicated.

266.   Kaufman, Edward, and Pauline Kaufmann, eds. **Family Therapy of Drug and Alcohol Abuse.** Foreword by E. Mansell Pattison. New York: Gardner Press; distr., Halsted Press, Division of John Wiley and Sons, Inc., 1979. 276p. bibliog. index. $24.95. LC 78-9346. ISBN 0-470-26385-7.

It seems that family therapy as treatment for addictive behaviors is a growing modality. Realization has come that behavior is the product of social systems, that a change in behavior is a result of social change. The book describes clinical methods for such changing social systems as marriage, parent-child systems, and nuclear family systems. The book shows that addictive behavior is a secondary problem; the primary one is social dysfunction in the social system of the addict's life.

Several fundamental assumptions are made in the presentation as follows: 1) addiction is a behavioral problem; 2) treatment methods that will "unlearn" behavioral patterns are needed; 3) drug abuse is considered a "syndrome" model of illness; 4) the addict is not considered as helpless; 5) whether a family generates addiction to a certain drug may be dependent on social style, availability, and peer practice; 6) family therapy extends beyond the nuclear family; 7) since the concept of family has been enlarged, so has the concept of therapeutic method; and 8) the therapist of social systems must function as an agent for system change.

The work is divided into two sections, drug abusers, and alcohol abusers. The 17 chapters are contributions of experts in the family therapy field.

267.   Kazdin, Alan E., and G. Terence Wilson. **Evaluation of Behavior Therapy: Issues, Evidence, and Research Strategies.** Cambridge, MA: Ballinger Publishing Co., a subsidiary of J. B. Lippincott Co., 1978. 227p. bibliog. index. $15.50. LC 77-12006. ISBN 0-88410-520-2.

The authors of this work are psychologists who attempt to clarify the field of behavior therapy which has had its proponents and its critics, some of whom feel that it is just one of the latest fads. It is hoped that the book will be useful to those interested in the therapeutic applications of behavior change procedures.

A number of disorders of behavior are considered, including addictive behaviors such as alcoholism, obesity, cigarette smoking, and drug addiction. Recent research is cited and discussed, and areas needing further investigation indicated.

The authors believe that behavioral methods are at least as effective, and often more effective, than alternative approaches.

268.   Langrod, John, Joyce H. Lowinson, and Lois Alksne. **Methadone Detoxification: Personality Correlates and Therapeutic Implications.** Oceanside, NY: Dabor Science Publications, 1977. 108p. + appendices. bibliog. index. $15.00. LC 77-21494. ISBN 0-89561-000-0.

The authors of this work organize the literature on methadone maintenance and detoxification and present a report of a study of the initiation of detoxification in 100 patients from a Bronx drug abuse program. In addition, psychotherapeutic methods that can be applied to detoxifying patients are discussed.

The book begins with a historical review of one of the main controversies in narcotic addiction treatment, whether detoxification of well-rehabilitated, methadone-maintained patients is a possible and realistic goal. The authors believe that under certain circumstances and in certain patients it is. Actually, few of the subjects studied were able to detoxify, although they had stated willingness to attempt it. Success depended on the patient's physiological state, his psychological readiness, his family, and his environment.

More specifically, the most important factors for successful detoxification were found to be: 1) a therapeutic milieu provided either by environmental change and/or drug program or community, 2) selected treatment with attention to diet and other health related education, 3) psychotherapeutic intervention, and 4) long-term treatment in group, family, or individual therapy.

269.   Larkin, E. J. **The Treatment of Alcoholism: Theory, Practice, and Evaluation.** 2nd ed. Toronto: Addiction Research Foundation, 1976. 101p. bibliog. index. $2.95pa. ISBN 0-88868-001-5.

A revision of an earlier work published in 1974, this book describes current issues and problems relating to the treatment of alcoholism. It is intended for clinical students, practitioners, and program directors.

Chapter 1, on causes and curses of alcoholism, discusses several theories about causes of the condition and provides an overview of the subject. Chapter 2 discusses the disease concept of alcoholism, a concept that provides a basis for many treatment approaches. Difficulties encountered in the concept and the programs based on it are pointed out. Chapter 3 presents the results that may be encountered in current treatment programs. Chapter 4 is a review of the literature relating to the problem of patients dropping out of outpatient treatment programs. Chapter 5 discusses behavior-modification techniques, particularly the possibility of teaching patients to drink in a socially acceptable manner. Although this approach is contrary to prevailing beliefs and practices, the possibility that it may develop into a useful treatment modality for some patients is considered. Chapter 6 describes three evaluation procedures designed originally for public health, government, and industry. In addition, a computerized evaluation system for outpatient treatment facilities is illustrated.

A useful and extensive bibliography is appended.

270.   Lipp, Martin R. **Respectful Treatment: The Human Side of Medical Care.** New York: Harper and Row, 1977. 232p. bibliog. index. $11.50pa. LC 77-21496. ISBN 0-06-141550-2.

This book is not about drug abuse per se, but it includes material on some important aspects of the drug problem. The intent of the author, who is a psychiatrist, is to offer factual information that will help physicians in practice deal with the suffering, hopeless, or disfigured patient as a human being. The author says that most of the problems he discusses are not soluble in the sense that most would prefer. Many are the product of our social and health care systems themselves. He focuses on matters such as patients who refuse care, those with chronic pain, and those in confused mental states due to age, alcoholism, or drugs.

In a chapter of special interest called "Pain and Addiction," suggestions are given on how to deal with a patient who is "addicted" to a life of pain and pain medication. A section of the chapter treats the problems of treating narcotic addicts who become hospitalized for various medical reasons, such as hepatitis, diabetes, or bacterial infections. Maintenance and withdrawal are discussed, and barbiturate addiction is given attention.

271.   Lowinson, Joyce H., and John Langrod. **Drug Detoxification: A Comprehensive Examination**. Oceanside, NY: Dabor Science Publications, 1977. 289p. bibliog. $15.00. LC 77-25246. ISBN 0-89561-049-3.

The 27 essays in this collection were written from 1967 to 1977. Most report on the authors' original research or their own clinical experiences. One, however, which concerns detoxification from methadone, is largely a literature review. Lowenstein and Langrod are members of the staff of the Bronx Psychiatric Center, Albert Einstein College of Medicine.

The material is presented under the following headings: 1) Drug abuse: some aspects of the problem, 2) Treatment approaches and problems, 3) Some characteristics of methadone maintenance, and 4) Special treatment populations.

Some of the topics covered include: the history of methadone maintenance, comparison with narcotic maintenance in other countries, changing patterns of street methadone use, the therapeutic community as adjunct to methadone maintenance, the role of religion in the treatment of opiate addiction, legal services and the addict, the resistance to the opening of drug treatment centers, and government policies and supportive services in drug abuse treatment.

The authors also offer insights into the treatment and responses of special types of patients such as the juvenile, pregnant woman, Hispanic addicts, and probationers.

272.   Marlatt, G. Alan, and Peter E. Nathan, eds. **Behavioral Approaches to Alcoholism**. New Brunswick, NJ: Rutgers Center of Alcohol Studies, 1978. 222p. bibliog. index. (NIAAA-RUCAS Alcoholism Treatment Series, No. 2.) $6.00pa. LC 77-620035. ISBN 0-911290-48-6.

This volume is part of a series jointly sponsored by the National Institute on Alcohol Abuse and Alcoholism, and the Rutgers University Center of Alcohol Studies. The aim of the series is to make available to those who treat alcoholism the best current knowledge on helping, treating, and rehabilitating alcoholics. The publication is based on presentations of a conference held in the summer of 1975 at the University of Washington entitled "Behavioral Approaches to Alcoholism and Drug Dependencies." An overview of the "state of the art" is presented.

The book is in three parts: 1) Behavioral theory, behavioral theories of alcoholism, and the scope of the problem, 2) Behavioral observation and assessment of drinking by alcoholics, and 3) Behavioral treatment of alcoholics.

The presentations make clear that advances have been made in extending knowledge of the behavioral aspects of social drinking and alcoholism, and it is likely that research on the subject will continue at a rapid rate.

273.   Newman, Robert G., in collaboration with Margot S. Cates. **Methadone Treatment in Narcotic Addiction: Program Management, Findings, and Prospects for the Future**. New York: Academic Press, 1977. 285p. bibliog. index. $19.50. LC 77-74059. ISBN 0-12-517050-5.

This book presents the history, policies, procedures, and experiences of two large addiction treatment programs, the Methadone Maintenance Treatment Program and the Ambulatory Detoxification Program of the New York City Department of Health. The author directed these efforts from their inception in 1970 until 1975. Considerable attention is given to the social, political, and therapeutic controversies that have traditionally divided the general public and professionals in the treatment field.

The book is in two parts. The first presents a rationale for maintenance and detoxification treatment. Following is a discussion of policy issues that are of concern to a wide group—workers in the field, physicians, sociologists, criminologists, political scientists, and possibly the general public. Ethical questions, particularly, such as forcing clients to accept treatment and confidentiality of records, are a concern of the author.

Part two presents and analyzes data from the two programs. The patients are described in terms of demographic, social, criminal, and drug abuse characteristics prior to enrollment. Their progress while in treatment and following discharge is analyzed.

The author acknowledges that the high hopes for treatment success in the early 1970s were unrealistic from the outset. Conditions have worsened since early 1974, and the pendulum has swung from treatment emphasis to law-enforcement emphasis. Newman hopes his book will facilitate a reasonable debate by providing perspective and by bringing into focus fundamental, substantive questions.

274.   Orford, Jim, and Griffith Edwards. **Alcoholism: A Comparison of Treatment and Advice, with a Study of the Influence of Marriage**. New York: Oxford University Press, 1977. 175p. bibliog. index. (Maudsley Monographs: 26.) LC 77-30166. ISBN 0-19-712148-9.

This book reports in detail a study of two groups of outpatient alcoholics. The first chapter describes alcoholism programs within the British National Health Service. Chapter 2 discusses current knowledge about alcoholism and marriage. Chapter 3 describes the project, which involved 100 marriages in which the husbands were alcoholics. The alcoholics were divided into two groups. One received a single counseling session only, and the other had several months of treatment. Chapter 4 presents the results of the study. Among other results, it was found that one year later there were no significant differences in outcomes between the two groups. Chapter 5 provides information about patterns of marriage that were related to the prognosis. The remaining chapters supply further details about the subjects and their marriages.

In general, the study shows that, although there was some improvement among the drinkers, alcoholism remains a chronic relapsing disease, relapse being the rule rather than the exception.

The last chapter discusses implications for treatment and further research. It is not suggested that all patients can benefit as much from on counseling visit as from an intensive treatment program. Possibly the patients who had only one clinic visit benefited to the point of needing no more in some instances.

The book makes a contribution in a previously unexplored area.

275.   Otto, Shirley, and Jim Orford. **Not Quite Like Home: Small Hostels for Alcoholism and Others**. New York: Wiley, 1978. 218p. illus. bibliog. index. $19.50. LC 77-12664. ISBN 0-471-99589-4.

The first part of this work is a review of the literature on hostels and halfway houses designed to treat people with such problems as alcoholism and drug addiction. In addition, twelve London hostels were surveyed.

The second part deals with the research the authors performed, which was a social and psychological analysis of two hostels set up in the mid-1960s in South London for the care of alcoholic men. The difficulties of such institutions are described along with such matters as their aims, management, and governance. The factors affecting the morale of the residents and the staff and their evaluation of each other is emphasized.

The book is important because it represents an attempt to define some of the factors that can make or break a hostel. Sociologists and psychologists particularly will be interested in the book.

276.   **Psychotherapy and Drug Addiction, I: Diagnosis and Treatment.** Papers by Charles P. Cohen, S. Robinson, Reginald G. Smart, et al. New York: MSS Information Corporation, 1974. 265p. illus. bibliog. index. $17.00. LC 11097. ISBN 0-8422-7143-0.

The articles in this collection, all of which were published previously in various journals, deal with the diagnosis and treatment of drug addiction, which includes studies on the personality of drug abusers, their motivations, and psychopathology. Also included are theoretical discussions on the psychotherapy of narcotic addiction, and comparisons of treatment for addicts and alcoholics. New techniques in treatment are discussed, including the use of videotape and recording equipment. In addition, treatment for those who have used hallucinatory drugs is included.

The work is in three sections: 1) Personality patterns of addicts, 2) Treatment of narcotic addiction, and 3) Research.

A companion volume is reviewed below.

277.   **Psychotherapy and Drug Addiction, II: Community and Institutional Care.** Papers by Irving Silverman, Robert S. Garber, Mitchell S. Rosenthal, et al. New York: MSS Information Corporation, 1974. 185p. bibliog. index. $17.00. LC 73-11097. ISBN 0-8422-7144-9.

This volume, a companion to the title reviewed above, deals with the recent use of therapeutic communities for the treatment of drug addicts. A number of such communities are discussed. In addition, the success of intensive, short term treatment in out-patient centers is assessed, as are other kinds of programs.

The titles of the articles, which have previously been published in various journals, are as follows: 1) Reaching for accountability in community practice, 2) The need for therapeutic and administrative partnerships, 3) Phoenix Houses: therapeutic communities for drug addicts, 4) Synanon: A therapeutic life style, 5) The Laguna Beach experiment as a community approach to family counselling for drug abuse problems in youth, 6) Drug addicts in a therapeutic community: outline on the California Rehabilitation Center Program, Corona, 7) A community-centered program for heroin addicts, 8) Civil commitment for addicts: the California program, 9) A hospital program for young adults, 10) Three-day hospitalization: a model for intensive intervention, 11) Plan for a drug-dependence service for New South Wales, background and management of the problem, 12) Heroin addiction: a comparison of two inpatient treatment methods, 13) An adolescent inpatient program: guidelines and ethics, 14) Predicting attrition during the outpatient detoxification of narcotic addicts, 15) Standard operating procedures and institutionalization on the psychiatric unit, and 16) Emergency psychiatric treatment during a mass rally: the march on Washington.

278.   Schecter, Arnold, ed. **Rehabilitation Aspects of Drug Dependence.** S. Joseph Mulé, editor-in-chief. Cleveland, OH: CRC Press, Inc., 1977. 181p. bibliog. index. $48.95. LC 77-12738. ISBN 0-8493-5108-1.

Along with its companion volume *Treatment Aspects of Drug Dependence* (*see* below), this book explores various approaches that have been used in rehabilitation of and therapy for drug abusers. This volume provides basic material and a theoretical base.

The following chapters, by noted experts, are presented: 1) Introductory thoughts regarding treatment and rehabilitation, 2) Historical evolution of the current drug treatment perspective, 3) Factors in the etiology of drug use and drug dependence, 4) Drug dependence: broad perspectives and international approaches, 5) The evolution of the federal drug policy: one perspective, 6) State and local relationships: the role of the single state agency for drug abuse, 7) The role of the city in responding to the problems of drug abuse, 8) The (negligible) role of the private physician, 9) Evaluation of treatment programs, and 10) The addict life cycle and problems in treatment evaluation.

In Chapter 8, author Rufus King, who is an attorney and legal scholar, is very critical of the way drug abuse treatment and rehabilitation is handled. His view is that physicians in the private sector have contributed little because they have been bullied and intimidated by the law enforcement bureaucracy. Chapter 9 emphasizes methadone maintenance, and the author, Frances R. Gearing, expresses the view that the mass media have emphasized negative features of the modality to the extent that addicts are deprived of needed treatment. Chapter 10, by I. F. Lukoff and P. H. Kleinman, presents criticisms of Gearing's work by pointing out that her studies were limited to older, better-educated patients and that their improvement may have been a natural "maturing out" process.

279.   Schecter, Arnold, ed. **Treatment Aspects of Drug Dependence.** S. Joseph Mulé, editor-in-chief. West Palm Beach, FL: CRC Press, Inc., 1978. 249p. illus. bibliog. index. (CRC Drug Dependence Series.) $59.95. LC 77-12402. ISBN 0-8493-5476-5.

This is a companion volume to *Rehabilitation Aspects of Drug Dependence* (*see* review above). The two volumes together cover legal, regulatory, and political aspects of the problem, the history and sociology of the field, clinical evaluation research methodology and findings, and perspectives by individuals from a number of disciplines. The contributors, experts in their fields, have provided material of value to physicians, psychologists, social workers, nurses, counselors, attorneys, and program administrators. This volume is confined mostly to treatment; the other volume contains mainly theoretical and basic material.

The following are the chapter headings: 1) The use of methadone in narcotic dependency, 2) LAAM, 3) Detoxification, 4) Chemotherapy: cyclazocine, 5) Naltrexone, 6) Oxilorphan, 7) Possible use of endorphins in the treatment of opiate addiction, 8) The therapeutic community: a treatment approach for drug abusers, 9) Adolescent drug abuse, 10) Psychiatric approaches to drug dependence, 11) Barbiturates and other sedative-hypnotics, 12) CNS stimulants, 13) Psychedelics, 14) Marijuana: a critical review of sociological, medical, and psychiatric questions, 15) Solvent abuse and its treatment, 16) Innovative methods of treatment in drug abuse, 17) Epidemiology and medical consequences of alcoholism, 18) Treatment of alcohol abuse: psychotherapies and sociotherapies, and 19) Treatment—past and future.

The last chapter points out that there is currently antipathy between proponents of methadone maintenance and those of therapeutic communities. It then discusses chronologically all treatment modalities that have been tried in the past. At the turn of the century it was believed that heroin could be used to treat morphine addiction. This failed. Other modalities used have been: the Town-Lambert treatment (a failure); U.S. Public Health Service Hospitals (failures); drug-free therapeutic communities of the 1960s (addiction was curable as long as the addict did not leave the community); methadone maintenance (the addict must stay on methadone); narcotic antagonists (some success, but have not lived up to early promise); and the multi-modality approach (still under study). There are a few experimental approaches on the horizon, but nothing really new, just refinements of old techniques. There is a movement toward more psychiatric input in therapeutic communities. The recent discovery of narcotic receptor sites and the endogenous opiate-like substances may give rise to new advances. Finally, the chapter author points out that treatment of narcotic addiction is in about the same state currently as treatment of other diseases that are treated by psychiatry, and successes may run parallel.

280.   Sells, Saul B., and D. Dwayne Simpson, eds. **The Effectiveness of Drug Abuse Treatment.** Vol. III, *Further Studies of Drug Users, Treatment Typologies, and Assessment of Outcomes During Treatment in the DARP.* Vol. IV, *Evaluation of Treatment Outcomes for 1971-1972 DARP Admission Cohort.* Vol. V, *Evaluation of Treatment Outcomes for 1972-1973 DARP Admission Cohort.* Cambridge, MA: Ballinger Publishing Co., 1974-1976. 3v. bibliog. index. $25.00 each. LC 74-1069. ISBN 0-88410-037-5 (v. 3); 0-88410-038-3 (v. 4); 0-88410-039-1 (v. 5).

These three volumes continue those reviewed earlier (*see* Andrews: *Bibliography of Drug Abuse*, 1977, entry 294). The Drug Abuse Reporting Program (DARP) is a patient reporting system whose data collection includes nearly 44,000 admissions to 52 treatment agencies during a four-year period. Volume III of the series of volumes describes the concept and design of the program and the data system and presents some original studies on outcome measurements and classification of the patients and the treatments. Volumes IV and V present evaluations of the treatment outcomes for the years indicated.

These books are said to be a major contribution to the assessment of social and mental health services, and the work will likely serve as a model for continuing efforts of this kind.

281.   Shaw, Stan, Alan Cartwright, Terry Spratley, and Judith Harwin. **Responding to Drinking Problems.** Baltimore, MD: University Park Press, 1978. 269p. bibliog. index. $24.50. LC 78-2422. ISBN 0-8391-1271-8.

Two medical sociologists, a psychiatrist, and a social worker report on research conducted by Maudsley Hospital in London between 1973 and 1977. The Maudsley Alcohol Pilot Project studied the responses of physicians, social workers, community agencies, and other personnel to individuals with drinking problems. Also studied were the attitudes of the problem drinkers toward those to whom they turned for help. Attention is given to how these responses can be improved.

The six parts of the book include some general sections also. Titles are: 1) Alcohol—its uses and abuses, 2) The nature of drinking problems, 3) The existing response, 4) Theories about improving the response, 5) Experiments in improving the response, and 6) Community response.

The work is intended for physicians, psychiatrists, psychologists, nurses, therapists, counselors, sociologists, social workers, probation officers, and all others who are involved with problems of alcohol.

282.   Sobell, Mark B., and Linda C. Sobell. **Behavioral Treatment of Alcohol Problems: Individualized Therapy and Controlled Drinking.** New York: Plenum Press, 1978. 225p. illus. bibliog. index. $16.95. LC 77-12381. ISBN 0-306-31057-0.

This book summarizes the research conducted by the authors over the eight years before the book was written. The reader is given a perspective on traditional concepts in the alcohol field and is then told why they are being challenged. The authors trace the development of their own clinical research which involved the study of "Individualized Behavior Therapy (IBT)" for alcoholics. The book is intended for those interested in behavior therapy and those interested in the treatment and treatment outcome evaluation of alcohol problems.

The following are the chapter titles: 1) The nature of alcohol problems, 2) Alternatives to abstinence: a departure from tradition, 3) The functional analysis of drinking behavior, 4) The early Patton studies: an empirical foundation, 5) Individualized behavior therapy (IBT): a broad-spectrum behavioral approach, 6) IBT: emergence of new treatment evaluation measures and procedures, 7) IBT: results, 8) IBT: interpretation of results, 9) IBT in retrospect, and 10) IBT in private practice and outpatient programs.

It is of note that the authors contradict the view that "once an alcoholic, always an alcoholic" and believe for some it is possible to engage in nonproblem drinking. It is concluded that there are a variety of potentially effective treatment strategies that can be used to treat alcoholism, but a case analysis must be made to suggest which strategy is best for a given client.

283.   U.S. Bureau of Narcotics and Dangerous Drugs. **Proceedings of the Alternatives to Drug Abuse Conference.** Santa Barbara, California, May 16-18, 1972. Prepared by the National Council on Crime and Delinquency Research Center. Washington: Bureau of Narcotics and Dangerous Drugs, 1972. 2v.

These two volumes contain the full proceedings of the conference and a 61 page summary. The purpose of the conference was to gather together people from the criminal justice system, the educational system, and community-based drug programs to discuss ways of preventing drug abuse using the "alternatives" strategy. Working programs are described, specific alternatives identified, and ways of initiating action suggested.

284.   U.S. Bureau of Narcotics and Dangerous Drugs. Office of Scientific Support, Drug Control Division. **Alternative Approaches to Opiate Addiction Control: Costs, Benefits and Potential.** By William H. McGlothlin, Victor C. Tabbush, Carl D. Chambers, and Kay Jamison. Washington: GPO, 1972. 1v. (various paging). bibliog. (SCID-TR-7).

This report is the second of a three-part series, preceded by a similar study of marijuana and one following on amphetamines, barbiturates, and hallucinogens.

The paper estimates the costs, benefits, and potential of various approaches to narcotics addiction control. For each of several approaches, the authors estimate the maximum number of addicts that may be treated, the cost of the treatment, and the social benefits derived. The control approaches examined are: 1) methadone maintenance—strict control, 2) methadone maintenance—dispensing only, 3) heroin maintenance, 4) therapeutic community, 5) detoxification, 6) civil commitment, and 7) combined civil commitment and other modalities. It appears that the combined civil commitment and other modalities has the most potential. A summary table is included showing the advantages and disadvantages of the seven treatment approaches. In addition, there are two substantial appendices as follows: 1) A model for estimating the social costs of narcotic addiction, and 2) Psychological and sociological perspectives on narcotics addiction.

285.   U.S. National Clearinghouse for Drug Abuse Information. **Child Care Provisions in Drug Abuse Treatment Programs.** Washington: GPO, 1979. 39p. bibliog.

[DHEW Publication No. (ADM) 79-830; National Institute on Drug Abuse. Report Series. Series 43, No. 1.]

This report is an initial effort to describe the range of child care services available for drug dependent parents and to identify such provisions in specific drug abuse treatment programs. The need for such services is discussed, then 21 selected programs are listed and described from the following states: California, Connecticut, Illinois, Louisiana, Minnesota, New Jersey, New York, Pennsylvania, and Texas. An attempt is made to show how it is possible with limited budgets and staff, to meet the need for child care services to addicted parents.

286.   U.S. National Clearinghouse for Drug Abuse Information. **Self-Sufficiency through Third Party Reimbursements: A Study of Six Drug Treatment Programs.** Washington: GPO, 1979. 28p. [DHEW Publication No. (ADM) 79-817; National Institute on Drug Abuse. Report Series. Series 41, No. 1.]

The study reported in this publication examined the experience and key characteristics of six drug abuse treatment programs that are largely self-sufficient. The hope is that the findings will assist others in the field so that stable funding for community drug abuse programs can be found. The "third parties" referred to are usually state and local governments and the clients themselves (instead of the federal government).

287.   U.S. National Institute on Alcohol Abuse and Alcoholism. **A Procedure for Estimating the Potential Clientele of Alcoholism Service Programs.** By Parker G. Marden. Washington: GPO, 1980. 21p. bibliog. [DHEW Publication No. (ADM) 80-908.]

A major problem in planning alcoholism treatment programs is determining how many persons are in need of the services in a given area. It is difficult to secure funding for programs when a valid estimate cannot be made.

This document discusses methods that have been used to calculate the figure, and then presents an improved procedure. A formula is developed considering such variables as age, sex, ethnicity, race, residence, and socioeconomic status.

288.   U.S. National Institute on Drug Abuse. **Alcohol and Illicit Drug Use: National Followup Study of Admissions to Drug Abuse Treatments in the DARP During 1969-1971.** Washington: GPO, 1977. 21p. bibliog. [DHEW Publication No. (ADM) 77-496; Services Research Report.] S/N 017-024-00606-8.

This document reports on a followup study of 1,409 persons interviewed 4-6 years after admission to drug treatment in the Drug Abuse Reporting Program (DARP). The study focused on variations in alcohol consumption associated with drug use and treatment status for clients after they left DARP.

Findings include the following: 1) a small segment of the sample group occasionally substituted between alcohol and opioid drugs; 2) persons who returned to drug treatment after DARP generally used less alcohol than persons who did not; and 3) the use of alcohol tended to accompany the use of non-opioid drugs (particularly marijuana), but not opioid drugs.

289.   U.S. National Institute on Drug Abuse. **Alternative Pursuits for America's 3rd Century: A Resource Book on New Perceptions, Processes, and Programs, With Implications for the Prevention of Drug Abuse.** Edited by Louisa Messolonghites. Washington: GPO, 1974. 233p. bibliog. [DHEW Publication No. (HSM) 73-9158.] $2.60pa. S/N 1724-00333.

This book deals with the concept of alternatives as a road to prevention and early intervention where drug abuse is concerned rather than as a treatment or rehabilitation technique. The view taken is that drug abuse represents an effort to achieve aspirations and fill experiential voids not being met for young people in society. The enhancement of opportunities and the kinds of experiences through which one can grow can be a major effort in drug abuse prevention.

The publication contains selections from the current literature on drug prevention that support the validity of the alternatives approach. It places emphasis on strategies that represent emerging options, such as new trends, institutions, processes, values, lifestyles, attitudes, points of view, and pursuits and programs for the future.

The selections are grouped under the following headings: 1) The case for alternatives, 2) Positive alternatives: perspectives and directions, 3) Building alternatives: tactics, tools, techniques and experiences, and 4) Alternative programs in action. Section 5 is a resource directory with bibliographic notes.

The selections are varied in subject matter, touching on a wide range of activities and viewpoints.

290.   U.S. National Institute on Drug Abuse. **Behavioral Analysis and Treatment of Substance Abuse.** Edited by Norman A. Krasnegor. Washington: GPO, 1979. 256p. bibliog. [DHEW Publication No. (ADM) 79-839; NIDA Research Monograph 25.] LC 79-600111. S/N 017-024-00939-3.

This monograph is a product of the National Institute on Drug Abuse's recognition of the importance of the substance abuse concept, a belief that behavioral patterns involved in any kind of substance abuse, whether it be a hard drug or just tobacco use or overeating, are basically related. A variety of views on methods of behavioral treatment and the analysis of the addictive behaviors are presented, all of which provide a foundation for improved theory and treatment strategies. In addition, recent research findings and investigations underway are discussed. Future needs in the area of research are mentioned.

The publication is in four parts: 1) Drugs, 2) Cigarette smoking, 3) Ethanol, and 4) Obesity. There are several papers in each part, most of them written by psychologists.

291.   U.S. National Institute on Drug Abuse. **Clinical Record System for Drug Abuse Treatment Programs.** Washington: GPO, 1978. 164p. [DHEW Publication No. (ADM) 78-689; Treatment Program Monograph Series, No. 5.] $4.75pa. S/N 017-024-00732-3.

It is important that a good client record system is maintained in drug abuse treatment programs because they are valuable treatment tools and a repository of program management information.

This publication describes the uses of good client recordkeeping systems, provides a core set of record forms, gives instructions for field personnel in establishing and maintaining a record system, and shows the application of such systems to various functions of program management.

292.   U.S. National Institute on Drug Abuse. **Conducting Followup Research on Drug Treatment Programs.** Edited by Lloyd D. Johnston, David N. Nurco, and Lee N. Robins. Washington: GPO, 1977. 191p. bibliog. [DHEW Publication No. (ADM) 77-487; Treatment Program Monograph Series, No. 2.] S/N 017-024-00631-9.

The eleven chapters in this work were written by research scientists. The book is intended for individuals who may want to initiate a follow-up study on clients who have been in drug abuse treatment programs (presumably directors of such programs) and for individuals who may carry out the research. Complex theories and controversial techniques have been presented in distilled form for use by local program staff members.

Following are the chapter titles: 1) Introduction to the use of follow-up studies, 2) Planning a follow-up study, 3) Selecting a study design, 4) Measurement content, 5) Ethical considerations, 6) Locating respondents, 7) Interviewing respondents, 8) Institutional sources of data, 9) Data preparation and descriptive analysis, 10) The examination of relationships, and 11) Reporting and utilizing the results of a follow-up study. In addition, much practical material has been appended, for instance, interview items, a sample letter of introduction for interviewers, and probing techniques for interviewers.

Follow-up studies are of great value as it is important to know what happens to clients when they leave treatment programs. Funding agencies in particular want to see improvement as a result of treatment.

293.   U.S. National Institute on Drug Abuse. **Cost Accountability in Drug Abuse Prevention.** By Robert L. Retka. Washington: GPO, 1977. 9p. bibliog. [DHEW Publication No. (ADM) 77-444; NIDA Technical Paper.] $0.90pa. S/N 017-024-00599-1.

This study examines whether cost effectiveness in primary drug abuse prevention is possible, given assumptions about the cost of programs, the groups to which they are directed, and the level of benefits that can be expected if they do prevent drug abuse.

The results of the study are somewhat inconclusive. A need is expressed for further research and follow-up studies. It is felt that long-range cost effectiveness in drug abuse prevention programs is achievable. However, cost-accountability is not the only factor to be considered in assessing the worth of such programs.

294.   U.S. National Institute on Drug Abuse. **Drug Treatment Histories for a Sample of Drug Users in DARP.** Washington: GPO, 1978. 42p. bibliog. [DHEW Publication No. (ADM) 78-634; Services Research Report.]

Before the effectiveness of treatment programs for drug abusers can be evaluated, it is necessary to have available the patient's total treatment history. The primary objective of the study reported in this publication was to assess the degree of relationship 1) between some attributes of PreDARP and DARP (*Drug Abuse Reporting Program* of the National Institute on Drug Abuse), 2) between some attributes of DARP and PostDARP treatment, and 3) between some attributes of both Pre- and PostDARP treatments and demographic characteristics.

A major conclusion reached was that the evaluation of a treatment program in terms of patient outcomes is inappropriate without accounting for its relationship to other treatment experiences. No single set of treatment predictors, i.e., either PreDARP, DARP, or PostDARP, accounted for large differences in outcome indices.

295.   U.S. National Institute on Drug Abuse. **Drug Treatment in New York City and Washington, D.C.: Followup Studies.** Washington: GPO, 1977. 77p. [DHEW Publication No. (ADM) 77-506; Services Research Monograph Series.] S/N 017-024-00638-6.

This monograph reports on the findings of two studies conducted in 1974-1975 that attempted to follow up clients discharged from New York City and Washington, D.C. multimodality drug abuse treatment programs. The report was prepared to increase an awareness of what rehabilitation efforts can accomplish and to add to the continuing process of treatment and evaluation techniques.

Results showed a decrease in drug use for reasons not entirely clear. It is possible that the community changed, or that changes in availability, purity, and price of illicit drugs may have been a factor. There was little difference between treatment and comparison groups, and demographic and background factors failed to explain success or lack thereof in treatment.

296. U.S. National Institute on Drug Abuse. **Evaluation of Drug Abuse Treatments, Based on First Year Followup.** National Followup Study of Admissions to Drug Abuse Treatment in the DARP during 1969-1972. Washington: GPO, 1978. 108p. bibliog. [DHEW Publication No. (ADM) 78-701; Services Research Monograph Series.] S/N 017-024-00741-2.

This study is based on statistics on over 2,000 males who were in DARP (Drug Abuse Reporting Program, supported by the National Institute on Drug Abuse) treatment agencies, and interviewed during 1975-1976. The treatments included methadone maintenance, detoxification programs, therapeutic communities, and drug free treatment. In addition, there was a comparison group considered who were admitted but who never returned to receive any treatment. The purpose of the study was: 1) to examine changes on specific criterion measures from before DARP treatment to the first year after; 2) to compare DARP treatment group on outcome measures in the first year post DARP; and 3) to evaluate the contributions of client and treatment characteristics to first year post DARP outcomes and to identify those that account for significant proportions of variance in the past DARP outcomes.

The implications of the findings are that the most favorable post DARP outcomes are associated with methadone maintenance, therapeutic communities, and drug free treatment. No significant improvements were found for those in detoxification programs and for those who had no treatment.

297. U.S. National Institute on Drug Abuse. **An Evaluation of the California Civil Addict Program.** By William H. McGlothlin, M. Douglas Anglin, and Bruce D. Wilson. Washington: GPO, 1977. 102p. bibliog. [DHEW Publication No. (ADM) 78-558; Services Research Monograph Series.] S/N 017-024-00691-2.

This publication is a report on a study which evaluated the California Civil Addict Program. A major aspect of the study involved follow-up interviews with 756 males who were admitted to the program in 1962-1963, 1964, and 1970. A comparison was made between the 1964 sample, which made up a treatment group, and a 1962-1963 sample of admissions discharged by writ. Another comparison was made between 1964 and 1970 admissions during periods of strict and more lenient control policies.

Among other findings, it was shown that the treatment program significantly reduced daily narcotic use and associated behavior among the 1964 sample during the commitment program. There was slight indication of lasting benefits subsequent to discharge. Drug dealing, criminal activity, and illicit income are closely coupled with frequency of narcotic use; employment shows an inverse relationship. Frequency of narcotic use and alcohol abuse are also inversely related. Property crimes produce about 50% of the addicts' income during periods of daily use. The data does not permit a clear evaluation of the more lenient control policies.

298. U.S. National Institute on Drug Abuse. **An Investigation of Selected Rural Drug Abuse Programs.** Washington: GPO, 1977. 20p. [DHEW Publication No. (ADM)

78-451; formerly 77-451; Services Research Report.] S/N 017-024-00586-4.

A report on two studies exploring drug abuse treatment issues as they affect the rural population of eight states, this publication is intended to shed light on the needs and concerns peculiar to treatment services in rural communities. The first study surveys the characteristics of rural as compared to urban drug abuse clients and the implications of those characteristics for treatment delivery. The second study explores treatment staffs' concerns about the delivery of services in rural settings.

Some of the findings are as follows: the rural drug abuser is younger than his or her urban counterpart; there is a relatively low volume of clients in certain areas; rural users do not use drugs as regularly as urban users but use more substances; and rural users make more use of mental health services. The foregoing suggest that adjustments in treatment regimen content may be in order; intervention with clients' families may be more important; and community education may be appropriate.

299.   U.S. National Institute on Drug Abuse. **The Learning Laboratory: The Door—A Center of Alternatives.** Washington: GPO, 1980. 49p. illus. bibliog. [DHHS Publication No. (ADM) 80-928; NIDA Services Research Monograph Series.]

Youths who drop out of high school, and who often are drug users, tend to be alienated from school, family, and peers, and usually lack self-esteem and self-confidence. Drugs are often used as a buffer against the stresses and strains rather than learning to cope realistically.

This report presents the findings and recommendations of the Learning Laboratory project, a study of an alternative education model designed to treat drug-abusing adolescents. The project was operated by The Door, a multiservice center for youths in New York City. The following are the section headings: 1) Background, 2) The program, 3) Curriculum, 4) Evaluation methodology, 5) Client characteristics, 6) Evaluation of progress, 7) Predictors of success, 8) Need for supplementary services, and 9) Significance and recommendations.

Results showed that participants in the program improved in educational progress, drug use patterns, and purposeful activities, and the results contrasted favorably with other types of programmatic interventions. Follow-up studies indicated a continual pattern of financial hardship, and a need for vocational skills training and further education.

300.   U.S. National Institute on Drug Abuse. **Management Effectiveness Measures for NIDA Drug Abuse Treatment Programs.** Vol. I, *Cost Benefit Analysis.* By Brent L. Rufener, J. Valley Rachal, and Alvin M. Cruze. Washington: GPO, 1977. 56p. bibliog. [DHEW Publication No. (ADM) 77-423; NIDA Technical Paper.] $2.10pa. S/N 017-024-00577-1.

This report is a tool for the development of cost effectiveness and benefit ratio for drug abuse treatment modalities. Material is based on these modalities: outpatient drug free; outpatient detoxification, inpatient defoxification; methadone maintenance; and therapeutic community. Chapter titles are: 1) Introduction, 2) Principles of cost benefit analysis, 3) Cost effectiveness measure of drug abuse treatment programs, and 4) Cost benefit measure of drug abuse treatment programs. An appendix presents calculations.

A companion report is reviewed below.

301.   U.S. National Institute on Drug Abuse. **Management Effectiveness Measures for NIDA Drug Abuse Treatment Programs.** Vol. II, *Costs to Society of Drug Abuse.* By Brent L. Rufener, J. Valley Rachal, and Alvin M. Cruze. Washington: GPO, 1977. 84p. bibliog. [DHEW Publication No. (ADM) 77-424; NIDA Technical Paper.] $2.30pa. S/N 017-024-00578-9.

This report serves as a tool for estimating the costs of drug abuse to society. It provides an estimate of the total economic costs experienced by society in 1975 due to the drug abuse problem. Chapter titles are: 1) Introduction, 2) Explanation and estimates of the economic costs to society of drug abuse, and 3) Summary. There are two appendices: 1) Methods and sources used; and 2) Review of other methods used to estimate the economic costs to society of drug abuse.

In summary, total costs were estimated to be between $8.4 and $12.2 billion in 1975. Approximately 48% of these were due to direct costs or expenditures. In addition, the authors believe that in actuality the costs are probably underestimated because of intangible costs. They believe, however, that the data assembled and costs estimated can provide a useful basis for social policy.

302.   U.S. National Institute on Drug Abuse. **National Drug Abuse Treatment Utilization Survey (NDATUS); National Drug Abuse Treatment: Insights and Perspectives.** Washington: GPO, 1979. 24p. illus. [DHEW Publication No. 79-778.] S/N 017-024-00880-0.

NDATUS is a federally mandated system, conducted by the National Institute on Drug Abuse, that measures the scope and use of drug abuse treatment in the United States. Data are collected from all U.S. treatment units, federally funded or not, on all levels, federal, state, and local. It is presumed that this information, when correlated with other data, permits management and policy-level into treatment programs. This report presents a review of the national treatment network.

There are sections on the following topics: 1) Introduction, 2) Policy and management summary, 3) History of the National Drug Abuse Treatment Program— program strategy and structure, 4) Transfer of funds and technical assistance— authorities and responsibilities of participants, 5) Treatment services—typical clinical settings and programs, and 6) Policy and management insights.

The last section discusses seven selected insights: 1) Effectiveness of the basic management and program strategy, 2) Continuing role of federal funding, 3) Adequacy of program treatment capacity, 4) Efficiency of use in program resources, 5) Trends in service resources, 6) Range of drug abuse problems treated and depth of services provided, and 7) Integration of drug abuse programs into the health care system.

303.   U.S. National Institute on Drug Abuse. **The Therapeutic Community.** Proceedings of Therapeutic Communities of America Planning Conference, January 29-30, 1976. Compiled and edited by George De Leon and George M. Beschner. Washington: GPO, 1977. 115p. [DHEW Publication No. (ADM) 77-464; Services Research Report.]

This publication presents the proceedings of a conference cosponsored by the National Institute on Drug Abuse and the Therapeutic Communities of America organization. Six panels as follows explored topics germane to therapeutic communities: 1) The nature of the therapeutic community, 2) Research and evaluation of the therapeutic community, 3) Accreditation and licensing: status, overt and covert issues, 4) The therapeutic community in the spectrum: articulation within the system, 5) The therapeutic community in the spectrum: expansion and innovations, and 6) Internal issues and problems.

The participants believe in this type of treatment modality, that is, individual change through self-help, requiring a unique communal-living milieu. However, problems that are inherent in therapeutic communities are pointed out. Financing is often inadequate, and internal problems identified include: 1) Sexuality, 2) Minorities, 3) Management, 4) Women (they have special needs), 5) Staff burn-out, and 6) Alcohol abuse.

304.   U.S. National Institute on Drug Abuse. **Withdrawal from Methadone Maintenance: Rate of Withdrawal and Expectation.** Washington: GPO, 1977. 19p. bibliog. [DHEW Publication No. (ADM) 77-475; NIDA Services Research Report.] S/N 017-024-00600-9.

The ultimate aim of the methadone treatment program for heroin abuse is to get the patient from heroin to methadone to abstinence. The success of the methadone to abstinence concept depends in large part upon an effective protocol for withdrawal. The investigation reported in this monograph attempts to assess consequences upon the individual and the treatment process of differing rates of detoxification from methadone. Focus is placed on the psychological and physiological components of withdrawal.

Results of the study indicate that withdrawal from methadone maintenance should be carried out relatively slowly, with a dose decrement of approximately three percent per week, and that patient preparation for withdrawal is desirable.

305.   U.S. National Institute on Drug Abuse. Office of Program Development and Analysis. **Drug Abuse from the Family Perspective: Coping Is a Family Affair.** Edited by Barbara Gray Ellis. Washington: GPO, 1980. 140p. bibliog. [DHEW Publication No. (ADM) 80-910.] $4.00pa. S/N 017-024-00999-7.

This is a collection of commissioned papers on the connection between the family and drug abuse. It is evident from the messages conveyed in them that the family is a powerful force capable of dramatically influencing the behavior of its members. The following are the titles of the papers: 1) Some overlooked aspects of the family and drug abuse, 2) Incomplete mourning in the family trajectory: a circular journey to drug abuse, 3) Hispanic family factors and drug abuse, 4) Family therapy and the Chicano drug abuser, 5) Treating adolescent drug abuse as a symptom of dysfunction in the family, 6) Why family therapy for drug abuse: from the clinical perspective, 7) The strata beneath the presenting problem, 8) Family counseling for low-income drug abusers, 9) The family-drug abuse relationship, 10) An argument for family research, 11) Drug use and families—in the context of twentieth century science, and 12) Report of a workshop on reinforcing the family system as the major resource in the primary prevention of drug abuse.

306.   U.S. National Institute on Law Enforcement and Criminal Justice. **Drug Programs in Correctional Institutions.** By Roger Smith. Washington: GPO, 1977. 81p. bibliog. S/N 027-000-00501-2.

This "prescriptive package" is intended primarily for correctional administrators and those who set policy and direct drug treatment programs at all levels. In many correctional institutions more than half the inmates have drug problems, and the administrator has to deal with them.

The publication reviews several key areas in correctional drug treatment programming. The following are the chapter titles: 1) Drug abuse treatment and rehabilitation programs in corrections, 2) Establishing goals for institutional drug treatment programs, 3) The social environment of institutional drug programs, 4) Approaches to institutional drug treatment, 5) Screening and selection of drug program participants, 6) Staffing institutional programs, 7) Institutional relationships, 8) Making the transition to the community, 9) After care, 10) Evaluation of programs, and 11) Planning, coordination, and funding considerations. Appendix A contains Law Enforcement Assistance Administration guidelines, and Appendix B is a substantial list of recommended readings listed to correspond with the chapters.

The preface indicates that some reviewers of the manuscript felt that this publication was unduly pessimistic regarding the value of drug treatment efforts with offenders. However, the point is made that one must be realistic about drug treatment. Unrealistic goals for social programs have often been set and had to be abandoned altogether when they did not live up to high expectations. Drug dependence may not be overcome in a few months or even a few years.

307.   Valle, Stephen K. **Alcoholism Counseling: Issues for an Emerging Profession.** With a Foreword by Harold Hughes. Springfield, IL: Charles C. Thomas, 1979. 167p. bibliog. index. $13.75. LC 78-23726. ISBN 0-398-03877-5.

Alcoholism counseling as an emerging profession is reviewed in the work. The author's viewpoint is that alcoholism counselors are the key to successful treatment of those with alcohol abuse problems. He considers the occupation a profession.

The first part of the book focuses on the occupation as a profession and includes discussions of credentialing, requirements for the workers, a helping model, and consumerism in counseling. The last part of the book takes up issues for the practitioner, such as the occupational hazard of "burn-out," ethics and values in counseling, obstacles to effective counseling, supervision, confrontation, counseling the reluctant individual, and termination of counseling.

308.   Wilmarth, Stephen S., and Avram Goldstein. **Therapeutic Effectiveness of Methadone Maintenance Programs in the Management of Drug Dependence of Morphine Type in the USA.** Geneva: World Health Organization, 1974. 53p. bibliog. (WHO Offset Publication, No. 3.) S Fr 17.00. LC 74-192889. ISBN 92-4-170003-3.

The purpose of this report is to assess the value of methadone maintenance in the United States as a companion effort to similar assessments of opiate maintenance in the United Kingdom and Iran. The literature of the field was searched and reviewed.

It is difficult to arrive at useful objective data on this subject because of lack of cooperation of the addict population and distorted self-reporting. However, the authors of the report have chosen to compare three methadone maintenance programs in different areas of the United States: the East Coast, the Midwest, and the West Coast. The three programs are described and the outcomes analyzed. A considerable amount of data are presented in graphic and tabular form.

Results show that it is difficult to get patients withdrawn from methadone maintenance and to abstain from drug use in more than a fraction of those who try. Part of the problem may be with the technique of withdrawal used. Some patients do succeed, however, and remain abstinent. The authors feel that an ideal methadone program might have the goal of periodically encouraging patients who are ready to withdraw (those who have perhaps altered their lifestyles), with the realization that a great deal of recycling may occur.

309.   Wurmser, Leon. **The Hidden Dimension: Psychodynamics in Compulsive Drug Use.** New York: J. Aronson, 1978. 635p. illus. bibliog. index. $25.00. LC 77-2456. ISBN 0-87669-308-1.

The author of this work is a professor of psychiatry and Scientific Director of the University Hospital's drug abuse programs at the University of Maryland. His viewpoint is that in no case of severe drug use does one form of treatment suffice; many modalities may have to be employed. Family dynamics should be considered, for instance. Particularly, he feels that psychiatric treatment is necessary because of the severe inner problems underlying the compulsive use of drugs of abuse in order to prop up defective defenses in the individual. Wurmser points out that bureaucracies frequently impose a single modality orientation in treatment programs that is doomed to failure.

The book presents individual case studies, most of them studied by the author himself, which serve as illustrations for some of the book's major points. The author attempts when possible to put the patients' experiences in the context of literary and other classic tradition, as can be seen by the contents: 1) The problem—"Thou are not what thou seem'st," 2) "My Shadow Ran Fast," 3) Knowledge spurned and power abused, 4) "Sweetness and horror" or "Fleurs du mal," 5) The "sixth culture": "Paideia" and the "heart of darkness," 6) "New directions"—or: "The little truth is better than the big lie."

310.   Zimberg, Sheldon, John Wallace, and Sheila B. Blume, eds. **Practical Approaches to Alcoholism Psychotherapy.** New York: Plenum Press, 1978. 288p. bibliog. index. $20.00. LC 78-15811. ISBN 0-306-40086-3.

There is a feeling prevalent that nothing works where the treatment of alcoholism is concerned. The contributors to this volume, each with a good deal of experience in treatment services, believe that there is a knowledge of what works. They describe therapeutic techniques based on a psychosocial philosophy. The focus is on a range of psychotherapeutic approaches. Theoretical and practical guidelines are provided, mainly intended for practitioners and students in alcoholism psychotherapy. Sub-populations of alcoholics, including adolescents, women, the elderly, and the socioeconomically deprived are considered, which highlights the fact that alcoholism is a complex illness that manifests itself differently among various populations. Extensive use of alcoholism case studies is made.

The following are the chapter titles: 1) Principles of alcoholism psychotherapy, 2) Working with the preferred defense structure of the recovering alcoholic, 3) Critical issues in alcoholism therapy, 4) Psychiatric office treatment of alcoholism, 5) Group psychotherapy in the treatment of alcoholism, 6) Psychodrama and the treatment of alcoholism, 7) Behavioral-modification methods as adjuncts to psychotherapy, 8) Family therapy of alcoholism, 9) Treatment of the significant other, 10) The folk psychotherapy of Alcoholics Anonymous, 11) The psychotherapy of alcoholic women, 12) Treatment of socioeconomically deprived alcoholics, 13) Psychotherapy of adolescent alcohol abusers, 14) Psychosocial treatment of elderly alcoholics, and 15) Evaluation of patient progress.

8

SELF-HELP

Self-help books have become popular, attesting to the fact that individuals are attempting to deal with their dependency problems themselves. The books listed below primarily deal with alcohol abuse, but similar approaches can be used to deal with other dependencies. Books on breaking the smoking habit are included in Section 21.

Miller's book (entry 316) deals with control of several bad habits, notably drinking, smoking, and overeating. The books by McCabe (entry 315) and Seixas (entry 318) offer encouragement to those whose lives are affected by problem drinkers. Several works discuss Alcoholics Anonymous methods, still the most successful of self-help, non-institutional treatment modalities.

311.   **Living Sober.** New York: Alcoholics Anonymous World Services, Inc., 1975. 87p. ISBN 0-916856-04-6.
Written by Alcoholics Anonymous members, this excellent booklet offers tips and methods that have been found successful for living without drinking. For instance, new habits to take the place of the drinking habit are suggested. In addition, the material offered may help put the reader in the proper frame of mind for not drinking. Much good practical advice is given.

312.   Lord, Eileen, and Luther Lord. **How to Communicate in Sobriety.** Illustrated by Virginia Karney. Center City, MN: Hazelden, 1976. 113p. illus. $3.50pa. LC 78-53142. ISBN 0-89486-046-1.
The authors of this booklet take the view that alcoholic persons too often fail to take charge of their lives and become the strong, assertive persons they should be. The publication contains somewhat simple but basically sound directives on how one can communicate effectively without being either overly passive or overly hostile. Clever cartoon pictures illustrate the personality characteristics under discussion. The basic philosophy expressed is that of Alcoholics Anonymous.

313.   Marshall, John Armstrong. **Find Your Perfect High.** Glendale, CA: Happy Eye Enterprises and Fullmer Enterprises, Inc. (1460 Grandview, Glendale, CA 91201), 1978. 197p. $5.95pa. LC 78-112715. ISBN 0-933426-00-3.
This is a self-help book written primarily for the person who wants to change his or her drinking patterns, but also of value to parents preparing their children for society, those who need a better understanding of a partner's drinking habits, and therapists who are sharing new insights with patients.

The author, who is a TV actor and producer, begins by discussing what he calls "The Great American Drinking Standard." Nobody, he says, knows what it is, but everyone pretends he does. Everyone is encouraged to drink, and the idea is so prevalent that even a person who never has a drink has a label: nondrinker. Next, the author relates the story of his own problem drinking and how he came to the turning point in his life that changed his habits.

Marshall develops the theory that a person "drinks like he thinks;" for example, one tends to over-rely on the half of the brain that keeps him rational, logical, and controlled. For most individuals, drinking enables the shutting off or depressing of this side of the brain in order to become more fun-loving and creative, the latter being controlled by the other side of the brain. If one can learn to shift emphasis from one hemisphere of the brain to the other one can experience a natural high.

There is, incidentally, scientific evidence to indicate that Marshall is correct in his theory. Psychologists have found that the left hemisphere of the brain specializes in logical thinking, the right in creative thinking. There is also evidence that alcohol and various other drugs affect one side of the brain or the other.

The book includes a description of a program Marshall has developed to teach individuals to use both sides of the brain more effectively. The point is made that the tendency toward any kind of overindulgence can be handled this way. The book is well-written with a good deal of flair and is interesting. The arguments are persuasive and the author perceptive.

314.   Maultsby, Maxie C., Jr. **A Million Dollars for Your Hangover: The Illustrated Guide for the New Self-Help Alcoholic Treatment Method.** Illustrations by Hank Chapman. Lexington, KY: Rational Self-Help Books, 1978. 240p. illus. bibliog. index. $10.95. LC 78-27736. ISBN 0-932838-00-6.

The author of this book, who is a physician, acknowledges the debt he owes Dr. Albert Ellis, who formulated Rational Emotive Therapy. Dr. Maultsby developed his Rational Behavior Therapy and Rational Self-Counseling, which are described in this book, as an extension of Dr. Ellis' techniques. Dr. Maultsby feels there is a definite need for such self-help treatment methods because only a small percent of alcoholics make use of Alcoholics Anonymous or treatment by health professionals. A course of study that teaches Dr. Maultsby's method is given several times a year at the Training Center for Rational Behavior Therapy and Emotional Self-Help, University of Kentucky Medical College, Lexington, Kentucky.

The book is in three sections. The first describes the facts and insights needed for understanding alcoholism. The second gives step-by-step instructions for learning and teaching the new techniques, and section 3 describes the Intensive Self-Help Alcoholic Treatment Program for public schools. Good cartoons, typical case histories, and question and answer sections are made use of.

In conclusion, the book stresses the importance of the use of rational self-counseling in public school classrooms. Positive attitudinal changes can be produced in students, it is claimed. The method is particularly efficient and economical for moderately distressed adolescents.

315.   McCabe, Thomas R. **Victims No More.** Center City, MN: Hazelden, 1978. 103p. bibliog. $3.95pa. LC 77-94792. ISBN 0-89486-049-6.

This book was written for the unfortunate individuals whose lives are affected by the problem drinker, especially the spouse and children. The author, who is a well-known consultant for alcoholism programs, takes the view that all family members interact in the degenerative process of the alcoholic and become components in a "family system disease." Family members often unconsciously perpetuate the drinking. A technique known as "the rational-emotive" is outlined to assist in constructive change.

The following chapters are presented: 1) The family system, 2) How the family system reacts, 3) How the family system maintains the drinking, 4) How the family can stop the merry-go-round, 5) How the family can intervene, 6) The family system in treatment, and 7) The family system reorganizing.

The book ends on the following note: if the spouse does everything the book suggests and the alcoholic member still does not seek treatment, the spouse, like the alcoholic, must take responsibility for his or her own recovery and no longer be a victim, i.e., the marriage should end.

316.   Miller, Peter M. **Personal Habit Control.** New York: Simon and Schuster, 1978. 253p. $8.95. LC 78-10623. ISBN 0-671-24068-4.

The author, who is a clinical psychologist, expresses the view in this book that the only way to gain control over smoking, drinking, and overeating is through major modification in behavior patterns and life styles. Current research results suggest that this is true. Behavior modification involves a process of unlearning old habits and learning new ones. This self-help book teaches the author's techniques for what he calls Personal Habit Control.

The chapter titles are: 1) You and your bad habits, 2) Why you overindulge, 3) Your self-control strategy, 4) Breaking your bad habits, 5) Personal relaxation training, 6) You may be your own worst enemy, 7) Your consummatory style: controlling your eating, smoking, and drinking, 8) How to help your family and friends help you, 9) Getting started, and 10) *Permanent* personal habit control.

The techniques offered should help the individual gain power over his or her habits and life in general. Benefits are the ability to relax, control thoughts, and deal more effectively with other people, as well as the acquisition of better habits.

317.   Robinson, David. **Talking Out of Alcoholism: The Self-Help Process of Alcoholics Anonymous.** Baltimore, MD: University Park Press, 1979. 152p. bibliog. index. $14.50. LC 78-20506. ISBN 0-8391-1371-4.

This book is an attempt to integrate the literature, personal observations, and a limited survey of Alcoholics Anonymous members in order to describe the self-help process of A.A. It is to a considerable extent a recounting of the practices of A.A., its traditions, and the opinions of its members.

318.   Seixas, Judith S. **Living With a Parent Who Drinks Too Much.** New York: Greenwillow Books, 1979. 197p. $6.95. LC 78-11108. ISBN 0-688-80196-X.

Intended for the young reader (age 9-12), this work describes alcoholism, the behavior of alcoholics, and the family problems that result from alcohol abuse. Children are advised how they can deal with these problems, how they can cope with the unexpected behavior of the parent, and how they can take responsibility for their own lives. Actual practical instructions about what to do in a number of situations are provided.

Since the possibility of beatings or sexual abuse exists for the child of the alcoholic, advice is included on a course of action, such as telling the other parent, the police, or a school counselor.

The fact is stressed that some responsibilities thrust on the child are unfair, but they must be carried out. Seixas emphasizes that the child is not alone in having

a drinking parent. She says an estimated 20 million children in the United States
live with at least one parent who has a serious drinking problem.

Community agencies that can help are pointed out, such as Alateen. Finally,
Seixas discusses what may happen if the child decides to turn to alcohol. Research
has shown that such children have good chances of developing drinking problems
themselves, although the reasons are not clear.

319.   Silverstein, Lee M. **Consider the Alternative.** With Jon Brett and Linda
Roberts. Foreword by Sidney B. Simon. Minneapolis, MN: CompCare Publications,
1977. 139p. illus. bibliog. $5.50pa. LC 77-87739. ISBN 0-89638-004-1.

Written by a recovered alcoholic, this book is a personal testament that
can serve as a guide to self-help and a manual to help those who counsel alcoholics.
Methods are described that Silverstein himself has found successful in working with
others. He was himself initially helped by Alcoholics Anonymous, then found that
involvement with other individuals had therapeutic value. Involvement rather than
detachment is the tool he suggests.

Each chapter of the book ends with exercises and sayings to assist the
reader. The book has been favorably received by those who are involved with assisting alcoholics.

320.   U.S. National Institute on Alcohol Abuse and Alcoholism. **Facing Up To
Alcoholism.** Washington: GPO, 1978. 8p. illus. [DHEW Publication No. (ADM)
78-568.] $0.80pa. S/N 017-024-00751-0.

This is merely a small pamphlet, but it is attractive and well done. Written
for the person who suspects he or she is an alcoholic, the nature, symptoms, and
treatment of the condition are discussed in a matter-of-fact manner that should
help the individual face up to the problem.

321.   Willoughby, Alan. **The Alcohol Troubled Person: Known and Unknown.**
Chicago: Nelson-Hall, 1979. 235p. index. $12.95; $7.95pa. LC 79-1173. ISBN 0-
88229-426-1.

The author of this self-help book says it is intended to provide hope and
encouragement to alcohol-troubled persons, their families, and those who treat
them. He takes the optimistic view that there is a higher success rate in treating
alcoholics than is generally believed. The chronic losers are so highly visible that
everyone overlooks the winners.

The book emphasizes techniques for getting out of difficulties and for
identifying the alcohol problem before it escalates. Also emphasized is the value
of multiple treatment methods. Willoughby does not believe special funds spent
for alcohol programs help very much. Alcoholism treatment should be provided
along with other health care. Use of Alcoholics Anonymous is recommended.

Willoughby, who is a clinical psychologist, has written in a refreshing, candid
style with a good deal of humor interspersed. There are many apropos quotations
from other works. This one, at the beginning of a chapter, is a good example:

If you absolutely cannot refrain from drinking, start a saloon in your
own home. Be the only customer, and you will not have to buy a
license. Give your wife $18 to buy a gallon of whiskey. There are
128 snorts in a gallon. Buy all your drinks from your wife at a dollar
and in four days—when the gallon is gone—your wife will have $100
to put in the bank and $18 to buy another gallon. If you live 10

years and buy all your booze from your wife and then die with
snakes in your boots, she will have $108,774.34 on deposit—
enough to bury you respectably, bring up the children, buy a
house and lot, marry a decent man and forget she ever knew you.

9

EDUCATION AND ATTITUDES

Efforts to influence the attitudes of young people about the use of drugs and alcohol have had only limited success. The results of the oft-maligned "scare tactics" and the more moderate information campaigns have both been disappointing. They have not, however, been total failures.

Listed here are publications offered to assist teachers, counselors, and those who administer drug education programs. Several publications attempt to evaluate the success of programs. The federal government has taken the initiative in the production of materials to assist personnel involved with drug education, and a number are listed. Several works emphasize such matters as "clarification of values" and "responsible use" of drugs and alcohol.

322.   Canada. National Planning Committee on Training of the Federal/Provincial Working Group on Alcohol Problems. **Core Knowledge in the Drug Field: A Basic Manual for Trainees.** Edited by Lorne E. Phillips, G. Ross Ramsey, Leonard Blumenthal, and Patrick Cranshaw. Toronto: distr., Ontario Institute for Studies in Education, 1978. 12v. bibliog. $23.00 in Canada; elsewhere $29.00. ISBN 0662-10316-6 (v. 1).

The material in this set of booklets can be considered a program as well as a publication. There are twelve parts, each of which presents an overview of current information and research on a particular aspect of the drug field. The presentations are set up as a series of major discussion points. Each is prefaced by a learning objective, and there is a least one learning activity presented as an aid to the trainer in communicating the material. As a program the material represents the basic knowledge required of those who work in the alcohol and drug services.

The following are the titles of the booklets: 1) Historical aspects and current developments, 2) Overview of alcohol/drug programs in Canada, 3) Law and social policy, 4) Economics and social costs, 5) Prevention, 6) Some definitions and parameters of addictions, 7) Classification and symptomatology, 8) Etiology, 9) Guide to pharmacology, 10) Treatment, 11) Ethics and professional attitudes, and 12) Evaluation.

This material should be quite effective for its intended purpose. Some of it pertains only to Canada, but this should not be a great drawback for readers in the United States and other places.

323.   Engs, Ruth C. **Responsible Drug and Alcohol Use.** New York: Macmillan Publishing Co., 1979. 287p. illus. bibliog. index. LC 78-14557. ISBN 0-02-333760-5.

This publication begins with a values clarification exercise. Then depressants, stimulants, hallucinogens, over-the-counter products, and prescription drugs are discussed with a focus on responsible use. Appended are U.S. drug regulations.

324.   Florida. University. College of Education. Institute for Development of Human Resources. Florida Alcohol Education Project. **Alcohol Education: Research Report and Recommendations on Educational Policy for the State of Florida**. Gainesville, FL: The University, 1977. 316p. (looseleaf). bibliog.

This report was prepared as a step in the implementation of Florida's comprehensive Health Education Act of 1973. The Act requires every district school system to schedule health education as part of the curriculum in every elementary, junior, and senior high school. In addition, the Act places priority on inservice education for teachers.

The report describes the project, which had three main tasks: 1) to collect and review existing materials for alcohol education and to evaluate the materials, 2) to select the best of the alcohol curriculum materials and field test them in the schools, and 3) to analyze the field test data and make recommendations for state policy and guidelines on alcohol education based on the outcomes of the project.

The report summarizes the findings and recommendations; reviews literature on alcohol abuse; organizes and evaluates existing materials; describes the teacher orientation, research methodology, and instrumentation; presents results of the field tests; and makes recommendations on alcohol curricula.

A good deal of practical information and material can be found in the publication.

325.   Goodstadt, Michael, ed. **Research Methods and Programs of Drug Education**. Toronto: Alcoholism and Drug Addiction Research Foundation of Ontario, 1974. 101p. bibliog. index. (International Symposia on Alcohol and Drug Addiction.) $6.25pa. LC 74-84406. ISBN 0-88868-002-3.

When it became evident that the value of drug education was being questioned, this symposium was convened to examine the problem and move toward rectifying the situation. The nine papers in this publication were presented by a group of researchers who had a strong commitment to research and a systematic approach in answering questions regarding human behavior. Several major concerns are emphasized in the papers: 1) various "models" for drug education efforts, 2) motivation for drug use, 3) research evidence concerning the effectiveness of drug education programs, and 4) a more balanced perspective for drug education as it relates to general health education and within the context of human behavior and society at large.

326.   Goodstadt, Michael S., Margaret A. Sheppard, Kristina Kijewski, and Linda Chung. **The Status of Drug Education in Ontario: 1977**. Toronto: Addiction Research Foundation, 1978. 128p. bibliog. $4.95pa. ISBN 0-88868-031-7.

As part of a larger survey, this publication reports on the status of drug education in elementary and secondary schools in Ontario, Canada, in 1977. The prevalence and nature of drug education is assessed; students' evaluations of the drug education they received are reported; their preferences for alternative curriculum and formats stated; and the relationship between respondents' characteristics and their opinions studied. Results and recommendations are summarized. The survey questionnaire is reproduced in appendix A, appendix B is made up of 32 tables of data, and appendix C lists the geographic regions covered.

327.   Manning, William O., and Jean Vinton. **Harmfully Involved.** Center City, MN: Hazelden, 1978. 156p. $4.95. LC 78-60062. ISBN 0-89486-056-9.

Intended for school administrators, teachers, counselors, parents, and other adults concerned about drug abuse prevention and education, this book will assist in setting up a program. Practical and specific information on developing a system of identification and handling of drug problems among young people is included, and early signs of alcohol and drug involvement are pointed out.

A description of a successful drug abuse program adopted by a large suburban public high school is described. It can serve as a model for others, and it does not require highly trained specialists to initiate it.

328.   Miles, Samuel A., ed. **Learning About Alcohol: A Resource Book for Teachers.** Washington: American Association for Health, Physical Education, and Recreation, a National Affiliate of the National Education Association, 1974. 168p. bibliog. $2.95pa. LC 73-93351.

This resource book has been prepared for classroom teachers who need a single source of practical material to assist them in developing effective approaches to alcohol education. The approaches presented are those believed to lead to responsible behavior in relation to alcoholic beverages; the teacher may choose from among them.

The material has been divided into three sections as follows: 1) The realities about people and alcohol, 2) The schools and alcohol, and 3) Ranges of behavior involving alcohol. There are, in addition, three appendices: 1) Manufacture and uses of alcohol, 2) A brief history of health and alcohol education, and 3) Teaching media and sources.

Many aspects of the subject are touched upon, including history, chemistry, pharmacology, physiology, medicine, psychology, sociology, and law. The book does not attempt to influence points of view. Emphasis is given to technique and the teacher's attitude.

329.   Milgram, Gail Gleason. **Coping with Alcohol.** Illustrated by Nancy Lou Gahan. New York: Richards Rosen Press, 1980. 108p. illus. bibliog. $7.97. LC 79-25817. ISBN 0-8239-0494-6.

Although this book is of most interest to young people, parents and educators can also make use of the information on alcohol, its use, effects, attendant problems, and ways to deal with it. The question and answer format is utilized after the introductory chapter in which the importance of clarifying values toward alcohol use is stressed. Sample values-clarifying exercises are provided.

The following topics are dealt with: types of alcohol and alcohol beverages, history of alcohol use, attitudes toward drinking, adult and teenage use, effects on the body, alcohol problems, alcoholism, and effects of alcoholism on family members. The rather simple presentation stresses the importance of making responsible decisions about alcohol use. The bibliography indicates audience level, and a list of resources for further information and a glossary are included.

330.   Sheppard, Margaret A., Michael S. Goodstadt, Gloria Torrance, and Mario Fieldstone. **Alcohol Education: Ten Lesson Plans for Grades 7 and 8.** Toronto: Addiction Research Foundation of Ontario in cooperation with the Toronto Board of Education, 1978. 58p. illus. $7.95pa.

Each lesson plan in this set deals with some aspect of alcohol use and was developed to provide the teacher with a foundation upon which to build a program.

The lessons are an attempt to aid the decision-making process regarding whether or not to drink by providing knowledge about values and possible consequences of behavior. The end result is to reduce the personal and social costs of alcohol use and/or abuse in society.

The plans were tested and evaluated and appear to have positive outcomes.

331.   Sheppard, Margaret A., Michael S. Goodstadt, Gloria Torrance, and Mario Fieldstone. **Alcohol Education: Ten Lesson Plans for Grades 9 and 10.** Toronto: Addiction Research Foundation of Ontario in cooperation with the Toronto Board of Education, 1978. 83p. illus. $7.95pa.

This publication is similar to the one above, except that the lesson plans presented are for higher grades.

332.   U.S. Drug Enforcement Administration. **Soozie Says "Only Sick People Need Drugs!"** Washington: GPO, 1978. 1v. (unpaged). illus. $1.20pa. S/N 027-004-0024-5.

This attractive "workbook" for children is intended to provide a basis for classroom and home discussion that will identify for them the purpose of medicine and help them to understand the dangers that accompany the use of any drug. A study guide for the parent or teacher has been included. Basically, the booklet is made up of pictures, a bit on the Sesame Street or Dr. Seuss style, which a child can color, cut out, or paste, and which contain a message. The intention is to encourage an attitude of caution but not fear where drugs are concerned. The work is nicely done and should appeal to a child.

333.   U.S. National Institute on Alcohol Abuse and Alcoholism. **Alcohol, Drug, and Related Mental Health Problems: A Pilot Curriculum for Primary Care Providers.** Developed by the National Center for Alcohol Education. Washington: GPO, 1980. 131p. bibliog. [DHHS Publication No. (ADM) 80-983.]

This publication presents a session-by-session outline of a workshop curriculum for providers of community health services to those with alcohol, drug, and related mental health problems. A good deal of practical material is provided, including assistance in the analysis of experience, and pre- and post-course assessments.

334.   U.S. National Institute on Alcohol Abuse and Alcoholism. **Participant Workbook, Planning Alcoholism Services: A Basic Course in Assessment, Program Design, Implementation, and Evaluation.** Developed by National Center for Alcohol Education. Washington: GPO, 1978. 150p. bibliog. [DHEW Publication No. (ADM) 78-714.] S/N 017-024-00828-1.

The course of study presented in this workbook is designed to build or improve the basic planning skills needed by persons responsible for program planning in alcohol service agencies. The course looks at community problems and suggests a framework for their resolution. Essential subject matter and session exercises are included.

335.   U.S. National Institute on Alcohol Abuse and Alcoholism. **Services for Alcoholic Women: Foundations for Change. Resource Book.** Developed by the National Center for Alcohol Education. Washington: GPO, 1979. 326p. bibliog. [DHEW Publication No. (ADM) 79-873.] S/N 017-024-00943-1.

The course of study presented here is designed primarily for people who are responsible for alcohol treatment program administration and decision making, and who wish to improve services. The emphasis is on the planning, implementation, and monitoring of such programs.

The book is in five sections as follows: 1) Course material, 2) Selected articles, 3) Treatment program resources, 4) Staff development resources, and 5) Client education resources.

The selected articles reprinted in section 2, and the annotated bibliographies and list of periodicals included in the work elsewhere are worthy of note. Many deal with women's roles and problems in society in a broad sense.

336.   U.S. National Institute on Alcohol Abuse and Alcoholism. **Services for Alcoholic Women: Foundations for Change. Session Outline Cards.** Developed by the National Center for Alcohol Education. Washington: GPO, 1979. 112p. [DHEW Publication No. (ADM) 79-872.] $5.50pa. S/N 017-024-00945-8.

This publication is a spiral-bound packet of cards that contain specific directions for conducting each session of the course described in the entries directly above and below. The goals and objectives, material, and equipment for the various learning activities are given.

337.   U.S. National Institute on Alcohol Abuse and Alcoholism. **Services for Alcoholic Women: Foundations for Change. Trainer Manual.** Washington: GPO, 1979. 1 v. (various paging). [DHEW Publication No. (ADM) 79-871.] S/N 017-024-00944-0.

A companion volume to the one reviewed directly above, this publication is designed to help the trainer prepare for and conduct the sessions of the course of study. A session-by-session overview is provided, as is refresher materials on methods and techniques, guidelines for training program management, sample recruiting materials, and masters for making handout materials.

338.   U.S. National Institute on Alcohol Abuse and Alcoholism. **Trainer Catalog of Alcohol and Drug Training Materials from the National Center for Alcohol Education and the National Drug Abuse Center.** Washington: GPO, 1978. 192p. (looseleaf). index. [DHEW Publication No. (ADM) 79-834.] S/N 017-024-00889-3.

This publication was prepared to inform trainees and course developers in the fields of alcohol and drug abuse about available training materials developed by the National Center for Alcohol Education and the National Drug Abuse Center. The material is presented in two sections: 1) Overviews of courses from the National Center for Alcohol Education, and 2) Overviews of courses from the National Drug Abuse Center. These course overviews include information about package source and publication date, package components, trainer requirements for presenting the course, intended audience, and instructional mode and setting. A list of course contents by unit is also provided.

339.   U.S. National Institute on Alcohol Abuse and Alcoholism, and the National Institute on Drug Abuse. **Medical Education in Drug and Alcohol Abuse: A Catalog of Sources.** Rockville, MD: National Clearinghouse for Alcohol Information, 1978. 1v. (various paging). index.

Since 1971 the National Institute on Alcohol Abuse and Alcoholism, and the National Institute on Drug Abuse have funded individuals as career teachers in medical schools to increase the quality and quantity of education in substance abuse received by medical students, residents, and practicing physicians. Individuals and the career teachers have developed products that relate to their work as educators in drug and alcohol abuse. These products are cataloged in this publication.

The book is organized into the following sections: 1) Introduction, 2) Curriculum objectives in drug and alcohol abuse, 3) Career teacher products, 4) Addresses of career teachers, centers, and institutes, and 5) Index. The career teacher products section contains a listing and descriptions of the following: course curricula, test items, books and chapters, journal articles and presented papers, A-V material, teaching aids and lectures, and other.

340.   U.S. National Institute on Drug Abuse. **Beyond the Three R's: Training Teachers for Affective Education.** Washington: GPO, 1975. 45p. bibliog. [DHEW Publication No. (ADM) 77-233, formerly 75-233.] S/N 017-024-00459-6.

As a response to past unsatisfactory approaches to drug abuse education, the guidelines presented here were developed to train teachers in becoming more effective agents of change. The Southern Regional Education Board has put together some of the best thinking about the school's role and responsibility in the area of drug abuse prevention. The material is presented under the following headings: 1) Conceptual issues, 2) The training process, 3) Implications and recommendations, and 4) Special concerns.

341.   U.S. National Institute on Drug Abuse. **Growing Up In America—A Background to Contemporary Drug Abuse.** By Anne MacLeod. Washington: GPO, 1975. 98p. bibliog. [DHEW Publication No. (ADM) 75-106.]

This publication assesses the drug problem and its social background as well. It is aimed at helping school personnel and others understand the world young people experience, particularly those of inner city and suburban environments. The text is based principally on studies of these groups, although there are applications for all communities.

The following chapters and appendices are included: 1) Growing up in America in the 1970's, 2) Growing up in the inner city, 3) Growing up in the suburbs, 4) The schools and their problems, 5) Bringing the worlds together; appendix I, Annotated bibliography for teachers, appendix II, Annotated bibliography for students.

The message the book has for teachers is that they are in a position to influence profoundly the direction and quality of a child's life. They can reveal to the child alternatives to drug use.

342.   U.S. National Institute on Drug Abuse. **Vanguards in Training.** Washington: GPO, 1977. 92p. index. [DHEW Publication No. (ADM) 77-297.] $1.65pa. S/N 017-024-00519-3.

Information on the National Training System's Training Grant Program, which is supported throughout the United States by the National Institute on Drug Abuse, is presented here in summary form. The purpose of the grants is to increase the skills, career mobility, and credentials of drug abuse prevention, treatment, and research personnel.

The first section of the document gives a resumé of the purposes, provisions, and requirements for the Training Grant Program. The next (and largest) section provides summaries, arranged by state, of the individual projects which have been funded under each type of grant. Three types are awarded, Developmental Training, Career Teacher, and National Research Service. The summaries include the title of the program, program director and other personnel, institutional address, dates, grant number, and a brief description of the program.

343.   U.S. National Institute on Drug Abuse. **Why Evaluate Drug Education? Task Force Report.** Washington: GPO, 1975. 32p. bibliog. [DHEW Publication No. (ADM) 77-234, formerly 75-234.] $0.85pa. S/N 017-024-00461-8.

This brief publication, which is of value to administrators of alcohol and drug abuse education programs, attempts to clarify the different levels of evaluation and the kinds of learning that can occur at each level. It outlines the components and considerations for evaluation, but does not give a step-by-step procedure. Four sections are included: 1) Why evaluate?, 2) Guidelines for impact evaluation, 3) Suggestions for process evaluation, and 4) Evaluation of drug programs.

344.   U.S. National Institute on Drug Abuse. Division of Resource Development. Manpower Training Branch. **Confidentiality of Alcohol and Drug Abuse Patient Records: A Self-Paced Programmed Instructional Course.** By Bettye Ann Moore, and others. Washington: GPO, 1979. 242p. (looseleaf). (Publication No. (NDACTRD) 79-501R.)

The purpose of this course of study is to teach the substance of and to explore the implications of the 1975 Federal Regulations on Confidentiality of Alcohol and Drug Abuse Patient Records. It is of interest to personnel in the alcohol and drug abuse prevention, treatment, and rehabilitation field who have access to patient records. The presentation is divided into these sections: 1) Introduction and general provisions, 2) Disclosures with patient consent, 3) Disclosures without patient consent and court orders, 4) Issues in confidentiality: patient education and ethical considerations, and 5) Joint Commission on Accreditation of Hospitals' Standards: a case study in application.

345.   U.S. National Institute on Drug Abuse. Division of Resource Development. Prevention Branch. **Come Closer Around the Fire: Using Tribal Legends, Myths, and Stories in Preventing Drug Abuse.** Prepared by the Center for Multicultural Awareness. Washington: GPO, 1978. 32p. illus. bibliog. [DHEW Publication No. (ADM) 78-741.] S/N 017-024-00821-4.

This unusual pamphlet is a guide showing how tribal stories, myths, and legends can be used as tools for preventing drug abuse among Native Americans. The strategy suggested is to provide alternative activities to drug use and to help Indian young people feel pride in themselves and their culture, and to increase their skill and confidence. Several stories are reproduced and a good bibliography provided.

346.   U.S. National Institute on Drug Abuse. Office of Communications and Public Affairs. **This Side Up: Making Decisions About Drugs.** By Maureen H. Cook, and Carol Newman. Washington: GPO, 1978. 64p. illus. [DHEW Publication No. (ADM) 78-420.] S/N 017-024-00776-5.

This profusely illustrated publication was developed as a source of information for young people faced with making decisions about drugs. Many examples of social situations a teenager may encounter are dealt with. The subject matter is presented in novel ways, such as cartoons, games, questions and answers, and personal testimonies.

347.   U.S. National Institute on Drug Abuse, and National Institute on Alcohol Abuse and Alcoholism. **Alcohol and Drug Abuse in Medical Education.** Edited by

Marc Galanter. Washington: GPO, 1980. 131p. bibliog. [DHEW Publication No. (ADM) 79-891.]

Recently it has become evident that more attention should be given to preparing physicians to treat drug or alcohol abusing patients. This book presents the "state of the art" of American medical education in this area. History, contemporary perspectives, and educational materials recently developed are presented.

Career teachers and members of the Association for Medical Education and Research in Substance Abuse collaborated on this publication, and it is planned that they will produce others in the future.

348.   U.S. Special Action Office for Drug Abuse Prevention. **The Media and Drug Abuse Messages.** Washington: GPO, 1974. 96p. bibliog. (Special Action Office Monograph. Series D, No. 1, April 1974.)

Although this is an older publication and some of the material in it is dated and of doubtful value, it deals with a subject of continuing importance in drug abuse education: how to deal with the problems encountered in the production and dissemination of drug abuse prevention messages. The contributors are noted authorities.

The following are the titles of the papers: 1) Communications, mass media and drug abuse—the issues and research findings, 2) The knowledge about drugs, attitudes towards them and drug use rates of high school students, 3) The pusher, 4) Popular music and drug lyrics: analysis of a scapegoat, 5) How to launch a nationwide drug menace, 6) Introduction to drug abuse films, 7) Guidelines for the use of existing materials and the preparation of new printed materials, 8) Federal guidelines for drug abuse prevention materials, and 9) Drug education through the news media: suggestions for reporters and drug program directors.

349.   Wenk, Ernst A. **Peer Conducted Research: A Novel Approach to Drug Education.** Davis, CA: Research Center, National Council on Crime and Delinquency (Available from Responsible Action, Inc., 1814 Redwood Lane, Davis, CA 95616), 1974. 31p. $1.00pa.

This booklet, which contains a paper presented to the First International Congress on Drug Education, outlines an experiment that the author hopes will provide a model for effective presentation and intervention in drug abuse problems. The method employed, called "Partnership in Research," involved subjects as partners and participant researchers in an attempt at self-study. The research objectives and method are defined and carried out by the participant researchers, providing a learning experience for them. The real goal of the endeavor is to involve students in observing and evaluating issues that have a significant impact on their lives. The consensus was that high quality drug education programs are of great importance, since inadequate programs only aggravate the situation.

10

DRUGS AND YOUTH

Emphasis is still given to the problem of youth and their use of drugs. A disturbing aspect of the matter is that younger and younger children are becoming habitual users of dangerous drugs such as marijuana, barbiturates, and hallucinogens. The problem is no longer restricted to inner cities, but has spread to the suburbs and rural areas as well.

However, it has become evident recently that alcohol is the number one drug of abuse, and a number of titles listed here reflect that awareness. Areas dealt with include social, cultural, and peer group influences, behavior, trends, and health effects.

350.   Beschner, George M., and Alfred S. Friedman, eds. **Youth Drug Abuse: Problems, Issues, and Treatment**. Lexington, MA: Lexington Books, 1979. 681p. illus. bibliog. index. $26.50. LC 78-21197. ISBN 0-669-02804-5.

This is a comprehensive work that examines most of the major issues in the field of youth and drug abuse. There are six major sections dealing with epidemiology, methodology, issues and aspects, special problems, special youth populations, and treatment. Most of the statistical data included was obtained from the national drug data bases, CODAP, DAWN, and DARP, and the recent National Youth Polydrug Study. The chapters, prepared by various authors, contain short synopses of the issues to be considered, interwoven data, subsections, and summary discussions. Some of the special topics considered are: female adolescent drug use, multiple drug-use patterns, the effects of youth drug abuse on education, the association of marijuana and heroin use, relationships between drug use and delinquent behavior, special youth populations (rural, Native American, black, Hispanic, and white), an appraisal of treatment services, and methods of reaching youth during the critical years.

The book is of special interest to the researcher, clinician, and educator. It has been well-received.

351.   Blane, Howard T., and Linda E. Hewitt. **Alcohol and Youth: An Analysis of the Literature, 1960-75**. Pittsburgh, PA: University of Pittsburgh, 1977. Prepared for the National Institute on Alcohol Abuse and Alcoholism (Available from the National Technical Information Service). 590p. bibliog. $16.50; microfiche, $3.00. PB 268 698.

The National Institute on Alcohol Abuse and Alcoholism commissioned this survey of the literature dealing with alcohol use and abuse by young people in order to obtain a picture of the way alcohol and youth interrelate and to serve as a basis for determining policy and for identifying research and social action needs.

The following chapters are provided: 1) Introduction, 2) Trends in high school drinking practices, 3) Influences on adolescent drinking, 4) College age drinking practices, 5) Children and alcohol, 6) Alcoholism and youth, 7) Juvenile delinquents, 8) Children of alcoholics, 9) Racial and ethnic variations, 10) Other special youth populations, 11) Theories of youthful drinking, and 12) Conclusions and recommendations.

A major finding of the study is that negative consequences related to the acute effects of alcohol are at their peak during late adolescence and early adulthood. The recommendation is made that research with this age group be accorded the highest priority.

An extensive bibliography (more than 1,000 references) has been provided with the report.

352.   Blane, Howard T., and Morris E. Chafetz, eds. **Youth, Alcohol, and Social Policy**. New York: Plenum Press, 1979. 424p. bibliog. index. $27.50. LC 79-9094. ISBN 0-306-40253-X.

The papers reprinted in this volume are from a conference organized by the Health Education Foundation which was held October 18-20, 1978 in Arlington, Virginia. They approach the diverse body of information dealing with alcohol use and alcohol-related problems among young people. An attempt has been made to provide recent information on the epidemiology of drinking behavior and drinking problems among the young, theories that may explain drinking behavior, social policy implications of youthful drinking, and a review of programs designed to reduce problems associated with alcohol.

The material has been divided into four sections: 1) Epidemiology of drinking practices among adolescents and young adults, 2) Theoretical models of drinking among adolescents and young adults, 3) Public policy implications of drinking problems among young, and 4) Strategies for reducing drinking problems among youth. Chapter titles are as follows: 1) Middle-aged alcoholics and young drinkers, 2) Patterns of alcohol consumption among the young: high school, college, and general population studies, 3) Alcohol problems among civilian youth and military personnel, 4) Developmental aspects of drinking through the young adult years, 5) Ecological factors in drinking, 6) Sex roles and adolescent drinking, 7) Priorities in minimizing alcohol problems among young people, 8) The impact of sociopolitical systems on teenage alcohol abuse, 9) Toward national policy for health education, 10) Strategies for reducing drinking problems among youth: college programs, 11) U.S. Military alcohol abuse prevention and rehabilitation programs, and 12) Behavioral strategies for reducing drinking among young adults.

It is hoped that the volume will lay the groundwork for establishing social policy aimed at reducing alcohol problems among the young. The suggestion is made that legal-drinking-age legislation is frequently ridiculous. To be effective (if it could be enforced anyway) the legal drinking age would have to be raised to 25 as it is the age group 21-25 that experiences the most drinking trouble.

353.   Bowker, Lee H. **Drug Use at a Small Liberal Arts College**. San Francisco, CA: R & E Research Associates, 1976. 133p. bibliog. $9.00. LC 75-38309. ISBN 0-88247-398-0.

The author of this research monograph gathered data on the use of legal and illegal drugs at a small liberal arts college by making use of questionnaires. The study was designed to relate incidence of use to the students' perceptions of their home and peer drug environments. In addition, self attitudes were studied and the distribution of drug use mapped using demographic variables.

In summary, it was found that drug use at the college was substantial, but less than might be supposed. Positive relationships were found between drug use and perceived home drug environment. A relationship was found between the perceived peer drug environment and self drug use. Several demographic variables were related to self drug use. Compared to the nonuser, the user of illegal drugs was more likely to be male, upper-middle class in origin, a non-attendee or identifier with an organized religion, an upperclassman in the social sciences holding liberal political values, and having a slightly lower degree of reported general health. Need profiles were constructed for all categories of drugs. It was found that marijuana, hallucinogens, and alcohol met a similar pattern of needs. A second pattern of needs was met by narcotics, barbiturates, tranquilizers, aspirin, and other legal drugs. Tobacco and amphetamines did not fit into either group of drugs.

354.   Cross, Wilbur. **Kids and Booze: What You Must Know to Help Them.** New York: E. P. Dutton, 1979. 180p. bibliog. index. (A Sunrise Book.) $5.95pa. LC 78-21105. ISBN 0-87690-314-6.

The author of this book, who is a recovered alcoholic, has been active in organizations dedicated to alcohol education and has written a good deal on a number of subjects. In this book he gives advice to parents, teachers, and others concerned with the drinking problems of young people. The material is presented in question-and-answer format, and many of the answers contain the testimony of young people about their own experiences. In addition, use is made of case studies.

In spite of the fact that the book attempts to give "answers," few clear-cut ones will be found. The author says he has no neat, workable formula. He can only help the reader focus on the nature of the problem and determine what steps to take to correct it.

One of the most likely suggestions comes at the conclusion of the book in a letter to the author from a young person. The suggestion is made that a community needs a program "that gets everyone involved, that brings the subject into the open, that treats alcohol and alcohol abuse as something every neighbor should be able to discuss. If your town was being demoralized and the inhabitants sickened by air pollution, you wouldn't get far by having each citizen or family trying to counteract it independently, in secret. You'd have meetings, enlist the aid of many people, hold discussions, and take action."

355.   du Toit, Brian M. **Drug Use and South African Students.** Athens, OH: Ohio University Center for International Studies, Africa Program, 1978. 127p. bibliog. (Papers in International Studies, Africa Series, No. 35.) $6.50pa. LC 78-21910. ISBN 0-89680-076-8.

The author of this study is a professor of anthropology who was born in South Africa. Between 1972 and 1974 he directed a research project on cannabis and its use in Africa. This report, which is on high school seniors and university students, is part of that study.

A questionnaire was administered to the students composed of these major sections: 1) Social background of the person, 2) History of cannabis use by the person, 3) Social aspects influencing use by the person, e.g., friends, parents, and values, 4) Attitudes regarding cannabis, its effects, its legal status, etc., and 5) Use of and attitudes regarding other drugs.

Since several ethnic groups are represented among South African students, it was expected that research findings would vary among them. The views did differ somewhat among the ethnic groups, but in general the African students were conservative in their responses. They had a relatively open mind concerning cannabis use, but turned conservative when the question of drug use pertained to persons with whom they were close. The reason most often given for this concern was the fear that drugs would damage the health. Also they tended to favor legal restrictions.

356.   Englebardt, Stanley L. **Kids and Alcohol, the Deadliest Drug.** New York: Lothrop, Lee & Shepard Co., a Division of William Morrow and Co., 1975. 64p. bibliog. index. $6.95. LC 75-20327. ISBN 0-688-41717-5.

This book was written for young people because alcohol abuse is a growing problem among them. The material included is authentic and very well-presented. Techniques such as the use of statistics on alcohol use and case histories are utilized.

Following are the chapter titles: 1) Alcohol, the drug of choice among young people, 2) What it is, and how it affects your body, 3) What drinking can do to your health, 4) How and why some people become "problem drinkers," 5) Are you a candidate for alcoholism?, 6) How to recognize, prevent, and treat alcoholism, and 7) Some questions and answers about alcohol.

357.   Hawker, Ann. **Adolescents and Alcohol: Report of an Enquiry into Adolescent Drinking Patterns Carried Out from October 1975 to June 1976.** London: B. Edsall and Co., Ltd., 1978. 65p. illus. bibliog. index. $12.00pa. LC 78-326342. ISBN 0-902623-21-4.

There has been a growing interest and increase in the amount of research carried out on the use of alcohol by young people. This volume makes a limited contribution to the understanding of the problem of youthful drinking. It reports on the outcome of a 59-item, self-administered questionnaire survey of approximately 7,000 young people, ages 13-16 in schools in England. Included in the questionnaire were questions on demographic background, leisure activities, group membership, cigarette smoking, and alcohol use. In regard to alcohol use, there were questions on the first drinking experience, family and peer models for use, and frequency, context, consequences, and reasons for drinking. Results are shown in a large number of tables and figures.

The data provided mainly relates to the epidemiology of adolescent alcohol use. Only a little discussion, interpretation, and analysis of the findings has been provided. Appendices include additional tables, questionnaires, and existing legislation in Great Britain.

358.   Maddox, George L., and Bevode C. McCall. **Drinking among Teen-Agers: A Sociological Interpretation of Alcohol Use by High-School Students.** New Brunswick, NJ: Rutgers Center of Alcohol Studies, 1964. 127p. bibliog. index. $6.00. LC 64-63392.

Although old, this book is still of interest because it shows how things regarding alcohol do not change and how repetitive the literature is. Teenage drinking was a problem in the 1960s as it is now and was before. The authors' conclusions are that youth do not have to invent the idea of drinking, they learn it. It is pointed out that if this is an obvious conclusion, the adult community has for many generations treated drinking by youth as if it were something that youngsters repeatedly invent anew.

The following chapters are included: 1) Teen-agers and alcohol, 2) Drinking is social behavior, 3) Patterns of drinking and abstinence, 4) Drinking and social norms, 5) Why people drink: a teen-age version, and 6) Some concluding observations. A copy of the questionnaire used is appended. Statistical data are presented throughout the text.

The conclusion is reached that some alcohol use is probably involved in growing up in a society in which most adults drink.

359.   McGrath, John H., and Frank R. Scarpitti, comps. **Youth and Drugs: Perspectives on a Social Problem**. Glenview, IL: Scott, Foresman and Co., 1970. 199p. bibliog. $3.95pa. LC 72-130190. ISBN 0-673-07558-3.

The articles in this anthology were chosen because they point out that there has been a radical change in types of drug use and in those who use drugs. The view of the compilers is that the societal reaction to deviant behavior is a more complex aspect of drug abuse than the biochemical mysteries. Deviants are under pressure to conform, but at the same time society is under pressure to change. The basic question is felt to be why so many young people feel the need to engage in drug use.

The work is in three sections, each containing several papers: 1) The problem and its setting, 2) Patterns and meanings in youthful drug use, and 3) Some implications for society. Each section begins with an overview essay. The papers have, for the most part, been reprinted from journals of the late 1960s.

The conclusion drawn by the compilers is that disciplined research into the many complex aspects of drug abuse is urgently needed. We need to know more about drug use before rational decisions can be made about what should be done or not done about it. At this writing, it would appear that at least some of the research called for has been carried out. However, more of it has been involved with physiological aspects than the social, and decisions on what to do about drug abuse as social policy are as perplexing as ever.

360.   Nawaz, Mohammad. **Pot Smoking and Illegal Conduct: Understanding the Social World of University Students**. Foreword by Edmund W. Vaz. St. Catharines, Ontario: Diliton Publications, Inc. (P. O. Box 1351, St. Catharines, Ontario, Canada L2R 7J8), 1978. 210p. bibliog. index. $15.95; $10.95pa. ISBN 0-920642-06-3; 0-930642-04-7pa.

This work is a sociological study of 4,510 students at a Canadian university. The author tests a series of logically derived hypotheses on marijuana use among the students. Anonymous questionnaires are made use of as well as personal attendance at pot parties and informal interviews with drug users.

The author's view is that drug use among students is not an occurrence prompted by anti-social impulses, but comes from a sustained participation in culturally accepted and approved activities. Marijuana smoking is looked on as a legitimate, normal socially defined role in the youth culture. When it comes to law violation, students (like others) engage in illegal acts selectively and discriminately. They perform acts that make sense to them. The data reveals, however, that "serious" infractions, such as assault, breaking and entering, or using or selling hard drugs, generally violates prevailing cultural values among students.

In addition to attitudes toward illegal drug use, such matters as formal religious participation, living arrangements, and self confidence are considered in relation to marijuana use.

There are five chapters as follows: 1) The problem, literature and theoretical perspective, 2) Formalizing relationships: youth culture activities and illegal conduct,

3) Methodology: collection and analysis of data, 4) Presentation and interpretation of the data, and 5) Conclusions and implications. In addition, appendices include additional statistical material and a research questionnaire.

361.   O'Connor, Joyce. **The Young Drinkers: A Cross-National Study of Social and Cultural Influences.** With a Foreword by D. L. Davies. London: Tavistock Publications, 1978. 312p. bibliog. index. £14.25. ISBN 0-422-76380-2.

Based on a thesis prepared in the Department of Social Science, University College, Dublin, this work is an attempt to contribute to the knowledge and understanding of drinking behavior. It is particularly concerned with the importance and interaction of factors which influence patterns of drinking behavior and attitudes among young people. The following matters are focused upon: 1) parental influences, 2) peer group influences, 3) social and personal influences, and 4) ethnic and cultural influences.

The work is in three parts. The first section is background. The second presents a picture of drinking among three different groups of young people, Irish, English, and Anglo-Irish (Irish immigrants to England and their children). The third section is concerned with the importance and relative influence of the factors mentioned in the preceding paragraph. Copious amounts of statistical data have been presented throughout the book.

The behavior of the Anglo-Irish is of special interest. They are very heavy drinkers. The author believes these young people are exposed to a dual culture in relation to drinking and attitudes toward it. The fact that they have not assimilated either the Irish or the English culture seems to have given rise to a heavy drinking and drunkenness pattern. They have perhaps accepted the Irish tendency toward drunkenness and the English tendency toward heavy drinking. O'Connor further believes that parental attitudes are the most important influence in the drinking behavior of the young. Her view is that the Anglo-Irish youth socialize with English friends and that their parents' attitudes toward drinking are not as negative as Irish parents' but not as permissive as English parents'.

362.   Smart, Reginald G. **The New Drinkers: Teenage Use and Abuse of Alcohol.** Toronto: Addiction Research Foundation of Ontario, 1976. 143p. illus. bibliog. (Program Report Series No. 4.) $3.95pa. ISBN 0-88868-004-X.

There was a need for this book in Canada (and elsewhere) because youthful drinking has risen greatly. The legal age for drinking was lowered from 21 to 18 or 19 in the years 1970 to 1974 in Canada, as was also a trend in the United States. This brought about much anxiety on the part of parents, educators, and others involved with the problem. This book attempts to answer the questions raised regarding youthful drinkers and pulls together information from recent research studies. In addition, matters such as reasons for drinking, the extent of drinking problems, and the steps parents and social institutions might take to solve problems are discussed.

Chapter headings are as follows: 1) What are the reasons for concern about drinking among young people?, 2) How many young people drink and how much do they drink?, 3) What do young people drink (and where)?, 4) What is the effect of parental drinking on children?, 5) How many young people have drinking problems?, 6) What can be done for young people with drinking problems?, 7) What is the effect of the new drinking age laws?, 8) Can parents prevent drinking problems?, 9) What can schools do to teach safe drinking habits?, 10) What can governments do about preventing drinking problems?, and 11) Where do we go from here with alcohol?

The view taken by the author is that there is a major need for educational, social policy, and familial changes which can lessen problems. However, he is generally hopeful, feeling that there are some encouraging signs that drinking problems among youth are still infrequent and the problem areas manageable.

363.   Snyder, Anne. **Kids and Drinking**. Illustrations by Susan Harlan. Minneapolis, MN: CompCare Publications, 1977. 47p. illus. $2.50pa. ISBN 0-89638-010-6.

This small book was designed for gradeschool-age children. It offers information about drinking and alcoholism by relating experiences of three children who were alcoholics and were recovering. The book is not intended as a "scare" book, but rather a source of information for youngsters who may already at ages 7-11 be faced with whether or not to take a drink.

Included is a 20-question self-quiz to help young people evaluate their own drinking habits. Also a parent/teacher guide section has been provided.

The author writes juvenile literature and is a teacher of creative writing.

364.   U.S. Bureau of Narcotics and Dangerous Drugs. Office of Scientific Support. Drug Control Division. **Patterns of Drug Use Among College Students in the Denver-Boulder Metropolitan Area: An Epidemiological and Demographic Survey of Student Attitudes and Practices**. By James T. Barter, George L. Mizner, and Paul H. Werme. Washington: GPO, 1971. 311p. bibliog. (SCID-TR-1.)

This publication is perhaps the first comprehensive account of a drug use survey conducted among a large population of college students in one metropolitan area. The study particularly investigated the patterns of drug use and their relationship with alienation and the milieu of the educational institution. Use of marijuana, amphetamines, and LSD was considered, as was the attitude toward their use.

Following are some of the findings: 1) 3 of every 10 students reported the use of marijuana, amphetamines, and/or LSD one or more times; 48% had used only marijuana; 14% only amphetamines; few had used only LSD. 2) Sixteen percent were using marijuana at the time of the study; 7% amphetamines; and 4% LSD. 3) Rates of drug use ranged from 16 to 35%. 4) Students who reported high parental education and income also reported the highest proportion of drug use. 5) Student drug use was related to restrictiveness of the residential setting. The more restrictive the setting the less likelihood there was of drug use. 6) Alienation in the sense of social isolation was not related to drug use, but dissatisfaction with college was. In addition there are many other findings of interest. Recommendations are included in the volume.

365.   U.S. National Institute on Drug Abuse. **Drug Abuse Among American High School Students 1975-1977**. By Lloyd D. Johnston, Jerald G. Bachman, and Patrick M. O'Malley. Washington: GPO, 1977. 238p. bibliog. [DHEW Publication (ADM) 78-619.]

The first of a series from the University of Michigan's Institute for Social Research (*see also* the next three entries), this volume presents detailed statistics on the prevalence in 1977 of drug use among American high school seniors and on trends in these figures since 1975. Information on 11 separate classes of drugs is presented in chapters 2-12. The overall results are summarized in chapter 1. Attitudes and beliefs about drug use are dealt with in chapter 13, and perceived availability of drugs in chapter 14. Appendices include questionnaire content and variable definitions, estimation of sampling errors, and like materials.

The following are the drug classes distinguished: marijuana/hashish, inhalants, hallucinogens, cocaine, heroin, other opiates, stimulants, sedatives, tranquilizers, alcohol, and cigarettes.

366.   U.S. National Institute on Drug Abuse. **Drugs and the Class of '78: Behaviors, Attitudes, and Recent National Trends.** By Lloyd D. Johnston, Jerald G. Bachman, and Patrick M. O'Malley. Washington: GPO, 1979. 335p. bibliog. index. [DHEW Publication No. (ADM) 79-877.] S/N 017-024-00954-2.

The second in a series of publications conducted by the University of Michigan's Institute for Social Research, this volume presents detailed statistics on the prevalence of drug use by American high school seniors in 1978 and trends since 1975. Alcohol and cigarettes are included, but all the other drug use discussed is illicit use. There are sections on the following illicit substances: marijuana/hashish, inhalants, hallucinogens, cocaine, heroin, other opiates, stimulants, sedatives, tranquilizers.

Drug use, attitudes about drugs, exposure to them, and perceptions about their availability are dealt with.

367.   U.S. National Institute on Drug Abuse. **Highlights from Drugs and the Class of '78: Behaviors, Attitudes, and Recent National Trends.** By Lloyd D. Johnston, Jerald G. Bachman, and Patrick M. O'Malley. Washington: GPO, 1979. 57p. [DHEW Publication No. (ADM) 79-878.] S/N 017-024-00933-4.

This document, which presents findings from a national program entitled "Monitoring the Future: A Continuing Study of the Lifestyles and Values of Youth" and conducted by the University of Michigan's Institute for Social Research, has been superseded by a later publication, *1979 Highlights: Drugs and the Nation's High School Students: Five Year National Trends* (see entry 368). A longer, more detailed report is also available: *Drugs and the Class of '78: Behaviors, Attitudes, and Recent National Trends* (see entry 366).

368.   U.S. National Institute on Drug Abuse. **1979 Highlights: Drugs and the Nation's High School Students: Five Year National Trends.** By Lloyd D. Johnston, Jerald G. Bachman, and Patrick M. O'Malley. Washington: GPO, 1979. 80p. [DHEW Publication No. (ADM) 80-930.] $3.25. S/N 017-024-00968-7.

This document presents findings from a national program conducted by the University of Michigan's Institute for Social Research for the National Institute on Drug Abuse. The publication is the third in a series reporting on drug use and attitudes of high school seniors in the U.S. It supersedes the previous report, *Highlights from Drugs and the Class of '78* (see entry 367); however, it does not supersede the longer report, *Drugs and the Class of '78: Behaviors, Attitudes, and Recent National Trends* (see entry 366). The latter contains more detail.

Sections headed as follows are presented: 1) Introduction, 2) Prevalence of drug use, 3) Recent trends in drug use, 4) Use at earlier grade levels, 5) Degree and duration of highs, 6) Attitudes and beliefs about drugs, and 7) The social milieu. Much statistical data has been included in graphs and tables.

Levels of drug use reported can be summarized as follows: 1) about 65% of seniors report illicit drug use at some time in their lives, although a substantial proportion used only marijuana; 2) over 1/3 report using an illicit drug other than marijuana at some time; 3) marijuana is by far the most widely used illicit drug, with 60% reporting use at some time; and 4) the most widely used class of other illicit drugs is stimulants.

369.   U.S. Special Action Office for Drug Abuse Prevention. **Looking Ahead: The Youth Health Center.** Edited by James A. Crupi, George C. Schwarz, and Charles F.

Weiss. Washington: GPO, 1975. 123p. bibliog. (Special Action Office Monograph. Series E, No. 1.)

In response to the need for increased attention to the health problems of adolescents as they relate to drug abuse, the Special Action Office for Drug Abuse Prevention and the Department of Defense set up a project in Frankfurt, Germany, that provided a comprehensive health plan for American adolescent dependents. This monograph provides background information on the Youth Health Center. The following chapters are presented: 1) Drug abuse in total adolescent health care, 2) Understanding, organizing and involving community support, 3) Setting up a youth health center, 4) Designing a program: two examples, 5) Clinical leadership: medical care, supervision and consultation, 6) Staff training and paraprofessional development, 7) Linkage with the judicial system.

The hope is that the monograph will assist others in efforts to maximize the quality of life and health for young people.

11

DRUGS AND OTHER SPECIAL GROUPS

In the 1960s many of the books regarding drug abuse focused attention on the use of drugs by young people. More recently it has become evident that others also have drug problems that require special understanding. Books in this section deal with drug and alcohol problems among these groups: women, homosexuals, writers, prostitutes, physicians, the elderly, Jews, blacks, and other minorities.

Although those who counsel women feel that alcoholism among them has been collectively ignored in the past, many of these titles concern women. The use of alcohol and other drugs by pregnant women has been found dangerous to unborn children; the fetal alcohol syndrome is a serious condition. Although males are the heaviest drug users, female use is increasing. This may be because of changing attitudes toward women's use of drugs, particularly alcohol, and their dissatisfaction with traditional roles in society. Nellis's book (entry 388) focuses on the tendency toward overprescribing mind-altering drugs for women instead of dealing constructively with their problems.

Five titles deal with the aged and drug or alcohol use. The elderly are a major group in the consumption of psychoactive drugs, a good deal of it for medical purposes. It is felt that there is considerable potential for misuse or abuse because of this.

370.   Bowker, Lee H. **Drug Use Among American Women, Old and Young: Sexual Oppression and Other Themes.** San Francisco, CA: R & E Research Associates, 1977. 86p. bibliog. LC 76-55964. ISBN 0-88247-434-0.

This monograph focuses on the interaction of women's studies and female drug abuse. The literature of the field was searched and examined, and a large bibliography is included in the publication. The data on sexual differences in drug use patterns is summarized and the theoretical material analyzed. The viewpoint expressed is that a recognition of sexual oppression is crucial to understanding the existing drug use differences between the sexes.

The following chapters are presented: 1) Sexual differentiation in drug use, 2) Female drug use in a rural county, 3) Alcoholism and narcotic addiction among women, 4) Housewife drug problems, 5) Males as carriers of drug use to females, and 6) Methodology of the field research.

Although males are the heaviest drug users, there is a trend toward convergence of the rates. There is some evidence to suggest that this may be an effect of "women's liberation," that is, sexual equality may encourage women to use drugs more often as they become more assertive and gain more freedom in their private lives. The sociological version of this view is that liberation has allowed women to increase their (masculine) deviant activity.

371.   Burtle, Vasanti, ed. **Women Who Drink: Alcoholic Experience and Psycho-therapy.** With Forewords by Phyllis K. Snyder, Jan DuPlain, and George Staub. Springfield, IL: Charles C. Thomas, 1979. 274p. bibliog. index. $21.00. LC 78-10401. ISBN 0-398-03854-6.

Recently, alcoholism as it relates to women has begun to be acknowledged and discussed, and much of the stigma that once surrounded the female alcoholism victim has been removed, probably largely because of the women's movement now prevalent. The book makes a contribution to the understanding of the woman who is an alcoholic and her special needs during the recovery process.

An overview of the causes of alcoholism and a multidisciplinary approach to treatment is presented. There are 15 chapters, by various authors, grouped under these headings: 1) Women and the alcoholic experience, 2) Issues in the therapy of women alcoholics, and 3) Special approaches of therapy for women alcoholics.

The first part includes background papers and personal accounts. Part 2 considers clinical experiences of alcoholism workers, issues in marriage and the family, and training needs of workers. Part 3 includes papers on a cognitive/behavioral approach to therapy, comprehensive psychoanalytic therapy, gestalt therapy, Jungian treatment, and Alcoholics Anonymous.

372.   Christenson, Susan, and Gayle Ihlenfeld. **Lesbians, Gay Men and Their Alcohol and Other Drug Use: Resources.** With assistance from Janice Kinsolving. rev. ed. Madison, WI: Wisconsin Clearinghouse for Alcohol and Other Drug Information, University of Wisconsin Hospital and Clinics (1954 East Washington Ave., Madison, WI 53704), 1980. 15p. $0.35pa.

The compilers of this pamphlet feel that lesbians and gay men with drinking problems require special understanding. It is estimated that up to one out of three gay individuals has an alcohol problem, and there are few professionals trained to help them.

This booklet lists and provides annotations of articles, pamphlets, and films available on the subject. In addition, names of a few organizations and places to go for help are also listed.

The publication is intended primarily for use by alcoholism counselors and members of the gay community concerned with the issue.

373.   Coney, John C. **Exploring the Known and Unknown Factors in the Rates of Alcoholism Among Black and White Females.** San Francisco, CA: R and E Associates, Inc., 1978. 94p. bibliog. $10.00pa. LC 77-090385. ISBN 0-88247-509-6.

This study explores known and unknown assumptions and bases for predicting rates of alcoholism for black females, with predicted rates for white females. The consensus is that there has been an increase in alcoholism among black females. The author consolidates available literature to answer specific research questions. Among the conclusions: the number of female alcoholics is unknown, but thought to be increasing; the ratio of males to females is also unknown, but thought to be narrowing; hidden drinking is indicative of middle and upper class women; the purported increasing rates among women may actually be the result of greater visibility; socio-economic variables influence drinking patterns, e.g., a high concentration is found in the lower classes; sex difference, marital status, and race also affect rates of alcoholism; there seems to be more black than white female alcoholics, although the whites may hide their drinking better.

A great many questions are raised by the study, and suggestions are made for further research.

374.   Coney, John Charles. **The Precipitating Factors in the Use of Alcoholic Treatment Services: A Comparative Study of Black and White Alcoholics.** San Francisco, CA: R and E Associates, Inc., 1977. 129p. bibliog. $9.00pa. LC 76-24721. ISBN 0-88247-414-6.

Apparently derived from an academic dissertation, this study explores the circumstances under which black alcoholics and white alcoholics utilize the same treatment program. Social and demographic profiles of those program members, black and white, who were receiving out-patient care at the Dimock Community Health Center Alcoholism Program in Roxbury, Massachusetts, are presented. The author's thesis is that such services are underused or not used at all by black alcoholics. The profiles provide illustrations of the similarities and differences between blacks and whites who use the program. In addition, a number of questions are answered in the areas of social and racial problems of black alcoholics, treatment utilization experiences, assessments of treatment and mental health services by alcoholics, the conceptual model, data collecting procedures, and study group characteristics.

375.   Curlee-Salisbury, Joan. **When the Woman You Love Is an Alcoholic.** St. Meinrad, IN: Abbey Press, 1978. 96p. illus. bibliog. (A When Book.) $1.95pa. LC 78-73017. ISBN 0-87029-143-2.

This book is for the husband, mother, father, sister, brother, son, daughter, or other person who must cope with a woman who is an alcoholic. The chapter headings are as follows: 1) Who is an alcoholic, 2) The problem of denial, 3) Out of denial, 4) When there are children, 5) When she wants help, 6) Road to recovery, and 7) Special problems.

The conclusion of the book is that one should learn about the options and programs open to alcoholic women and try to find the best treatment setting for the victim. A list of organizations that offer help has been included as well as a bibliography of self-help materials.

376.   Dowsling, Janet, and Anne MacLennan, eds. **The Chemically Dependent Woman; Rx: Recognition, Referral, Rehabilitation.** Toronto: Addiction Research Foundation, 1978. 115p. $4.95pa. ISBN 0-88868-026-0.

This publication presents the proceedings of a conference sponsored by the Donwood Institute, Toronto, June 4, 1977. Special issues of women in need of assistance were discussed by women actively involved in dealing with women.

In addition to a panel discussion, "Putting the Chemically Dependent Woman in Touch with Alternatives," the following papers were presented: 1) The chemically dependent woman: an overview of the problem, 2) Special issues of women in therapy, 3) Getting in touch with the chemically dependent women, 4) Women and psychotropic drug use, 5) The chemical trap: a patient's view, 6) The chemical trap: a physician's perspective, 7) Women problem drinkers: anonymous alcoholics, 8) Personal reflections on women and alcohol, and 9) Feminist counselling: new directions for women.

A chief concern expressed by participants revolved around the question of feminist counselling and how it related to chemical dependency. Also, it was felt that dissatisfaction with traditional roles in society may be causing some chemical dependency problems in women.

377.   **Four Authors Discuss: Drinking and Writing**. New York: The New York City Affiliate, Inc. of The National Council on Alcoholism, 1980. 52p. $4.50pa.

The papers and discussions in this publication are from a special seminar on the link between alcoholism and America's creative writers, held October 30, 1979. These four noted authors presented material on the subject, based on their own experiences and research: Ian Hunter, Roger Kahn, Ring Lardner, Jr., and Jill Robinson. A number of famous writers of the past who were known alcoholics were discussed. These include: John Steinbeck, William Faulkner, John O'Hara, Ernest Hemingway, Sinclair Lewis, Eugene O'Neill, Edgar Allan Poe, Stephen Crane, Theodore Dreiser, Sherwood Anderson, Edna St. Vincent Millay, and Ambrose Bierce.

The presentations do not go into great depth, but they are interesting and insightful. Some of the conclusions drawn are: the writing profession might encourage alcoholism, but a predisposition comes first; alcoholics who are writers should be treated as other alcoholics; and writer's block cannot be freed by alcohol.

378.   Fraser, Judy. **The Female Alcoholic**. Revised by Lavada Pinder. Toronto: Addiction Research Foundation of Ontario, 1976. 15p. illus.

An earlier version of this article was published in the journal *Addictions* in 1973.

The author points to the increased use of alcohol by women, discusses the reasons they may become alcoholics, and explores the special problems they may encounter.

The following matters are dealt with: the effects of the women's liberation movement, the "double standard" that still remains in social attitudes toward women's drinking, special treatment of women by law officers and judges, the relative instability of life's institutions today, the difference of attitude toward the spouse of the alcoholic depending on whether the inebriate is male or female, and the high incidence of psychological disorders among women alcoholics.

The author hopes that as women gain a better understanding of themselves, their hopes and aspirations, and more often realize their potentials, they can better come to grips with the alcohol problem.

379.   Goldstein, Paul J. **Prostitution and Drugs**. Lexington, MA: Lexington Books, 1979. 190p. bibliog. index. $18.95. LC 78-24766. ISBN 0-669-02833-9.

The author of this publication points out that drug use and prostitution are forms of deviant behavior rife with myth, folklore, and assumptions. Recently many of the myths have been shattered by the social scientists, the medical profession, and organizations of prostitutes. The intent of this study is to address a gap in the knowledge and understanding of the relationship between drug use and prostitution by women in order to influence treatment or rehabilitation programs and contribute toward more reasonable legislation. The research conducted attempted to answer these questions: 1) What is the role of drug use in becoming a prostitute?, 2) What are the functions and dysfunction of drug use for prostitutes?, and 3) How does the nature and scope of drug use serve to differentiate socially the subculture of prostitution?

Chapter headings are as follows: 1) Introduction, 2) Methodology, 3) Defining and operationalizing key variables I: What is prostitution?, 4) Defining and operationalizing key variables II: What is drug use?, 5) Drug barterers and ex-addict mistresses: two aspects of the relationship between drug use and prostitution, 6) Associations between specific forms of drug use and prostitution: quantitative and sequential perspectives, 7) The relationship between prostitution and drug addiction, 8) The role of drug use in becoming a prostitute, 9) Drug use as a deterrent to becoming a prostitute, 10) Functions and dysfunctions of drug use for prostitutes, 11) Can the data be trusted?, and 12) Summary, conclusions, and implications.

One conclusion drawn from the study is that drug use is prevalent in any business where there is a certain amount of emotional trauma involved.

380.   Gordis, Enoch, and Mary Jeanne Kreek. **Alcoholism and Drug Addiction in Pregnancy**. Chicago: Year Book Medical Publishers, 1977. 48p. bibliog. (Current Problems in Obstetrics and Gynecology, v. 1, No. 3, November, 1977.)

This publication is an issue of a journal in the field of obstetrics and gynecology. An overview of the problems of alcoholism and drug abuse in pregnancy is provided. The material is presented under these headings: 1) Addiction, tolerance, and physical dependence, 2) Diagnosis and treatment of alcoholism and sedative and narcotic addiction in pregnancy, 3) Effects of addicting drugs on reproductive physiology, pregnancy and obstetric management, 4) Effects of addiction and therapies on the fetus and neonate.

381.   Green, Robert C., George J. Carroll, and William D. Buxton. **The Care and Management of the Sick and Incompetent Physician**. Springfield, IL: Charles C. Thomas, 1978. 101p. bibliog. index. $10.00. LC 77-21401. ISBN 0-398-03727-2.

This monograph compiles information that the authors, as officers of the Virginia State Board of Medicine, have defined as problems of physicians whose incompetence has caused them to come within the purview of the board's official concern. The purpose of the work is to present an in-depth study of the sick, incompetent, or unethical physician with the hope that it will provide an impetus to better management of the problem.

There are chapters on the drug-addicted physician and alcoholism among physicians. The authors state that the incidence of drug addiction is generally conceded to be high among physicians, an estimated ratio of 1:100 physicians as compared to 1:3000 in the general population. In their opinion this estimate is probably low and represents only a fraction of all physician addicts. In regard to alcoholism among physicians, the authors believe it is currently one factor among many that may account for the lowered public esteem of the medical profession. Addiction of both types, of course, often results in inadequate care of patients.

Other specific conditions discussed are psychiatric illness and behavioral problems.

382.   Hornik, Edith Lynn. **The Drinking Woman**. New York: Association Press, 1977. 191p. bibliog. index. $8.95. LC 77-10940. ISBN 0-8096-1909-1.

This work, by a free-lance writer, is one of several on the subject of the special problems of the alcoholic woman to appear recently. Like most of the others, it seeks to help the victim, the family, and the alcoholism counselor. The focus is on the psychological and social dynamics of the woman alcoholic, brought about through interviews in halfway houses and with women's groups.

Many aspects of the subject are covered: the role of the family; feminist attitudes that may contribute to the problem; the role of Alcoholics Anonymous and other treatment programs; stress brought on by family living, a bad marriage, or pregnancy; the fetal alcohol syndrome; attitudes of the employee, husband, and physician; self-esteem and related emotional states; dependency needs; and sexual problems.

The author feels that a woman alcoholic is more difficult to treat than a male alcoholic; however, the reasons she gives for arriving at this conclusion may not convince everyone.

383.   Hugunin, Mary B., ed. **Helping the Impaired Physician.** Proceedings of the AMA Conference on "The Impaired Physician: Answering the Challenge," February 4-6, 1977. Chicago: American Medical Association, Department of Mental Health, 1977. 95p. bibliog.

Presented here are the proceedings of the second national conference sponsored by the American Medical Association on physicians impaired by alcoholism, drug dependence, and mental illness. The first conference, held in 1975, called attention to the dilemma of the impaired physician; the second reviewed the successes and shortcomings of medical society, licensing board, and hospital programs for such physicians. The publication contains digests of papers, panel discussions, and workshop sessions.

384.   Kayne, Ronald G., ed. **Drugs and the Elderly.** revised. Los Angeles, CA: Ethel Percy Andrus Gerontology Center, University of Southern California, 1978. 156p. bibliog. $4.00pa. LC 78-52886. ISBN 0-88474-045-5.

A revision and expansion of an earlier compilation of meeting papers, this work is intended to broaden the reader's perspective regarding the principles involved in the safe, effective, and rational use of drugs by the elderly. It does not provide a detailed description of all the individual drugs the elderly may use; further, it is not concerned exclusively with the common drugs of abuse, but many of the substances considered (e.g., psychotropic drugs and alcohol) fall in that category.

The following are the chapter headings: 1) Drugs and the elderly, 2) Self-medication by the elderly, 3) Effective drug administration as viewed by a physician-administrator, 4) Nursing responsibilities in drug administration, 5) Use of drugs which influence behavior in the elderly, 6) Issues in psychotropic drug misuse, 7) Alcohol and the elderly, 8) Psychoactive drug misuse among the elderly: a review of prevention and treatment programs, 9) Drug interaction with the changing physiology of the aged, and 10) Effect of aging on pharmacokinetics.

The book is of particular value to those who provide medication to the aged (physicians, pharmacists, and nurses) as it will help them better understand, recognize, manage, and prevent drug-related problems.

385.   Kimball, Bonnie-Jean. **The Alcoholic Woman's Mad, Mad World of Denial and Mind Games.** Center City, MN: Hazelden, 1978. 69p. $3.50pa. LC 77-94793. ISBN 0-89486-048-8.

One aspect of the alcoholism problem is the focus of this work: the denial by the person affected that he or she is an alcoholic. Although there seems to be little difference in the way women and men handle this phase of addiction, this book is concerned with the alcoholic woman only. The author's view is that society encourages women's denial and delusion.

The book's message is that by looking squarely at the many levels of denial concerning women and chemical dependency in our culture, we can see and perhaps avoid certain impediments to recovery and rehabilitation. The Alcoholics Anonymous program is recommended. The dependent woman must learn to accept the reality of her condition and take responsibility for herself. Spiritual guidance is also called for.

386.   MacLennan, Anne, ed. **Women: Their Use of Alcohol and Other Legal Drugs. A Provincial Consultation—1976.** Compiled by Lavada Pinder. Toronto: Addiction Research Foundation of Ontario, 1976. 144p. bibliog. $5.00pa. ISBN 0-88868-017-1.

This book is essentially a report of a meeting, the First Provincial Consultation on Women and Addictions, held in Ottawa, Canada, on September 29-30 and October 1, 1975. The aim of the meeting was to bring together a small group of knowledgeable people to discuss women and their use of alcohol and other legal drugs. The hope was to contribute to the understanding of and to generate interest in what was felt to be a neglected area.

The following papers were presented: 1) The changing role of women, 2) On women and on one woman, 3) The alcoholic woman: attitudes and perspectives, 4) Women and legal drugs: a review, and 5) Women and psychotropic drugs. In addition, the book summarizes discussions held at the meeting and lists twelve recommendations formulated at the meeting and distributed to various health, social service, and educational bodies in Canada.

The overall viewpoint of the participants was that many of the problems of women are social and require social rather than chemical solutions. They expressed the belief that attempts at prevention or treatment will be inadequate if the social structure that limits women's full participation in society is not changed.

387.   Mishara, Brian L., and Robert Kastenbaum. **Alcohol and Old Age.** New York: Grune and Stratton, 1980. 220p. bibliog. index. (Seminars in Psychiatry.) $22.00. LC 79-3777. ISBN 0-8089-1226-7.

This work brings together much of the existing knowledge concerning the use of alcohol by older persons. Research is reviewed from medical, physiological, psychological, sociological, epidemiological, and historical perspectives.

The first chapter, "Alcohol and the Elderly: Five Thousand Years of Uncontrolled Experimentation," surveys alcohol use by the elderly over a long time span. The view is taken that the development of alcoholic beverages for medicinal and sacred purposes took some unfortunate turns, leading to alcohol problems in the population in general. Following chapters review physiological effects of ethanol, the extent of alcohol use in old age, problem drinking, treatment, health in old age, possible benefits of alcoholic beverages, and the effects of wine on elderly people who are self-sufficient. An appendix on "Research Methodology by Phase" has been included, as has a summary and recommendations.

388.   Nellis, Muriel. **The Female Fix.** Boston: Houghton Mifflin Co., 1980. 212p. $8.95. LC 79-23971. ISBN 0-395-27786-8.

The author of this book is well-qualified to write it; she has directed the National Alliance of Regional Coalitions: Drugs, Alcohol, and Women's Health, and has served on the President's Commission on Mental Health. She examines the experiences of women that make them vulnerable to treatment by drugs, treatments that often involve overuse, overprescribing, and perhaps even addiction to mind-altering substances. Three-quarters of all the prescriptions written for such drugs are written for women.

The following are the chapter titles: 1) The unadmitted problem, 2) Valium for the lump in your throat, 3) The unprepared mother, 4) Working women, 5) Her husband's career, 6) The older woman, 7) Male doctors, female patients, 8) The drugs and how they work, 9) The big mood-altering business, 10) The search for help, and 11) Finding yourself without drugs.

Nellis blames a number of groups for the tragedies of women caught in the "female fix." This includes society in general, the health care system, physicians, medical schools, and pharmaceutical companies. Each chapter contains a case history or two that illustrate the problem discussed. Appended is a good section on "Where to Find Help." There are lists of state programs, treatment resources, and self-help organizations.

In general, the work is well done, although there is some tendency to blame others when women themselves have used poor judgment. There is little doubt, though, that women especially need better medical counseling where prescription drugs of this kind and alcohol are concerned.

389.   Ostrea, Enrique M., Jr., with Cleofe J. Chavez, and Joan C. Stryker. **The Care of the Drug Dependent Pregnant Woman and Her Infant**. Lansing, MI: Department of Public Health, 1978. 83p. bibliog. index. $2.00pa.

The aim of this book is to consolidate available information concerning the special problems of pregnant women who are drug dependent and to make recommendations on the care of the woman and her infant.

The work is in four sections: 1) The drug dependent woman during pregnancy, 2) Neonatal addiction to narcotic drugs, 3) Neonatal addiction to non-narcotic drugs (hypnosedatives and alcohol), and 4) The prognosis of infants of drug dependent women (long-term outcome).

Drug dependent women are not as fertile as nonaddict women, and when pregnancy does occur medical and obstetrical problems are frequent. The authors believe that with proper guidance and supervision, addicted mothers are able to provide reasonable care for their infants. However, a long followup is required to be positive of this. More deaths, medical problems, and symptoms of child abuse are found among these infants, particularly when the mothers exclusively care for the children.

390.   Petersen, David M., Frank J. Whittington, and Barbara P. Payne, eds. **Drugs and the Elderly: Social and Pharmacological Issues**. With a Foreword by Peter G. Bourne. Springfield, IL: Charles C. Thomas, 1979. 255p. bibliog. index. $23.75. LC 77-17617. ISBN 0-398-03758-2.

This work is based on a Conference on Drugs and the Elderly held at Georgia State University in February 1975. Experts, a number of them from Georgia, with a wide range of backgrounds contributed the papers. The fields of medicine, psychiatry, pharmacology, pharmacy, sociology, social work, the ministry, and nursing home administration were represented. The book is primarily for the professional practitioner, although the academician will find it of value for courses in gerontology and drug abuse.

The Foreword points out that drug use has usually been considered a youth phenomenon. This is misleading as most of the 50 million people who use some kind of psychoactive drug on a regular basis do so under medical guidance and have some degree of legitimate use for them. Older people consume disproportionately more of all kinds of drugs than the rest of the population.

The 14 papers are presented in three sections. Section 1, "Perspectives on Elderly Drug Use," includes an overview of the problem, a survey of the existing literature, and papers on alcohol and the elderly and on acute drug reactions. Section 2, "Pharmacology, Pharmacy, and the Elderly Patients," includes papers on side effects and drug interactions in the elderly, pharmaceutical services available, self-medication problems, and drug misuse in nursing homes. Section 3, "Clinical and Community Response to Elderly Drug Use," presents papers on the appropriate responsibility of health care professionals, strategies for educating the elderly drug user, and social concerns.

The book presents a good comprehensive overview of the field, a matter of growing concern.

391.   Rementeria, Jose Luis, ed. **Drug Abuse in Pregnancy and Neonatal Effects.** St. Louis, MO: C. V. Mosby Co., 1977. 299p. illus. bibliog. index. $18.95. LC 77-3541. ISBN 0-8016-4108-X.

This is a timely, welcome work as it is becoming increasingly evident that drug abuse, or even use, by pregnant women may have ill effects on their infants. Further, the neonatal mortality rate in the babies of addicted mothers is approximately four times the average. Twenty chapters are provided by 35 contributors who are well-known authorities in various aspects of the subject; those contributors include pediatricians, gynecologists, obstetricians, pharmacologists, social workers, psychiatrists, and public health workers. Many of the chapters contain reports of original work as well as a review of the literature. There is some overlap (and some differing opinions) included, but the subject is covered comprehensively and in depth.

The presentations are grouped in five sections as follows: 1) The pregnant drug addict, 2) The infant of the drug-addicted mother, 3) Drug abuse in pregnancy with agents other than narcotics, 4) Pharmacologic aspects: various problems, and 5) The social aspects. Topics such as the following are covered: the fetal alcohol syndrome, the infant in withdrawal, sudden infant death syndrome, late complications in passively addicted infants, the effect of prenatal exposure to narcotics on the central nervous system, teratogenic aspects, and drug abuse and the law.

The work should be of considerable value to many—physicians, nurses, psychologists, social workers, legislators, drug counselors, and students.

392.   Robe, Lucy Barry. **Just So It's Healthy: New Evidence that Drinking Can Harm Your Unborn Baby.** Minneapolis, MN: CompCare Publications, 1977. 96p. bibliog. $2.75pa. ISBN 0-89638-099-2.

This concise book contains summarized information on the hazardous effects of alcohol and other chemicals on fetal development. This is a problem that is receiving growing attention. Fetal alcohol syndrome is said to be the third most common neurological birth defect. Even moderate drinkers may have infants with the condition.

In addition to the emphasis on alcohol, the book lists other drugs such as antibiotics, antihistamines, hormones, sedatives, amphetamines, tranquilizers, aspirin, antacids, laxatives, vitamins, and nasal sprays indicating damage their use may cause.

The book has been well-received and has frequently been recommended for medical and nursing students, health professionals, and health classes, as well as for pregnant women.

393.   Sandmaier, Marian. **The Invisible Alcoholics: Women and Alcohol Abuse in America**. New York: McGraw-Hill, 1980. 298p. bibliog. index. $12.95. LC 79-17819. ISBN 0-07-054660-6.

The primary purpose of this book is to show that women's alcohol problems cannot be treated like men's; they must be understood within the context of the social conditions of women's lives. Links are found between women's social roles and all aspects of their alcohol problems. The author's views are based on a review of available literature and interviews with various groups: teenage girls, minority women, business-women, housewives, lesbians, and Skid Row women. Some of the interviews have been recorded to illustrate similarities and differences in women's drinking experiences.

The author attempts to show why women drink, what treatments work and what do not, and why women alcoholics experience more depression, polydrug addiction, and suicide than men alcoholics.

There are chapters that focus on women's special needs in treatment. In addition, there is a special chapter that traces the history of societal attitudes toward women's drinking from classical Greece to today. Although attitudes are changing, the prevailing trend has been to stigmatize and punish heavy drinking women rather than help them. These attitudes affect women's dealing with men, marriage, sex, children, job, and help systems. The latter are likely to be inadequate for her needs.

The book has some self-help elements: there is a chapter on getting help for a drinking problem, and it identifies helping organizations and information sources.

394.   Snyder, Charles R. **Alcohol and the Jews: A Cultural Study of Drinking and Sobriety**. Glencoe, IL: The Free Press, 1958. 226p. bibliog. index. LC 57-6760.

This classic work was republished in 1978 by the Southern Illinois University Press with a new short preface. The Yale Center of Alcohol Studies sponsored the original edition.

The book covers in depth the use of alcohol by Jews. It conceptualizes a wide variety of data based upon research into the ancient documents of Judaism, demographic sources, personal interviews, and group interviews. In addition, it ties these abstract research processes to practical questions associated with problem drinking.

At the time the book was written there was evidence to show that among Jews drinking problems were low. (Whether this is still true is not clear.)

Chapter headings are as follows: 1) Problem and approach, 2) Jewish drinking patterns, 3) Ceremonial orthodoxy, 4) Regional background, generation and class, 5) Ingroup-outgroup relations, and 6) Signs of alcoholism. Appended is the text of a sample interview.

The quality of the research reported is high. However, the reissued edition of the work has been criticized because it does not bring the subject up to date and does not report on research to show whether or not problem drinking among Jews has increased as they have become assimilated and have moved up the ladder of success.

395.   U.S. Alcohol, Drug Abuse, and Mental Health Administration. **Shattering Sex Role Stereotypes . . . Foundations for Growth**. Washington: GPO, 1977. 50p. bibliog. [DHEW Publication No. (ADM) 77-570.] $2.25pa. S/N 017-024-00688-2.

Alcohol and drug abuse are considered along with other issues in this packet of 25 two-page summaries dealing with women's psychological problems that emerge from sex role stereotyping.

A comparison is made between the traditional view of sex roles and a new perspective. The new perspective suggests that there are sex differences on some traits, but there is considerable overlap. Psychological differences are biologically based in part, but are nonetheless highly trainable and influenced by environment. Recent research on the matter is outlined and literature references given, as are names and addresses of researchers to contact in regard to the various new findings.

This is a very good material.

396.   U.S. Bureau of Alcohol, Tobacco, and Firearms. **The Fetal Alcohol Syndrome: Public Awareness Campaign. Progress Report Concerning the Advance Notice of Proposed Rulemaking on Warning Labels on Containers of Alcoholic Beverages and Addendum.** Washington: GPO, 1979. 254p. bibliog.

This document consists of the text of the progress report regarding a public awareness campaign on the fetal alcohol syndrome and a much longer addendum that presents scientific reports and comments on the possible dangers that alcohol consumption by pregnant women has on the unborn child.

The bureau concluded that there is a need for public awareness about the fetal alcohol syndrome. It was less clear about how to educate the public, but the bureau decided to encourage the alcoholic beverage industry to work with the government and private interest groups to this end. If this does not prove successful, it will reconsider the proposal to require warning labels on alcoholic beverage containers.

397.   U.S. National Clearinghouse for Alcohol Information. **Alcohol Programs for Women: Issues, Strategies and Resources.** By Marian Sandmaier. Washington: GPO, 1977. 26p. bibliog.

The author of this manual takes the position that drinking problems of women have been neglected in the past, but that recently awareness of the special problems involved has grown. Guidance is given in the publication for developing prevention and treatment programs for women. Groups such as community task forces, women's centers, volunteer organizations, and professional program planners will find the work of value.

The following sections are included: 1) Introduction, 2) Women and alcohol: the issues, 3) Treatment programs for women, 4) Prevention/education programs for women, 5) Funding your program, and 6) Resources.

The last section contains some useful lists as follows: 1) Program development and funding resources, 2) Alcohol organizations and agencies: local and regional, 3) Alcohol organization and agencies: national, 4) Women's organizations/centers, 5) Women's alcohol programs, 6) Organizing tools for women, and 7) Bibliographies: women, alcohol and health.

398.   U.S. National Institute on Alcohol Abuse and Alcoholism. **Alcoholism Treatment and Black Americans.** By Frederick D. Harper. Washington: GPO, 1979. 124p. bibliog. [DHEW Publication No. (ADM) 79-853.] S/N 017-024-00967-9.

This report summarizes three workshops held in April 1978 by the National Institute on Alcohol Abuse and Alcoholism. It is hoped that the report will increase public awareness of alcohol problems in the black community. Major areas of clinical, management, funding, and related concerns were identified.

There is a review and analysis of the literature on alcohol use and alcohol treatment and blacks. Then the three workshops as follows are summarized and discussed: 1) Black alcoholism programs, 2) Predominantly white alcoholism programs, and 3) Organizations, institutions, and agencies with an interest in black alcoholism. The publication concludes with an analysis and recommendations.

399.   U.S. National Institute on Drug Abuse. **The Aging Process and Psychoactive Drug Use.** Washington: GPO, 1979. 91p. bibliog. [DHEW Publication No. (ADM) 79-813; Services Research Monograph Series.] S/N 017-024-00866-4.
        Three separate reports of research involving drug misuse by the elderly constitute this monograph. The first study, "The Aging Process and Psychoactive Drug Use in Clinical Treatment," examines the literature on the physiological and psychological changes attendant to the aging process and the relationship of these changes to drug use. The second report, "Patterns of Psychoactive Drug Use among the Elderly," reflects the difficulties of dealing with this topic. Findings of available research do not show a substantial problem of drug abuse by the elderly, but they are a major group in the consumption of psychoactive drugs. It is felt that a closer examination of the problem is needed. The third study, "Psychoactive Drug Misuse among the Elderly: A Review of Prevention and Treatment Programs," seeks to identify operating programs that deal with drug abuse by the elderly. There are few.
        Two appendices are included: 1) Researchers involved in psychoactive drug use by the elderly, and 2) Programs specifically designed to intervene in psychoactive drug misuse/abuse by the elderly. In addition, there are literature references with each report and two general bibliographies, one well-annotated.

400.   U.S. National Institute on Drug Abuse. **Drugs and Minorities.** Edited by Gregory A. Austin, Bruce D. Johnson, Eleanor E. Carroll, and Dan J. Lettieri. Washington: GPO, 1977. 210p. index [DHEW Publication No. (ADM) 78-507; NIDA Research Issues No. 21.] S/N 017-024-00745-5.
        This volume contains summaries of the latest research that focuses on the extent of drug abuse among racial and ethnic minorities and the factors influencing it. Much of the research conducted in the last 15 years is brought together, making it possible to compare and examine studies critically. Studies dealing with the ritual use of peyote among American Indians have been excluded.
        The summaries section is in two parts, multi-drug and opiates. In each of the 90 entries the literature reference is given, then a table giving drug name, sample size, sample type, age, sex, ethnicity, geographic area, methodology, data collection instrument, dates conducted, and number of references. Also included are statements of purpose, methodology, and results and conclusions.

401.   U.S. National Institute on Drug Abuse. **Multicultural Perspectives on Drug Abuse and Its Prevention: A Resource Book.** By Louisa Messolonghites. Washington: GPO, 1979. 149p. bibliog. [DHEW Publication No. (ADM) 78-671.] $4.00pa. S/N 017-024-00887-7.
        The first part of this presentation, "Perspectives," examines drug and alcohol abuse among minority group members. Native Americans, Asian American and Pacific Islanders, black Americans, Mexican Americans, Puerto Ricans, children and youth, and women are considered. A group called the "Invulnerables" also is discussed, young people living in mean social and economic environments who, despite stressful lives, are healthy and stable.
        The second section of the book is an information and education resource guide. There are bibliographies on, for, and about cultural and ethnic groups; also listed are multimedia materials, children's folklore, Spanish-language material, and

periodicals about drugs. In addition, a list of publishers and booksellers, and federal and other sources of information is included.

402.　　U.S. National Institute on Drug Abuse. **A Study of Legal Drug Use by Older Americans.** By David Guttmann. Washington: GPO, 1977. 14p. bibliog. (DHEW Publication No. 78-495; formerly 77-495; Services Research Report.) $0.90pa.

This study was conducted to explore patterns of behavior and problems associated with the medical and nonmedical use of drugs by older Americans. Use of prescription (ethical) and over-the-counter drugs and alcohol were investigated. A rather thorough study of the subject was made.

One of the major findings was that there are specific demographic and psychosocial variables associated with the older individuals who use or refrain from using ethical and over-the-counter drugs. Patterns of legal use vary according to marital status, sex, age, living arrangements, and self-perception. Ethical drugs are used heavily by the respondents, and most heavily by elderly women who are living alone and not married. Another finding was that the great majority use legal drugs appropriately, although a danger may exist in the use of drugs in combination. Finally, more and better information needs to be developed on the legal drug-taking behavior of older Americans.

The report is of special interest because it deals with a problem of growing concern.

403.　　U.S. National Institute on Drug Abuse. **A Woman's Choice: Deciding About Drugs.** Sponsored by the Task Force on Women. Washington: GPO, 1979. 28p. illus. bibliog. [DHEW Publication No. (ADM) 79-820.] S/N 017-024-00867-2.

Written to help women deal with stress in the modern world, this unique pamphlet begins by pointing out the times in a woman's life that may be particularly stressful and indicates alternatives to drug use for handling the problems. Brief information is included on the effects of commonly misused drugs. Also included are lists of organizations and state agencies that have programs of assistance to women.

The presentation is brief but well done.

404.　　U.S. National Institute on Drug Abuse. Division of Resource Development. Services Research Branch, and Center of Comprehensive Health Practice, New York Medical College. **Symposium on Comprehensive Health Care for Addicted Families and Their Children; May 20 and 21, 1976.** Compiled and edited by George Beschner, and Richard Brotman. Washington: GPO, 1977. 122p. bibliog. [Services Research Report; DHEW Publication No. (ADM) 77-480.] S/N 017-024-00598-3.

This symposium was organized to bring together investigators who were working with the problem of maternal and neonatal narcotic addiction. The aim was to share findings, experiences, and problems. Also, more appropriate methods and means of transmitting newly gained information were sought. The publication contains introductory material and 12 research papers.

Despite the recent overall reduction in the birth rate in the United States, there has been an increase in the number of births to drug-addicted mothers. Children born to such mothers experience more physiological problems and higher mortality rates than children born to nonaddicted mothers from the same socioeconomic class.

405.　　Youcha, Geraldine. **A Dangerous Pleasure.** New York: Hawthorn Books, 1978. 251p. bibliog. index. $10.95. LC 78-53486. ISBN 0-8015-1922-5.

This work examines the use of alcohol by women and provides information on the problems it creates. The author, who is a journalist, has pulled together research, opinion, and experiences to present a view of the problem female drinker. Areas covered include: drinking habits, physiological effects, women alcoholics, alcohol and the family, pregnancy and alcohol, and treatment. Controversial areas and proven concerns are both mentioned. The appendix provides a guide to sensible alcohol use, a checklist on alcohol use, and sources of treatment and information.

This well-written book is intended for laymen, but it might also be useful for social workers, nurses, and other health professionals seeking a synthesis of the subject.

12

PSYCHO-SOCIAL ASPECTS

The major portion of the books listed in this section are concerned with the use of alcohol. Many deal with the lifestyles and behavior of heavy users of the substance. The titles by Marshall and Moore (entries 414 and 416) present views of alcohol use in other cultures. There are titles on such matters as family problems and suicide and their relation to substance abuse. A somewhat unique publication is Bylinsky's book on mood control by drugs (entry 408). Another unusual work is *Theories on Drug Abuse*, issued by the U.S. National Institute on Drug Abuse (entry 423).

Titles dealing more specifically with social policy and law are listed in the following section.

406.   Archard, Peter. **Vagrancy, Alcoholism, and Social Control.** New York: Macmillan Publishing Co., 1979. bibliog. index. (Critical Criminology Series.) ISBN 0-333-23190-2; 0-333-23191-9 pa.

This research study looks into the life style of homeless alcoholics and society's reaction to the skid row inhabitant. Attention is focused on the social relationships among alcoholics and their guardians. While it has been said that skid row is a phenomenon peculiar to the United States, this is not true, according to Archard, who is writing here about Great Britain. Similar institutions, men, and life styles exist in Britain, although they are not ecologically concentrated as in the United States; rather, they are spread intermittently or are located in small pockets within working class and commercial districts.

The following are the chapter titles and subheadings: 1) Skid row in Great Britain (society's response to the skid row alcoholic), 2) Perspectives on skid row, (researchers and participants define the alcoholic and his situation), 3) Strategies of survival (the alcoholic makes out on skid row), 4) Drinking schools (the social organisation or drinking on skid row), 5) The penal revolving door (interaction in the world of law enforcement), 6) The rehabilitation network (interaction in the world of treatment), 7) Social policy and the skid row alcoholic (the rediscovery of a social problem), 8) Vagrant alcoholics and their guardians (skid row as social interaction), and 9) Research perspective and method (an outline and critical commentary).

This is an interesting, well-documented sociological study, although a good deal of the material is difficult to comprehend. The conversations with skid row individuals contain British slang unfamiliar to Americans. In addition, much of the terminology of the field is difficult for the general reader.

407.   Blumberg, Leonard U., Thomas E. Shipley, Jr., and Stephen F. Barsky. **Liquor and Poverty: Skid Row as a Human Condition**. New Brunswick, NJ: Rutgers Center of Alcohol Studies, 1978. 289p. bibliog. index. (Rutgers Center of Alcohol Studies, Monograph No. 13.) $14.00. LC 76-620080. ISBN 911290-46X.

This book casts skid row in a somewhat new light. It compares the Philadelphia skid rows with those of other places (Detroit and San Francisco), documents the history of their development, and concludes that skid row is not really a place but a human condition. It is a lifestyle found particularly among those who are poor and who are alcoholics.

The work is presented in three parts: 1) The origins of skid row, 2) Where will skid row move? and 3) Skid-row-like people.

The book identifies several sources of possible skid row residents, but has emphasized the ways that skid row as a social institution interacts with the larger society. Recommendations are made on how to bring skid row, its residents, and skid-row-like people into the normal political and social mainstream.

408.   Bylinsky, Gene. **Mood Control**. New York: Charles Scribner's Sons, 1979. 169p. index. $9.95. LC 78-929. ISBN 0-684-15586-9.

Selections from this work have appeared in *Fortune* magazine in a slightly different form. The author's view is that drug technology is moving very rapidly, and chemical modification of behavior may soon become so commonplace that we are on the edge of a choose-your-mood society. He has drawn heavily from studies into the workings of the nervous system in such fields as depression, longevity, control of anger, improvement of memory, cognition, and cure of impotence and enhancement of sex.

In conclusion, Bylinsky says that the capacity to control emotions and behavior is already here. The question is, how far we want to carry behavior and mood control with drugs. He concedes that there are obvious opportunities for misuse of such drugs, and he points to the controversy mood-control drugs have produced. However, he believes that, guided into constructive channels, advances in mood and mind control can lead one to a happier, fuller life by enhancing emotions and sharpening capabilities.

409.   Coltoff, Philip, and Allan Luks. **Preventing Child Maltreatment: Begin with the Parent. An Early Warning System**. New York: The Children's Aid Society and The New York City Affiliate, Inc., National Council on Alcoholism, 1978. 53p. bibliog.

This report points out the close association between child abuse and alcoholism and other "warning signs." The problem is identified and solutions sought. The data collected in this study suggests that many cases of child abuse and neglect could be prevented if staffs of government and nonprofit agencies were trained to identify and deal with parents who have problems with their children. The incidence of child abuse and neglect is not explored; the focus is instead on the way institutions deal with clients who show signs of problems.

Included is a course outline that should help the human service worker. Recommendations are given, parent interview procedures outlined, and sample questionnaires provided. The publication will be of most value to the many workers in institutions who come in contact with the victim.

410.   Coombs, Robert H., Lincoln J. Fry, and Patricia G. Lewis, eds. **Socialization in Drug Abuse**. Cambridge, MA: Schenkman Publishing Co., 1976. 478p. bibliog. $11.25. LC 75-37067. ISBN 87073-488-1; 87073-489-X pa.

This work comprises a collection of articles selected to represent published materials dealing with the socialization of the drug abuser and to illustrate a conceptual model which may provide a basis for new approaches to the drug abuse problem. The editors feel the assumption commonly held about drug abuse is that it is primarily a product of underlying emotional pathology; hence the addict is treated as a "patient." In their judgment such an assumption misses the point. The addict's life, they say, requires a great deal of personal resourcefulness, ingenuity, motivation, and hard work. Also, drug abusers usually find purpose and meaning in their lives. (They allow that drug abuse is a destructive activity, however.) The model proposed in the book suggests that drug abuse is a "social career" into which persons are recruited, learn roles, and rise in status as they achieve success according to the values of this social system.

The articles are presented under three section headings: 1) Preconditions affecting drug abuse, 2) Developmental stages in drug careers, and 3) Implications for the future.

The hope of the editors is that insights and perspectives gained from their approach will stimulate new methods of dealing with drug abusers, provide acceptable responses to their personal needs, and serve as a basis for public policy and institutional approaches to the drug problem.

411.   Gottheil, Edward, A. Thomas McLellan, and Keith A. Druley, eds. **Substance Abuse and Psychiatric Illness.** Proceedings of the Second Annual Coatsville-Jefferson Conference on Addiction. New York: Pergamon Press, 1980. 210p. illus. bibliog. index. $25.00. LC 79-25407. ISBN 0-08-025547-7.

The 1978 conference represented in this volume was intended as a forum for the discussion of issues involving concurrent psychiatric and substance abuse disorders.

The book presents papers on the conceptualization of the problems, clinical experiences, directions for clinical approaches and research, and practical aspects of treatment. Specific topics covered include: psychopathology and substance abuse, problem drinking in psychiatric hospitals, psychiatric illnesses of alcoholics, drug addiction and psychiatric illnesses, and the use of psychotropic medication in the treatment of drug abuse. A case study of a concurrent psychiatric and substance abuse disorder is also included.

412.   Lettieri, Dan J., ed. **Drugs and Suicide: When Other Coping Strategies Fail.** Beverly Hills, CA: Sage Publications, 1978. 303p. bibliog. index. (Sage Annual Reviews of Drug and Alcohol Abuse, v. 2.) $18.50; $7.95pa. ISBN 0-8039-1037-1; 0-8039-1038-X pa.

The contributors to this volume approach behaviors such as drug abuse, alcoholism, and suicide as life-sustaining or life-enhancing activities for those who are unable to cope with the stresses of their lives. The work is of particular value to psychiatrists, social workers, psychologists, and sociologists.

The 12 chapters are presented in four sections: Perspectives and theoretical orientations, Behavioral and symptomatic alternatives, Research strategy, and Social issues. Chapter titles are as follows: 1) Theories of suicide, 2) Theories of drug abuse, 3) Gambling with death, 4) Self-attitudes and multiple modes of deviance, 5) Prostitution and drug use as a means of coping with underlying psychodynamic conflict, 6) Stigma, interpersonal relationships, and information control: a coping equilibrium, 7) Sensation seeking and drug use, 8) Suicide and drug abuse, 9) Self-destruction: suicide and drugs, 10) Single organism research and the representative case method, 11) Use of licit drugs and other coping alternatives, and 12) Pot and pills: toys or therapy?

The papers focus on various apsects of what is called the "symptom" theory, which essentially accepts that individuals have certain native givens, but that these are easily transmutable potentialities, and do not firmly shape themselves into clear syndromes. Addiction, suicide, prostitution, etc., are all alternative behaviors.

413.   Marshall, Mac. **Weekend Warriors: Alcohol in a Micronesian Culture.** Palo Alto, CA: Mayfield Publishing Co., 1979. 170p. illus. bibliog. index. (Exploration in World Ethnology.) $4.95pa. LC 78-64597. ISBN 0-87484-455-X.

The Preface of this work points out that during the nineteenth century the inhabitants of the island of Truk acquired a reputation for ferocity and bravery in their dealings with outsiders. By the early twentieth century the German colonial government caused the Trukese to surrender firearms and cease all warfare. At the present time, young Trukese males have once again acquired a reputation for ferocity and bravery, this time in drunken brawls with each other.

The purpose of this book, which is an ethnological study by an anthropologist, is to examine contemporary Trukese drinking behavior. The idea is developed that today's drunkenness, and its associated violence, is a present-day substitute for the traditional warfare. The author concerns himself with the way traditional beliefs allow behavior that would be unacceptable in society if it were not carried out under the influence of alcohol.

The women of Truk behave in a manner opposite to the men. The males are assertive, take risks, smoke, and drink. Women are subservient, remain in the home, look after the family, and are guardians of the drunks. Alcohol enables the men to build a public reputation in keeping with basic Trukese values. The male is looked upon as superior. (It is interesting to note, however, that personality tests administered by outside researchers showed that the men were notably more anxious than women and would tend to respond less adequately in any situation of conflict or doubt.)

The work concludes with the comment that Americans who come to Truk have been blind to the fact that they tend to judge the young Trukese men by alien standards. If alcohol treatment programs are to be successful, account must be taken of Micronesian customs and values.

414.   Marshall, Mac, ed. **Beliefs, Behaviors, and Alcoholic Beverages: A Cross-Cultural Survey.** Ann Arbor, MI: University of Michigan Press, 1979. 490p. bibliog. $7.95pa. LC 78-31552. ISBN 0-472-08580-8.

The compiler of this collection of articles, a professor of anthropology, feels that this volume fills a gap in the social science literature on alcohol use and abuse around the world. Most of the contributions were written since 1965, and more than half since 1970. The hope is that the book will serve as a sourcebook for students and professionals. The material shows how cultural factors define and limit the attitudes, values, and behaviors that accompany drinking.

Marshall's introduction reviews the available literature on the subject. His view is that in order to solve the complicated riddle of alcoholism, studies of the great variety of drinking beliefs and behaviors within and across cultural boundaries must be made as well as studies of the biomedical and psychological aspects.

The articles are arranged under the following headings: 1) Overview of alcohol studies and anthropology, 2) Alcohol use in Mesoamerica, Latin America, and the Caribbean, 3) Alcohol use by North American Indians, 4) Alcohol use in the Pacific Islands, 5) Alcohol in Asia, 6) Africans and alcohol, and 7) Alcohol use in Euro-American societies.

The editor has provided a final chapter of conclusions, which presents some important and well-thought-out generalizations about alcohol and humanity based on the articles in the book. A bibliography of 32 pages is appended. This is an outstanding book.

415.   Miles, C. G., ed. **Experimentation in Controlled Environment: Its Implications for Economic Behaviour and Social Policy Making.** S. L. Lambert, general editor. Toronto: Alcoholism and Drug Addiction Foundation of Ontario, 1975. 170p. bibliog. index. $9.00; $6.00pa. ISBN 0-88868-010-4.

The papers presented in this symposium volume examine the effects of chronic cannabis smoking, and to some extent alcohol use, on human subjects in such areas as social, economic, psychological, and spending and saving behavior. The researchers who presented the papers represent a number of fields: experimental psychology, economics, psychiatry, statistics, ecology, architecture, clinical psychology, pharmacology, animal behavior, and anthropology. An important new interdisciplinary approach was created by the participants, which could be called behavioral economics.

One of the main thrusts of the research reported was to create as natural a controlled environment as possible and to reproduce experimentally the "amotivational syndrome" in "normal" cannabis smokers. Results of some of the studies showed that use of cannabis resulted in lower productivity; reduction of the intake raised productivity. Some indications of "amotivational syndrome" were found present, but no evidence of physiological damage was yielded by medical examinations, at least with short-term use.

Titles of the papers are as follows: 1) An experimental study of the effects of daily cannabis smoking on behaviour patterns, 2) Practical difficulties in the management of a micro-economy, 3) The effects of cannabis and negotiated wage rate changes on income and job performance in an experimental token economy, 4) Income, consumption and saving in controlled environments: further economic analysis, 5) Analysis of individual behaviour in controlled environments: an economist's perspective, 6) Methodological and conceptual issues in testing economic theory of consumer demand in a token economy, 7) Toward a behavioural ecosystems technology, 8) The microcosm of the mental hospital, 9) A programmed environment for the experimental analysis of individual and small group behaviour, 10) Research with Gibbons in a designed environment, and 11) What are the variables necessary for training environmental designers?

416.   Moore, Joan W. **Homeboys: Gangs, Drugs, and Prison in the Barrios of Los Angeles.** With Robert Garcia, and others. Philadelphia, PA: Temple University Press, 1978. 239p. bibliog. index. $15.00. LC 78-11808. ISBN 0-87722-121-9.

This book is one of a group of publications of the Chicano Pinto Research Project, which was funded in 1974-1975 by the National Science Foundation and the National Institute on Drug Abuse. The data on which the book is based came from that project.

Chicanos who serve sentences in California prisons tend to come from territorially-based youth gang backgrounds, and to have been imprisoned for offenses that involve narcotics. Called homeboys, they are the subject of this book. Slang terms are used regarding them: pinto, meaning convict or ex-convict; barrio, meaning the neighborhood and/or the gang; and tecato, meaning addict. The pinto-tecato-barrio subculture is suspicious of research, but its members collaborated with the academic group carrying out the Pinto Project.

The book begins with background information about Los Angeles and its Mexican American population. It then presents the issues of barrio life in terms of the ideas and viewpoints of participants. The gang members supplied much of the material. To them, their lives of community gangs, drug marketing structures, and prisoner structures were everyday, normal, and routine affairs. The Chicano gangs' involvement with drugs, both as users and dealers, is unlike that of other groups in other cities.

The book contains the following chapters: 1) The problem, 2) The Chicano gang in context, 3) Three barrio gangs, 4) Drugs and the barrios, 5) Prisons and the barrios, 6) Chicano self-help, 7) Square and deviant in the barrio, and 8) A policy for the barrios. Also, there are several appendices containing survey data.

The author concludes that in spite of the difficulties there are a great many reasons for optimism regarding the future of the Chicano gang members. Not all are deviants in their outlook. Further, prison self-help groups have been carried over into barrio social movements with very little help from traditional social agencies. New identities are being found. A measure of understanding from professionals is long overdue.

417.   Paolino, Thomas J., Jr., and Barbara S. McCrady. **The Alcoholic Marriage**: **Alternative Perspectives**. New York: Grune and Stratton, 1977. 211p. bibliog. index. $14.50. LC 77-14954. ISBN 0-8089-1024-8.

This is an important book for all who seek to understand the interrelationships of alcoholic men and their wives. The authors have dealt only with marriages in which the husband is an alcoholic and the wife is not, and the focus is on the married couple rather than on the family as a whole.

The authors very thoroughly explore the literature on alcoholic marriages. They attempt to establish "facts" about the marriages and to provide an understanding of the ways that have been and can be used to look at this and other clinical phenomena. Psychoanalytic theory, sociological stress theory, learning principles, and systems theory are all considered. Emphasis is placed on the necessity for researchers and clinicians to possess a knowledge of alternative orientations to this kind of problem. The concluding chapter deals with theoretical implications. Four major areas are discussed: 1) Entering treatment and motivation for treatment, 2) Assessment of the alcoholic marriage, 3) The delivery of treatment, and 4) The therapeutic relationship. A range of potential intervention strategies for therapists are suggested.

The book has been highly praised for its comprehensiveness of the literature review, its treatment of research methods, and its conceptualizations.

418.   Pittman, David J., and Charles R. Snyder, eds. **Society, Culture, and Drinking Patterns**. New York: John Wiley and Sons (Available from Southern Illinois University Press), 1962. 616p. bibliog. index. $6.95. LC 62-15188.

This widely read work has remained in print for a number of years. It collects under a single cover a wide selection of material reporting significant social science research on drinking patterns, normal and pathological. Major emphasis is on the work of sociologists, but also included are some studies in cultural anthropology and social psychology. Thirty-five chapters are presented. Twelve are excerpts or reprintings of previously published material, but the rest are original contributions written for this book.

The contributions are arranged in the following sections: 1) Drinking in anthropological perspective, 2) General observations on the modern setting, 3) Social structure, subcultures, and drinking patterns, 4) The genesis and patterning of alcoholism, and 5) Responsive movements and systems of control.

419.   Plant, Martin A. **Drinking Careers: Occupations, Drinking Habits, and Drinking Problems.** London: Tavistock Publications, 1979. 167p. bibliog. index. $22.00. ISBN 0-422-76590-2.

The primary concern of this work is the relationship between drinking habits of an individual and the social setting. Drinking habits and alcohol-related problems of two groups of Scottish male manual workers in "high-" and "low-risk" occupational settings and a follow-up study are presented. Results show that drinking patterns are associated with social or occupational group, and that the immediate social enrironment overshadows the influence of such factors as family background. Also it is shown that alcoholism is not a clear-cut illness, but the final stage of drinking behavior. However, problem drinking may not be permanent, and some drinkers resolve their own difficulties.

The first chapter summarizes the properties of alcohol, describes social aspects of drinking behavior, and defines alcoholism. Chapter 2 reviews the literature, which indicates that some occupational groups have unusually high rates of alcohol problems. Chapter 3 discusses the inadequacy of information available about drinking habits and alcoholism. Chapter 4 describes the study of the male workers. Chapters 5-7 describe the characteristics of the subjects as they move to new jobs, become unemployed, or move into different work situations. The last chapter reviews the empirical and theoretical implications of the results of the study. The interview schedules used are appended.

420.   Ray, Oakley. **Drugs, Society, and Human Behavior.** 2nd ed. St. Louis, MO: C. V. Mosby Co., 1978. 457p. bibliog. index. $9.50pa. LC 77-20660. ISBN 0-8016-4094-6.

This new edition of a 1972 book incorporates many new scientific and technical advances that have been made since that date and continues the historical perspective on the psychosocial issues that come about by changes in scientific knowledge and society. New topics covered oral contraceptives, drug education, and dealing with bad trips.

Like the first edition, there are seven parts on the following topics: Introduction and review; Fundamentals of the nervous system, neurotransmitters, general mechanism and drug actions, addiction, and the categories of drugs; The nondrug drugs (e.g., alcohol, nicotine, caffein, over-the-counter drugs, and oral contraceptives); Psychotherapeutic drugs; Narcotics; Phantasticants (hallucinogens); and the Conclusion, which is a rational look at drug use.

The author, who is a professor of psychology, has produced a book suitable as a text for courses designed to teach drug education. There are many literature references, tables, and figures to support the material presented. The major emphasis is on facts and themes that will enable the reader to reach a rational point of view on drug use. The last chapter contains the author's views on what determines and what is the extent of drug use, how safe drugs are, and what view society might take about the matter.

421.   Rubin, Vera, ed. **Cannabis and Culture.** The Hague: Mouton Publishers; distr., Aldine, 1975. 598p. illus. bibliog. index. (World Anthropology.) $24.95. ISBN 90-279-7669-4; 0-202-01152-6 (Aldine).

The papers in this volume were originally presented at a Conference on Cross-Cultural Perspectives on Cannabis, held in Chicago in 1973, during the Ninth International Congress of the International Union of Anthropological and Ethnological Sciences.

The papers help provide an understanding of the sociocultural differences in reactions to the ancient and widespread substance, cannabis. Also, the volume introduces new botanical classifications and presents data on clinical studies of cannabis users. Scientists from a number of disciplines participated—anthropologists, botanists, geneticists, pharmacologists, psychiatrists, and sociologists.

The 35 papers are arranged under the following section headings: 1) Ethnobotany and diffusion, 2) Sociocultural aspects of the traditional complex, 3) Medical, pharmacological and ethnometabolic studies, 4) Traditional usage of other psychoactive plants, and 5) The modern complex in North America. An abstract is included with each paper.

The work makes apparent the fact that psychoactive plants have been used for a variety of purposes in the world, secular as well as sacred, to serve a wide range of human needs, and that different emphases have been placed on the use of such substances in various cultures.

422.   U.S. National Institute on Drug Abuse. **Consequences of Alcohol and Marijuana Use: Survey Items for Perceived Assessment**. Edited by Joan Dunne Rittenhouse. Washington: GPO, 1979. 227p. bibliog. [DHEW Publication No. (ADM) 80-920.] $5.00pa. S/N 017-024-00971-7.

It has been established that millions of Americans currently use alcohol and marijuana, and the possible public health consequences are of growing concern. This monograph presents a strategy to measure perceived consequences and/or beliefs where abuse of these substances is concerned. A review of background research on the physiological and social-psychological consequences is included, and survey questionnaires are presented. A large number of literature references are included.

423.   U.S. National Institute on Drug Abuse. **Theories on Drug Abuse: Selected Contemporary Perspectives**. Edited by Dan J. Lettieri, Mollie Sayers, and Helen Wallenstein Pearson. Washington: GPO, 1980. 488p. bibliog. [DHHS Publication No. (ADM) 80-967; NIDA Research Monograph 30.] LC 80-600058.

There has been a striking upsurge in the models and theories attempting to explain the problems of drug abuse. In response to the need for a reference volume outlining these theories, this work was prepared. It presents 43 theoretical perspectives from the social and biomedical sciences.

The format of the book is somewhat unusual. The contributions, written by the theorists themselves, make up part 1 and are arranged under these headings: 1) Theories on one's relationship to self, 2) Theories on one's relationship to others, 3) Theories on one's relationship to society, and 4) Theories on one's relationship to nature. Part 2, "Theory Components," provides a brief working definition and classification of the theories. Five components were defined as follows: 1) Why people begin taking drugs, 2) Why they maintain their drug-taking behaviors, 3) How or why drug-taking behavior escalates to abuse, 4) Why or how people stop taking drugs, and 5) What accounts for the restarting of the drug dependence behavior or cycle once stopped. Also included are five "guides," which are charts or tables presenting condensed information: 1) A list of the theorists, 2) Theory classification, 3) Disciplinary foci of the theories, 4) Organization of the volume, and 5) Theory boundaries.

13

PRODUCTION, CONTROL, PUBLIC POLICY, AND LEGAL FACTORS

As is the case in the earlier bibliography, Andrews: *A Bibliography of Drug Abuse* (1977), there are a large number of titles in this section, attesting to the fact that control of drugs is still a major problem.

These specific subjects are dealt with here: drugs and their relation to crime; prosecution and defense of drug cases; effects of drug laws; illicit manufacture and trafficking in drugs; control of production and distribution of drugs (including international agreements); public policy regarding drug enforcement and treatment (including propaganda efforts); and drug use and highway safety.

Drug use is widespread and difficult to control. Some experts think relatively heavy usage is here to stay and that society should learn to live with it. A counter trend, however, against drug use is evident, and a shift in the value system is foreseen. Some groups (such as Alcoholics Anonymous) take the view that abusers must be helped or they will perish. It is of note that the dramatic rise in funding for drug abuse prevention a few years ago at the federal level has ended.

The emphasis of the publications in this area of the drug abuse field has never been on penalties for drug use. Treatment and understanding are still the foremost concerns. The real world, however, may be different.

424.   Baridon, Philip C. **Addiction, Crime, and Social Policy**. Lexington, MA: D. C. Heath and Co., 1976. 126p. bibliog. index. $14.00. LC 75-32221. ISBN 0-669-00342-5.

More than 60 years have passed since the non-medical use of opiates was made a criminal offense. This book attempts to analyze certain aspects of the relationship between addiction and crime. Reform in social policy is suggested.

The principal issues studied are as follows: 1) Is there a positive correlation between the price of opiates and crime?, 2) What is the addicts' personal response to spiraling drug costs?, 3) Is there evidence that our drug control policies are creating additional deviance?, 4) What is the role of age in the interdependence of addiction and crime?, 5) What is the nature and extent of preaddict crime?, and 6) What differences are there between addict and nonaddict crime?

The author's view, supported by the data presented in the book, is that the criminalization of opiate drug use has brought about the connection between crime and addiction. He points to the fact that the rate of addiction to opiates at the turn of the century (when use was legal) was the same as it is now. Although realizing that intense opposition to his proposal would result, he suggests that addicts should have inexpensive and unfettered access to opiates as they choose. In such a case the supportive subculture would gradually vanish and hopefully the number of dependent persons decline.

425.   **Basic Drug Manufacture: Easy to Follow Instructions for Synthesizing Cocaine-Mescaline-Psilocybin, LSD-DMT-MDA-STP-THC.** New York/Hermosa Beach, CA: High Times/Golden State Publishing, 1973. 32p. illus. bibliog. $2.00pa.

This booklet contains information on the procedures for producing the illegal drugs mentioned in the title. In addition, it includes information on the starting chemicals called for, such as toxicity and fire hazards, chemical and physical properties, legal risks, alternate uses, and advice on handling. Following are the chapter headings: 1) Introduction, 2) Mescaline, 3) MDA (3 methods), 4) STP, 5) LSD, 6) Psilocin and psilocybin, 7) DMT (dimethyltryptamine), 8) Cocaine, 9) THC, 10) Chemicals, 11) Obtaining chemicals, 12) Equipment, 13) Explanation of certain procedures, 14) Recrystallization using solvent pairs, and 15) Working with a catalyst.

The reviewer is somewhat skeptical that just anyone, without chemical background, could follow the instructions in this booklet and manufacture the drugs of abuse named. However, some are relatively easy to produce, evidently, because many of the starting materials have common uses, are readily available, and little further chemical manipulation is necessary. But attempted purchase of other chemicals called for is sure to draw the attention of authorities.

426.   Bernheim, David. **Defense of Narcotic Cases.** New York: Matthew Bender, 1972. 1 looseleaf v. $50.00. LC 72-89203. (Kept up to date with supplements and revisions.)

This publication is a practical work, intended primarily for the attorney giving legal advice or defense or serving on a public body dealing with the narcotic problem. Virtually every aspect of narcotic cases is covered. Many examples are drawn from real cases, and step-by-step help for difficult areas is provided. An exhaustive discussion of federal and many state laws is given. In addition, some special materials have been included such as a table "Drugs at a Glance," a glossary of addict jargon, and a national directory of drug abuse programs.

Partial contents includes the following: 1) Introduction, 2) Pretrial proceedings, 3) Motions to suppress illegally obtained evidence, 4) Identification of drugs, 5) The trial, 6) Alternatives to standing trial, 7) Drugs and addiction, 8) Compulsory commitment, 9) Defense of a narcotic addict.

The author is an authority on the defense of narcotic cases. He is a member of the New York Bar and is in private practice in New York City.

427.   Bonnie, Richard J., and Michael R. Sonnenreich, eds. **Legal Aspects of Drug Dependence.** Cleveland, OH: CRC Press, 1978. 367p. bibliog. index. $59.95. LC 74-28375. ISBN 0-87819-061-9.

Part of a series on various aspects of drug dependence, this book presents philosophical views of the legal structure and the drug user, the interrelationship between the legal system and treatment of drug dependence, and federal and state drug laws, and a discussion of new and future developments in legal and drug abuse interrelationships. The editors and contributors, who are attorneys, are well-known for their work in this field.

Most of the papers included have been extracted from other sources. Titles of the contributions are as follows: 1) Legal intervention and the drug user, 2) Reaching out: origins of the interventionist strategy, 3) Therapeutic justice, 4) The role of the law in treatment, 5) A legal history of the Narcotic Addict Rehabilitation Act of 1966, 6) Analysis of drug treatment laws in the 50 states and 5 territories, 7) Maintenance of opiate-dependent persons in the United States: a legal-medical history, 8) Confidentiality: the *Sine Qua Non* of a voluntary treatment strategy, 9) The Uniform Drug Dependence Treatment and Rehabilitation Act and commentary, and 10) A proposed federal drug dependence treatment and rehabilitation act.

428.   Bruun, Kettil, and others. **Alcohol Control Policies in Public Health Perspective.** A collaborative project of the Finnish Foundation for Alcohol Studies, the World Health Organization Regional Office for Europe, and the Addiction Research Foundation of Ontario. New Brunswick, NJ; distr., Rutgers University Center of Alcohol Studies, 1975. 106p. bibliog. (The Finnish Foundation for Alcohol Studies, v. 25.) $8.00pa. ISBN 951-9191-29-1; 951-9191-30-5 pa.

This report is the outcome of a collaborative project aimed at collecting information on and analyzing one neglected aspect of prevention of alcohol related problems, alcohol control policies and their relation to public health, Representatives of Finland, Canada, Norway, the United Kingdom, and the United States took part in the project. The report presented here is a position or "state-of-the-art" paper.

Chapter headings are as follows: 1) Introduction, 2) Heavy alcohol consumption and physical problems, 3) Consumption, heavy use and mortality in populations, 4) Alcohol statistics, 5) Trends in alcohol consumption and production, 6) Alcohol control policies, 7) International control, and 8) Conclusions. In addition, there are two appendices: 1) Abridged version of the questionnaire used in the inquiry on alcohol statistics, and 2) Areas of further inquiry.

The main argument of the report is that changes in the overall consumption of alcohol have a bearing on the health of people in any society. Alcohol control measures can be used to limit consumption; thus, control of alcohol availability becomes a public health issue. The final conclusions reached support this argument.

429.   Cochin, Joseph, and Louis Harris. **Synthetic Substitutes for Opiate Alkaloids: A Feasibility Study.** Washington: Drug Abuse Council, Inc., 1975. 77p. bibliog. $5.00pa. LC 75-8492.

The Bureau of Narcotics and Dangerous Drugs (later the Drug Enforcement Agency) asked the National Academy of Sciences to carry out the study reported in this publication. It was initiated at a time of national emergency—heroin addiction had reached nearly epidemic proportions.

Some felt that the banning of opium poppy growing would result in the elimination of "street" heroin. Further, it was believed that synthetic drugs existed which could be substituted for the opiates in clinical practice and that these drugs were much less likely to be illegally produced and abused.

The contents of the publication are as follows: 1) Introduction and scope, 2) Purpose of the study, 3) Recognized opiates and derivatives, 4) Therapeutic products synthesized from opiates, 5) Possible synthetic equivalents—current research, 6) Banning opium—possible consequences, and 7) Summary and conclusions. In addition, the following appendices are included: 1) Further documentation of morphine and certain congeners vs. synthetic analgetics with respect to pharmacology, side effects, and costs, 2) The need for opiates in medicine, 3) Stockpiling narcotics, and 4) Survey of drug prescribing patterns, a preliminary report by the American Medical Association.

In summary, the conclusions of the study are as follows: there is reason to believe that banning opium production would not significantly affect problems of narcotic abuse even if adequate substitutes for the opium-derived drugs were available; most of the synthetic analgesics also have potential for abuse, and there is no synthetic available as potent and efficacious as morphine.

430. Davis, Hamilton. **Mocking Justice: America's Biggest Drug Scandal.** New York: Crown Publishers, Inc., 1978. 242p. $8.95. LC 77-27370. ISBN 0-517-52895-9.

This book is the tale of a dishonest narcotics agent of St. Albans, Vermont, Paul Lawrence. Before he was brought to justice Lawrence evidently had framed a number of young people by reporting that they had made undercover narcotics sales to him. The sales were never made. The agent planted drugs that he got from an unknown source, and evidently kept the drug-buy money the authorities gave him to make the purchases.

The book is an interesting account of the curious dealings of Lawrence and of the officials who unraveled the case, which was a black mark against law enforcement generally.

431. Distilled Spirits Council of the United States, Inc. **The Beverage Alcohol Industry: Public Attitudes and Economic Progress. DISCUS Facts Book, 1978.** Washington: Distilled Spirits Council of the United States, Inc., 1979. 29p. illus. bibliog. Free. ISSN 0160-1504.

This annual publication is the 25th edition made available to researchers, educators, students, economists, and others seeking concise information and statistical data about the distilled spirits industry. Emphasis throughout the report is on the contribution made by the industry to economic growth; health, safety, and education issues associated with drinking; and civic concern and social responsibility.

The section headings are: 1) Foundations of an American industry, 2) Social attitudes and prevention, 3) Consistent economic benefits, 4) Patterns of price stability, 5) Consumer's tax burden, 6) Lethal rotgut, 7) Sound health approaches, 8) Economic outlook, 9) Materials available from DISCUS, and 10) Statistics.

432. Drug Abuse Council. **The Facts About "Drug Abuse."** New York: Free Press, a division of Macmillan Publishing Co., 1980. 291p. bibliog. $14.95. LC 79-54668. ISBN 0-02-907720-6.

The Drug Abuse Council that prepared this work was established in 1972 to provide independent analysis of public drug policies and programs. The book, called the final report, is one of the results of their efforts. The last formal meeting of the board of directors of the council was held in June 1978, and its operations are being phased out.

The publication being reviewed was undertaken because the council felt that society should be informed about the complexities of the issues and evidence surrounding the drug abuse problem in order to deal with it more constructively.

Following are some of the findings. Despite all the "get tough" views and strict legislation, use of psychoactive substances is greater than ever (although use of certain drugs, such as heroin, has declined). The emphasis on marijuana and cocaine use has shaped policies and opinions based on misconceptions. Alcohol and nicotine problems have been de-emphasized too much. Prohibiting the supply of one drug will result in increased use of another (such as alcohol, which is readily available). The use of psychoactive drugs is pervasive, but misuse is much less frequent. Adverse social conditions and drug abuse are highly correlated. Finally, Americans should not blame their drug abuse problems on the trafficking of foreign countries; our problems are peculiar to our own national experience. The problem will not yield to single or simplistic solutions or approaches. Local options rather than reliance on national drug policy is suggested.

The following are the chapter headings of the council staff contributions: 1) Federal government's response to illicit drugs, 1969-1978, 2) Drug-law enforcement efforts, 3) Heroin treatment: development, status, outlook, 4) The influence of public attitudes and understanding on drug education and prevention, 5) Marijuana and cocaine: the process of change in drug policy, and 6) American heroin policy: some alternatives. An appendix lists the activities of the Drug Abuse Council.

Perhaps the most significant aspect of the council's recommendations is their divergence from prevailing policies and attitudes regarding drug abuse.

433.   **The Effects of Alcoholic-Beverage Control Laws.** Washington: Medicine in the Public Interest, Inc., 1979. 96p. bibliog. $4.00pa. LC 79-51853.

This publication is a summary version of a two-volume report, *A Study in the Actual Effects of Alcoholic Beverage Control Laws,* a project carried out for the National Institute on Alcohol Abuse and Alcoholism. Written by Stuart M. Matlins, M. D. Greenberg, and R. J. Bonnie, it was published in 1975 and is available from the National Technical Information Service (PB-262-641/AS and PB-242-642/AS). The issuing body of the summary report hopes it will stimulate the interest and action needed to achieve a maximally effective alcoholic-beverage-control system in the United States.

The position of the NIAAA prior to the study was that the present system of alcoholic controls in the United States is a chaotic relic. It provides little support in mitigating alcohol problems and possibly induces a counterproductive ambivalence among the public. The two basic purposes of the study were as follows: 1) to determine relationship between the laws and the incidence, patterns, and circumstances of alcoholic-beverage consumption, and 2) to make recommendations that will assist in identifying changes that should be made in existing laws and regulations in order to discourage alcohol misuse.

The recommendations made relate to creating a climate that is amenable to the consideration of law change in general and those that relate to determining the specific direction the change should take, the specific policies needed to guide that change, and the specific laws and other activities required to implement it.

434.   Epstein, Edward Jay. **Agency of Fear: Opiates and Political Power in America.** New York: G. P. Putnam's Sons, 1977. bibliog. index. $9.95. LC 14443. ISBN 399-11656-7.

The author of this work, who writes popular articles for periodicals, takes the position that politicians have, since the turn of the century, summoned up the specter of "dope fiends" and drug addiction out of control in order to obtain votes for themselves or serve some other personal political end.

A number of government bureaus and well-known political figures are criticized. These include Richard Pearson Hobson, the Spanish-American War veteran and anti-drug crusader; Nelson Rockefeller, who is accused of inventing thousands of fictional junkies; and Richard Nixon who, among other misdeeds, is accused of attempting to provide a national secret police force responsible only to the White House.

Epstein's story and the points he makes are difficult to follow. The tangled tale of the Watergate scandal is woven into the account. Some of the evidence cited was obtained from Watergate figures.

Possibly the book offers illuminating insights into the use of drug abuse for political gain, and possibly some political figures have overreacted to the problem. However, the book is not entirely convincing. There is little reason to think that anyone would need to "invent" a drug problem. It has obviously been with us for some time. In addition, it does not seem logical to accuse political figures of exaggerating the illegal use of drugs. News media figures have a far better opportunity of doing that, and have done so in the recent past. The most sensational books on the subject of drug abuse written in the late 1960s were by journalists.

435. Erwin, Richard E., and Marilyn K. Minzer. **Defense of Drunk Driving Cases: Criminal–Civil**. 3rd ed. New York: Matthew Bender, 1971. 2 looseleaf v. $97.50. LC 72-166435. (Kept up to date with cumulative supplements and replacement pages.)

Originally published in 1963, this publication is a useful reference for the defense attorney and the prosecuting attorney as well. It is a source for the legal and scientific knowledge needed to protect clients. Included is material on motions to suppress, motions to strike prior conviction, pretrial discovery, suggestions on selecting a jury, facts on constitutional objections to self-incrimination, unlawful search and seizure, and a good collection of helpful charts, tables, photographs, and diagrams. In addition, material on instruments used to detect alcohol is presented in layman's terms.

436. Haberman, Paul W., and Michael M. Baden. **Alcohol, Other Drugs and Violent Death**. New York: Oxford University Press, 1978. 134p. illus. bibliog. index. $13.95. LC 78-2752. ISBN 0-19-502359-5.

This work deals with alcohol and narcotics abuse among adults who died unnaturally in New York City during a one-year period. A study was made of 1,954 cases investigated by the Chief Medical Examiner's Office. In the study there were more than 500 homicide victims, 300 suicides, about 400 fatalities in motor vehicle or other accidents, and over 600 who died directly of alcoholism and/or narcotism. Among the cases, about 600 were identified as alcoholics, over 300 as narcotic abusers, and some 200 as having both conditions.

Chapter headings of the book are as follows: 1) Highlights of study findings, 2) Background, 3) Classifying decedents as alcoholics and narcotics abusers, 4) Multiple drug use, 5) Suicides, homicides, and fatal accidents, 6) Familial drinking and drug-use problems, and 7) Implications and recommendations.

The study demonstrates the relationship between substance abuse and unnatural deaths. Alcohol and drugs not only contribute significantly to such deaths, but are obviously the most common underlying factor. In addition, patterns of substance abuse by decedents and their close relatives are interpreted.

The authors feel that drinking and drug problems are underreported in death records and that a new standard death certificate should be utilized which will reflect the contribution of alcohol and other drugs to the cause of death.

437. Hauge, Ragnar, ed. **Drinking and Driving in Scandinavia**. Oslo: Universitetsforlaget; distr., Columbia University Press, 1978. 143p. bibliog. (Scandinavian Studies in Criminology, v. 6; Scandinavian University Books.) $14.00. LC 79-305557.

The Scandinavian use of jail sentences for persons convicted of drinking and driving offenses has attracted attention, particularly among those who are interested in the deterring effect of such practices. All four Scandinavian countries are considered, and there are some differences in the situation among them. The history of the legal framework of each is summarized. Information on public opinion about the issue is provided, collected from opinion polls. It is interesting that in Denmark drunken driving is considered inexcusable, on the same level with rape. In Norway it is less acceptable than housebreaking and forgery. In Sweden it is worse than smuggling or burglary. It is of note, however, that some of the results of the polls are old, and opinion may be changing.

438.   International Narcotics Control Board, Geneva. **Comparative Statement of Estimates and Statistics on Narcotic Drugs for 1977 Furnished by Governments in Accordance with the International Treaties.** New York: United Nations, 1979. 41p. (E/INCB/45.) $3.00pa. Sales No. E/F/S.79.XI.3.

This publication contains preliminary remarks; an index of countries and territories; and a long table (No. XI) which lists substances covered by the international treaties, by country, and showing amounts available, amounts utilized, and the balance. Tables I-X are included each year in another document, *Statistics on Narcotic Drugs for [year] furnished by Governments in Accordance with the International Treaties and Maximum Levels of Opium Stocks* (*see* entry 441).

439.   International Narcotics Control Board, Vienna. **Estimated World Requirements of Narcotic Drugs in 1980.** Statement issued by the International Narcotics Control Board in accordance with the international treaties on narcotic drugs. New York: United Nations, 1979. 58p. index. (E/INCB/46.) $6.00pa. Sales No. E.80.XI.1.

This publication is a reference document for national administrations responsible for narcotic drug control and for international bodies concerned.

Included is a short introductory note and estimates of narcotic requirements for medical and scientific purposes, and world totals of estimated requirements of the narcotic drugs from 1975 to 1980. The bulk of the publication, however, is taken up by four comprehensive tables as follows: 1) Estimated world requirements of narcotic drugs in 1980, 2) Estimates of opium production for 1980, 3) Estimates of the cultivation of the opium poppy for purposes other than the harvesting of opium in 1980, and 4) Estimated manufacture of synthetic drugs in 1980. There is an index by country and non-metropolitan territories.

Monthly supplements to this annual document are issued which transmit to governments amendments made during the month prior to the publication date of each supplement.

440.   International Narcotics Control Board, Vienna. **Report of the International Narcotics Control Board for 1979.** New York: United Nations, 1979. 39p. (E/INCB/ 47.) $5.00pa. Sales No. E.80.XI.2.

This is the third annual report submitted by the International Narcotics Board. The responsibilities of this board under the drug control treaties are to endeavor to limit the cultivation, production, manufacture, and utilization of narcotic and psychotropic drugs to the amount needed for medical and scientific purposes only, to ensure that necessary quantities are available, and to prevent the illicit use of these substances. Governments are to provide the board with relevant information to enable it to perform its task.

This report contains sections on operation of the board, world requirements of opiates, developments in illicit traffic, and an analysis of the world situation, country by country.

441.   International Narcotics Control Board, Vienna. **Statistics on Narcotic Drugs for 1978 furnished by Governments in Accordance with the International Treaties and Maximum Levels of Opium Stocks.** New York: United Nations, 1980. 99p. (E/INCB/48.) $9.00pa. Sales No. E.80.XI.4.

The first section of this publication contains text material on trends in the licit movement of narcotic drugs. It is in two parts: the first on raw materials, their alkaloids and the derivatives of the alkaloids, and the second on synthetic narcotic drugs. Then follows tables containing the principal statistical information. For comparison, statistics for four previous years have been included.

Tables are headed as follows: 1) Opium production, 2) Manufacture of morphine, 3) Conversion of morphine, 4) Manufacture of the principal narcotic drugs other than morphine, 4a) Manufacture of narcotic drugs other than those specified in table 4, 5) Coca leaves: production and export declared by producing countries, 5a) Coca leaves: utilization for chewing, 6) Manufacture of cocaine, 7) Consumption of the principal narcotic drugs falling under the convention, 7a) Utilization of cocaine, codeine, dihydrocodeine, diphenoxylate, ethylmorphine, morphine and pholcodine in the manufacture of preparations of schedule III of the 1961 convention, 7b) Consumption of narcotic drugs other than those specified in table 7, 7c) Consumption of narcotic drugs, 8) Total stocks of opium, 9) World trade in 1978, and 10) Seizures of narcotic drugs in 1978.

The last section indicates maximum levels of opium stocks which countries may hold.

442.   International Narcotics Control Board, Vienna. **Statistics on Psychotropic Substances for 1978 furnished by Governments in Accordance with the Convention of 1971 on Psychotropic Substances and Resolution I of the United Nations Conference for the Adoption of a Protocol on Psychotropic Substances and Resolution 1576 (L) of the Economic and Social Council.** New York: United Nations, 1979. 89p. (E/INCB/49.) $10.00pa. Sales No. E/F/S.80.XI.3.

Psychoactive substances under international control are divided into four schedules. Practically all countries have schedule I drugs under control, and they are the least utilized. Schedule II drugs are under control in most countries, and are somewhat utilized. In regard to substances in schedules III and IV, the competent authorities do not control all the substances in these classes in many countries. Schedule IV drugs are most widely used, and they have not been brought under control in a large number of countries.

One hundred and twelve countries furnished statistics for this report, an update of a periodical publication. An introductory section lists the countries providing statistics and those that did not. The drugs are listed by schedule number, and information is given about their production, particularly comparisons with earlier figures. Then follows four comprehensive tables that contain information about the drugs in each of the schedules, such as movement in manufacturing countries and international trade, by country and date.

Some of the material appears in French and Spanish as well as in English.

443.   **International Statistics on Alcoholic Beverages: Production, Trade and Consumption 1950-1972.** A collaborative project of the Finnish Foundation for Alcohol Studies and the World Health Organization Regional Office for Europe. Helsinki: Finnish Foundation for Alcohol Studies, 1977. 231p. bibliog. (The Finnish Foundation for Alcohol Studies, v. 27.) ISBN 951-9191-45-3; 951-9191-46-1 pa.

This work was compiled because there was felt to be a need for accurate and up-to-date information on world alcohol consumption particularly since consumption seems to be increasing.

A small part of the book contains text material on such matters as background, definitions and classifications of beverages, sources of information, methodological problems, and coverage. The bulk of the work is made up of extensive tables as follows: 1) Global and continental production of wine, beer and distilled alcoholic beverages 1960-1972, 2) National production, exports, imports and consumption of alcoholic beverages 1950-1972, 3) Average alcohol content of consumption statistics, 4) Per capita consumption of alcohol beverages 1950-1972, and 5) Supply and utilization of alcoholic beverages 1972. In addition, there are two appendices: 1) Abridged version of the questionnaire used in the inquiry and 2) Unregistered consumption.

The work was undertaken at the request of the World Health Organization in order to make relevant data available for a public-health-oriented alcohol policy.

444.   Israelstam, S., and S. Lambert, eds. **Alcohol, Drugs, and Traffic Safety.** Proceedings of the Sixth International Conference on Alcohol, Drugs, and Traffic Safety, Toronto, September 8-13, 1974. Toronto: Addiction Research Foundation of Ontario, 1975. 939p. bibliog. $30.00. ISBN 0-88868-011-2.

The 93 papers reprinted in this large volume were presented at the Conference named above in association with the International Committee on Alcohol, Drugs, and Traffic Safety, and the International Council on Alcohol and Addictions. Papers were presented by specialists from more than 30 countries, and a variety of subject fields were represented. These include such areas as social, biological, and physical sciences, counseling, education, technology, medicine, and law.

The papers are divided into five sections: 1) The epidemiology of alcohol and drug related traffic accidents, 2) Pharmacological, physiological, and psychological aspects relevant to driving impairment, 3) Analytical aspects, 4) Control and prevention, and 5) Public education and information.

Most papers report current research but also deal with history, problems, and criticism of work in this field. Some papers suggest areas where further research is needed.

445.   Lee, Dick, and Colin Pratt. **Operation Julie: How the Undercover Police Team Smashed the World's Greatest Drugs Ring.** London: W. H. Allen, 1978. 382p. illus. £4.95. ISBN 0-491-02176-3.

Operation Julie was a police investigation in Great Britain that led to the uncovering of a secret LSD operation, the largest ever discovered. More than two years of undercover work, which led to the arrest of 120 people in 1977, is described. The detectives infiltrated the underworld distributors, mounted round-the-clock observations, and developed a fine surveillance team. Federal agencies in the United States and police in Switzerland and France assisted. Huge sums of money were involved. The account sheds light on British police methods and on smuggling activities.

It was presumed in 1974 that LSD was seldom used anymore. The senior author, who led the investigation, found that it was being manufactured and distributed on a much larger scale than had been supposed. Enough of the drug was confiscated to provide 18,000,000 "trips."

At the end of the book Lee pondered on the rights and wrongs of the operation, and felt sorry to a degree about the sentences imposed on the principals in the operation. The people had university and academic backgrounds, and some had excellent professional qualifications. He felt a flash of anger at them, though—why had they done it? They were not fools and must have known where it would end. Lee asked himself whether it had all been worthwhile to break the ring. Then his answer came in the form of a letter from a couple who had lost two teenage daughters by overdose of LSD. The team was congratulated on their efforts. Lee reminded himself to remember these and other victims; of course it had been worth it.

446.   Lentini, Joseph R. **Vice and Narcotics Control**. Beverly Hills, CA: Glencoe Press, 1977. 200p. illus. bibliog. index. LC 14924.

The topics treated in this book include gambling, loan sharking, prostitution, and sex offenses as well as narcotics. There are two chapters on narcotics, which treat the following aspects of the subject: 1) Terms relating to narcotics and drug addiction, 2) Recognizing the addict, 3) Classification of drugs, 4) Glossary of narcotics terms, 5) Technical terms, 6) Slang terms associated with today's youth and their drugs of abuse, 7) The use of informants, 8) The drug search, 9) Drug concealment in the home, on the person, and in the automobile.

The aim of the work is to provide basic knowledge of vice activities and the various methods used to suppress them. Also, these consensual crimes are placed in perspective among the activities of professional, organized criminals.

447.   Levin, Gilbert, Edward B. Roberts, and Gary B. Hirsch. **The Persistent Poppy: A Computer-Aided Search for Heroin Policy**. Cambridge, MA: Ballinger Publishing Co., 1975. 229p. bibliog. index. $16.50. LC 75-4656. ISBN 0-88410-031-6.

Written by a psychiatrist and two management experts, this book provides a framework for examining the forces that encourage and discourage the growth of heroin use, particularly in cities and suburbs. The authors have developed a mathematical model to assist in this endeavor. In addition, they have analyzed the psychological, social, and economic causes of addiction and evaluated the possible corrective strategies and trade-offs among them.

The work is in three parts: an overview, the heroin system in detail, and policy experiments and recommendations. The chapter headings are as follows: 1) The persistent poppy, 2) The heroin system in brief, 3) Becoming addicted, 4) The punitive response, 5) Alternatives for coping, 6) Alternative heroin futures, and 7) What to do. In addition, there is an appendix of about 85 pages: "A Comprehensive System Dynamics Model of Heroin and the Community."

The conclusions consist of a number of "do's" and "bewares." In brief, the view is that while inaction is not desirable, overreaction in any direction is perilous.

The book should be of value to professionals in the field of drug abuse treatment and enforcement and to anyone concerned with public policy in this area. The computer model included will interest social scientists. The language of the text is reasonably nontechnical, and the computer simulation may serve as an introduction to the technique for the uninitiated reader.

448.   Liu, Hsien Chou. **The Development of a Single Convention on Narcotic Drugs** (A Historical Survey for the International Cooperation in Solving the Crucial

Problem of Narcotic Drugs). Bangkok: Academy of New Society (294 Plabplachai Road, Bangkok, Thailand), 1979. 70p. bibliog. index.

The problem of international control over narcotic drugs is a critical one, and international collaboration for the eradication of the use of such drugs for non-medical purposes can be traced to the Shanghai Conference of 1909.

The work under review was written before the adoption of a single convention on narcotic drugs which took place in 1961. This convention incorporated the nine existing conventions into a single treaty with 74 governments participating.

This book is a historical survey of the previous treaties. It is presented in three parts as follows: 1) Conference prior to the formation of the League (of Nations), 2) The league's efforts of international control, and 3) The UN's struggle for a single convention.

The viewpoint of the author is that efforts to control the narcotic problem have never been entirely successful, mainly because of an uncooperative attitude among nations. He believes a study of previous treaties is necessary before a perfect text can be contemplated, and consequently has made this book available.

449.   Logan, Frank, ed. **Cannabis Options for Controls.** Report of a Study Group, for the Institute for the Study of Drug Dependence. Sunbury, Middlesex, Great Britain: Quartermaine House Ltd., 1979. 135p. illus. bibliog. £3.50pa. ISBN 0-905898-05-2.

This report attempts to present in unbiased fashion opinions from experts on various alternatives to the present system of cannabis control in Great Britain and on the problems the alternatives might cause. There has been much controversy over whether or not marijuana is as harmful as alcohol and tobacco. Those who claim it is not believe present controls in Great Britain are ineffective and advocate new legislation, decriminalization, or licensing. On the other side of the question, tighter restriction on trafficking, possession, and use are urged by many.

The book defines the options available. Changes in penalties are discussed; decriminalization in the light of American experience is examined; and licensing systems are considered. The suggestion is made that cannabis might be controlled and distributed from pharmacies because pharmacists understand poison control laws, are accustomed to keeping records, and have scientific knowledge of drugs. (Some reviewers have commented that this suggestion may not be acceptable to pharmacists.) The problems involved with new legislation and possible complications caused by Great Britain's international obligations with respect to the drug are considered.

An appendix of papers by a panel of experts has been included. The problems surrounding the issue are well-presented.

450.   Lowry, W. T., and James G. Garriott. **Forensic Toxicology: Controlled Substances and Dangerous Drugs.** New York: Plenum Press, 1979. 445p. bibliog. index. $37.50. LC 78-26439. ISBN 0-306-40124-X.

This is a timely book. With the rapid spread of drug abuse, there is a growing need for information to assist with legal matters surrounding the problem. The federal and state laws are complex, and there is an increasing demand for expert chemists and toxicologists in the courtroom. In addition, attorneys need toxicological information in order to handle drug cases.

The book is intended primarily for the active forensic chemist or the student. The material included should provide the scientific expert with the necessary information to testify in court; the attorney should find enough to assist in prosecuting or defending a case; and the physician should find information that will assist in maintaining proper records and prescription practices.

Practical material is presented. The first section discusses new drugs, advertising, adulterated drugs, misbranded drugs, and drug nomenclature. The second section describes the various pharmaceutical dosage forms (17 in all), such as capsules, creams, elixirs, aerosols, powders, tablets, etc. The third section explains the classification of schedules substances. There are five schedules, ranging from schedule I, which contains drugs with the highest potential for abuse, to schedule V, which includes the lowest. Section 4 is on the regulation of controlled substances. The next sections, on excluded substances, excepted substances, and drug isomers and derivates, are mainly lists. Section 8 is a brief outline of techniques and instrumentation for analysis of drugs.

Section 9, the last, makes up about 2/3 of the book. It is an alphabetical (by generic name) listing of "Controlled and Noncontrolled but Commonly Abused Substances." There is a short monograph on each drug. Information provided about each usually includes: synonymous names, trade names, products that contain the drug, a diagram of the chemical structure, general comments, toxicology-pharmacology, and biochemistry.

The general intent of the book is to bridge the gap between scientific and legal matters in the field of controlled and dangerous drugs. The title of the work is somewhat misleading; it does not contain material usually considered to be in the area of forensic toxicology in the classic sense.

451. Mattila, M., ed. **Alcohol, Drugs and Driving.** Basel: S. Karger, 1976. 101p. bibliog. index. (Modern Problems of Pharmacopsychiatry, v. 11.) $19.00. ISBN 3-8055-2349-1.

The papers reprinted in this volume were originally presented at a Satellite Symposium of the 6th International Congress of Pharmacology on Alcohol, Drugs and Driving, held in Helsinki on July 26-27, 1975. Most of the contributors are of Scandinavian origin.

Reviews are presented on the epidemiological, practical, legal, clinical, pharmacological, and psychomotor performance aspects of the problem. In addition, techniques for documenting the effects of drug and alcohol use are presented. The need for standardization of testing and evaluating methodologies is stressed, as is the need for international coöperation. A good deal of statistical and technical material has been included.

The subject is important because a major problem in all western countries is that more and more fatal traffic accidents are caused by young drivers under the influence of alcohol and/or drugs.

452. McLennan, Ross J. **Booze, Bucks, Bamboozle, and You! Propaganda vs. Facts.** Oklahoma City, OK: Sane Press, 1978. 143p. $2.95pa.

The author of this small book has for a number of years lectured to groups, particularly young people, on alcohol and narcotics and has been involved in legislative action on the matter. In this book he has sought to expose the liquor industry's and other propaganda efforts to promote the use of alcohol. He says the propaganda has been based on half-truths, innuendos, superstition, and out-right lies.

The material is arranged under the following headings: 1) Propaganda regarding alcohol, 2) Beer propaganda, 3) Wine propaganda, 4) Laws, rights, taxes, and liquor conglomerates, 5) Prevention and rehabilitation propaganda, and 6) The prohibition era.

The format used is the presentation of a statement and then several paragraphs to refute it. Following are examples of some of the statements: "Alcoholism is a disease;" "I can handle booze—and drive a car," "Alcohol aids digestion," "We need to develop a concept of responsible drinking," "Beer is food," "People drank more during prohibition," and many more.

453.   Messick, Hank. **Of Grass and Snow: The Secret Criminal Elite.** Englewood Cliffs, NJ: Prentice-Hall, Inc., 1979. 190p. illus. $9.95. LC 78-31553. ISBN 0-13-630558-X.

The author of this work, a journalist, shows how a new criminal elite has emerged in the United States, the dealers in illegal and addictive drugs. This tale of current drug trafficking, particularly in marijuana and cocaine, presents a view of complex crime networks and the part law enforcement officials have been playing in attempting to handle the problem. Changing tactics of detection, pursuit, and prosecution are described.

The book is interesting, though written in a somewhat sensational journalistic style. It is also confusing. It is impossible to tell very much about accuracy, although it is evident that an illustration is incorrectly labelled as a "cola plant, source of cocaine." It is the coca, not cola, plant from which cocaine comes.

The viewpoint of the author seems to be that legalization of drug use is necessary to break up crime syndicates, because the present laws are unenforceable, much as was the case with Prohibition. In addition, he believes that in a more perfect society the demand for drugs would cease, an oft-repeated statement.

454.   Moskowitz, Herbert, ed. **Drugs and Driving.** New York: Pergamon Press, 1976. 79p. bibliog. (Special Issue of *Accident Analysis and Prevention*, v. 8, No. 1, Feb. 1976.) $8.00pa. ISBN 0-08-020537-2.

This publication evolved from a symposium on Drugs and Driving presented in 1975 at the annual meeting of the U.S. Transportation Research Board, sponsored by the Committee on Road User Characteristics. Ten papers are included. The first five review current literature on five different classes of drugs regarding the potential driving safety hazards associated with them. Amphetamines, tranquilizers, barbiturates, narcotics, and cannabis are the classes considered. The other papers are as follows: 6) Drug use and driving risk among high school students, 7) Traffic accident rates among Finnish outpatients, 8) Marihuana: effects on simulated driving performance, 9) Statistical evaluation of the effectiveness of "alcohol safety action projects," and 10) A critique of the paper "Statistical evaluation of the effectiveness of alcohol safety action projects."

The five review papers reveal the sparseness of data regarding the nature and extent of the effects of drugs on psychomotor performance and perceptual changes, but it appears that tranquilizers, barbiturates, and cannabis are definitely likely to lead to driving impairment. The three papers following are representative of research studies being conducted. The last two papers point out the difficulties in choosing effective countermeasure programs.

Taken together the papers are representative of the state of the art in the field of drugs and driving, a growing problem of ever-widening portions of the population.

455.   Platt, Jerome J., Christina Labate, and Robert J. Wicks, eds. **Evaluative Research in Correctional Drug Abuse Treatment: A Guide for Professionals in**

Criminal Justice and the Behavioral Sciences. Lexington, MA: Lexington Books, D. C. Heath and Co., 1977. 203p. bibliog. index. $18.00. LC 12687. ISBN 0-669-00724-2.

There has been a growing awareness that difficult policy issues confront the field of corrections and the drug abuse treatment area in particular. The belief has prevailed that evaluative research is too difficult or too expensive to set up, and there has been question as to the merit of expending the effort to conduct it. Recently, however, funds have been withheld pending evaluation of existing programs. Consequently, correctional administrators and drug program directors are attempting to become familiar with evaluative research.

This book, then, fills a need, and it has been set up to provide those interested with a guide to initiating and understanding the research and assessment process. Both theory and application are emphasized. The work is presented in three parts: 1) Basic concepts of evaluative research in correctional drug abuse treatment, 2) Three basic evaluative research issues, and 3) Evaluative research in correctional drug abuse treatment: an illustrative example.

Chapter headings are: 1) Evaluative research in correctional drug abuse treatment: practical issues, implications, and questions, 2) Basic principles of evaluation methodology in correctional drug abuse treatment, 3) Management information systems for drug abuse programs, 4) Evaluating outcome in correctional drug abuse rehabilitation programs, 5) Predicting parole outcome in correctional drug abuse treatment, 6) Evaluation of the Wharton Tract Narcotics Treatment Program, 7) Evaluation of the Wharton Tract Narcotic Treatment Program: a methodological analysis, and 8) Wharton Tract Narcotics Treatment Program: parole outcome and related studies.

Critics of correctional programs have characterized the field as having nothing to look back to with pride or to look forward to with hope. The editors and authors of this work believe there is potential for generating both pride and hope at a critical time in the history of the corrections field.

456. Regier, Marilyn. **Social Policy in Action: Perspectives on the Implementation of Alcoholism Reforms.** Foreword by Roland L. Warren. Lexington, MA: Lexington Books, D. C. Heath and Co., 1979. 177p. bibliog. index. $18.95. LC 78-20274. ISBN 0-669-02716-2.

The study reported here examines how the participants of a social reform effort negotiate the implementation of it. In this instance the social policy involved is the Uniform Alcoholism and Intoxication Treatment Act of 1971. The attitudes and behaviors of those who execute the decriminalization process are looked at particularly. Over a period of 19 months three groups were observed: skid rowers, medical personnel, and the police.

The author allows that the recent literature of the social sciences abounds with analyses of faltering and defunct social programs. The book attempts to determine what lies between policy intent and a successful program.

Chapter headings are as follows: 1) Introduction, 2) A policy in perspective, 3) Policy validation: models of idealism, 4) Policy critique: models of experimentation, 5) Policy rationalization: models of pragmatism, 6) The displaced reform: a final look, and 7) On the correspondence of ideas and actions.

The author concludes with the hope that the analysis she has made of the process experienced at the operational level by service recipients and providers will have application to other social reforms as well as to the alcoholism field.

457.   **The Rights of Alcoholics and Their Families.** New York: The New York City
Affiliate, Inc., National Council on Alcoholism, 1976. 42p. bibliog.

This brief publication, written in a question and answer format, provides an
overview of laws and regulations in many areas that concern alcoholics and their
families. It is based mainly on New York State laws. Intended for the general public
and for professionals, it is subtitled "A Handbook for social workers, treatment
facilities, attorneys, therapists, individuals, government agencies, personnel directors,
and all other persons who work and are concerned with alcoholics and their families."

The first section, "The Family," contains the following chapters: 1) Domestic
relations (marriage, divorce, custody), 2) Insurance (health, life), 3) Commitment,
and 4) Capacity (contracts, wills). The second part, "The Individual," contains these
chapters: 1) Employment (hiring, firing, disability), 2) Licenses, 3) Public assistance,
4) Criminal law, 5) Confidentiality, 6) Driving while intoxicated, 7) Public intoxication, 8) Treatment, and 9) Immigration and citizenship.

The handbook serves a dual purpose. It explains the rights people have and
do not have, and the compilers hope it will help society question whether the weigh-
ing it has done in alcoholism has been correct.

458.   Rutledge, Barbara, and E. Kaye Fulton, eds. **International Collaboration:
Problems and Opportunities.** Toronto: Addiction Research Foundation, 1978. 206p.
bibliog. $14.95.

This publication contains the proceedings of a symposium held in Toronto
on the occasion of the designation by the World Health Organization of the Addiction
Research Foundation as a Collaborating Centre for Research and Training on Drug
Dependence. Included are papers and remarks presented by well-known authorities
representing a number of countries. The contributions have been divided into sections
as follows: 1) Designation ceremonies, 2) Epidemiology of alcohol and other drug-
related problems, 3) Alcohol and drug-related problems, 4) Control strategies, and
5) International collaboration in drug abuse programs.

The emphasis of a number of the papers is on international strategies and
cooperation, and the role of the World Health Organization in drug dependence programs is stressed.

459. Schwartz, Michael A. **Prescription Drugs in Short Supply: Case Histories.** New
York: Marcel Dekker, Inc., 1980. 130p. bibliog. index. (Drugs and the Pharmaceutical
Sciences. v. 8.) $17.50pa. LC 79-24783. ISBN 0-8247-6910-4.

It has recently become evident that shortages of certain major prescription
drugs have been occurring. This book tells the story of these real or threatened shortages of vital drugs between the years 1973-1976. The author analyzes the measures
being taken to deal with such problems and makes recommendations for averting
future situations of this nature.

Several drugs are discussed that are not drugs of abuse, although a chapter
on opium and opium-derived drugs makes up about 1/3 of the book. Several reasons
are given for the critical shortage of opium drugs in 1972. These include increased
demand in the United States; the U.S. policy of ending cultivation to prevent abuse
of the drug; poor crops in India, the major supplier; ban on cultivation of the opium
plant in Turkey because of diversion into illegal channels; and the Soviet Union's
buying the drug on the open work market when they had formerly produced it
themselves. The situation is cited as a good example of how a complex of political,
economic, and social factors, along with reliance on foreign sources of a natural
product, can influence the supply-demand balance of a drug.

The book describes the steps being taken to alleviate the problem. These include research to improve crop yields and the development of synthetic replacements. The role of the federal government in regulating production of drugs in general is discussed.

The book will interest pharmacists, physicians, pharmaceutical manufacturers, government officials, and those concerned with health care.

460.   Trebach, Arnold S., ed. **Drugs, Crime, and Politics.** New York: Praeger Publishers, 1978. 178p. bibliog. $19.50. LC 78-5735. ISBN 0-03-042286-8.

The papers in this publication were selected from those presented at the 1975 Annual Meeting of the American Society of Criminology. The following papers are included: 1) Introduction by Arnold S. Trebach, 2) From morphine maintenance to methadone maintenance, 1919-75: the history, promise, and problems of narcotic clinics in the United States, by John M. Martin, 3) The politics of a heroin maintenance proposal in New York City, by Cyril D. Robinson, 4) Working bases for corruption: organizational ambiguities and narcotics law enforcement, by Peter K. Manning and L. J. Redlinger, 5) Trends in narcotics use and treatment in Toronto, by Al Everson and Ruth Segal, 6) Pretreatment client roles and therapeutic environment as correlates of in-treatment "success": the case of the nonopiate user, by T. J. Keil, T. V. Rush, and F. B. Dickman, 7) The role of buying and selling in illicit drug use, by Eric Single and Denise Kandel, 8) Deterrence and deviance: the example of cannabis prohibition, by Patricia G. Erickson, and 9) The potential impact of "legal" heroin in America, by Arnold S. Trebach.

The publication is most noteworthy for its reflection of the growing mood of pessimism that characterizes works on the social problems of drug abuse. The programs, treatments, and policies that have been tried at home and abroad have not been very effective.

461.   United Nations. **Convention on Psychotropic Substances 1971.** New York: United Nations, 1977. 33p. $2.50pa. Sales No. E.78.XI.3.

This book contains the "Final Act and Resolutions, as agreed by the 1971 United Nations Conference for the Adoption of a Protocol on Psychotropic Substances, and the Schedules Annexed to the Convention." The *Convention* contains 33 articles covering such topics as use of terms, scope of control of substances, special provisions regarding control of preparations and scope of control, limitation of use to medical and scientific purposes, special administration, licenses, prescriptions, warnings on packages and advertising, records, international trade, reports, measures against abuse of substances, illicit traffic, penal provisions, and related matters.

462.   U.S. Bureau of Narcotics and Dangerous Drugs. Office of Scientific Support. Drug Control Division. **Drug Usage and Arrest Charges: A Study of Drug Usage and Arrest Charges Among Arrestees in Six Metropolitan Areas of the United States.** By William C. Eckerman, and others. Washington: The Bureau, 1971. 388p. + appendices. (SCID-TR-4.)

Because of the acceleration of crime and of drug addiction in recent years, there has been speculation about the relationship between them. The study reported in this publication is a contribution by the Bureau of Narcotics and Dangerous Drugs to determine what relationship, if any, exists. The following chapters are presented: 1) Introduction, 2) A brief review of earlier research on the relationship between drug usage and criminal behavior, 3) Study objectives and methodology, 4) Selected characteristics of arrestees in the study, 5) The analytical approach and the stages of analysis adopted for this report, 6) Drug usage and arrest charge—all drug users irrespective of drug, 7) Drug usage and arrest charges by specific drug as determined by the urine analysis, 8) Drug usage and arrest charges by specific drug as determined by both questionnaire data and urine analysis, 9) Drug usage and arrest charges by study site as determined by cumulative urine sample and questionnaire data, 10) Drug usage and other related variables, 11) Correspondence among different measures of illicit drug usage, 12) Trends in drug use and arrest charges, and 13) Summary and conclusions.

Briefly, the conclusions are that there is no relationship for crimes of violence; there are just as many arrests among nonusers as drug abusers, although with robbery or property crimes a different pattern emerges; and there are significantly more of these crimes among addicts, enough to constitute a clear and present threat of disturbing proportions.

463.   U.S. Comptroller General. **The Drinking-Driver Problem—What Can Be Done About It?** Report to the Congress. Washington: General Accounting Office, 1979. 53p.

The drinking-driver problem is a matter of long-standing concern; it is the single largest factor in highway deaths. Chapter headings in this necessary report are: 1) Introduction, 2) Recent efforts to reduce the drinking-driver problem, 3) Obstacles to a successful anti-drinking-driver campaign, and 4) Conclusions, recommendations, and agency comments. Appended is a drinking-driver program questionnaire.

The conclusions are reached that society's general acceptance of drinking and driving is the main obstacle to a successful anti-drinking-driver campaign, and that before accidents can be reduced, a long-term, continuous educational commitment will be necessary, possibly lasting for generations. The report suggests that the Secretary of Transportation should lead in an effort to change attitudes.

464.   U.S. Comptroller General. **A Report on Gains Made in Controlling Illegal Drugs, Yet the Drug Trade Flourishes.** Submitted by Senator Ernest F. Hollings to the Committee on Appropriations, United States Senate. Washington: GPO, 1979. 214p. $5.50pa. S/N 052-070-05203-1.

This report is an assessment of the federal government's drug enforcement and supply control efforts during the past ten years. Section headings are as follows: 1) Introduction, 2) Reducing drug availability in the United States: efforts have had no lasting benefits, 3) International narcotics control: some progress but task is formidable, 4) Border management problems need to be resolved, 5) Immobilizing major drug violators: an elusive goal, 6) Bail and sentencing practices further weaken immobilization efforts, 7) Mobilizing state and local resources is easier said than done, 8) Agency comments and our evaluation, and 9) Scope.

Although federal agencies have fought hard to reduce the impact of drugs of abuse on society, the problem persists largely because of the enormous supply of and demand for drugs. Positive results have been achieved in reducing drug related deaths and injuries. In addition, heroin supplies have been reduced. However, other types of drugs are being substituted.

The hope is that effective law enforcement, drug crop eradication, and other controls will cause shifts and disruptions in trafficking and use, and time can be gained to concentrate on long-term solutions. It is suggested that the U.S. take a tougher and more consistent stance on the subject, and that branches of the government form a partnership to carry out a consistent national policy on the problem.

465.   U.S. Congress. 95th, Second Session. House of Representatives. **Prevention of Drug Abuse.** Hearings before the Select Committee on Narcotics Abuse and Control. April 18, 20, 25, May 16, 25, 1978. Washington: GPO, 1978. 412p.

The committee, through the testimonies and prepared statements presented in this document, undertook a comprehensive review of the entire federal effort to control narcotics and drug abuse. Noted authorities in the field, in government and other agencies, contributed the material. Basically answers to the following specific questions were sought: 1) What agencies are involved in drug abuse prevention programs?, 2) Are these programs working?, 3) What evidence is there that they are working?, and 4) What new scientific approaches to drug abuse prevention should be tried?

466.   U.S. Drug Enforcement Administration. **Drug Abuse and the Criminal Justice System: A Survey of New Approaches in Treatment and Rehabilitation.** Prepared for Preventive Programs Section, Drug Enforcement Administration by the ANLFY (A New Life For You) staff, Research Center, National Council on Crime and Delinquency. Washington: Drug Enforcement Administration, 1974. 221p.

This document provides a survey designed to make available to all communities information on and technical assistance in implementing an array of alternatives to drug abuse. Several effective community-based programs dealing with treatment and rehabilitation of drug abusers were identified and evaluated. In addition, a low-cost, comprehensive evaluation strategy was designed and developed.

Part I, "Diversion by Criminal Justice Systems to Treatment and Rehabilitation," describes nine successful programs. Part II, "Drug Offenders and the Criminal Justice System: Methods and Models," discusses strategies that were found effective.

467.   U.S. Drug Enforcement Administration. **Drug Abuse Warning Network (DAWN 1 Analysis).** Washington: GPO, 1973. 137p.

This report on phase I of Project DAWN (Drug Abuse Warning Network) marks the close of a historic era in the collection of drug abuse statistical data. It is intended that DAWN will be a continuing effort which will constantly be reviewed and modified to obtain information upon which federal regulatory decisions are based.

The publication contains an introduction and three chapters containing general information, drug abuse modal values, and report reviews.

Although the report is presented in confused format, a good deal of valuable statistical information is included that identifies drugs currently being abused and existing patterns of drug abuse, provides an assessment of the relative abuse hazards to health, and gives data needed for regulatory control of drugs.

468.   U.S. Drug Enforcement Administration. **Drug Abuse Warning Network, Phase II Report. (DAWN 2 Analysis).** Washington: GPO, 1974. 292p.

The subject of this comprehensive report is the second phase of the DAWN Project (Drug Abuse Warning Network), a nationwide program set up by the Drug Enforcement Administration to provide a drug abuse "early warning" system of collecting information to be used as a barometer to assist those concerned with drug abuse problems. Also, the project assists the Drug Enforcement Administration in mounting enforcement and regulatory programs. The period covered by the report is July, 1973 through March, 1974.

A great many things can be determined by making use of DAWN statistics given in the report. For instance: the leading therapeutic classes and individual drugs of abuse (nationwide and by city), abuse trends by therapeutic class, motivation for abuse, demographic patterns, drug episodes involving polydrug abuse, new product appearances, source of drug, dosage form, and drug deaths.

469.   U.S. Drug Enforcement Administration. **Drug Enforcement**, v. 5, No. 2, September, 1978. Special Issue on Federal Interagency Cooperation. Washington: GPO, 1978. 41p. illus. (part col.).

This special issue of *Drug Enforcement* outlines the activities of a number of federal agencies that cooperate in the area of drug enforcement. There is a section on each of the following agencies: The Federal Bureau of Investigation; Immigration and Naturalization Service; Customs; Internal Revenue Service; Bureau of Alcohol, Tobacco and Firearms; U.S. Coast Guard; Federal Aviation Administration; and the Army Criminal Investigation Command. In addition, there is a section on the Administrative Procedure Act which covers activities of the Bureau of Narcotics and Dangerous Drugs and the Drug Enforcement Administration.

470.   U.S. Drug Enforcement Administration. **Instrumental Applications in Forensic Drug Chemistry.** Proceedings of the International Symposium, May 29-30, 1978. Edited by Michael Klein, Alice V. Kruegel, and Stanley P. Sobol. Washington: GPO, 1979. 290p. bibliog. S/N 027-000-00770-8.

This publication contains papers presented by 24 experts from eight countries highlighting the state-of-the-art of instrumental advances in the areas of spectrometry, computers, and chromatography applied to drug analysis and such topics as drug standards, scanning electron and light microscopy, immunoassays, and toxicology. The aim of the symposium was to provide a forum for the sharing of scientific information that could be applied to forensic work and help support international law enforcement attempts to deal with illegal drugs.

471.   U.S. Drug Enforcement Administration. **Source Debriefing Guide.** Prepared by Office of Intelligence, Office of Enforcement, Office of Science and Technology of the Drug Enforcement Administration. Washington: GPO, 1975. 44p.

Prepared to assist the investigator in formulating questions concerning international and domestic drug traffic, this brief guide is intended as a resource document to supplement the interrogative skills and knowledge of the investigator in the areas of drug production, processing, and distribution. There are four parts. The first is designed to identify the areas of knowledge of the person being questioned. Part 2 consists of five subject sections as follows: 1) Production, processing and distribution of opium-heroin and coca-cocaine, 2) Production, processing and distribution of dangerous drugs, 3) Questions for persons with detailed knowledge of laboratories, 4) Questions for persons with specific knowledge of smuggling or transporting drugs, and 5) Persons apprehended at a border while smuggling contraband. Part 3 regards conspiracy as stated in the Comprehensive Drug Abuse Prevention and Control Act of 1970, and part 4 is a listing of all DEA regional offices.

472.   U.S. Drug Enforcement Administration. Office of Compliance and Regulatory Affairs. **A Model Health Professions Practice Act and State Regulatory Policy.** Washington: GPO, 1977. 60p. $1.25pa. S/N 027-004-00022-9.

This publication was prepared by Arthur Young and Company for a study on state regulation, regulatory agencies, and professional associations as they relate to the Controlled Substances Act of 1970. It is volume two of a comprehensive study on the subject and addresses the statutory issues and problems which affect licensing in the health care professions. A Model Practice Act is presented as part of the volume. In addition, the following areas are also discussed: Summaries of recommendations and findings, Need for a model practice act, A problem situation, Model administrative procedures act, Model policies, practices, and objectives for regulatory boards and interacting entities, and Conclusions.

The conclusions state that the various states of the United States may choose to: 1) adopt the basic substance of the model act as it reads by simply adding, modifying, or deleting the appropriate provisions, or 2) adopt the basic jurisprudential philosophy underlying the act and develop a new model act premised on this philosophy.

473.   U.S. Drug Enforcement Administration. Office of Program Planning and Evaluation. **Drug Enforcement Administration: A Profile.** Washington: GPO, 1980. 34p.

An official statement of the mission and responsibilities of the Drug Enforcement Administration and a diagram of its organizational history begin this booklet. Other sections cover operations, organization, funds, personnel, and other resources. A great deal of information is provided, particularly statistical data, including charts and graphs of drug arrests, heroin retail purity and price, drug related deaths and injuries, drugs removed from the illicit market, laboratory analyses, and training personnel. Also included are charts of organizational structures, lists of regional and foreign offices, forensic science laboratories, and internal security field offices. The DEA's computerized and automated data systems are described, and lastly data on the aircraft and vehicle fleets is supplied.

474.   U.S. General Accounting Office. Comptroller General of the United States. **Retail Diversion of Legal Drugs—A Major Problem with No Easy Solution.** Report to Congress. Washington: GAO, 1978. 43p. $1.00. Available on microfiche.

The problem of legal drugs being diverted from the dispensing or retail level is addressed in the report. It is presumed that perhaps seven of every ten drugs abused have been obtained from such sources, most of these diverted by practitioners such as pharmacists and physicians. It is also felt that the Drug Enforcement Administration is unable to control retail diversion because of a lack of statutory authority, weak regulatory requirements, and inadequate resources. States also are not equipped to combat such diversion, according to the report.

The General Accounting Office recommends actions that could reduce such diversion. Congress is asked to change the Drug Enforcement Administration's role by authorizing it either to exercise direct regulatory authority over retail-level practitioners or to implement grant programs for assisting states in controlling the problem. In addition, because of potentially large costs involved, the Attorney General should study the costs and benefits of these approaches.

The report has been criticized for the impression it leaves that substantial proportion of medical practitioners are unethical, criminal types and for the questionable evidence given to support the claim.

475.   U.S. House of Representatives. **Liquor Laws.** Compiled by Gilman G. Udell, Superintendent, Document Room, House of Representatives. Washington: GPO, 1978. 452p. S/N 052-001-00153-2.

This publication is a compilation of the texts (or extracts) of the U.S. laws relating to liquor from the year 1890 through 1978. The legislative history is included for the more recent acts.

476.   U.S. National Highway Traffic Safety Administration. **Alcohol and Highway Safety: A Review of the State of Knowledge, Summary Volume, 1978.** Washington: GPO, 1979. 87p. bibliog. index. (DOT HS-805-172.) $3.50pa. S/N 050-003-00376-0.

This is a condensed version of a more detailed report that summarizes the results of a study sponsored by the National Highway Traffic Safety Administration and conducted by the University of Michigan's Highway Safety Research Institute. The objective of the study was to review, evaluate, and summarize existing knowledge on alcohol and highway safety in the United States.

The report is presented in the following sections: 1) Introduction, 2) General approaches and methodological problems, 3) Defining the alcohol-crash problem, 4) Dealing with the alcohol-crash problem, 5) Future directions of the alcohol-crash problem, and 6) Conclusions and recommendations. A comprehensive bibliography of 15 pages is included. Emphasis is on research conducted since 1968.

The last section lists significant findings on the present state of knowledge about the nature and extent of the alcohol-crash problem and what has been done about it so far. Measures are proposed to develop better responses to the problem in the future, and insights on the implications of the study's findings for operational agencies are given.

477.   U.S. National Highway Traffic Safety Administration. **Alcohol and Highway Safety Laws: A National Overview.** Washington: GPO, 1980. 81p. (DOT HS 85-173.)

Information on how the various states of the United States treat certain traffic violations and incidents is provided in this publication. The material is presented primarily in maps and charts as follows: map 1 and chart 1—Preliminary breath test laws; chart 2—Blood alcohol concentration (BAC) tests: statutory authority; chart 3—BAC tests required after traffic accidents: fatal and non-fatal; chart 4—BAC tests: scope of police authority; chart 5—BAC tests: defendant's options; map 2 and chart 6—Illegal *per se* and presumptive BAC laws: May 31, 1979, and BAC levels as evidence in state courts; chart 7—Driver screening, rehabilitation and sanctions; and chart 8—Legal age for consumption of beer, wine, and distilled spirits.

478.   U.S. National Highway Traffic Safety Administration. **A Report to Congress: Marijuana, Other Drugs and their Relation to Highway Safety.** Washington: GPO, 1980. 36p. bibliog. (DOT-HS-805-229.) $2.25pa. S/N 050-003-00382-4.

The following chapters are presented in this report: 1) Introduction, 2) The frequency of drug use among drivers and its relation to highway safety, 3) Legal approaches to the control of drug use by drivers, 4) Federal and state activity in the detection and prevention of inappropriate drug use by drivers, and 5) Conclusion, recommendations and DOT programmatic actions.

In brief, it was concluded that with the exception of alcohol, no drug has been established as a high priority highway safety concern; the frequency with which drug-impaired drivers drive, are arrested, or involved in auto crashes is not known; prescription and over-the-counter drugs may impair driving; information on marijuana and driving is incomplete; and roadside surveys to determine the nature and extent of drug use by drivers will be continued by the Department of Transportation.

479.   U.S. National Highway Traffic Safety Administration. **Results of National Alcohol Safety Action Projects.** Washington: GPO, 1979. 118p. bibliog. (DOT-HS-804-033.)

Historically, there has been a low rate of arrests and convictions for drinking drivers. Consequently, law enforcement agencies have responded actively to special enforcement countermeasures of the Alcohol Safety Action Program. This work reports on projects carried out nationally.

The following sections are included: 1) Enforcement, 2) Adjudication, 3) Rehabilitation, 4) Public information and education, 5) Management: project financing, and 6) Management: project administration. In addition, there is a summary report bibliography included.

In general, the projects showed that cost-effectiveness can be readily achieved by: training, analysis of police and court procedures, a high degree of motivation provided by top police management, and regular liaison with prosecutors and the court system.

480.   U.S. National Institute on Drug Abuse. **Criminal Justice Alternatives for Disposition of Drug Abusing Offender Cases. Defense Attorney.** Washington: GPO, 1978. 39p. + appendices. bibliog. [DHEW Publication No. (ADM) 78-744.] S/N 017-024-00770-6.

This publication is one of three reports developed by the Criminal Justice Branch, Division of Resource Development of the National Institute on Drug Abuse to assist judges, prosecutors, and defense attorneys in planning responses to the treatment needs of the drug abuser who is criminally involved.

The following sections are presented: 1) Introduction, 2) The criminal justice process, 3) Treatment intervention options, 4) Role of the defense attorney, 5) Implementing intervention options, and 6) Developing intervention options. In addition, there are five appendices as follows: 1) Resources, 2) Single state agencies for drug abuse prevention, 3) Bibliography, 4) Additional readings, and 5) Glossary.

Two companion volumes, one for the judge and one for the prosecutor, are almost identical to the one under review except for section 4, which is addressed specifically to the judge and prosecutor respectively instead of to the defense attorney.

481.   U.S. National Institute on Drug Abuse. **Drug Users and the Criminal Justice System.** Edited by Gregory A. Austin, and Dan J. Lettieri. Washington: GPO, 1977. 150p. bibliog. index. [DHEW Publication No. (ADM) 77-510; NIDA Research Issues No. 18.] $3.00pa. S/N 017-024-00629-7.

A companion volume to Number 17 in the Research Issues Series (*see* following entry). This document also presents summaries of major research and theoretical studies on the subject of drug use, criminal behavior, and the law. Sixty-seven summaries are presented, divided into two sections: 1) Drugs and the law and 2) Treatment and rehabilitation of the drug offender.

The first section contains studies in three broad areas: Attitudes toward drug laws, Effects of drug laws, and Patterns of enforcement. The second section is devoted to the following kinds of studies: general readings, community-based compulsory treatment, civil commitment in California and New York, the halfway house, prison-based treatment, and drug offenders on parole.

482.	U.S. National Institute on Drug Abuse. **Drugs and Crime: The Relationship of Drug Abuse and Concomitant Criminal Behavior**. Edited by Gregory A. Austin, and Dan J. Lettieri. Washington: GPO, 1976. 268p. bibliog. index. [DHEW Publication No. (ADM) 77-393; NIDA Research Issues No. 17.] $3.45pa. S/N 017-024-00556-8.

The first of two publications presenting abstracts of major research and theoretical studies that explore the relationship between drug abuse and criminal behavior, this volume addresses the relationship of drug use and criminal acts other than possession of, or trafficking in, illicit drugs. The second volume, *Drug Users and The Criminal Justice System* (*see* entry above), focuses on drug-related offenses such as drug use, possession, and trafficking, and the effect of the criminal justice system on the drug user.

This volume includes abstracts of 107 studies divided into seven topics as follows: 1) Reviews and theories, 2) Drug use and criminal behavior, 3) Addiction and criminal behavior, 4) Drugs and delinquency, 5) Crime and female drug users, 6) The impact of treatment modalities, and 7) The economics of drugs and crime.

483.	U.S. National Institute on Drug Abuse. **Drugs and Driving**. Edited by Robert E. Willette. Washington: GPO, 1977. 137p. bibliog. [DHEW Publication No. (ADM) 77-432; NIDA Research Monograph 11.] $1.70pa. LC 77-70426. S/N 017-024-00576-2.

It has become increasingly evident that drug use causes impairment of driving skills and that such impairment dramatically raises the risks of highway accidents. This monograph presents a critical review of the available literature relating drug use to driving and other complex human performance. In addition, it offers recommendations for the future. The material was prepared by a panel of nationally recognized experts on the behavioral effects of drug usage.

Chapter 1 of the publication is an introduction; chapter 2 is a synopsis of the issues and recommendation developed by the experts; chapter 3 is a summary of the position papers prepared by the panelists; and chapter 4 presents the nine individual papers of the panel members.

484.	U.S. National Institute on Drug Abuse. **Methadone Diversion: Experiences and Issues**. By James A. Inciardi. Washington: GPO, 1977. 104p. bibliog. [DHEW Publication No. (ADM) 77-488; Services Research Monograph Series.] $2.50. S/N 107-024-00615-7.

There has long been concern that a supply of methadone (a synthetic narcotic drug used in heroin addiction treatment) is being diverted from licit sources to the drug abusing community. This monograph describes the phenomenon of methadone diversion, clarifies issues around the matter, and provides guidance to treatment administrators and program planners regarding efforts to monitor the phenomenon.

It is interesting that the greatest amount of illicit methadone is used by the addict for self-treatment.

485.	U.S. National Institute on Drug Abuse. **Utilization of Third-Party Payments for the Financing of Drug Abuse Treatment**. Washington: GPO, 1977. 26p. [DHEW Publication No. (ADM) 77-440; NIDA Services Research Report.]

For a number of years the federal government has provided financial aid to drug abuse treatment programs. This assistance was intended to be "seed money" or the initial investment needed to fund programs until they could expand their sources of support. Third parties were envisioned as an important source. However, limited progress has been made in capturing such funds, for reasons which have been unclear.

This publication reports on two studies designed to explore reasons for the failure to obtain funds. The conclusion reached was that such funding is most often not available now because of client ineligibility. It is suggested that Medicaid agencies and private health insurange carriers should relax their requirements.

486.   U.S. National Institute on Drug Abuse. Office of Program Development and Analysis. **Purchase Predictions of Schedule II Drugs under the Controlled Substances Act of 1970.** By Fred Streit, Mark J. Nicolich, and Michael S. Backenheimer. Washington: GPO, 1976. 223p.

The Controlled Substances Act of 1970 was passed by Congress in order to minimize the amount of drugs of abuse available to high risk persons. Manufacturing quotas were set by the Drug Enforcement Administration with guidance from the Food and Drug Administration for schedule I and II drugs. Schedule I drugs have high abuse potential and no known medical uses. They are for research purposes only. Schedule II drugs have high abuse potential also, but possess legitimate medical uses. Setting the schedule II quotas was a problem, and the National Institute on Drug Abuse was called upon to provide an assessment of the needs. Their estimates have been well-received by both the Drug Enforcement Administration and the pharmaceutical industry.

This publication contains projections for 27 schedule II drugs based upon data collected from drug stores, hospitals, and the federal government.

487.   U.S. National Institute on Law Enforcement and Criminal Justice. **The Nation's Toughest Drug Law: Evaluating the New York Experience.** Final report of the Joint Committee on New York Drug Law Evaluation. Washington: GPO, 1978. 162p. LC 77-89054. S/N 027-000-00648-5.

Presented here are the results of a three-year study of the impact of the strictest drug law passed by the New York State Legislature in 1973. Emphasis was placed on heroin abuse. The presentation is in two parts. The first contains conclusions, the second supporting data. Section headings are: 1) What are the effects of the 1973 drug law?, 2) What accounts for the disappointing results of the 1973 drug law?, 3) Observations and lessons for the future. Appended are a summary of the major provisions of the law and a glossary.

The evidence of the study shows that the drug abuse problems are still with us. General observations made are that problems as complex as drug abuse do not yield to simple solutions. The misuse of all drugs, including the prescribed, constitute "the drug problem." Drug use is rooted in deep social maladies. And finally, it is implausible that social problems of this sort can be solved by criminal law.

A companion volume, *Staff Working Papers of the Drug Law Evaluation Project*, is reviewed below.

488.   U.S. National Institute on Law Enforcement and Criminal Justice. **Staff Working Papers of the Drug Law Evaluation Project.** A companion volume to the Final Report of the Joint Committee on New York Drug Law Evaluation. Washington: GPO, 1978. 322p. LC 77-89054. S/N 027-000-00647-7.

This volume presents papers prepared during the course of the Drug Law Evaluation Project. It is hoped that the data and methodologies presented in them will contribute to research and analysis of the issues related to controlling drug use and to operating criminal justice systems.

Titles of the four staff working papers are as follows: 1) The effects of the 1973 drug laws on heroin use in New York State, 2) Crime committed by narcotic users in Manhattan, 3) The effects of the 1973 drug laws on the New York State courts, 4) Sentencing patterns under the 1973 New York State drug laws.

489.   U.S. Office of Drug Abuse Policy. **1978 Annual Report.** Washington: GPO, 1978. 91p. $2.20pa. S/N 014-010-00032-1.

In March, 1976, Congress enacted Public Law 94-237, amending the Drug Abuse Office and Treatment Act of 1972 to establish the Office of Drug Abuse Policy in the Executive Office of the President. President Carter activated the office in March, 1977 with Dr. Peter G. Bourne as director.

This booklet gives a brief history of federal concern in the field of drug abuse prevention and control and discusses the establishment of the Office of Drug Abuse Policy as a coordinating and policy-making body. The report comments on the objectives, major activities, and accomplishments of the office. In addition, an accounting of funds expended is included.

The report ends with a discussion of the transfer of the office's responsibilities and functions to the Domestic Policy Staff, provided for under a reorganization plan. The office was in operation for 6½ months during fiscal (Mar.-Sept.) 1977 and October 1977-March 1978. It will be recalled that the controversial Dr. Bourne left the office after he received bad publicity for writing false prescriptions for controlled drugs.

490.   Vingilis, Evelyn, Lorne Salutin, and Godwin Chan. **R. I. D. E. (Reduce Impaired Driving in Etobicoke): A Driving-While-Impaired Countermeasure Program; One-Year Evaluation.** Toronto: Addiction Research Foundation, 1979. 97p. bibliog. $4.95pa. ISBN 0-88868-036-8.

This publication reports on a program to reduce drunken driving conducted in a borough of metropolitan Toronto. Based on the concept of deterrence, and involving both enforcement and education, the program showed some positive indicators of success. Results showed that the number of impaired drivers on the road decreased; there was increased risk perception for being caught while drinking and driving; and increased knowledge about drinking and driving was obtained. In addition to text material, a large amount of statistical data is presented, making use of tables and graphs.

491.   Weissman, James C. **Drug Abuse: The Law and Treatment Alternatives.** Cincinnati, OH: Criminal Justice Studies, Anderson Publishing Co., 1978. 339p. index. $14.50pa. LC 78-67245. ISBN 0-87084-928-X.

The author of this work is experienced in criminological and legal research, program evaluation, training, diversion, programming, rehabilitative service delivery, and teaching in the drug abuse field. The book was prepared primarily to give the reader, particularly criminal justice students, a comprehensive and balanced perspective regarding the socio-legal aspects of the subject.

Common drugs of abuse are discussed with brief sketches of their discovery, the history of their use, and their legitimate medical applications. Various patterns of abuse are outlined, including the end results and unfortunate side effects. A typology of five styles of drug use is developed (the nonuser, experimental user, social-recreational or situation users, involved user, and dysfunctional user). The book elaborates on the problem of social control of drugs and mentions current trends toward decriminalization of possession of marijuana, severe punishment of pushers, and recognition of a right to treatment for drug dependent persons. The author explores why these seemingly contradictory approaches are being pursued. The book can be used additionally as a case study of intergovernmental relations on all levels and as a study on the general issue of limitation of discretion in the justice system. Other matters discussed are judge-made law ("judicial gloss"), and treatment and prevention of drug abuse.

This comprehensive work, covering many aspects of the subject, is divided as follows: The problem, drugs of abuse, patterns of behavior, legal aspects, law enforcement, rehabilitation and correction, and prevention. In addition, a glossary, a selected list of drug offender case profiles, and a table of cases have been appended. A list of discussion questions are provided at the end of each chapter.

492. Weppner, Robert S., ed. **Street Ethnography: Selected Studies of Crime and Drug Use in Natural Settings.** Beverly Hills, CA: Sage Publications, 1977. 288p. bibliog. index. (Sage Annual Reviews of Drug and Alcohol Abuse, v. 1.) LC 76-50446. ISBN 0-8039-0808-3; 0-8039-0809-1pa.

This study of life in city streets was carried out by individuals who went into urban areas where deviances exist in abundance and talked to addicts, dealers, fences, prostitutes, and other law-breakers, as well as to public health officials and officers of the law. A primary concern of the book is the ethics involved in such research methods. When observing and recording crimes and other illegal acts, the researcher enters the gray area between right and wrong. The book attempts to justify and explain this area.

The 11 chapters are grouped under three headings: 1) Methodology and theory, 2) Ethical considerations, and 3) Descriptive studies. Various social scientists are authors of the chapters: 1) Street ethnography: problems and prospects, 2) In search of the class cannon: a field study of professional pickpockets, 3) Gettin' it together: some theoretical considerations on urban ethnography among underclass people, 4) Methodological notes on the employment of indigenous observers, 5) Network analysis as a methodological approach to the study of drug use in a Latin city, 6) Ethnography in the streets and in the joint: a comparison, 7) Workin' the corner: the ethics and legality of ethnographic fieldwork among active heroin addicts, 8) Ethnography and social problems, 9) Field ethics for the life history, 10) Methadone, wine, and welfare, and 11) A neighborhood history of drug switching.

The book should provide insights and understanding of addicts and criminals that may lead to improved programs of treatment and more humane policies.

493. World Health Organization Expert Committee on Drug Dependence. **Twenty-First Report.** Geneva: World Health Organization, 1978. 49p. bibliog. (WHO Technical Report Series No. 618.) $2.70pa. ISBN 92-4-120618-7.

In 1977 The World Health Organization Expert Committee on Drug Dependence was faced with the task of making realistic recommendations to the United Nations Commission of Narcotic Drugs regarding substances to be controlled under the 1971 Convention on Psychotropic Substances. Many of the substances in question have been used in medical practice, and the convention required that therapeutic value of the psychotropic substances be balanced against the risk to public health arising from their use. This report provides a survey of the problem.

The report begins with a discussion of the techniques used in animal studies and human pharmacology; then an assessment of public health and social problems caused by the abuse of a drug is presented. Therapeutic usefulness is assessed, and the decision-making process considered. The report ends with a discussion of the problems that might result if the convention extended controls to include substances such as salts, esters, ethers, isomers, and precursors of psychotropic substances. An addendum includes scientific background material on this complex question.

A list of recommendations is included in the report.

14

PHARMACOLOGY, CHEMISTRY, RESEARCH, AND MEDICAL ASPECTS

The large number of titles listed here is impressive evidence of the extent and nature of the recent research efforts regarding drug and alcohol abuse. There are many outstanding works, some highly technical and scientific and suitable primarily for a scientifically trained reader.

Areas that have received research attention are: the dependence and addictive process, effects of a wide variety of abuse substances, treatment methods, the action of drugs, behavior of drug users, brain studies, stimulus properties of drugs, withdrawal, methods of research, epidemiological studies, metabolism, diagnosis, long-term drug use, and structure-activity relationships. There are several volumes that report on recent advances and developments in drug and alcohol abuse research. Perhaps the research area of most promise at this time, and one that has received wide attention, is the investigation of the endorphins, enkephalins, and drug receptors. The titles by Costa, Gráf, Herz, Losterlitz, Loh, Snyder, Usdin, Van Ree, and Way all deal with this subject.

Recent recognition of the gravity and extent of alcoholism as a human problem has influenced the number of research efforts in this area. Virtually all aspects of the problem are under study.

494.   Adler, Martin W., Luciano Manara, and Rosario Samanin, eds. **Factors Affecting the Action of Narcotics.** New York: Raven Press, 1978. 774p. bibliog. index. (Monograph of the Mario Negri Institute for Pharmacological Research, Milan.) $39.50. LC 78-2999. ISBN 0-89004-272-1.
      This volume contains the proceedings of a meeting held at the Mario Negri Institute for Pharmacological Research to review current findings on the pharmacology of narcotics, particularly the variety of modes of action of the drugs. Experts from many parts of the world contributed scholarly research-level papers. The underlying hope of the participants was that biomedical research of the kind reported plays a fundamental role in protecting society from the modern epidemic of drug abuse.

      Narcotics are very important drugs, especially in the treatment of pain. They do have serious drawbacks of tolerance and dependence, and their nature has still to be fully understood. Like most drugs they elicit their effects by interacting with specific receptors. Insights into this aspect of their nature have recently come to light.

      This volume focuses on the many experimental variables that can influence the effect of a narcotic drug. Some of the variables considered are: the genetic factors, the developmental stage of the experimental animal, housing conditions, ambient temperature, light, route of administration, patterns of distribution, binding, metabolism, and interactions with other agents. It is also shown that factors related to the methodology employed can influence narcotic action.

The book is of particular interest to those involved with research in the fields of pharmacology, physiology, neurosciences, experimental psychology, and psychopharmacology.

It is of note that the conference ended with a discussion of the problems of publication, particularly how most effectively to make the scientific community aware of what is happening in a rapidly moving field.

495.   **Advances in Behavioral Pharmacology.** Vol. 1. Edited by Travis Thompson, and Peter B. Dews. New York: Academic Press, 1977. 267p. bibliog. index. $21.00. LC 74-10187. ISBN 0-12-004701-2.

The field of behavioral pharmacology has reached such a point in its development that the need for a series of volumes synthesizing knowledge about it has been felt. This is the first volume of such a series. It is intended to provide synthetic and analytic reviews of significant areas of the field, prepared by competent individuals.

In this initial volume papers providing historical background and a brief review of the current and anticipated future of the discipline are included. Also, reviews of specific classes of compounds and papers on specific mechanisms of action are presented. It is intended that the volumes contain papers which are in-depth analyses rather than summaries of research literature.

Most of the contributions deal with substances that are commonly abused. The contents of the work are as follows: 1) Behavioral pharmacology of the tetrahydrocannabinols, 2) Ethanol self-administration: infrahuman studies, 3) The discriminative stimulus properties of drugs, 4) Drugs, discrimination, and signal detection theory, 5) Rate-dependency of the behavioral effects of amphetamine, 6) Behavioral pharmacology: a brief history, and 7) Current status of behavioral pharmacology.

496.   **Alcohol Dependence and Smoking Behaviour.** Edited by Griffith Edwards, M. A. H. Russell, David Hawks, and Maxine MacCafferty, on behalf of The Addiction Research Unit, Institute of Psychiatry, University of London. Farnborough, England, and Lexington, MA: Saxon House/ Lexington Books, 1976. 268p. bibliog. index. (Saxon House Studies.) $17.50. LC 75-30137. ISBN 0-347-01127-6.

The research reports collected in this book primarily have come from the Addiction Research Unit's work. The intent is to present an assemblage of material and a perspective on the subjects under consideration. Questions suitable for interdisciplinary research, possible methods to be employed, and problems to be encountered are pointed out.

The presentation is in three sections: 1) Drinking studies, 2) Smoking studies, and 3) The research position. The drinking section is further divided into three parts, surveys of drinking behavior, surveys of special groups, and hospital treatment studies. An appraisal section follows each part of the book which identifies the unsolved and underlying questions discussed in the papers.

The work is of most value to social and behavioral scientists. The editors feel that the questions of why people by hundreds of thousands damage themselves with socially accepted drugs and why the drugs are socially accepted call for much more study.

497.   Anisman, Hymie, and Giorgio Bignami, eds. **Psychopharmacology of Aversively Motivated Behavior.** New York: Plenum Press, 1978. 564p. bibliog. index. $35.00. LC 77-17998. ISBN 0-306-31005-4.

This work was planned to meet the needs of the scientist and researcher interested in understanding the neurochemical mechanisms that underlie aversively motivated behavior, as well as drug effects thereon.

The following chapters are included: 1) Aversively motivated behavior as a tool in psychopharmacologic analysis, 2) Behavioral genetics and animal learning, 3) Neurochemical changes elicited by stress: behavioral correlates, 4) Cholinergic mechanisms and aversively motivated behaviors, 5) Monoamines and aversively motivated behaviors, 6) Hallucinogens, 7) Effects of neuroleptics, ethanol, hypnotic-sedatives, tranquilizers, narcotics, and minor stimulants in aversive paradigms, 8) Stimulus attributes of drugs, and 9) A comparative neurochemical, pharmacological, and functional analysis of aversively motivated behaviors: caveats and general considerations.

As is often the case with books of this nature, animal investigations play a large part.

498.   Avogaro, Pietro, Cesare R. Sirtori, and Elena Tremoli, eds. **Metabolic Effects of Alcohol.** Proceedings of the International Symposium on Metabolic Effects of Alcohol held in Milan, June 18-21, 1979. Amsterdam: New York: Elsevier/North-Holland Biomedical Press, 1979. 430p. illus. bibliog. index. (Developments in Nutrition and Metabolism, v. 1.) $56.00. LC 79-21596. ISBN 0-444-80174-X.

The papers contained in this publication were written by specialists on the health and nutritional aspects of alcohol. The Nutritional Foundation of Italy sponsored the meeting where the papers were presented. A number of aspects of alcohol use and abuse were examined. The first section is on alcohol, health, and society. Included are papers on social contexts, epidemiology, composition of alcohol beverages and the fate of their components, microbiology and biochemistry, fetal alcohol syndrome, and altered properties of brain ribosomes following chronic alcohol use.

Other sections deal with the effects of alcohol on the endocrine system, alcohol interaction with drugs, alcohol and lipids and lipoproteins, alcohol effects on liver function and pathology, and renal and cardiovascular systems and alcohol.

The papers are highly scientific and technical, but emphasis is given throughout to the social and epidemiological aspects of the alcohol problem.

499.   Bennett, A. E. **Alcoholism and the Brain.** New York: Stratton Intercontinental Medical Book Corp., 1977. 86p. illus. bibliog. $9.75. LC 76-54392. ISBN 0-913258-45-8.

The author of this short monograph is a neurologist and psychiatrist who wrote the book primarily to provide physicians with a better understanding of alcoholism, its serious consequences, and treatment. He hopes physicians will face up to their medical responsibility and more adequately treat the compulsive, addicted alcoholic. He has avoided discussion of moral, social, and economic aspects of the problem, although he believes alcohol abuse has reached such proportions that it is seriously threatening our national character.

The specific facets of brain function are considered in relation to alcoholism as a brain disease. Bennett believes that alcoholism is a brain disease of itself and that it causes other brain diseases. It is long-term in duration and there is a deterioration through its progress and consequences. There is an intermediate stage of illness, which the physician may not recognize, when the patient usually struggles with the illness, not receiving medical help.

The book is of most value to physicians, but paramedical professionals who attempt to help alcoholics may use it also.

Chapter headings are: 1) Alcoholism as a disease, 2) Pharmacology and physiological action of alcohol on the brain, 3) Neuropathology of alcoholism, 4) Value of electroencephalography and psychological testing in alcoholic brain disease, 5) Associated systemic diseases; morbidity and mortality; medicolegal problems in alcoholism and industry, 6) Psychiatric alcoholic brain disorders, 7) Developing constructive relationships between psychiatry, general medicine and Alcoholics Anonymous, and 8) Rehabilitation and treatment of acute and chronic alcoholism of the brain.

500. Berde, B., and H. O. Schild, eds. **Ergot Alkaloids and Related Compounds**. Berlin; Heidelberg; New York: Springer-Verlag, 1978. 1003p. bibliog. index. (Handbuch der experimentellen Pharmakologie, Vol. 49, Heffter-Heubner, New Series.) $140.00. LC 77-14126. ISBN 3-540-08475-4.

This monumental work reviews the progress made during the past four decades on ergot research. In addition, a synopsis of the whole field is included although emphasis is on recent work.

Ergot compounds have many uses, but since some of them (e.g., LSD) have hallucinogenic properties, it seemed advisable to include this title with other drug abuse materials.

The following chapters, written by noted researchers, are included: 1) Introduction to the pharmacology of ergot alkaloids and related compounds as a basis of their therapeutic application, 2) Chemical background, 3) Basic pharmacological properties, 4) Effects on the uterus, 5) Actions on the heart and circulation, 6) Effects on the central nervous system, 7) Clinical pharmacology of ergot alkaloids in senile cerebral insufficiency, 8) Some compounds with hallucinogenic activity, 9) Influence on the endocrine system, 10) Metabolic effects, 11) Biopharmaceutical aspects: analytical methods, pharmacokinetics, metabolism and bioavailability, and 12) Toxicological considerations.

501. Birnbaum, Isabel M., and Elizabeth S. Parker, eds. **Alcohol and Human Memory**. Hillsdale, NJ: Lawrence Erlbaum Associates; distr., Halsted Press, a division of John Wiley and Sons, 1977. 220p. bibliog. index. $12.95. LC 77-15653. ISBN 0-470-99339-1.

The papers reprinted in this volume were originally presented at a conference sponsored by the National Institute on Alcohol Abuse and Alcoholism, September 9-10, 1976, in Laguna Beach, California. The meeting was designed to stimulate new approaches for understanding the effects of alcohol on behavior by bringing together researchers from the fields of experimental psychology of learning and memory and the investigation of alcohol and cognitive processes. Promising directions for the expansion of knowledge on the subject were explored and new research reported.

The work is in five parts as follows: 1) Introduction, 2) Approaches to the study of alcohol and memory, 3) Memory and alcohol intoxication, 4) Alcohol and state dependency, and 5) Memory in alcoholics and Korsakoff patients.

502. Blackman, D. E., and D. J. Sanger, eds. **Contemporary Research in Behavioral Pharmacology**. New York: Plenum Press, 1978. 506p. bibliog. index. $32.50. LC 77-16206. ISBN 0-306-31061-9.

The nine monographs in this book, which were written by specialists, review various aspects of psychopharmacology. The work is not limited to discussions involving drugs of abuse, but since such drugs, among others, affect behavior, they are given considerable attention. For instance, chapter 6 is concerned with alcohol.

Titles of the contributions are as follows: 1) Schedule-controlled behavior and the effects of drugs, 2) The effects of drugs on behavior controlled by aversive stimuli, 3) Stimulus control and drug effects, 4) Drug-induced stimulus control, 5) The effects of drugs on adjunctive behavior, 6) Schedule-induced self-administration of drugs, 7) Drugs as reinforcers, 8) Behavioral tolerance, and 9) Behavioral toxicology. Each contribution is followed by a summary and an extensive bibliography.

503.   Blum, Kenneth, ed. **Alcohol and Opiates: Neurochemical and Behavioral Mechanisms.** Diana L. Bard and Murray G. Hamilton, associate editors. New York: Academic Press, 1977. 403p. bibliog. $19.25. LC 77-1930. ISBN 0-12-108450-7.

This book contains the Proceedings of a Conference called The Neurological and Behavioral Mechanisms of Alcohol and Opiate Dependence, held in New York, March 26-28, 1976. The 22 papers, presented by leading experts, are divided into two sections: alcohol and opiates.

The book illustrates the kinds of issues that basic researchers are concerned with. One can see what advances are being made in understanding the addictive process, the nature of dependence and withdrawal, and the mechanisms of tolerance. In addition, such areas as opiate receptors, the effects of narcotics on behavior, metabolic aspects of opiate agonists and antagonists, and research on endorphins are discussed.

504.   Bradley, P. B., and E. Costa, eds. **Studies of Narcotic Drugs.** A symposium held at the XXVI International Congress of Physiological Sciences, New Delhi, 1974. Oxford, England: Pergamon Press, 1975. 72p. bibliog. (Special issue of *Neuropharmacology*, v. 14, No. 12, Dec. 1975.) $7.50. ISBN 0-08-0205658.

The highly technical scientific papers in this publication were presented at the meeting mentioned above. A biochemical characterization of the profile of the neurochemical action of central analgesics was presented. The action of analgesics was differentiated from that of antipsychotics and amphetamines. Morphine was considered at a synaptic level, and evidence was presented that helps characterize the location of the opiate receptors and other matters pertaining to them.

505.   Broadhurst, P. L. **Drugs and the Inheritance of Behavior: A Survey of Comparative Psychopharmacogenetics.** New York: Plenum Press, 1978. 206p. bibliog. index. $30.45. LC 78-3617. ISBN 0-306-31105-4.

The subject under consideration in this work is a blend of psychology, pharmacology, and genetics. It is the genetical analysis of behavior as modified by drugs, or the genetics of drug responsivity as measured by behavioral methods. The book reports on research in the interdisciplinary field, a great deal of it laboratory animal research.

The chapter headings are: 1) Introduction, 2) Sex differences, 3) Pharmacogenetical selection, 4) Other selections, 5) Strain differences I: amphetamine and other stimulants, 6) Crossbreeding: diallel cross, 7) Strain differences II: nicotine, anxiolytics, convulsants, and amnesiacs, 8) Recombinant inbred strains, 9) Strain differences III: alcohol, opiates, and barbiturates, and 10) Overview.

The book is highly technical. A good deal of emphasis is given to techniques of research in the field.

506.   Colpaert, Francis C., and John A. Rosecrans, eds. **Stimulus Properties of Drugs: Ten Years of Progress**. Amsterdam; New York: Oxford, Elsevier/North Holland Biomedical Press, 1978. 572p. bibliog. index. $93.26. LC 78-21532. ISBN 0-444-80087-5.

This work presents the papers of the First International Symposium on Drugs as Discriminative Stimuli, which was held in Beerse, Belgium, July 3-5, 1978, and was sponsored by the Janssen Research Foundation. This new field of chemical substances as discriminative stimuli is now a legitimate branch of neuro- and psychobiology, although a wide variety of other disciplines relate to the field. There are many practical benefits of the subject. Using appropriate experimental design, one can now determine, making use of experimental animals, whether a new chemical is like amphetamine, morphine, alcohol, or some other drug.

The highly scientific and technical papers are presented in three sections: 1) Drug discrimination, 2) State-dependency, and 3) Stimulus control.

In conclusion, it is pointed out that the stimulus properties of drugs may explain the problem of drug dependency. For example, a narcotic addict who has undergone treatment may remain drug free while in a certain locale, but will likely resume narcotic use when the environment is usual to the drug taking habit. The volume contains a representative sampling of current research on state-dependency learning, a related area.

507.   Committee on Problems of Drug Dependence, Inc. **Problems of Drug Dependence, 1978**. Proceedings of the Fortieth Annual Scientific Meeting, Committee on Problems of Drug Dependence, Inc., Lord Baltimore Hotel, Baltimore, Maryland, June 3-6, 1978. 805p. bibliog. index.

Most of these papers report on ongoing research. About 45 contributions are included, grouped under session headings as follows: Plenary, Committee on Problems of Drug Dependence Reports, Chemistry and biochemistry, Clinical, Pharmacology, Sociological, Self-administration, Addenda, and Read by title.

508.   Conklin, Marie E. **Genetic and Biochemical Aspects of the Development of Datura**. Basel: S. Karger, 1976. 170p. illus. bibliog. index. (Monographs in Developmental Biology, v. 12.) $29.00pa. ISBN 3-8055-2307-6.

This monograph was prepared primarily to report on research work done on the plant *Datura* (jimsonweed or thorn apple) from 1960 until the time the book was published. The work presents genetic and biochemical aspects of the growth and development of the plant including studies on tissue growth *in vitro*, androgenesis, isozyme production, gene mapping, protoplast hybridization and the biosynthesis of alkaloids of pharmacological importance. The latter is of most interest to those concerned with drug abuse because the plant contains intoxicants sometimes abused. The work is highly technical and suitable only for researchers.

509.   Costa, Erminio, and Marco Trabucchi, eds. **The Endorphins**. New York: Raven Press, 1978. 379p. bibliog. index. (Advances in Biochemical Pharmacology, v. 18.) $28.00. LC 76-5661. ISBN 0-89004-226-8.

The 32 papers in this volume were presented at a symposium on endorphins held in Italy in August 1977. There is a feeling at the present time that these recently discovered biochemical substances hold great promise, and some of the most important papers available at this writing are presented here. There are revolutionary implications for the field of drug abuse; for instance, non-addictive pain relievers may be designed and the mechanism of addiction elucidated.

The contributors to the volume are the leading experts and researchers in the field, and they survey the latest findings on physiological, pharmacological, and pathogenic implications of endorphins.

The subject is very complex, and it is evident that many questions remain and that much research will follow. However, the following are some of the aspects of the subject treated in the book: a historical review of neuropeptide research; the development of the concepts of opiate receptors and their ligands; the biochemistry of the endorphins; their cellular distribution within specific neural pathways; interactions between endorphins; catecholamine metabolism and the control of pituitary hormone release; interactions between endorphinergic neurons and those containing other neurotransmitters; the localization of opiate receptors and their differential ligand affinity in various brain regions; the comparative effects of the endorphins and their involvement in psychiatric disorders; brain endorphins and the sense of well-being; morphine-like factors in cerebrospinal fluid of headache patients; and the possible role of endorphins in acupuncture-induced analgesia.

510.   Fishman, Jack, ed. **The Bases of Addiction**. Report of the Dahlem Workshop on the Bases of Addiction, Berlin 1977, September 26-30. Berlin: produced for Dahlem Konferenzen by Abakon Verlagsgesellschaft, 1978. 535p. bibliog. index. (Life Sciences Research Report 8.) $32.00pa. ISBN 3-8200-1210-9.

The intent of this workshop was to survey the present state of knowledge about all aspects of addiction with the hope of gaining new insights into the problem. Because addiction is usually perceived as a complex mixture of biological mechanisms and behavioral drives, both behavioral and biological papers have been included.

The focus of the workshop was on seeking commonalities in the addiction to different substances and any specific differences that distinguished individuals who become addicted from those who do not under the same circumstances.

Twenty-six papers by experts are included. Several are group reports.

511.   Ford, Donald H., and Doris H. Clouet, eds. **Tissue Responses to Addictive Drugs**. Proceedings of a workshop session for the International Society for Neuroendocrinology, Downstate Medical Center, State University of New York, June, 1975. New York: SP Books Division of Spectrum Publications, Inc.; distr., Halsted Press, 1976. 704p. bibliog. index. $50.00. LC 76-21325. ISBN 0-470-15192-7.

One of the basic aims of recent studies of drug dependence has been an understanding of the mechanisms of drug action and of the phenomena of tolerance and dependence. This book deals with problems of drug disposition in the brain and other tissues and the possible nature of the drug receptors. It contains 41 scientific papers presented by experts in the fields of anatomy, physiology, biochemistry, pharmacology, and endocrinology.

New information is provided in relation to the effect of morphine on protein synthesis in the central nervous system. In addition, studies are presented on anatomical localization, endocrine effects in relation to development, and clinical effects of drugs.

The work is of most interest to those working in drug-related research.

512.   Gibbins, Robert J., and others, eds. **Research Advances in Alcohol and Drug Problems**. Vol. 3. New York: John Wiley and Sons, 1976. 476p. bibliog. index. $32.75. LC 73-18088. ISBN 0-471-29736-4.

One volume in this series is published every year, although it is not an "annual review" in the usual sense. Instead, the aim is to present a number of critically evaluative papers dealing with topics in which special progress has been made or which require analysis and clarification.

The following chapters are presented, each by a noted expert: 1) Tobacco smoking and nicotine dependence, 2) Caffeine as a drug of abuse, 3) Psychiatric syndromes produced by nonmedical use of drugs, 4) Drinking patterns and the level of alcohol consumption: an international overview, 5) Cannabis and experimental studies of driving skills, 6) Current trends in prescribed psychotropic drug use, 7) Death in amphetamine users: causes and estimates of mortality, 8) Behavioral modification techniques in the treatment of alcoholism: a review and critique, 9) Nonabstinent drinking goals in the treatment of alcoholics, and 10) Sex differences in criminality among drug abuse patients in the United States.

513.   Gottheil, Edward L., A. Thomas McLellan, Keith A. Druley, and Arthur I. Alterman, eds. **Addiction Research and Treatment: Converging Trends.** Proceedings of the First Annual Coatesville-Jefferson Conference on Addiction, held in October 1977. New York: Pergamon Press, 1979. 146p. bibliog. $15.00. LC 78-23703. ISBN 0-08-023025-3.

This volume presents selected conference papers presented by experts in the addiction field. Recent advances that illustrate the mutual contribution of research and treatment in addiction are stressed. The papers are grouped under two headings: treatment as a resource for meaningful research, and translating research into clinical practice.

Titles of the papers are as follows: 1) Some relationships between experimental theoretical and clinical approaches to alcoholism, 2) The relationship between depression and alcoholism, 3) LAAM vs. methadone: advantages and disadvantages, 4) Hallucinogenic drugs—psychopharmacology, clinical effects and management of adverse reactions, 5) Problem solving training: a structured therapeutic modality for new drug and alcohol admissions, 6) Alcohol and other substance abuse in adolescents, 7) Addictive disorders—an interface between medicine and politics, 8) An overview of craving disorders, 9) Compulsive smoking—a new look at an old addiction, 10) One year experience with combined treatment of drug and alcohol abusers, 11) A comparative study of levo-alpha acetylmethadol and methadone in the treatment of narcotic addiction, 12) Sleep quality reported by drinking and non-drinking alcoholics, 13) Effective inpatient treatment of older alcoholics, 14) Conditioning as a cause of relapse in narcotic addiction, 15) Alcoholics' drinking decisions: implications for treatment and outcome, and 16) Developing an effective collaboration between substance abuse treatment and research.

514.   Gráf, L., M. Palkovits, and A. Z. Rónai, eds. **Endorphins '78.** International Workshop Conference, Budapest, Hungary, 2-6 October, 1978. Amsterdam; Oxford: Excerpta Medica, 1978. 336p. bibliog. (International Congress Series, No. 471.) $58.50. ISBN 90-219-0395-4.

The subject of endorphins has provoked considerable interest of recent years, and this volume makes a contribution to a better understanding of the biological function of endorphins, substances that may reveal some of the mysteries of addiction. The participants in the conference were judiciously selected, and the papers are highly scientific and suitable only for the research-level reader.

Fifteen papers are presented under the following headings: 1) Structure and function, 2) Biosynthesis, 3) Distribution and release, 4) Receptor and function, and 5) Pharmacology and clinical aspects. Discussions follow each paper.

515.   Gross, Milton M., ed. **Alcohol Intoxication and Withdrawal—IIIa; Biological Aspects of Ethanol**. New York: Plenum Press, 1977. 652p. bibliog. index. (Advances in Experimental Medicine and Biology. v. 85A.) $47.50. LC 77-21537. ISBN 0-306-39085-X.

This volume contains the proceedings of the first half of the Third Biennial International Interdisciplinary Symposium of the Biomedical Alcohol Research Section, International Council of Alcohol and Addictions, held in Lausanne, Switzerland, June 7-11, 1976. The contributors are well-known researchers in the field.

The 40 papers, which are highly scientific and technical, are grouped in the following sections: 1) Genetics and alcohol, 2) Macromolecules, membranes, and alcohol, 3) Biochemical studies on the metabolism of ethanol and acetaldehyde, 4) Cytotoxic effects of alcohol, 5) Neurochemistry and alcohol, and 6) Sleep and alcohol. An abstract has been included with each paper.

516.   Gross, Milton M., ed. **Alcohol Intoxication and Withdrawal—IIIb; Studies in Alcohol Dependence**. New York: Plenum Press, 1977. 646p. bibliog. index. (Advances in Experimental Medicine and Biology. v. 85B.) $49.50. LC 77-21537. ISBN 0-306-39086-8.

The second of two volumes (*see* above) presented here are the proceedings of the second half of the Third Biennial International Interdisciplinary Symposium of the Biomedical Alcohol Research Section, International Council of Alcohol and Addictions, held in Lausanne, Switzerland, June 7-11, 1976. As with the first volume the scientific papers were contributed by experts in the field.

Forty papers are grouped under the following numbered headings: 7) Relevance of animal models of physical dependence to the alcohol dependence syndrome in humans, 8) Comparative mechanisms of tolerance to and dependence on alcohol, barbiturates, and opiates, 9) Additional studies in non-human animals, 10) Additional studies in humans, 11) Operant conditioning and alcohol intake, and 12) Craving and alcohol intake. An abstract has been provided for each paper.

517.   Herz, Albert, ed. **Developments in Opiate Research**. New York: Marcel Dekker, 1978. 432p. bibliog. index. (Modern Pharmacology-Toxicology, v. 14.) $35.00. LC 78-9745. ISBN 0-8427-6762-4.

This volume presents recent developments in the field of opiate pharmacology, an area where notable scientific advances have been made the past five years or so. An extensive coverage of the literature is not offered; instead, attention is focused on a few topics where most significant progress has been made.

The following chapters are presented, each written by a noted author or authors: 1) The opiate receptors, 2) Endogenous ligands of opiate receptors (endorphins), 3) Sites of opiate action in the central nervous system, 4) Actions of opioids on on single neurons, 5) The use of isolated organs to study the mechanism of action of narcotic analgesics, 6) On the role of brain catecholamines in acute and chronic opiate action, 7) Opioids and cyclic nucleotides, and 8) Opiate tolerance and dependence: some concluding remarks.

The last chapter is a good, brief, and reasonably understandable review of what is now known and what is yet to be learned about opiate tolerance and dependence.

518.   Ho, Beng T., Daniel W. Richards III, and Douglas L. Chute, eds. **Drug Discrimination and State Dependent Learning**. New York: Academic Press, 1978. 392p. bibliog. index. $23.00. LC 77-2027. ISBN 0-12-350250-0.

An interdisciplinary work, this book is intended primarily for researchers in the fields of pharmacology and experimental pharmacology. The chapters, written by leading researchers, are divided into three sections: Mechanism of drugs as discriminative stimuli, Research methods and new techniques, and State dependent phenomena. Overview chapters have been included for background and to place the material in context, providing a rationale for the use of drugs to study behavior.

While the book is not about drug abuse per se, the chapter titles show that the drugs involved in the studies are psychotropic drugs commonly abused. Chapter titles are as follows: 1) Pharmacology of discriminative stimuli, 2) Current trends in the study of drugs as discriminative stimuli, 3) Discriminative properties of mescaline, 6) Stimulus properties of ethanol and depressant drugs, 7) The discriminative stimulus properties of N- and M-cholinergic receptor stimulants, 8) The discriminative stimulus properties of cannabinoids: a review, 9) Dual receptor mediation of the discriminative stimulus properties of pentazocine, 10) Stimulus properties of narcotic analgesics and antagonists, 11) Attributes of discriminative pentobarbital stimulus immediately after intravenous injection, 12) Experimental design and data analysis in studies of drug discrimination: some general considerations, 13) Statistical and methodological considerations in drug-stimulus discrimination learning, 14) A functional analysis of the discriminative stimulus properties of amphetamine and phentobarbital, 15) Discriminative control of behavior by electrical stimulation of the brain: a new neuropharmacological research strategy, 16) Intragastric self-administration of drugs by the primate, 17) Major theories of state dependent learning, 18) State dependent retrieval based on time of day, 19) The engram: lost and found, and 20) Human state dependent learning.

The book is of value to psychopharmacologists, physiologists, researchers in learning and memory, neuropharmacologists, and behavioral pharmacologists.

519.   Hunt, Leon Gibson. **Assessment of Local Drug Abuse.** Lexington, MA: Lexington Books, D. C. Heath and Co., 1977. 153p. bibliog. index. $17.50. LC 76-42694. ISBN 0-669-01053-7.

The author of this book is a mathematician who has written several works on mathematical epidemiology and public health demography as related to drug abuse. He has made a contribution to the field by getting drug abuse experts to pay attention to numerical data. He has found, for instance, that the year a client first used a particular drug is significant in understanding the spread of drug use. The book shows that data systems and surveys are useful, but that the most valuable data may be easiest to get, for example, questioning the drug abuser who seeks treatment.

The material is presented in four sections: 1) Public perception of drug abuse, 2) Empirical measures of drug use, 3) Detecting abused drugs, and 4) Responses and priorities. The chapter titles are as follows: 1) Introduction, 2) Anatomy of the drug problem, 3) Measuring community drug use, 4) Spread of drug use: applications of incidence of first use analysis, 5) Incidence of first use of a drug: significance and interpretations, 6) Incidence of first use: examples of local differences, 7) Age of first use of drugs: empirical data and interpretations, 8) Extent of drug use: estimates of prevalence, 9) Extent of use: types of users and changes in level of use, 10) Other indicators of drug abuse, 11) What is an abused drug?, 12) Overdoses: a second look, 13) A note on progression, 14) Criteria for abused drugs, 15) Public responses to drug use, and 16) Conclusions.

520. Hunt, Leon Gibson, and Carl D. Chambers. **The Heroin Epidemics: A Study of Heroin Use in the United States, 1965-75**. New York: SP Books Division of Spectrum Publications, Inc.; distr., Halsted Press, 1976. 145p. bibliog. index. $12.95. LC 75-42343. ISBN 0-470-15231-1.

This book treats the heroin problem from a different point of view from that usually taken. It is an epidemiological point of view, employing standard methods and new mathematical techniques to investigate the spread of the use of the drug. The conclusions are based on empirical data that are analyzed and interpreted mathematically. The extent and the spread of heroin use are both considered; also, prediction of future developments is made.

The material is presented in three parts: 1) Incidence of new heroin users, 2) Prevalence of active heroin users, and 3) Treatment and prevention policy.

In summary, the authors present characteristics of a successful primary prevention program. Realistic programs must do the following: 1) anticipate the locales of new use, 2) focus on the individual new user, 3) identify the new user early, and 4) discover a way to induce the new unaddicted user to give up heroin. The authors believe society can accomplish the first three, but know of no workable approach to the last task.

521. Ideström, Carl-Magnus, ed. **Recent Advances in the Study of Alcoholism**. Proceedings of the First International Magnus Huss Symposium, Stockholm, 2-3 September 1976. Organized by the Department of Clinical Alcohol and Drug Research, Karolinska Institutet. Amsterdam: Excerpta Medica, 1977. 135p. bibliog. index. (International Congress Series, No. 407.) $22.95pa. ISBN 90-219-0332-6.

The participants of this symposium discussed various aspects of alcohol research and also the treatment of alcoholics. The editor of the publication points to the enormous worldwide problem of alcohol abuse, its great economic impact, and the variety of treatments possible, all of which have low success rates. About 20 papers are presented. Some of the specific topics covered are: The mechanism of action of alcohol, long-term effects, correlation of personality and risk of alcoholism, the alcoholic female, and a number of treatment approaches, including the pharmacological.

522. Institute of Medicine. Division of Mental Health and Behavioral Medicine. **Sleeping Pills, Insomnia, and Medical Practice: Report of a Study**. Washington: National Academy of Sciences, 1979. 198p. bibliog. LC 79-87705. ISBN 0-309-02881-7.

In 1977, President Carter called for a study to review the safety and usefulness of hypnotic drugs and to examine physician prescribing practices with respect to them. The Institute of Medicine undertook the study for the White House and the National Institute on Drug Abuse. This publication reports on the results of the investigations.

Both clinical issues and public health problems associated with the prescribing of hypnotic drugs are reviewed. The major emphasis is on drugs prescribed as sleeping pills, but some effort also is made to assess the use of certain anti-anxiety drugs, such as diazepam (Valium), and anti-depressants, such as amitriptyline (Elavil). Alcohol is not discussed in depth except to document its inefficiency as a hypnotic agent and the addictive nature of its undesirable effects when consumed with hypnotic drugs.

The following chapters are presented: 1) An overview of sleep and medication, 2) Epidemiology of sleep complaints and prescribing practices, 3) Public health problems associated with the use of hypnotic drugs, 4) Insomnia: research findings, diagnostic approaches, and therapeutic options, 5) Sleep disturbance in the elderly, and 6) Conclusions. In addition, there is an appendix, "Assessing the Hazards and Benefits of Hypnotic Drugs."

The conclusions chapter covers the following considerations: prudent prescribing, patient information, suicide prevention, toxicology, epidemiology, professional education, advertising and labeling, research needs, and initiation and coordination of federal efforts.

523.   International Symposium on Alcohol and Aldehyde Metabolizing Systems, 1st, Stockholm, 1972: 2nd, University of Pennsylvania, 1976. **Alcohol and Aldehyde Metabolizing Systems**. Edited by Ronald G. Thurman, and others. New York: Academic Press, 1974-77. 3 v. illus. bibliog. index. (Johnson Research Foundation Colloquia.) $72.50 the set. LC 73-5316. ISBN 0-12-691450-6; 0-12-691402-8; 0-12-611403-6.

Volume 1 of this set contains papers presented at the first symposium; volumes 2-3, papers of the second. Volume 2 has the special title "Enzymology and Subcellular Organelles"; volume 3, "Intermediary Metabolism and Neurochemistry."

The purpose of the meetings was to bring together experts in the field from wide backgrounds in an attempt to gain clarity and insight into the problems of alcohol metabolism. Hundreds of papers on the topic are produced annually, and the hope was to focus on this literature, bring discoveries into perspective, and elucidate controversial issues. The papers are highly technical, and generally deal with the underlying biochemical mechanisms of alcohol and aldehyde metabolism rather than clinical aspects. The intended audience includes those in the fields of biochemistry, pharmacology, neurochemistry, and others interested in alcoholism.

The following are the section headings: Volume 1, 1) Enzymology of alcohol dehydrogenase, 2) Enzymology and localization of aldehyde dehydrogenases, 3) Properties of catalase in situ, 4) Hydrogen peroxide production in cellular organelles, 5) The role of catalase in microsomal ethanol oxidation, 6) Interaction of ethanol with fatty acid synthesis and degradation, 7) Influence of ethanol upon intermediary metabolism, and 8) Ethanol metabolism in vivo. Volume 2, 1) Enzyme structure and mechanism, 2) Alcohol and aldehyde dehydrogenase, 3) Subcellular organelles and their distribution, and 4) Peroxisomes and mocrosomes. Volume 3, 1) Biochemical compartmentation, 2) Intermediary metabolism, 3) Neurochemistry and neuropharmacology, and 4) Acetaldehyde and withdrawal.

524.   Israel, Yedy, and others, eds. **Research Advances in Alcohol and Drug Problems**. Vol. 4. New York: Plenum Press, 1978. 497p. bibliog. index. $39.50. LC 73-18088. ISBN 0-306-34424-6.

This volume is another in a series that presents critical reviews and assesses current developments in the field. Evaluative papers on topics in which enough recent progress has been made to alter the general scope of a particular area are presented.

The following chapters are included, each written by an expert or experts: 1) Biological significance of the endogenous opioid peptides and the opiate receptors, 2) Brain reinforcement centers and psychoactive drugs, 3) Animal studies of alcohol withdrawal reactions, 4) Acetaldehyde—its metabolism and role in the actions of alcohol, 5) Patient characteristics as predictors of treatment outcomes for alcohol and drug abusers, 6) The social history of the tavern, 7) Level of consumption and

social consequences of drinking, 8) Alcohol use among North American blacks,
9) The etiologic relationship between drug use and criminality, 10) Decriminalization
of public drunkenness, and 11) The treatment of cigarette dependence.

525.   Iversen, Leslie L., Susan D. Iversen, and Solomon H. Snyder, eds. **Drugs of
Abuse.** New York: Plenum Press, 1978. 420p. bibliog. index. (Yearbook of Psychopharmacology, v. 12.) $32.50. LC 75-6851. ISBN 0-306-38932-0.

This work is a volume in a series dealing with psychopharmacology. Although
it is part of a section on human psychopharmacology, several of the chapters contain
data obtained from animal studies.

There are seven chapters: 1) Drug self-administration: an analysis of the
reinforcing effects of drugs, 2) Analgesics and their antagonists: structure-activity
relationships, 3) Opiates: human psychopharmacology, 4) Sedative-hypnotics: animal
pharmacology, 5) Alcohol and human behavior, 6) Cannabis: structure-activity relationships, and 7) Marihuana: human effects. Stimulants are considered in another
volume of the series.

Each chapter presents a reasonably comprehensive, rather technical review
of the topic under consideration. In addition, various approaches and methodologies
for research are presented. The reader needs some working knowledge of both psychology and pharmacology in order to understand the material.

526.   Jones, Kenneth R., and Thomas R. Vischi. **Impact of Alcohol, Drug Abuse
and Mental Health Treatment on Medical Care Utilization: A Review of the Research
Literature.** From the Office of Program Planning and Coordination, Alcohol, Drug
Abuse and Mental Health Administration, Rockville, Maryland. Philadelphia, PA:
J. B. Lippincott Co., 1979. 82p. bibliog. (*Medical Care*, Supplement, v. 17, No. 12,
December 1979.) $5.00pa.

It has been presumed of recent years that the treatment of alcoholism, drug
abuse, and mental illness results in a subsequent reduction in treatment necessary
for other health problems. Research has been carried out that addresses this supposi-
tion. This monograph reviews and assesses 25 research studies that examine the hypothesis. Some of the studies do not indicate any dollar amounts saved nor the extent
to which such savings lower the net additional costs of alcoholism, drug abuse, or
mental illness, but virtually all found that a reduction did take place. The range was
5-85% with the median being 20%.

The publication contains the following sections: 1) Introduction, 2) Findings,
3) Research conclusions, 4) Policy implications, 5) Methodological recommendations
for future studies, and 6) Summary table for twenty-five studies. In addition, there
is a long appendix, which presents a review and critique of each of the studies and
a few additional ones that are currently underway. Most of the studies reported
involve mental health or alcoholism only; just a few consider drug abuse also.

The authors make a strong recommendation for further more rigorous
research in this area.

527.   Keller, Mark, ed. **Research Priorities on Alcohol.** Proceedings of a Symposium sponsored by the Rutgers Center of Alcohol Studies and Rutgers University.
New Brunswick, NJ: Center of Alcohol Studies, Rutgers University, 1979. 342p.
bibliog. index. (Journal of Studies on Alcohol, Supplement No. 8, November 1979.)
ISBN 911290-03-6.

This publication presents the papers of the meeting, prepared responses to them, and discussions. The participants are well-known researchers in the alcohol field. The presentations are grouped under the following headings: 1) Alcohol studies as a discipline, 2) Psychology, 3) The biological perspective, 4) Social sciences, and 5) Conclusion.

A highlight of the conference is the first paper, which presents a somewhat novel viewpoint. The author believes that the field of alcohol studies should be treated as a distinct discipline rather than an "interdisciplinary" subject. The term "alcoholo-gy" is suggested by the editor. In the last paper, in which research priorities are discussed, the author suggests that emphasis be placed on answerable questions.

528.   Khanna, J. M., Y. Israel, and H. Kalant, eds. **Alcoholic Liver Pathology.** S. L. Lambert, general editor. Toronto: Alcoholism and Drug Addiction Research Foundation of Ontario, 1975. 369p. illus. bibliog. index. (International Symposia on Alcohol and Drug Addiction.) $25.00; $17.00pa. ISBN 0-88868-005-8.

This work contains the proceedings of the Liver Pathology Section of the International Symposia on Alcohol and Drug Research held in Toronto on October 15-18, 1973. Of the 21 papers, the first sessions were devoted to clinical and epidemiological data that would sort out the role of alcohol per se, as distinct from malnutrition or other factors in the development of alcoholic liver disease. Next, consideration was given to the liver as a complex organ influenced by blood flow, oxygen supply, hornomes, and biochemical events elsewhere in the body. Then ethanol metabolism was dealt with, and lastly the sequence of events initiated by cell death and eventually irreversible and fatal cirrhosis. Concluding summary remarks have been included in the volume, but not the free discussions by the participants. The papers are scholarly and highly technical.

529.   Kissin, Benjamin, Joyce H. Lowinson, and Robert B. Millman, eds. **Recent Developments in Chemotherapy of Narcotic Addiction.** New York: New York Academy of Sciences, 1978. 315p. bibliog. (New York Academy of Sciences. Annals. v. 311.) $40.00. LC 78-15373. ISBN 0-89072-067-3.

This volume is based on a conference held November 3-4, 1977, cosponsored by the New York Academy of Sciences and PACT-NADAP, a voluntary agency located in Manhattan. The conference brought together a group of leading experts, clinicians and basic scientists, to report and discuss research progress relevant to substance dependency. The main thrust is on biochemistry and clinical management of chemotherapeutic approaches to opiate addiction, with particular emphasis on neurohumoral discoveries, epidemiology, and the problem of tracking those exposed to various treatments. Substances used to treat opiate dependence, such as methadone, LAAM, and narcotic antagonists, are stressed; and a section on opiate receptors and endorphins is included.

Section headings are as follows: 1) Epidemiology and characteristics of drug abuse, 2) Opiate receptors and endorphins, 3) Tolerance and physical dependence on drugs, 4) Medical aspects of methadone maintenance, 5) Rational approach to detoxification from methadone maintenance, 6) LAAM and narcotic antagonists, 7) Evaluation of treatment effectiveness, and 8) Current trends in narcotic addiction treatment.

The contributions are of very high quality.

530.   Kornetsky, Conan. **Pharmacology: Drugs Affecting Behavior.** New York: John Wiley and Sons, 1976. 275p. illus. bibliog. index. (A Wiley-Interscience Publication.) $20.00. LC 76-6062. ISBN 0-471-50410-6.

The aim of this book is to provide the clinical psychologist and others in the mental health professions a basic understanding of the principles and methods of pharmacology, and to present information on the major classes of drugs that affect behavior, either licitly or illicitly used. Much of the basic pharmacology presented can be found in standard pharmacology textbooks, but those trained in the behavioral sciences usually do not have the necessary background in chemistry and physiology to comprehend them. The author of this work has assumed that his readers have only rudimentary knowledge of these subjects.

In addition to the pharmacology, several chapters have been included of special interest to those in the drug abuse field, and which may be considered individual studies. For instance, there are chapters on narcotic analgesics, hypnotics and sedatives, alcohol, the amphetamines, and the nonmedical use of drugs. A glossary of street terms has also been provided.

The author, who is a psychologist, has done a noteworthy job of providing the nonmedical reader with an understanding of the subject. As an added feature he has also examined to some extent the social and psychological aspects of illicit drug use.

531.   Kosterlitz, H. W., ed. **Opiates and Endogenous Opioid Peptides.** Proceedings of the International Narcotics Research Club Meeting, Aberdeen, United Kingdom, 19-22 July 1976. Amsterdam: North Holland Publishing Co., 1976. 456p. bibliog. index. $36.50. ISBN 0-7204-0599-8.

This is evidently the first book-length work devoted to the enkephalins, substances now known generally as the endorphins. Since the appearance of this work, the editor was one of three who received the Albert and Mary Lasker Foundation's Basic Research Award for his work in this field (the award was made in November 1978).

The volume contains a large number of research papers presented at a conference. They are highly technical contributions of an international group of researchers, suitable only for a research-level audience. Because of rapid progress in the field, all offered papers were accepted for the meeting.

Enkephalins were identified in the body and synthesized in late 1975. Since that time research in the field has accelerated rapidly, and a large number of laboratories are involved in research on the acute and chronic effects of opiates. The discovery of the enkephalins portends great promise in a number of respects. They are part of the body's protective biochemical system for coping with pain and stress. They also help explain narcotic addiction, and subsequently may point the way toward alleviating it.

532.   Kosterlitz, H. W., H. O. J. Collier, and J. E. Villarreal, eds. **Agonist and Antagonist Actions of Narcotic Analgesic Drugs.** Baltimore, MD: University Park Press, 1973. 290p. bibliog. index. $19.50. LC 72-12612. ISBN 0-8391-0725-0.

This work is a record of the proceedings of an international symposium held at Aberdeen, Scotland, in July 1971. It is of interest because it is still not known how opium alkaloids and their modern counterparts exert their analgesic action and why they so readily produce dependence and tolerance in users. The following aspects of the subject are covered: chemistry, structure-activity relationships, acute and chronic effects, neurochemical mechanisms, and psychological dependence. There are several technical research papers in each category.

The work is important because nonmedical use of this class of drugs has increased rapidly of recent years. In addition, research workers have expended a great deal of effort, with only limited success, to find new substances that have analgesic but not addictive properties.

533.   Kurland, Albert A. **Psychiatric Aspects of Opiate Dependence.** West Palm Beach, FL: CRC Press, 1978. 273p. bibliog. index. (CRC Drug Dependence Series.) $59.95. LC 77-18030. ISBN 0-8493-5056-5.

Written primarily for those involved with the clinical management of addicted individuals, this book contains guidelines and is intended as an introduction to the subject. The author is a psychiatrist who has served in a clinic devoted to investigational studies of the felon parolee narcotic addict.

The following are the chapter titles: 1) Historical notes, 2) The "natural history" of the narcotic addict, 3) The experimental model, 4) The drug choice, 5) Personality, 6) Psychodiagnostics, 7) Prognosis, 8) Psychodynamics, 9) Deaddictive mechanisms, 10) Clinical issues and case histories, and 11) The future of narcotic addiction.

The book is quite well-written and interesting and is suitable for the well-educated layman as well as the professional. Some of the comments in the closing chapter are of note. The author feels that the hope for a "cure" for addiction emerging from the advances in biochemical pharmacology becomes more remote as the understanding of the disorder deepens. Also, the promise of psychotherapy has not materialized as was hoped, largely because of the time-consuming procedures. Kurland names five major categories of present approaches: 1) the measures designed to control the traffic in illicit drugs, 2) prevention through public education about the hazards of drug abuse, 3) social reforms to enhance the quality of life, 4) the expansion of treatment resources, and 5) research. All have limitations. However, some possibility exists that a means will be found for facilitating treatment. Kurland believes that a treatment form may evolve in a series of brief treatment experiences that will remake these personalities into potentially more rewarding individuals both to themselves and to society.

534.   **Legal and Illicit Drug Use: Acute Reactions of Emergency-Room Populations.** By James A. Inciardi, Duane C. McBride, Anne E. Pottieger, Brian R. Russe, and Harvey A. Siegal. New York: Praeger Publishers, 1978. 185p. bibliog. index. $20.95. LC 78-19743. ISBN 0-03-046701-2.

This work takes up drug abuse research and data collecting from a different point of view. The authors use hospital emergency room statistics as an indicator of drug abuse prevalence in a community. They are concerned with abuse of legal prescription drugs as well as with illicit drug use, and they find that treatment for the former is seldom available. A case is made for the development of emergency room-based treatment programs as a means of intervention in a drug abuse and/or alcoholism career. A great deal of statistical information has been presented in the work.

535.   Lemberger, Louis, and Alan Rubin. **Physiologic Disposition of Drugs of Abuse.** New York: SP Books, a division of Spectrum Publications, Inc., 1976. 401p. bibliog. index. (Monographs in Pharmacology and Physiology, v. 1.) $29.50. LC 76-13. ISBN 0-470-15021-1.

This book was written by research pharmacologists for other pharmacologists, psychiatrists, psychologists, and those in the other basic and clinical fields who need to know about how a drug acts in the body and how the body acts on the drug.

The following chapters are presented: 1) Fundamental principles of drug distribution, 2) Amphetamine, 3) Mescaline and chemically related phenylalkylamines, 4) LSD and related indolealkylamines, 5) Morphine and morphine substitutes, 6) Barbiturates and methaqualone, 7) Recreational drugs of abuse: caffeine, nicotine, and alcohol, 8) The cannabinoids, 9) Cocaine and miscellaneous drugs of abuse, and 10) Tolerance.

The material is well-organized and readable although highly technical in some sections. It shows clearly that the matter of drug disposition in the body is a complex set of circumstances.

536.   Lieber, Charles S., ed. **Metabolic Aspects of Alcoholism**. Lancaster, England: MTP Press Limited, 1977. 308p. bibliog. index. $24.50. ISBN 0-85200129-0.

A number of specialists collaborated with the editor to produce this work, which is an investigation of the metabolic effects of continued excessive use of alcohol. The approach used is a combination of clinical, biochemical, physiological, and pathological. How the body handles alcohol and how it affects liver, intestine, heart, muscle, brain, bone, and the endocrine and hematopietic systems are considered. The book also reviews the way the alcoholic, as a result of changes produced by alcohol, does not respond normally to alcohol, other drugs, or even other toxic agents.

The work is of particular value for those who treat alcoholism and other diseases that afflict the alcoholic. In addition, clinical and basic researchers such as biochemists, pharmacologists, pathologists, and psychologists should find it of interest.

537.   Lindros, K. O., and C. J. P. Eriksson, eds. **The Role of Acetaldehyde in the Actions of Ethanol**. Satellite Symposium to the Sixth International Congress of Pharmacology, July 26, 1975, Helsinki, Finland. New Brunswick, NJ: Rutgers University Center of Alcohol Studies, 1975. 239p. illus. bibliog. (The Finnish Foundation for Alcohol Studies, v. 23.) $37.50pa. ISBN 951-9191-23-2.

The 16 papers in this volume are based on presentations at the international meeting mentioned above. The partly controversial questions of the quantitative and qualitative role of acetaldehyde in the actions of alcohol are discussed. (Acetaldehyde is the primary metabolite in ethyl alcohol oxidation.) Many aspects of the subject are reviewed, the most important ones being: the question of the possible formation in the intact organism of condensation products between acetaldehyde and biogenic amines, which resemble morphine and related alkaloids; the mechanism involved in acetaldehyde's effect on the regulation of voluntary intake; and how ethanol influences metabolic pathways. The papers are highly technical, suitable for the research scientist.

538.   Loh, Horace H., and David H. Ross, eds. **Neurochemical Mechanisms of Opiates and Endorphins**. New York: Raven Press, 1979. 563p. bibliog. index. (Advances in Biochemical Psychopharmacology, v. 20.) $39.00. LC 78-24623. ISBN 0-89004-166-0.

This work of 21 chapters by 39 notable researchers provides a comprehensive review of the latest developments in the rapidly growing and promising research areas of opiate receptors and neurochemical mechanisms of the opiate peptides and narcotic analgesics. The literature of the field is well-covered and the authors' own research findings reported. Long bibliographies have been included.

The first paper is a review and an overview of narcotic research covering the past 40 years. The author, E. Leong Way, points out what he considers the most profitable avenues for researchers to follow in the next decade, with the hope that the mechanism of action of the opiates will be made entirely clear. The remaining papers are grouped in the following sections: 1) Opiate-endorphin-receptor interactions, 2) Chemistry and neurobiology of endogenous opiate peptides, 3) The role of messenger systems in opiate actions, 4) Opiates and neurotransmitter function, 5) Macromolecules, membrane function, and opiate mechanisms, and 6) Summary and perspectives.

At this writing, the book probably represents the most up-to-date and comprehensive collection of information on the topic. The material is too advanced for the average reader, or even undergraduates in the biological sciences, but neurochemists, pharmacologists, and all neuroscientists involved in opiate research will find it quite valuable.

539.   Majchrowicz, Edward, and Ernest P. Noble, eds. **Biochemistry and Pharmacology of Ethanol**. New York: Plenum Press, 1979. 2 v. illus. bibliog. index. $90.00. LC 79-292. ISBN 0-306-40125-8 (v. 1); 0-306-40130-4 (v. 2).

The editors of this impressive work point out that in the past, particularly since the repeal of Prohibition, there has been little effort to do research on the deleterious effect of alcohol, in spite of the fact that its abuse represents a major health, social, and economic problem of the world. This comprehensive treatise provides a scholarly, scientific, timely, and critical review of the biochemistry and pharmacology of alcohol, progressing from the action at the molecular level to effects at higher levels of biological organization. It is presumed that the behavioral effects of alcohol reflect the consequences of its molecular interactions. The list of contributors to the work is long and impressive.

The publication is in 13 sections, each containing several chapters dealing with various aspects of the topic. The section headings are as follows: 1) Distribution and elimination of ethanol, 2) Enzymology and metabolism of ethanol, 3) Effects of ethanol on intermediary metabolism, 4) Biochemistry of ethanol-induced liver damage and disease, 5) Effects of ethanol on the metabolism of brain, 6) Metabolic effects of ethanol on various organs of the body, 7) Ethanol and electrolyte metabolism, 8) Influence of ethanol on biological membranes, 9) Interaction of ethanol with hormonal functions, 10) Interaction of ethanol with neurotransmitters, 11) Ethanol and neuronal electrophysiology, 12) Interaction of ethanol with drugs, and 13) Physiology, behavior, and animal models of alcohol dependence.

540.   Marks, Vincent, and John Wright, eds. **Metabolic Effects of Alcohol**. London; Philadelphia; Toronto: W. B. Saunders Co., 1978. 466p. bibliog. index. (Clinics in Endocrinology and Metabolism, v. 7, No. 2, July 1978.) LC 77-182439.

Although this special issue of a serial publication covers the subject under consideration in a selective manner, it deals with some of the most important clinical aspects of alcohol use. It is estimated that alcoholic drinks account for six percent of the mean daily energy intake of individuals in the United Kingdom, and in countries such as France and Italy consumption is twice as great. This high consumption accounts for many of the metabolic abnormalities in heavy drinkers (in addition to other harmful effects such as the psychiatric disturbances).

The chapters, written by various experts, are headed as follows: 1) The metabolism of alcohol, 2) Alcohol and its metabolic interactions with other drugs, 3) Clinical biochemistry of alcoholism, 4) Alcohol and the abnormalities of lipid metabolism, 5) Alcohol and carbohydrate metabolism, 6) Endocrine effects of alcohol, 7) Alcohol and nuerotransmitters, 8) Alcohol and the nervous system, 9) Alcohol and nutrition, 10) Alcohol and the alimentary system, and 11) Alcohol and the haemopoietic system.

541.   Martin, William R., ed. **Drug Addiction I: Morphine, Sedative/Hypnotic and Alcohol Dependence.** New York; Heidelberg; Berlin: Springer-Verlag, 1977. 748p. bibliog. index. (Handbuch der experimentellen Pharmakologie: New Series; v. 45, pt. 1.) $103.50. LC 77-24381. ISBN 0-387-08170-4.

This volume, the first of a two-volume set, addresses the general problem of drug addiction from several points of view. The main thrust of the work, however, is exploration of the possibility that drug abusers have an organic dysfunction of the brain. It is hoped that the presentation will stimulate experimental therapists to become more involved in the general problems of psychopathy and the particular problem of drug abuse. A portion of the work is devoted to the description of the effects of drugs of abuse on the function of the brain and body; another portion is devoted to methods and to description of endeavors that the pharmacologist can make in treating and limiting drug abuse.

This volume of the work treats dependence on morphine, sedative/hypnotic drugs, and alcohol. Part 2 of the work (*see* entry below) treats other substances. Tobacco and cocaine have not been treated at all. The chapters that have been included, like other contributions in the *Handbuch* series, were written by noted experts, are of high quality and comprehensive, include excellent bibliographies, and treat the subjects under consideration in depth. Further, they are of scholarly research level.

The following are the chapter titles: 1) General problems of drug abuse and drug dependence, 2) Neuropharmacology and neurochemistry of subjective effects, analgesia, tolerance, and dependence produced by narcotic analgesics, 3) Assessment of the abuse potential of narcotic analgesics in animals, 4) Assessment of the abuse potentiality of morphinelike drugs (methods used in man), 5) Psychiatric treatment of narcotic addiction, 6) Chemotherapy of narcotic addiction, 7) Detection of drugs of abuse in biological fluids, 8) The pharmacology of sedative/hypnotics, alcohol, and anesthetics: sites and mechanisms of action, 9) The assessment of the abuse potentiality of sedative/hypnotics (depressants) (Methods used in animals and man), 10) Clinical aspects of alcohol dependence, and 11) Abuse of non-narcotic analgesics.

542.   Martin, William R., ed. **Drug Addiction II: Amphetamine, Psychotogen, and Marihuana Dependence.** New York; Heidelberg; Berlin: Springer-Verlag, 1977. 502p. bibliog. index. (Handbuch der experimentallen Pharmakologie: New Series; v. 45, pt. 2.) $87.40. LC 77-24381. ISBN 0-387-08334-0.

This volume continues the work of Volume 1 (reviewed above), treating other substances.

The chapter headings are as follows: 1) General pharmacology of amphetamine-like drugs, A. Pharmacokinetics and metabolism, B. Effects of amphetamine in animals, C. Effects of amphetamines in humans; 2) Amphetamine dependence; clinical features; 3) Pharmacology and classification of LSD-like hallucinogens; 4) Cannabis, its chemistry, pharmacology, and toxicology.

543.   Martini, G. A., and Charles Bode, eds. **Metabolic Changes Induced by Alcohol.**
Berlin; Heidelberg; New York: Springer-Verlag, 1971. 217p. bibliog. $21.20. LC 77-
142386. ISBN 3-540-05296-8 (Berlin); 0-387-05296-8 (New York).

A symposium volume, this publication brings together 26 papers presented
by scientists involved in the development of new concepts about metabolic disorders
caused by alcohol. Biochemists, physiologists, pharmacologists, pathologists, and
clinicians from eight European countries and the United States have made contributions.

For many years the concept was accepted that alcoholic liver disease was of
nutritional origin and only indirectly related to alcohol comsumption and metabolism. As can be seen in the papers in this volume, opinion has changed; alcohol itself
is seen as being responsible for many metabolic disorders, an important development
in research in this field.

The papers are arranged under these headings: 1) Metabolism of alcohol
and alcohol dehydrogenase, 2) Ethanol induced ultrastructural alternations in the
liver, 3) Effect of ethanol on microsomal functions, 4) Effect of ethanol on metabolites and coenzymes of the energy producing metabolism, 5) Effects of ethanol on
carbohydrate metabolism, and 6) Effect of ethanol on hormone metabolism.

544.   Mendlewicz, J., and H. M. van Praag, eds. **Alcoholism: A Multidiscplinary**
Approach. Basel: S. Karger, 1979. 138p. bibliog. index. (Advances in Biological
Psychiatry, v. 3.) $33.00pa. ISBN 3-8055-2977-5.

The 11 scientific papers reprinted in this volume were originally presented
at a symposium on alcohol, held in Amsterdam in 1978. There has been a rapidly
increasing amount of biological research on alcoholism, and these contributions
update knowledge through an interdisciplinary approach. The orientation is toward
understanding the etiology and pathogenesis of alcoholism and on improving
treatment.

The papers are arranged in three categories: clinical therapeutic aspects,
biological aspects, and behavioural and social aspects. Titles of the papers are: 1) Alcoholism, a many-sided problem, 2) The treatment of alcoholism: a reevaluation of the
rationale for therapy, 3) Alcoholism, seizures and cerebral atrophy, 4) Major concepts
and trends in alcoholism, some issues in clinical and experimental biomedical research,
5) Genetic aspects of alcoholism, 6) Animal models of alcohol dependence, 7) Neuropharmacological aspects of ethanol tolerance and dependence, 8) Biochemical and
metabolic basis of alcohol toxicity, 9) Epidemiological studies in alcoholism, illustrated by studies in Iceland, 10) Drinking patterns in the course of alcoholism, and
11) The importance of psychosocial factors in the genesis and prognosis of alcoholism.

The publication is of most value for those conducting research on the subject
or for those interested in basic therapeutic aspects.

545.   Meyer, Roger E., and Steven M. Mirin. **The Heroin Stimulus: Implications**
for a Theory of Addiction. New York: Plenum Press, 1979. 254p. bibliog. index.
$22.50. LC 78-13634. ISBN 0-306-40104-5.

Although heroin has been synthesized and available for over three-quarters
of a century, little has been discovered that can point the way to successful therapy
for victims of its use. There has been a period of taboo on the direct study of human
heroin use, but this book reports on a project where a team observed the evolution
of addictive behaviors of individuals using the drug. The subjects were volunteers who
were housed in a research ward environment.

The project had two goals: 1) to define the nature of opioid reinforcement through an interdisciplinary study of the effects of unblocked and blocked (using a narcotic antagonist) heroin consumption upon mood, behavior, and several physiological factors, and 2) to assess the effects of narcotic antagonists upon heroin self-administration in a research ward setting and later in the community in order to devise a possible model for the use of narcotic-blocking drugs in the rehabilitation of addicts.

Following are the chapter titles: 1) Overview, 2) The study of heroin use in human subjects, 3) Ward management in a research-treatment setting, 4) Operant analysis, 5) Psychopathology and mood during heroin use, 6) Behavioral and social effects, 7) The effects of unblocked heroin upon catecholamine metabolism: preliminary findings, 8) Effect of opiates on neuroendocrine function: plasma cortisol, growth hormone, and thyrotropin, 9) Effect of opiates on neuroendocrine function: testosterone and pituitary gonadotropins, 10) Family studies, 11) Community outcome on narcotic antagonists, and 12) Implications.

The authors feel that their findings concerning narcotic antagonists may also help clarify certain aspects of other heroin treatment modalities, as well as other behavioral and substance abuse disorders.

546.   Miller, Peter M. **Behavioral Treatment of Alcoholism**. New York: Pergamon Press, 1976. 188p. bibliog. index. (Pergamon General Psychology Series, v. 60.) $12.00; $5.75pa. LC 75-22415. ISBN 0-08-01919-9; 0-08-019518-0 pa.

This work is concerned with alcoholism treatment therapies and assessment techniques based on behavior modification. It attempts to organize and present the various methodologies such as aversion therapies, assertion training, social skills training, relaxation training, self-management procedures, operant approaches, and marital therapy. New techniques that have been developed to teach controlled, moderate drinking are also described.

The book will interest all those generally interested in the field of behavior modification as well as those working in the alcoholism field. The latter include psychologists, psychiatrists, social workers, physicians, nurses, counselors, sociologists, law enforcement officers, mental health workers, and personnel managers. Academic professionals and students can make use of the work as a textbook.

The author concludes that probably the most important contribution of behavior modification to the field of alcoholism lies in its emphasis on the merger between treatment and research. Treatment methods are evaluated simultaneously with their clinical application. He also believes that behavioral research data may eventually have relevance to prevention of alcoholism. For example, behavioral techniques that teach controlled social drinking patterns may be effective. In addition, early intervention could be emphasized in populations most likely to abuse alcohol.

547.   Nathan, Peter E., G. Alan Marlatt, and Tor Løberg, eds. **Alcoholism: New Directions in Behavioral Research and Treatment**. Proceedings of a NATO Conference on Experimental and Behavioral Approaches to Alcoholism, held in Os, Norway, 1977. New York: Plenum Press, 1978. 403p. bibliog. index. (NATO Conference Series: III, Human Factors, v. 7.) $35.00. LC 78-11876. ISBN 0-306-40058-8.

Fifteen papers make up this volume. The contributions were written by scientists invited to present material on experimental and behavioral topics of relevance to alcoholism. There are five sections: 1) Assessment, etiology, and models of alcoholism, 2) Behavioral treatment methods, 3) Behavioral treatment methods, evaluation of treatment outcome, and surveys of drinking behavior, 4) Cognitive and social factors, and 5) Special presentation.

Titles of the papers are as follows: 1) Comments on the many faces of alcoholism, 2) Etiology of alcoholism: interdisciplinary integration, 3) Toward a multivariate analysis of alcohol abuse, 4) Alternative skills training in alcoholism treatment, 5) Treatment for middle income problem drinkers, 6) Studies in blood alcohol level discrimination, 7) Alternatives to abstinence: evidence, issues and some proposals, 8) Relationships between drinking behavior of alcoholics in a drinking-decisions treatment program and treatment outcome, 9) Subcultural differences in drinking behavior in U.S., national surveys and selected European studies, 10) Alcohol treatment outcome evaluation: contributions from behavioral research, 11) Craving for alcohol, loss of control, and relapse: a cognitive-behavioral analysis, 12) Booze, beliefs, and behavior, cognitive processes in alcohol use and abuse, 13) Craving and loss of control, 14) Relationship of social factors to ethanol, self-administration in alcoholics, and 15) A nonbehaviorist's view of the behavioral problem with alcoholism.

548. Nickerson, Mark, John O. Parker, Thomas P. Lowry, and Edward W. Swenson. **Isobutyl Nitrite and Related Compounds.** San Francisco, CA: Pharmex, Ltd., 1979. 95p. bibliog. LC 79-62920.

This brief publication is intended for scientific, industrial, and governmental use. The authors are physicians and/or scientists at academic institutions. For the past several years some concern has been shown regarding the use of butyl nitrite in consumer products (such as room odorizers) because of the possibility of abuse and subsequent danger of personal injury. Nitrites such as amyl, butyl, and isobutyl are sometimes inhaled for their physiological effect. Some individuals use them as aphrodisiacs.

The authors undertook this study in order to help consolidate, clarify, and expand pharmacological, toxicological, and social data regarding the substances. Some of the nitrites have a legitimate place in medicine, such as amyl nitrite as a vasodilator (used in angina treatment).

It was found that despite substantial and increasing uncontrolled sale and use of amyl nitrite during the 1960s, very few reports of injuries were recorded. Amyl nitrite is one of the safest medications, and the action of other volatile nitrites is almost identical. Therefore regulation or control was deemed unnecessary.

The book contains substantial appendices that bring together statistical information on problem reports and results of research on the effects of nitrite inhalation.

549. Pattison, E. Mansell, Mark B. Sobell, and Linda C. Sobell, eds. **Emerging Concepts of Alcohol Dependence.** New York: Springer Publishing Co., 1977. 369p. bibliog. index. $18.95. LC 77-4115. ISBN 0-8261-1950-6.

This book takes the view that traditional concepts of alcoholism should be revised in the light of new experimental evidence. Part 1 of the book covers traditional concepts in conflict with new data, and part 2 is a revised model of alcohol dependence.

The emerging concepts can be outlined as follows: 1) alcohol dependence summarizes a variety of syndromes that are best considered a serious health problem; 2) an individual's pattern of alcohol use can be considered as lying on a continuum, ranging fron nonpathological to severely pathological; 3) any person who uses alcohol can develop a syndrome of alcohol dependence; 4) the development of alcohol problems follows variable patterns over time and does not necessarily proceed to severe fatal stages; 5) recovery from alcohol dependence bears no necessary relation to abstinence, although such a concurrence is frequently the case; 6) the consumption of a small amount of alcohol by one once labeled as "alcoholic" does not initiate physical dependence or a physiological need for more alcohol by that individual; 7) continued drinking of large doses of alcohol over an extended period of time is likely to initiate a process of physical dependence that will eventually be manifested as an alcohol withdrawal syndrome; 8) the population of persons with alcohol problems is multivariant, and correspondingly, treatment services should be diverse; 9) alcohol problems are typically interrelated with other life problems, especially when alcohol dependence is long established; 10) an emphasis should be placed on dealing with alcohol problems in the environment in which they occur; and 11) Treatment services should be designed to provide for a continuity of care throughout the lengthy process of recovery from alcohol problems.

The authors feel that the revised model of alcoholism, differing from the traditional, has profound implications for treatment. They caution, however, that since there are several areas where data is too ambiguous or insufficient to draw firm conclusions, they will offer no entirely unrelenting set of new concepts. Many will find the new evidence convincing as well as interesting. The book can be used by a variety of readers, laymen to research scientists.

550.   Pickens, Roy W., and Leonard L. Heston, eds. **Psychiatric Factors in Drug Abuse**. New York: Grune and Stratton, 1979. 379p. bibliog. index. $19.50. LC 79-3087. ISBN 0-8089-1214-3.

This publication contains the proceedings of a Conference on Psychiatric Factors in Drug Abuse, sponsored by the Psychiatric Research Unit, University of Minnesota, Minneapolis, on March 4-6, 1979. The purpose of the conference was to explore and review findings in the area of clinical research in the field of alcoholism and drug abuse. Diagnosis and treatment were both considered. Investigators in a range of disciplines were invited to present papers. These disciplines included such fields as psychiatry, psychology, genetics, anthropology, and pharmacology.

The following are some of the topics discussed: psychopathology and drug abusers, the role of depression in narcotic addiction and alcoholism, personality characteristics of drug abusers, treatment by psychotherapy and psychopharmacology, genetic factors, diagnosis, and psychoses resulting from drug intoxication.

551.   Pirola, R. C. **Drug Metabolism and Alcohol: A Survey of Alcohol-Drug Reactions—Mechanisms, Clinical Aspects, Experimental Studies**. Baltimore, MD: Univeristy Park Press, 1978. 175p. bibliog. index. $29.50. LC 77-18759. ISBN 0-8391-1228-9.

The use of alcohol is so widespread that perhaps a majority of patients who are prescribed a medication are also alcohol users. This book is designed to acquaint health professionals and researchers with the influence of alcohol on total body metabolism, emphasizing the mechanics of alcohol effects on drug pharmacokinetics and pharmacologic responses and on the resulting implications. The author discusses pertinent reports from the literature and points out evidence that is not conclusive or that is contradictory, and attempts to resolve the differences. A great deal of complex material has been drawn together in the book and organized in a manner understandable to practicing health professionals. A large number of literature references (27 pages) has been included.

The following are the chapter titles: 1) Introduction, 2) Absorption, 3) Drug metabolism, 4) Factors affecting the rate of drug metabolism, 5) Ethanol metabolism, 6) General metabolic and pharmacological consequences of ethanol metabolism, 7) Specific alcohol-drug interactions, 8) The congeners of alcoholic beverages, and 9) Miscellaneous experimental aspects.

The book has been well-received by readers.

552.   Platt, Jerome J., and Christina Labate. **Heroin Addiction: Theory, Research, and Treatment**. New York: John Wiley and Sons, 1976. 517p. bibliog. index. $21.25. LC 76-5794. ISBN 0-471-69114-3.

Though emphasis on psychology comes through, this book surveys the whole field of approaches to heroin addiction, covering contributions from psychiatry, social work, pharmacology, physiology, medicine, criminology, and psychology. The work is in four major parts: 1) The historicolegal context of heroin addiction in the United States, 2) The physiology and pharmacology of heroin addiction, 3) Explaining heroin addiction, and 4) Treatment of the heroin addict. In addition, there are two appendices: 1) Recent and current trends in the prevalence and incidence of heroin addiction, and 2) Scales used specifically in the assessment and study of drug addiction. A notable feature of the book is that it contains a comprehensive list of about 500 references referred to in the text and a supplementary list of about 500 more citations published since 1970.

The chapters are directed toward showing where we stand currently in our understanding of heroin addiction, each focusing on a particular aspect of the problem.

The authors find no easy answer to the heroin addiction problem and no perfect therapeutic process. The best methods seem to be those that focus on similar ways of working through specific inabilities to cope. They all have in common an emphasis on recognizing the consequences of one's behavior and on defining ways in which one needs to change. In addition, the use of role models as a therapeutic tool may be useful.

The book is quite well done and should be very useful for psychologists, psychiatrists, social workers, program administrators, and those involved in the administration of criminal justice.

553.   Rankin, James G., ed. **Alcohol, Drugs, and Brain Damage**. Proceedings of a Symposium: Effects of Chronic Use of Alcohol and other Pscyhoactive Drugs on Cerebral Function. Toronto: Alcoholism and Drug Addiction Research Foundation of Ontario, 1975. 101p. illus. bibliog. index. $8.00; $5.50pa. ISBN 0-88868-009-0.

The papers in this publication were originally presented at a symposium the objectives of which were to examine the present state of knowledge about the effects of chronic use of alcohol and other psychoactive substances on cerebral function, particularly intellect, learning, and memory, and to explore and define research questions and needs. The 21 participants included pharmacologists, psychologists, psychiatrists, neurologists, and specialists in internal medicine from several different countries. The eight papers are divided into three subject areas as follows: 1) Clinical features, pathology and epidemiology, 2) Pathogenesis, and 3) Preventative and therapeutic implications.

The following were identified as important research topics, needs, or approaches: improvement in techniques to identify and measure sub-clinical or early clinical brain damage; clarification of the nature and basis of reversible abnormalities in psychological tests of cerebral function which are commonly observed in alcoholic patients; further studies of the natural history of brain damage associated with alcohol and drug use; more extensive use of laboratory animals to determine the effects of alcohol and drug use on the brain.

554.　　Rumack, Barry H., and Emanuel Salzman, eds. **Mushroom Poisoning: Diagnosis and Treatment.** West Palm Beach, FL: CRC Press, 1978. 263p. illus. (part col.). bibliog. index. $62.95. LC 77-21633. ISBN 0-8493-5185-5.

This publication is an outgrowth of the annual Aspen Mushroom Conferences. The purpose of these conferences has been to coordinate activity and facilitate exchange of information between mycologists and physicians who treat poisoned patients with the aim of improving treatment of mushroom poisoned victims. The book should interest those involved in drug abuse work because of the increased use of mushrooms by those seeking hallucinogenics effects.

The book contains 15 chapters divided into three sections as follows: 1) Mushroom identification, 2) Mushroom toxicology, and 3) Mushroom hallucination. The four chapters of the last section are entitled: 12) Hallucinogenic mushrooms, 13) The present status of Soma: the effects of California *Amanita Muscaria* on normal human volunteers, 14) The abuse of drug terminology, and 15) Recreational use of hallucinogenic mushrooms in the United States. The latter chapters have some popular appeal (and may, in fact, appeal to drug abusers), but, like the rest of the book, are rather scientific and technical. All chapters include extensive documentation.

555.　　Schering Corporation. **Infections in Alcoholic and Drug-Abusing Patients.** Kenilworth, NJ: Schering Corporation, 1977. 29p. illus. bibliog. (Schering Infectious Disease Hospital Handbook No. 6.)

The abuse of alcohol and other drugs is directly or indirectly responsible for a high percentage of problems encountered in hospital practice. Those related to alcohol alone may be anticipated in over 25% of general hospital patients. Rates of morbidity and mortality are higher than in normal patients.

The purpose of this compact handbook is to review diagnostic and pathogenic features of the infections frequently seen in substance-abusing patients and to present management guidelines for them.

The contents are as follows: 1) Introduction: patients and problems in hospital practice, 2) Pathogenesis of infection: microbial invasion and immunologic impairment, 3) Infections associated with alcoholism or drug abuse, and 4) Management of bacterial infections: acute bacterial endocarditis, acute bacterial pneumonia. The bibliography contains 40 references, and some Schering product data is appended.

556.　　Seitner, Philip G. **Survey of Analgesic Drug Prescribing Patterns.** Assisted by Beverly C. Martin, American Medical Association, Center for Health Services Research and Development, in consultation with Joseph Cochin and Louis Harris. Washington: Drug Abuse Council, 1975. 274p. $9.00pa. LC 75-8491.

The results of more than 5,000 responses to a survey by the American Medical Association on physicians' use of narcotic analgesics are presented in this volume. The objective of the study was to provide information on the frequency with which physicians prescribe, dispense, or administer opiate drugs and their alternates, and to solicit opinions about the adequacy of the substitution of synthetics for opiates. The ultimate aim of the study was to aid in establishing a responsible position regarding the therapeutic importance of opiate drugs based on the experience and opinion of doctors.

The publication presents the results of the study in considerable detail, much of it in tabular or graphic format.

Among other results, it was found that most physicians considered codeine and morphine indispensable, and felt that the quality of care would decrease if such opiates were to become unavailable.

An interesting aside: the physicians rated drug information sources as having marked or moderate influence in the following sequence: medical journal literature, *Physicians' Desk Reference* and package inserts, colleagues, reference books, *AMA Drug Evaluations*, the *Medical Letter*, detailmen, advertising in journals, pharmacists, and advertising by direct mail.

557.   Seixas, Frank A., ed. **Currents in Alcoholism. Vol. 1, Biological, Biochemical, and Clinical Studies.** New York: Grune and Stratton, 1977. 495p. bibliog. index. $21.50. LC 76-30552. ISBN 0-8089-1007-8.

This volume contains Track Papers from the Seventh Annual Medical-Scientific Conference of the National Alcoholism Forum, jointly conducted by the National Council on Alcoholism and the American Medical Society on Alcoholism, held May 6-8, 1976, in Washington, D.C. The papers submitted for the meeting fell into four groups: Biological and biochemical; Clinical; Psychiatric; and Social and epidemiological. The biological, biochemical and clinical papers are included in this volume; the others are presented in a second volume (*see* entry below).

Among the 35 papers in volume 1, several are significant. Among others, these include a presentation on a new chemical test for alcoholism; a new concept of the metabolic change in fatty liver; the membrane effects of alcohol in the brain and its effect on cyclic AMP; and further exploration of new animal models. In addition, the question of whether there is a racial difference in alcohol's effect is further explored. There are papers examining innovations in the hospital; for instance, the emergency room, the prenatal clinic, and the surgical floors. The evaluation of methods of withdrawal continues to be a central concern.

558.   Seixas, Frank A., ed. **Currents in Alcoholism. Vol. 2, Psychiatric, Psychological, Social and Epidemiological Studies.** New York: Grune and Stratton, 1977. 548p. bibliog. index. $21.50. LC 76-30552. ISBN 0-8089-1008-6.

This volume contains Track Papers on psychiatric, psychological, social, and epidemiological studies presented at the Seventh Annual Medical-Scientific Conference of the National Alcoholism Forum, jointly conducted by the National Council on Alcoholism and the American Medical Society on Alcoholism. The other papers presented at the conference appear in volume 1 of the work (*see* entry 557). The editor believes users of the volumes will find that they serve as a yearbook on alcoholism.

The 39 papers are presented under the following headings: 1) Alcoholism and affective disorders, 2) Aspects of treatment, 3) Cognitive studies, 4) Medical education about alcoholism, 5) Do methadone patients become alcoholics?, 6) Populations of alcoholics, 7) Ethnic and other differences, 8) Identifying heavy drinkers, 9) Interrelationships with alcoholism, 10) Reasons with characteristics, and 11) Evaluations.

Significant papers deal with such areas as the role of lithium in treating alcoholics and/or those with depression; the measurement, extent, and reversibility of alcohol-related brain damage; the possibility of treating alcoholics with a goal of cutting down rather than eliminating their drinking.

559.   Seixas, Frank A., ed. **Currents in Alcoholism. Vol. 3, Biological, Biochemical, and Clinical Studies.** New York: Grune and Stratton, 1978. 601p. bibliog. index. $31.50. LC 76-30552. ISBN 0-8089-1089-2.

This volume contains Track Papers of the Eighth Annual Medical-Scientific Conference of the National Alcoholism Forum, jointly conducted by the National

Council on Alcoholism and the American Medical Society on Alcoholism, held May 2-4, 1977 in San Diego, California. The volume contains papers on biomedical and clinical topics only; volume 4 contains psychological, psychiatric, and epidemiological papers. Together they make up a yearbook on alcoholism as did volumes one and two for the year 1976.

More than 40 papers are presented grouped under the following headings: 1) Animal studies and neurological findings, 2) Neurochemistry, 3) Causes and effects, 4) Metabolism of ethanol—a hypermetabolic state?, 5) Three explorations of technique, 6) Pharmacological interactions, 7) Effects on the heart, 8) Parameters of alcohol actions on the body, 9) Alcohol and performance, 10) Diagnosis of alcoholism, and 11) Treatment and withdrawal.

The Introduction points out that the most important landmark in research in 1977 was the passage by Congress of a bill authorizing the creation of several research centers on alcohol and the awarding of grants to them. Much new material is included in the volume.

560.   Seixas, Frank A., ed. **Currents in Alcoholism. Vol. 4, Psychiatric, Psychological, Social, and Epidemiological Studies.** New York: Grune and Stratton, 1978. 498p. bibliog. index. $26.50. LC 76-30552. ISBN 0-8089-1101-5.

A companion volume to volume 3 of the same title (*see* entry 559), this work contains additional Track Papers of the Eighth Annual Medical-Scientific Conference of the National Alcoholism Forum, jointly conducted by the National Council on Alcoholism and the American Medical Society on Alcoholism, held May 2-4, 1977, in San Diego, California. This volume presents papers on psychiatric, psychological, social and epidemiological studies, while volume 3 contains biomedical and clinical papers.

About 35 papers are included grouped under the following headings: 1) Alcoholic families, 2) Adolescents: psychiatric percepts, 3) Addiction complicated by alcoholism, 4) Psychiatric management, 5) Affective disorders, 6) Cognitive performance, 7) Social class and station, 8) Family position and its effect, 9) Casefinding, planning, and data gathering, and 10) Outcome.

There is a good deal of emphasis on the effects of alcoholism on children and the family.

561.   Sellers, E. M., ed. **Clinical Pharmacology of Psychoactive Drugs.** Toronto: Alcoholism and Drug Addiction Research Foundation, 1975. 226p. bibliog. index. (International Symposia on Alcohol and Drug Addiction.) $13.50; $10.00pa. ISBN 0-88868-007-4.

The 16 papers in this publication constitute the proceedings of a symposium held October 22-24, 1973 at the Clinical Institute Addiction Research Foundation in Toronto. The papers were presented during three sessions: 1) Etiology and epidemiology, 2) Factors influencing toxicity, and 3) Clinical and molecular drug interactions. The purposes of the symposium were to focus on somewhat unexplored areas of research, to review important developments, and to   discuss methodological problems. The papers, which were prepared by experts, are highly technical and cover a wide range of clinical areas.

562.   Sharp, Charles W., and Leo G. Abood, eds. **Membrane Mechanisms of Drugs of Abuse**. Proceedings of a Conference held at Silver Spring, Maryland, March 16-17, 1978. New York: Alan R. Liss, Inc., 1979. 272p. illus. bibliog. index. (Progress in Clinical and Biological Research, v. 27.) $22.00. LC 78-19682. ISBN 0-8451-0027-0.

Although this field is in its infancy, it offers potential for increasing the understanding of drug action, a complex mechanism. Most of the research so far on membrane receptors has dealt with drugs of abuse, particularly opiates, tetrahydrocannabinoids, and ethanol. This book covers these substances and also nicotine, barbiturates, and a few others. The focus is on new research findings.

The papers, by experts, are grouped under five headings: 1) Drug receptors, constituents and environment, 2) Drugs and neurotransmitter interactions with excitatory membranes, 3) Drug receptors—effects of interactions, 4) Drug effects on membrane fluidity, confirmation and ion interaction, and 5) Interpretation of drug effects through tissue culture systems. In addition, a review of the conference has been appended which summarizes the contributions and provides insight into the concept being studied.

The reports are timely, and some of the best known investigators in the field participated in the conference. The book is suitable for research scientists in neurobiology, pharmacology, and those concerned with cellular and subcellular actions of drugs of abuse.

563.   Sinclair, J. D., and K. Kiianmaa, eds. **The Effects of Centrally Active Drugs on Voluntary Alcohol Consumption**. Satellite Symposium to the Sixth International Congress of Pharmacology, July 26, 1975, Helsinki, Finland. Helsinki: Finnish Foundation for Alcohol Studies; distr., Rutgers University Center of Alcohol Studies, 1975. 162p. illus. bibliog. (The Finnish Foundation for Alcohol Studies, v. 24.) $7.00pa. ISBN 951-9191-24-0.

The 11 research papers in this publication are concerned with the ways in which substances with a pharmacologic action on the brain are able to influence the motivation for the use of alcohol. Most of the papers fall in one of these three areas of interest: 1) the possibility that centrally active substances already commonly used, such as caffeine or medically prescribed drugs, may affect the desire for alcohol; 2) the use of experimental drugs that alter the functioning of the central nervous system as a tool for studying the bases for alcohol drinking; and 3) the search for centrally active substances that may have a therapeutic use in reducing the motivation for alcohol in alcoholic individuals.

564.   Singh, Jasbir M., and Harbans Lal, eds. **Drug Addiction**. Vol. 3, **Neurobiology and Influences on Behavior**. New York: Stratton Intercontinental Medical Book Corp., 1974. 386p. bibliog. index. $18.95. LC 72-189180. ISBN 0-88372-025-8.

This volume contains papers and discussion from the Second International Symposium on Drug Addiction, held in New Orleans. Like others in the series, this volume takes a multidisciplinary approach to the problem of drug abuse. There are 30 scientific papers, prepared by established workers in the field, which present recent findings in the area of neurology and influences on behavior as the result of drug addiction. The presentations are arranged under the following subject headings: 1) Aggression, 2) Self-stimulation, 3) Conditioning, and 4) Electrophysiological.

565.   Singh, Jasbir M., and Harbans Lal, eds. **Drug Addiction**. Vol. 4, **New Aspects of Analytical and Clinical Toxicology**. New York: Stratton Intercontinental Medical Book Corp., 1974. 286p. bibliog. index. $17.95. LC 72-189180. ISBN 0-88372-059-0.

This volume contains selected papers and discussions from the Second International Symposium on Drug Addiction, held in New Orleans. Like the previous volumes in the series, it takes a multidisciplinary approach and provides further in-depth examination of scientific evidence regarding drug abuse. The emphasis in this volume is on toxicological, analytical, and clinico-sociological aspects.

The following are under scrutiny: morphine, barbiturates, amphetamines, LSD, heroin, marijuana, tranquilizers, and methadone treatment. Twenty-four papers are presented of special interest to those in the fields of psychology, pharmacology, toxicology, psychiatry, physiology, anatomy, chemistry, sociology, neurology, and public health.

566.   Snyder, Solomon H., and Steven Matthysse, with others. **Opiate Receptor Mechanisms: Neurochemical and Neurophysiological Processes in Opiate Drug Action and Addiction.** Based on a Work Session of the Neurosciences Research Program. Cambridge, MA: MIT Press, 1975. (Published simultaneously as v. 13, No. 1, February 1975, of the *Neurosciences Research Program Bulletin*.) 166p. illus. bibliog. index. $9.95. LC 75-7828. ISBN 0-262-19132-6.

This book reviews important new discoveries on the pharmacology, physiology, and biochemistry of the action of opiates on the brain. It has been established that opiates act on the brain cells by combining with particular protein molecules on their membranes. The opiate receptors in the brain interact in a highly specific and selective manner with the opiate molecules, which causes a disturbance and brings about behavioral changes. These findings have many implications for addiction and pain research. For instance: drug antagonists hold much promise of leading to an eventual cure of drug addiction; agonist-antagonist combinations may be the key to developing nonaddictive analgesics; and it may be possible to better predict the properties of a drug proposed for clinical testing.

These and other research projects and results are discussed in the book in a highly technical fashion. The chapters are grouped under the following subject headings: 1) Introduction, 2) Biochemical identification of receptors, 3) Agonist-antagonist interactions, 4) Neural mechanisms, 5) Biochemical phenomena in opiate action and addiction, 6) Addiction, 7) Future research: discussion review, and 8) A model of opiate receptor function with implications for a theory of addiction.

567.   Spano, P. F., and M. Trabucchi, eds. **Ergot Alkaloids.** International Workshop on Ergot Alkaloids, Rome, December 6-7, 1976. Basel: S. Karger, 1978. 213p. illus. bibliog. index. (Pharmacology: International Journal of Experimental and Clinical Pharmacology, v. 16, Suppl. 1, 1978.) ISBN 3-8055-2769-1.

Held under the sponsorship of the Italian Brain Research Foundation, the purpose of this workshop was to provide an integrated overview of the current knowledge of the basic and clinical aspects of the classic and new ergot derivatives. The 19 papers presented were selected to encompass all aspects of the subject related to an understanding of the regulation and control of brain functions by this class of drugs.

Although once considered a dreaded poisonous contaminant, ergot is today an extraordinarily rich source of valuable pharmaceuticals, a source not yet exhausted.

The papers are for the most part highly scientific and technical, and suitable only for the research audience. Since LSD is an ergot drug, the papers are of some interest to those curious about this hallucinogenic substance. The first paper, "Historical View on Ergot Alkaloids," is by Dr. A. Hofmann, the discoverer of LSD. His paper presents an interesting background to the current investigation of ergot compounds.

568.   Stimmel, Barry. **Cardiovascular Effects of Mood-Altering Drugs.** New York: Raven Press, 1979. 290p. illus. bibliog. index. $23.00. LC 77-91582. ISBN 0-89004-287-X.

The view taken by the author of this work is that the effectiveness and usefulness of modern mood-altering drugs have resulted in focus on their psychotropic actions, with little attention given to their systemic effects, particularly effects on the cardiovascular system. The book was written to provide knowledge of this kind to physicians prescribing these medications, treating persons abusing drugs, or giving advice to patients concerning the use of the readily available "social" drugs, such as alcohol, nicotine, caffeine, and marijuana. The effects of the drugs are reviewed, attention being given to possible drug interactions between the agents and cardiac medications.

The chapter headings are as follows: 1) Psychotropic drug use: defining the problem, 2) Pharmacologic considerations, 3) Anxiety, stress, and cardiovascular disease, 4) Alcohol 1: acute and chronic effects on the heart and vasculature, 5) Alcohol 2: alcohol-related cardiomyopathies, 6) Barbiturates, other sedatives, and minor tranquilizers, 7) The major tranquilizers, 8) Drugs used for affective disorders, 9) Marijuana, 10) Hallucinogenic agents, 11) Narcotic analgesics 1: synthetic opiates, and narcotic antagonists, 12) Narcotic analgesics 2: heroin addiction, 13) The stimulants 1: the amphetamines, cocaine, and methylphenidate, and 14) The stimulants 2: caffeine and nicotine.

The volume is of value to cardiologists, psychopharmacologists, psychiatrists, internists, family practitioners, and physicians working in the alcohol and/or drug abuse field.

569.   Tarter, Ralph E., and A. Arthur Sugerman, eds. **Alcoholism: Interdiscipilinary Approaches to an Enduring Problem.** Reading, MA: Addison-Wesley Publishing Co., Advanced Book Program, 1976. 857p. bibliog. index. $27.50; $13.50pa. LC 76-12551. ISBN 0-201-08146-6; 0-201-08145-8 pa.

An interdisciplinary approach is taken and extensive documentation has been provided in this review of developments in research on alcoholism through 1975.

The 22 chapters are presented under three headings: 1) Orientation and perspective, 2) Processes in alcoholism, and 3) Treatment approaches. The first section discusses the history of alcoholism, definitional issues, models, and theories. The second section emphasizes neuropsychological aspects of the subject. Alcoholism and its relation to psychological deficits, cognitive style, sleep disturbances, and behavior and motivational patterns are discussed. Genetic determination and epidemiological and social factors associated with problem drinking are given attention. And, in addition, effects on the liver and the nervous system are reviewed. The last section discusses various treatment techniques such as group psychotherapy, family therapy, behavioral and pharmacologic approaches, Alcoholics Anonymous, and community programs.

The work is suitable for psychiatrists and other professionals involved with treatment of alcoholics.

570.   Thompson, Travis, and Klaus R. Unna, eds. **Predicting Dependence Liability of Stimulant and Depressant Drugs.** Baltimore, MD: University Park Press, 1977. 328p. bibliog. index. $19.50. LC 77-7581. ISBN 0-8391-1147-9.

This volume presents the proceedings of a conference held April 19-21, 1976 at the National Academy of Sciences, Washington, D.C., sponsored by the Committee on Problems of Drug Dependence, NAS-NRC, Drug Enforcement Administration,

Food and Drug Administration, and the National Institute on Drug Abuse. The conference objective was to outline the methods to be used in animal screening programs aimed at finding the dependence liability of amphetamines and barbiturates, as well as recommend whether a screening program is needed, similar to that used with narcotics. Recent findings (many of which are reviewed in this work) suggest that the concept of drug dependence is changing, placing greater emphasis on the control the dependence-producing drug gains over a user's behavior as compared to the addiction produced by drugs of the morphine type.

The 21 papers included consider four basic procedures that predict the abuse liability of central nervous system stimulants and sedative-hypnotics: 1) physical dependence methods in animals and man, 2) human psychological and behavioral methods, 3) animal behavior predictors and toxicological tests, and 4) infrahuman self-administration procedures. The last chapter, prepared by the Committee on Problems of Drug Dependence, contains conclusions and recommendations based on a review of the evidence.

The work should be of value to scholars and researchers working on the problem of drug dependence, particularly pharmacologists, psychologists, and physicians.

571.   U.S. National Institute on Drug Abuse. **Behavioral Tolerance: Research and Treatment Implications.** Edited by Norman A. Krasnegor. Washington: GPO, 1978. 191p. bibliog. [DHEW Publication No. (ADM) 78-551; NIDA Research Monograph 18.] $2.75. LC 77-93034. S/N 017-024-00699-8.

The papers in this monograph were given at a meeting held June 23-24 at the National Institute on Drug Abuse. Present and past research findings on behavioral tolerance (nonpharmacological factors) in substance abuse were presented; theoretical and experimental approaches to investigation in the field were compared; an attempt was made to develop a working definition of behavioral tolerance as it applies to drug abuse; and new possibilities for investigating the concept in research settings were discussed.

Eleven papers are included grouped under the following headings: 1) Conceptualization, 2) Narcotics, 3) Ethanol, 4) Marihuana, 5) Stimulants, and 6) Depressants.

572.   U.S. National Institute on Drug Abuse. **Data Analysis Strategies and Designs for Substance Abuse Research.** Edited by Peter M. Bentler, Dan J. Lettieri, and Gregory A. Austin. Washington: GPO, 1977. 226p. illus. bibliog. index. [DHEW Publication No. (ADM) 78-389; NIDA Research Issues, No. 13.] $3.00pa. S/N 017-024-00562-2.

This publication contains ten original papers that discuss methodologies applicable to performing psychosocial research on substance abuse. The intent is to make available basic information on some of the latest and most relevant research techniques. Each paper was written by a noted methodologist. Eight data analysis strategies are discussed by the authors: automatic interaction detection, actuarial prediction, cluster and typological analysis, path analysis, factor analysis, general multiple regression and correlation analysis, multivariate analysis of variance, and discriminant analysis. In addition, two relevant research designs are dealt with: single-organism designs and longitudinal designs. An attempt has been made to keep the discussions as nontechnical as possible. Each paper includes a description of the rationale, procedures, assumptions, advantages, and disadvantages of the methodology.

573.　U.S. National Institute on Drug Abuse. **Drug Users and Driving Behaviors.**
Edited by Gregory A. Austin, Robert S. Sterling-Smith, and Dan J. Lettieri. Washing-
ton: GPO, 1977. 173p. bibliog. index. [DHEW Publications No. (ADM) 78-508; NIDA
Research Issues, No. 20.] $3.25pa. S/N 017-024-00640-8.

　　Summaries of the latest experimental and epidemiological research on the
relationships between drug use and driving behaviors are provided in this volume. The
experimental studies included deal with the effects of drugs on cognition, coordination,
reaction time, and other psychomotor functions related to driving performance. The
epidemiological studies primarily deal with drug-involved auto accidents. Seventy-six
abstracts are included.

574.　U.S. National Institute on Drug Abuse. **Drugs and Personality: Personality
Correlates and Predictors of Non-Opiate Drug Use.** Edited by Gregory A. Austin, and
Dan J. Lettieri. Washington: GPO, 1976. 121p. bibliog. index. [DHEW Publications
No. (ADM) 77-390; NIDA Research Issues, No. 14.] $2.00pa. S/N 017-024-00531-2.

　　This volume presents abstracts of 59 current research and theoretical studies
that explore the relationships between non-opiate drug use and personality. Particularly, the focus is on personality predictors and correlates of adolescent drug use.
Each abstract conveys what was done, why it was done, the methodology employed,
the results, and conclusions.

575.　U.S. National Institute on Drug Abuse. **Drugs and Psychopathology.** Edited
by Gregory A. Austin, Mary A. Macari, Patricia Sutker, and Dan J. Lettieri. Washington: GPO, 1977. 140p. bibliog. index. [DHEW Publication No. (ADM) 77-509; NIDA
Research Issues, No. 19.] $3.00pa. S/N 017-024-00630-1.

　　A companion volume to Number 14 in the NIDA Research Issues series,
Drugs and Personality, this document summarizes 57 studies dealing with both opiates
and nonopiates and with all age groups. The studies are arranged alphabetically by
author under the following headings: 1) Reviews and theories, 2) Opiates, 3) Cannabis,
4) Hallucinogens/LSD, 5) Amphetamines, and 6) General drug research. Each summary
is a page or so in length and gives purpose, methodology, results, and conclusions.

　　The publication serves the purpose of bringing together the latest thinking
and research on the relationship between drug abuse and incidence, type, and degree
of psychopathology. In addition, it contains hypotheses for testing and lays the
groundwork for future research in the area.

576.　U.S. National Institute on Drug Abuse. **The International Challenge of Drug
Abuse.** Edited by Robert C. Petersen. Washington: GPO, 1978. 349p. bibliog. [DHEW
Publication No. (ADM) 78-654; NIDA Research Monograph 19.] LC 78-60498.

　　This monograph comprises papers presented at the Sixth World Congress
of Psychiatry, held in Honolulu August 28 to September 3, 1977, by the Drug Dependence Section.

　　The 30 papers are grouped under the following headings: 1) The international challenge of drug abuse, 2) Biological aspects of drug dependence, 3) Psychobiology
of drug abuse and affect disorders, and 4) Treatment. Several treatment modalities
are discussed: multimodal, LAAM, and Naltrexone.

577.　U.S. National Institute on Drug Abuse. **International Drug Use.** Edited by
Gregory A. Austin, Mary A. Macari, and Dan J. Lettieri. Washington: GPO, 1978.
166p. bibliog. [DHEW Publication No. (ADM) 79-809; NIDA Research Issues No.
23.] S/N 017-024-00874-5.

This publication presents 95 summaries of research projects on drug use carried out in countries other than the United States. The geographical areas covered are: the United Kingdom, continental Europe, Scandinavia, Africa and the Near East, Asia, and Latin America and the Caribbean. A wide range of topics is covered. A great many of the studies are epidemiological, and research on cannabis is heavily represented. The coverage is not intended to be comprehensive but rather to provide basic familiarity with patterns of drug use in other parts of the world.

Each summary includes such information as purpose of the study, methodology, results, and conclusions.

578.   U.S. National Institute on Drug Abuse. **Problems of Drug Dependence, 1979.** Proceedings of the 41st Annual Scientific Meeting, The Committee on Problems of Drug Dependence, Inc. Edited by Louis S. Harris. Washington: GPO, 1980. 483p. bibliog. index. [DHEW Publication No. (ADM) 80-901; NIDA Research Monograph 27.] LC 80-600008. S/N 017-024-00981-4.

The Committee on Problems of Drug Dependence, which was formerly affiliated with the National Academy of Sciences—National Research Council, each year presents a comprehensive group of reports of ongoing research relating to various aspects of drug abuse. These papers present new knowledge of agents involved in drug abuse or significantly affecting the central nervous system, including their pharmacologic action, biological disposition, abuse potential, safety, tolerance liability, clinical usefulness, and related methodology in the experimental or clinical areas. In addition to the 44 papers presented, there is a section that provides summaries of a special satellite session on khat and the annual progress of new compounds. Also included is a group of seven "Papers Read by Title But Not Presented" at the meeting.

This collection of papers by noted authorities makes a significant contribution in reporting scientific activities in drug abuse and the neurosciences.

579.   U.S. National Institute on Drug Abuse. **Psychodynamics of Drug Dependence.** Edited by Jack D. Blaine, and Demetrios A. Julius. Washington: GPO, 1977. 187p. bibliog. [DHEW Publication No. (ADM) 77-470; NIDA Research Monograph 12.] $2.75pa. LC 77-77369. S/N 017-024-00642-4.

The 11 papers in this monograph constitute a pioneering effort toward discovering the part played by a person's own psychodynamics in drug dependence. The papers were written by psychiatrists who have had a considerable experience with drug abusing patients and have consequently developed a feeling for the complexity of the problem. Some of the papers are theoretical, some clinical; some treat broad issues and some precise limited areas. As with other monographs in this series, this volume provides clues to the current state of the art.

580.   U.S. National Institute on Drug Abuse. **QuaSAR: Quantitative Structure Activity Relationships of Analgesics, Narcotic Antagonists, and Hallucinogens.** Edited by Gene Barnett, Milan Trsic, and Robert E. Willette. Washington: GPO, 1978. 487p. index. [DHEW Publication No. (ADM) 78-729; NIDA Research Issues No. 22.] LC 78-600104. S/N 017-024-00786-2.

This publication contains the proceedings of a meeting held by the National Institute on Drug Abuse on April 20-22, 1978. Use of a wide variety of scientific methods and techniques is demonstrated as a significant aid in understanding the basic mechanisms of drug action at the molecular level. The papers, prepared by experts, are divided into four sections: 1) Pharmacochemical methods, 2) Hansch analysis and other empirical methods, 3) Molecular mechanics, and 4) Spectroscopic methods. Techniques discussed include quantum mechanics, molecular spectroscopy, tissue and receptor binding studies, chemical modification of molecular structures, and correlation analysis. The papers concentrate on questions of molecular structure, correlation of molecular properties with biological activity, and molecular interactions with the receptor or receptors. They demonstrate that progress is being made in achieving basic understanding of drug action, but it was agreed by the experts that there is still a long way to go before full knowledge is gained.

581.   U.S. National Institute on Drug Abuse. **Report of the Task Force on Comparability in Survey Research on Drugs.** Edited by Joan Dunne Rittenhouse. Washington: GPO, 1978. 89p. bibliog. [DHEW Publication No. (ADM) 78-750; NIDA Technical Paper.] S/N 017-024-00788-9.

This volume is one of a series of publications aimed at enhancing the comparability of research in the drug abuse field under sponsorship of the National Institute on Drug Abuse. An earlier publication, *Operational Definitions in Socio-Behavioral Drug Use Research, 1975* (NIDA Research Monograph No. 2), edited by Jack Elinson and David Nurco, called upon investigators to review the array of definitions being applied to drug abuse research and to develop standard definitions. This current report is an attempt to further the development of common methods that will encourage comparability of results of research.

There are three chapters as follows: 1) Drug use, 2) Demographic correlates, and 3) Consequences of drug use.

An Epilogue states that the work will contribute substantially to measurement in the universe of drug use and demography. Other volumes will follow to clarify successively and to define survey research in drug abuse.

582.   U.S. National Institute on Drug Abuse. **Research Issues Update, 1978.** Edited by Gregory A. Austin, Mary A. Macari, and Dan J. Lettieri. Washington: GPO, 1979. 308p. illus. bibliog. index. [DHEW Publication No. (ADM) 79-808; NIDA Research Issues No. 22.] S/N 017-024-00876-1.

This document contains summaries of research studies on topics previously covered by other numbers in the Research Issues Series. The purpose of the volume is to update numbers 1-7, 15, 17-20 of the series.

One hundred thirty-five abstracts are included, covering these topics: family-peer influence, attitude change, personality, psychopathology, addict lifestyles, employment, criminal behavior, drug laws and the criminal justice system, sexual behavior, pregnancy, driving behaviors, death, and cocaine.

583.   U.S. National Institute on Drug Abuse. **Review of Inhalants: Euphoria to Dysfunction.** Edited by Charles William Sharp and Mary Lee Brehm. Washington: GPO, 1977. 347p. bibliog. [DHEW Publication No. (ADM) 77-553; NIDA Research Monograph 15.] $4.25. LC 77-089150. S/N 017-024-00650-5.

The papers composing this monograph provide a thorough review of the literature on inhalants and critical assessment of the state of knowledge. In addition, a bibliography of 100 pages is included.

It should be pointed out that the practice of inhaling psychotropic substances and vapors for mind altering purposes has not recieved the interest and support that other drug abuse problems have. The drug culture, as well as the general populace, has looked down on the practice, and many of the solvents used have been considered safe and harmless in the past. The inhalants considered in this publication do not include cocaine or marijuana (which may be used in ways other than inhaling) because of more complete treatment elsewhere.

The papers, written by noted experts, are arranged under the following headings: Sociocultural-epidemiological aspects; Clinical evaluation; Preclinical; Pharmacology and toxicology; Preclinical behavioral dysfunctions; and Summary.

The following are the chapter titles: 1) Inhalant abuse: an overview of the problem, 2) Notes on the epidemiology of inhalants, 3) Clinical evaluation of psychological factors, 4) Medical evaluation of inhalant abusers, 5) Specific neurological evaluation of inhalant abusers: clinical and laboratory, 6) Occurrences of volatile agents, 7) Abuse of inhalation anesthetics, 8) Toxicology or alcohols, ketones, and esters—inhalation, 9) Review of the aliphatic and aromatic hydrocarbons, 10) Preclinical pharmacology and toxicology of halogenated solvents and propellants, 11) Nervous system damage from mixed organic solvents, 12) Preclinical behavioral toxicology of inhalant solvents, and 13) Approaches to the problem.

584.   U.S. National Institute on Drug Abuse. **Self-Administration of Abused Substances: Methods for Study.** Edited by Norman A. Krasnegor. Washington: GPO, 1978. 246p. bibliog. [DHEW Publication No. (ADM) 78-727; NIDA Research Monograph Series No. 20.] $10.75. LC 78-63094.

Based on papers presented at a conference, this monograph explores the possibility that there may be a commonality inherent in the use patterns of four substances: cigarette smoking, alcohol drinking, excessive caloric intake, and illicit drug use, and that there may be a set of basic processes that underlie these four behaviors. The papers included address one aspect of the quest to determine empirically whether there are indeed commonalities among these substance abuse behaviors. The focus is on methodological approaches used to study self-administration of abused substances by humans under controlled laboratory conditions.

The papers are presented in two sections: 1) Drugs and ethanol, and 2) Food and tobacco.

This unique monograph can be used as a point of reference for those who wish to conduct similar research on this subject. Also, it is hoped that further studies will be initiated to help elucidate other aspects of this emerging field.

585.   Usdin, Earl, William E. Bunney, Jr., and Nathan S. Kline, eds. **Endorphins in Mental Health Research.** New York: Oxford University Press, 1979. 618p. illus. bibliog. index. $46.50. LC 78-13849. ISBN 0-19-520110-8.

This work contains more than 50 scientific papers presented at a conference held in Puerto Rico in December 1977. The recent discovery of opiate receptors in animal and primate brains and the identification of endogenously produced opioid peptides have been of great interest to scientists. While the book under review is not concerned with drug abuse per se, most of the hypotheses concerning the functions of endorphins are derived from years of investigation of morphine, and the substances possess opiate-like activity. In addition, the most common strategy currently in clinical use (and reported in the book) involves the use of the narcotic antagonists, nalozone and naltrexone.

The book stresses the use of endorphins in mental health, although studies are underway on the role of endorphins in such matters as pain, sleep, respiration, sexual activity, endocrine regulation, and Parkinson's disease.

The papers are grouped in the following sections: 1) Localization, assay and structure of endorphins, 2) Biosynthesis and degradation of endorphins,

3) Functions and interactions of endorphins, 4) Endorphin antagonists, 5) Therapeutic use of endorphins, and 6) Endorphins in body tissues.

586.   Valzelli, L. ed. **Psychopharmacology of Aggression.** Basel: S. Karger, 1978. 180p. bibliog. index. (Modern Problems in Pharmacopsychiatry, v. 13.) $71.00. ISBN 3-8055-2751-9.

Hostile and destructive aggressiveness is a common aspect of modern life, and it seems to be increasing. It is hoped that research can bring about a method for control of such behavior. Such control must, however, have respect for human mind and personality. There are several drugs that can either block or facilitate agressive behavior. The aim of this volume is to trace, through the contributions of ten experts, the profiles of drugs suitable for controlling aggressive behavior. A number of these drugs are commonly abused substances. Questions such as the following are dealt with on the research level: How do these drugs act on aggression? On what kind of behavior are they most effective? What about side effects? To what extent can they be beneficial?

The following are the chapter titles: 1) Effects of sedatives and major tranquilizers on aggressive behavior, 2) Benzodiazepines and aggressive behavior, 3) Antidepressants and aggressive behavior, 4) The effect of lithium and other ions on aggressive behavior, 5) Effects of central stimulants on aggressive behavior, 6) Effects of cannabinoid compounds on aggressive behavior, 7) Effects of psychodysleptics on aggressive behavior of animals, 8) Narcotic analgesics and aggression, 9) Pharmacological management of human violence, and 10) Pathological aggressiveness in man: some theoretical and practical considerations.

587.   Van Ree, Jan M., and Lars Terenius, eds. **Characteristics and Functions of Opioids.** Proceedings of the International Narcotic Research Conference, held in Noordwijkerhout, The Netherlands on July 23-27, 1978. Amsterdam: Elsevier/North Holland Biomedical Press, 1978. 520p. illus. bibliog. index. (Developments in Neuroscience, v. 4.) $60.00. ISBN 0-444-80076-X.

Since the discovery of endorphins, morphine-like substances in the brain which are opioid receptors, there has been a better understanding of brain function. This book contains about 125 scientific research papers presented at an international meeting where some insights into the functional significance of endorphins emerged and the importance of their role in mental illness realized. Also, some papers deal with classical opioids, their specific effects and their interference with biological functions.

The papers are arranged under the following headings: 1) Mechanism of opioid tolerance dependence, 2) Neurotransmitter role of endorphins, 3) Functional role of endorphins, 4) Chemical and structural aspects of opioids, 5) Biosynthesis, release and metabolism of endorphins, 6) Neurochemical and endocrine effects of opioids, 7) Behavioral aspects of opioids, and 8) Opioids receptors.

588.   Warburton, David M. **Brain, Behaviour and Drugs: Introduction to the Neurochemistry of Behaviour.** London and New York: John Wiley and Sons, 1975. 280p. bibliog. index. $15.30. LC 74-20789. ISBN 0-471-91991-8.

This book is intended primarily as a textbook for advanced students in psychology, pharmacology, and allied medical fields. The approach taken is to attempt to explain behavior in terms of the basic neurochemical systems in the brain. As a result of this approach the presentation is organized around the neurochemical systems instead of around various classes of drugs.

The chemistry of synaptic transmission is discussed first, then the effect of drugs on transmission. Following are chapters on the control of hemeostatic motivation, the biochemical basis of mood, control of attention, motor control, and sleep and dreams. The last five chapters consider the ways in which neural systems can explain the phenomena of hallucination and psychoses, drug dependence, memory, intelligence, and anxiety.

Obviously, a great deal more than drug dependence is considered in this book, but most of the drugs discussed are commonly abused substances such as LSD, opiates, amphetamines, cannabis, barbiturates, and alcohol.

589.   Way, E. Leong. **Endogenous and Exogenous Opiate Agonists and Antagonists.** Proceedings of the International Narcotic Research Club Conference, June 11-15, 1979, North Falmouth, Massachusetts. New York: Pergamon Press, 1979. 590p. bibliog. index. $60.00. LC 79-20821. ISBN 0-08-025488-8.

An introductory chapter of this work outlines the role of the World Health Organization in dealing with drug addiction. Then, 139 meeting papers are presented, arranged under the following headings: structure-activity relationships; receptor binding; localization and characterization of active sites; ligands and receptor isolation; neurochemical interactions; disposition and metabolism; analgetic mechanisms; neuroendocrine relationships; behavioral effects; and tolerance and physical dependence.

The research topics covered are of current importance.

590.   Williams, Edward Huntington. **Opiate Addiction: Its Handling and Treatment.** New York: Arno Press, 1976. (Reprint of the edition published by Macmillan in 1922). 194p. index. (Social Problems and Social Policy: The American Experience.) $12.00. LC 75-17250. ISBN 0-405-07524-3.

This early work on opium addiction was written by a physician who reports his own experience with addiction cases. No literature references are given. The author's view was that medical aspects of addiction had been neglected and too much attention given to law enforcement.

The following chapters are presented: 1) The nature of opiate addiction, 2) Gradual reduction treatment of drug addictions, 3) Useful hypnotics, 4) Rapid withdrawal methods, 5) Characteristics of hyoscin delirium, and 6) Comments and observations.

The basic views and observations presented are not much different from those of today. Unfortunately things have not changed very much where drug abuse is concerned.

591.   Zarafonetis, Chris J. D., ed. **Drug Abuse: Proceedings of the International Conference.** Philadelphia, PA: Lea and Febiger, 1972. 616p. illus. bibliog. index. $20.00. LC 72-154243. ISBN 0-8121-0366-1.

The papers in this volume were originally presented to a conference held at Ann Arbor, Michigan, November 9-13, 1970. The primary purpose of the symposium was to help practicing physicians deal with the drug abuse problem. A number of aspects were considered: the physician-patient relationship and the role of the physician in community action programs, with school officials, courts, and representatives of social agencies. Most of the contributors are well-known experts in the field of drug abuse. Scientific aspects of drug abuse were considered as well as sociological concerns.

There is a good summary of the proceedings included. It is of note that some heated debate took place on whether marijuana should be released from legal controls. There was agreement that penalties should be mitigated. There was also agreement that drug dependence or abuse is a medical problem and that it should be treated accordingly. However, just what was meant by "medical problem" was not entirely clear, since self-help units have been somewhat successful, as have some other treatments not strictly "medical." Another point of general consensus was that social and recreational use of drugs extracts a price among users. Finally, attention was drawn to the fact that there are large numbers of fully addicted drug users who do not respond to any treatments available.

592. Zimmerman, Emery, and Robert George, eds. **Narcotics and the Hypothalamus.** New York: Raven Press, 1974. 272p. illus. bibliog. index. (Kroc Foundation Symposia No. 2.) $24.00. LC 74-83453. ISBN 0-911216-87-1.

This work is dedicated to the late David M. Hume, who was a pioneer in studies of the concept of neuroendocrine control. It contains scientific papers that summarize recent progress in the study of effects of drugs of abuse on hypothalamic function. There has been a great deal of interest in the subject as it has become increasingly evident that the effects of narcotics, such as tolerance and physical dependence, involve changes in neuroendocrine and automatic regulatory processes.

The following are the titles of the papers: 1) General overview of theories of opiate tolerance and dependence, 2) Behavioral and neurohormonal relationships to thermoregulatory adaptive changes in morphine abstinence, 3) The role of the lateral hypothalamus in opiate dependence, 4) Sites of action of narcotic analgesics in the hypothalamus, 5) Morphine effects on neurons of the median eminence and on other neurons, 6) Theoretical problems in localizing drugs actions and origins of withdrawal syndromes in the central nervous system: the glass-eye booby trap, 7) Effects of drugs of abuse on motivated behavior and magnocellular neuroendocrine cells, 8) A new technique for studying neuroendocrine systems, 9) Transhypothalamic effects of drugs of abuse on the secretion of pituitary hormones, 10) Drug-induced alternations in gonadotropin and prolactin release in the rat, 11) Effects of narcotic analgesics, anesthetics, and hypothalamic lesions on growth hormone and adrenocorticotropic hormone secretion in rats, 12) Some endocrinologic observations in narcotic addicts, 13) Effect of central acting drugs on the onset of puberty, 14) Long-lasting effects of prepuberal administration of morphine in adult rats, 15) Barbiturates and sexual differentiation of the brain, 16) Drug penetration of the blood-brain barrier, 17) Maturation of the blood-brain and blood-cerebrospinal fluid barriers and transport systems, and 18) Narcotic analgesics and the neuroendocrine control of anterior pituitary function.

Most of the contributors are well-known experts.

593. Zinberg, Norman E., ed. **Alternate States of Consciousness.** New York: The Free Press, a Division of Macmillan Publishing Co., 1977. 294p. bibliog. index. $14.95. LC 76-46722. ISBN 0-02-935770-5.

This volume contains the papers of a conference held in April, 1975, sponsored by the Drug Abuse Council. It was the second meeting so sponsored to consider the "high" states of consciousness as a subject of scientific inquiry. A group of ten well-known individuals from the fields of psychiatry, anthropology, psychology, and pharmacology contributed papers, each from the point of view of his particular discipline.

Several of the papers are not concerned directly with psychoactive drugs. Some of the authors believe that alternate states of consciousness are phenomena that occur to every individual, with or without drugs, and they describe such phenomena.

The papers and authors are as follows: 1) The study of consciousness states: problems and progress, by Norman E. Zinberg, 2) The marriage of the sun and moon, by Andrew T. Weil, 3) "High States" in culture-historical perspective, by Peter T. Furst, 4) Ongoing thought: the normative baseline for alternate states of consciousness, by Jerome L. Singer, 5) A framework for describing subjective states of consciousness, by Caryl Marsh, 6) A biofeedback strategy in the study of consciousness, by David Shapiro, 7) Putting the pieces together: a conceptual framework for understanding discrete states of consciousness, by Charles T. Tart, 8) Some observations on the organization of studies of mind, brain, and behavior, by Karl H. Pribram, 9) The missing center, by Arthur Deikman, and 10) Subjective and objective observation in psychiatry: a note toward discussion, by Joel Elkes.

15

EMPLOYEE PROBLEMS IN BUSINESS AND INDUSTRY

The matter of drug and alcohol abuse and its effect on the worker and the workplace is a matter of continuing concern. About half of the publications listed here deal with the alcoholic employee; the others consider substance abuse of all kinds. It is considered important to salvage as many employees as possible from dependence and addiction, and many companies sponsor treatment and rehabilitation programs. Another matter of concern is finding employment for ex-addicts.

594.   Brisolara, Ashton. **The Alcoholic Employee: A Handbook of Useful Guidelines.** New York: Human Sciences Press, 1979. 168p. illus. bibliog. index. $11.95. LC 78-15763. ISBN 0-87705-327-8.

This handbook is intended to serve as an aid to those involved with the problem of excessive drinking in industry. Written by a person experienced in counseling, the book approaches the problem in a practical manner and tells how to implement a company program to assist the troubled employee. The following chapters are presented: 1) Industrial alcoholism, 2) Alcohol, 3) Drugs, 4) Industrial alternatives, 5) Policy, 6) The supervisory force, 7) Approaching the troubled employee, 8) Case histories, 9) Company educational projects, 10) Referral, 11) Resources, and 12) Conclusion.

Although the book offers few, if any, new ideas on alcohol treatment, it gives good suggestions on identifying the problem employee and what measures can be taken toward rehabilitation. Specific do's and don'ts are presented. The philosophy of the author is opitmistic but also reasonable. Probably, following the instructions laid out can do much to reduce crisis situations, minimize absenteeism, salvage employees, and increase production in industry.

595.   Bureau of National Affairs. **Alcoholism and Employee Relations: A BNA Special Report.** Washington: Bureau of National Affairs, 1978. 20p. $2.50pa. LC 78-111351.

This report explores the implications of stated statistics that show a need for effective employee programs on alcoholism. In addition, it discusses the Hathaway-Williams legislation (which would require federal contractors to provide alcoholism programs for their employees) and other legal developments, and analyzes the ways in which government, business, and labor have in the past attempted to alleviate the problems of alcoholics.

The following are the section headings: 1) Introduction, 2) Hathaway-Williams Bill, 3) Private industry programs—general, 4) Examples of private industry programs, 5) Insurance coverage, 6) Role of supervisors, 7) Labor-management cooperation, 8) Government programs, and 9) Legal developments.

596.   Caplovitz, David. **The Working Addict.** White Plains, NY: M. E. Sharpe, Inc., 1978. 168p. $12.50. LC 77-94070. ISBN 0-87332-116-2.

Written by a professor of sociology, this work is concerned with drug abuse in industry. More than 500 addicts who held full-time jobs for an extensive period of time while addicted were interviewed. The following factors were studied: 1) social characteristics of working addicts, 2) drug history of working addicts, 3) work history of working addicts, 4) labor force participation and the drug habit, 5) the impact of drugs on the job, 6) the drug culture at the work place, and 7) involvement in the broader drug culture.

The author's view is that there is a need for reexamining the drug user's place in society. He suggests that the illegality of drug use is the greatest barrier to successful careers for addicts. Coplovitz summarizes the research done, emphasizing the inaccuracy of some societal stereotypes of addiction, points out areas for further research, and suggests social policy implications.

597.   Follman, Joseph F. **Alcoholics and Business: Problems, Costs, and Solutions.** New York: AMACOM, 1976. 246p. bibliog. index. $12.95. LC 75-40270. ISBN 0-8144-5410-0.

This publication, which was published by a division of the American Management Association, contains a comprehensive group of facts, figures, and opinions on alcoholism and the work place. The author recognizes that no effective alcoholism program can be established in industry without the involvement of unions, and he addresses his book to them as well as to management.

Follman points out the human and economic costs of alcoholism. To industry it is impaired production, labor turnover, and increased costs of operation. The alcoholic employee pays by loss of wages, job, family, and perhaps life. Many progressive leaders in industry have dealt with alcoholism as a disease. They have not fired or covered for the victim, but have provided help, treatment, and insurance. The author considers this to be the proper solution to the problem.

598.   Heyman, Margaret M. **Alcoholism Programs in Industry: The Patient's View.** New Brunswick, NJ: Rutgers Center of Alcohol Studies, 1978. 88p. bibliog. index. (Monographs of the Rutgers Center of Alcohol Studies, No. 12.) $8.50. LC 77-620066. ISBN 911290-45-1.

This book is somewhat unique in that it is concerned with research on the actual effects of alcohol programs in industry instead of merely on "action." Real data are presented. The emphasis is on how employees on the receiving end of programs have viewed them. Their motivations, perceptions, and reactions are examined. Five employer-sponsored programs in the New York City area supplied the data for individual case studies.

The following chapters are presented: 1) Purpose, method and sample, 2) Patients' perceptions associated with work improvement, 3) Referrals to outside treatment resources, 4) Education and interaction with treatment resources, 5) Patients' perceptions in coming to the program, 6) Five types of patients, 7) Analysis of Program B, and 8) Summary and conclusions.

The conclusions of the study point to the need for the following: early identification and referral of problem drinkers, union-management cooperation, education of patient and family, training of counselors, use of community resources, and "constructive confrontation" in dealing with employees.

599.   Schramm, Carl J., ed. **Alcoholism and Its Treatment in Industry.** Baltimore,
MD: Johns Hopkins University Press, 1977. 191p. bibliog. index. $12.00. LC 77-
4783. ISBN 0-8018-1973-3.

The work-related costs of alcoholism due to lost productivity is very high.
Government agencies, employers, and labor unions all have become increasingly concerned with establishing treatment programs in business and industry. This book serves
as a guide for those involved in setting up, administering, and evaluating such programs.

Eleven essays by various authors are presented, and together they provide a
state-of-the-art review of the subject. Titles are as follows: 1) Occupational alcoholism:
a review of issues and a guide to the literature, 2) The work-related costs of alcohol
abuse, 3) Differential use of an alcoholism policy in federal organizations by skill level
of employees, 4) Unionism and alcoholism: the issues, 5) Kennecott's INSIGHT program, 6) The program for alcoholism at Metropolitan Life, 7) Evaluating the New York
City Police Department Counseling Unit, 8) The evaluation of occupational alcoholism
programs, 9) The development of a successful alcoholism treatment facility, 10) Social
stability, work force behavior, and job satisfaction of alcoholic and nonalcoholic blue-
collar workers, and 11) Job-based risks and labor turnover among alcoholic workers. As
can be seen, a number of existing programs are described. Many facts and figures are
provided.

The contributors are a varied group and include academics, social service
employees, union officials, and treatment program directors.

600.   Schramm, Carl J., Wallace Mandell, and Janet Archer. **Workers Who Drink:
Their Treatment in an Industrial Setting.** Lexington, MA: Lexington Books, D. C.
Heath and Co., 1978. 153p. bibliog. index. $16.95. LC 76-58248. ISBN 0-669-
01342-0.

This book reports on results of a demonstration and research project undertaken to explore a new concept in alcoholism treatment services in industry and to
develop data on the labor force behavior of workers who are alcoholics. Professional
and managerial problem drinkers were not considered. The employees of 12 private
companies and government agencies and 14 local labor unions participated in the
study.

Chapter titles are as follows: 1) Background, goals, and scope of the study,
2) History of the program, 3) Identification and referral, 4) Treatment, 5) Description of the study population, 6) Comparison of Employee Health Program Study
workers and their non-problem-drinking peers, 7) Job retention and clinical attendance of the study population, and 8) Summary and recommendations. The intake
questionnaire has been appended.

Among other findings, a need was felt for early identification and referral
of problem drinkers and for constituency support. It was noted that alcoholic workers
expressed much higher levels of overall life-goal frustrations than did nonproblem
drinkers.

601.   Trice, Harrison M., and Paul M. Roman. **Spiritis and Demons at Work: Alco-
hol and Other Drugs on the Job.** 2nd ed. Ithaca, NY: New York State School of
Industrial and Labor Relations, Cornell University, 1978. 268p. bibliog. index. (ILR
Paperback No. 11.) $8.95pa. LC 78-23804. ISBN 0-87546-072-0.

The first edition of this work appeared in 1972. Since then there has been
considerable growth in the field known as occupational alcoholism programming.
The authors felt that their original work was still useful, so the text of the first edition has been reissued with only a new introduction added. In the introduction the

contents of the book are reviewed in terms of relevance to the current scene, and a few new topics are discussed.

The new topics considered include: the neglect of the female work force in occupational program design, the development of occupational alcoholism as a subfield among established health care activities, the emergence of new occupational specialties associated with this work, and the declining emphasis on the preventive potential of work-based programs. Further attention is also given to what the authors consider the core of programming efforts, constructive confrontation.

For a review of the first edition *see* entry 555 in Andrews: *A Bibliography of Drug Abuse* (1977).

602.   U.S. National Institute on Drug Abuse. **Developing an Occupational Drug Abuse Program: Considerations and Approaches.** Washington: GPO, 1978. 94p. bibliog. [DHEW Publication No. (ADM) 78-692; Services Research Monograph Series.] S/N 017-024-00757-9.

Prepared to provide general conceptual and practical guidelines for companies interested in establishing drug abuse programs, this document presents information based on a review of relevant business and professional literature, consultation with experts in occupational programming, and onsite interviews with officials and program staff of companies and unions with operating programs.

The presentation is divided into four sections as follows: 1) Drug abuse and industry: current state, 2) Preliminary considerations in developing an occupational drug abuse program, 3) Implementing a drug abuse program, and 4) Occupational drug abuse program models. In addition there is a good bibliography and several useful appendices: 1) Sample policy statements, 2) Sample program descriptions, 3) State drug authorities and program contacts, 4) Regional support centers, and 5) Selected annotated references.

This kind of publication has considerable value as employers are becoming aware that the provision of such services can effect cost savings and allow for the retention of valued employees.

603.   U.S. National Institute on Drug Abuse. **Developing and Using a Vocational Training and Education Resource Manual.** Washington: GPO, 1977. 24p. [DHEW Publication No. (ADM) 77-516; Services Research Report.] S/N 017-024-00639-4.

It has become increasingly evident that in order to be effective, rehabilitation programs must help clients find a legitimate way to earn money, that is, find and hold a job. This guide focuses on the necessity of the individual's possessing a viable skill. It shows how training and educational program manuals can be developed, how to locate training programs, how to compare the merits of all available programs, and how to refer the clients to the programs most advantageous to them.

604.   U.S. National Institute on Drug Abuse. **Drug Use in Industry.** Washington: GPO, 1979. 38p. bibliog. [DHEW Publication No. (ADM) 79-811; NIDA Services Research Report.] S/N 017-024-00852-4.

This report summarizes the results of a study on the extent and nature of drug use in industry nationwide. The following matters were investigated: 1) the nature and extent of current drug use in industry, 2) the impact of drug use including effect on job performance, 3) the extent, nature, and success of drug education and treatment programs in industry, and 4) the policies and practices of companies with regard to job applicants and employees using drugs.

Rather significant findings are reported. It is of note that in the few compan-ies that have programs for employed drug users, few employees are aware that they exist (less than ten percent). However, management perceives its programs as successful.

605.   U.S. National Institute on Drug Abuse. **Employment Discrimination and How to Deal With It: A Manual for People Concerned With Helping Former Drug Abusers.** By the Legal Action Center, New York. Washington: GPO, 1977. 1 v. (various paging). [DHEW Publication No. (ADM) 77-532; NIDA Services Research Report.]
        Prepared by attorneys to assist others in preparing clients for the search for employment, this manual contains basic advice on what should be reviewed with drug abuse clients before they approach employers, what should be learned about potential employers, what action should follow rejection, and when and how to find an attorney. Guidance regarding the legal tools that exist is provided.
        It is important in the rehabilitation process for individuals who have been drug users to find employment. This publication should provide the counselor and drug treatment program manager significant aid.

606.   U.S. National Institute on Drug Abuse. **Securing Employment for Ex-Drug Abusers: An Overview of Jobs.** Washington: GPO, 1977. 15p. [DHEW Publication No. (ADM) 77-467; Services Research Report.] S/N 017-024-00585-1.
        This document reports on a demonstration program to explore the feasibil-ity of securing employment for ex-drug abusers through centralized job placement units. A formal evaluation study and later follow-up staff interviews are both described.
        The conclusion is that a concentrated job development and placement effort is helpful for ex-addicts who have stabilized in treatment and who have moderately good work histories, but have never held more than entry-level positions in the past. Although many employers were reluctant to participate in the program at first, most were willing to continue because they were reasonably well-satisfied with the clients and because of the project's efforts to respond to employer concerns regarding the screening and follow-up procedures.

16

RELIGION AND DRUGS

There are a few recent books on the role of drugs, hallucinogens particularly, in religious rites and ritual in various societies and cultures. The intent of several of the books listed here is to give readers a better understanding of this role in the past and at the present time.

A work by Carlos Castaneda on the use of psychotropic plants by Mexican Indians, and a critical book about his work are reviewed in Andrews: *A Bibliography of Drug Abuse*, 1977 (entries 561 and 563). Four sequels to Castaneda's book are included here (entries 607-610). The series has generated a good deal of interest, probably primarily because of the mystical philosophy presented, a philosophy that has been adopted by many proponents of hallucinogenic drug use. The books by Wasson on hallucinogens (entries 618 and 619) are classics.

607. Castaneda, Carlos. **Journey to Ixtlan: The Lessons of Don Juan.** New York: Simon and Schuster, 1972. 315p. LC 72-83221. ISBN 0-671-21399-7.

This is the third book in the series about Don Juan, the Mexican Indian "sorcerer," who makes use of three psychotropic plants, jimson weed, peyote, and hallucinogenic mushrooms in his religious ritual. The author has been serving an apprenticeship with Don Juan, becoming endoctrinated into the beliefs of the cult, or what he calls "sorcery." This "sorcery" seems to be a philosophy, the main belief of which is that the world of everyday life is not real; it is only a "description" of the real world, which exists in the mind of an individual, particularly when assisted by the influence of the hallucinogens and properly instructed by a full-fledged sorcerer such as Don Juan. (Most readers will recognize this philosophy in which reality exists only in the mind as being similar to such systems as idealism and transcendentalism.)

In this book Castaneda becomes involved with what he calls "stopping the world." The final three chapters of "Journey to Ixtlan" are his field notes, which culminated in his "stopping the world." After this step the next was to be "seeing" which is achieved in the next book of the series. (*See* reviews below.)

608. Castaneda, Carlos. **The Second Ring of Power.** New York: Simon and Schuster, 1977. 316p. (A Touchstone Book.) $9.95; $3.95pa. LC 77-22107. ISBN 0-671-22942-7; 0-671-24851-0 pa.

This is another in the series about Don Juan, the Mexican Indian medicine man and sorcerer and the use of hallucinogenic drug plants in the religious experiences of the Yaqui Indians (*see* the entries above and below). This work concerns the use of sorcery (which had been taught to other Yaquis by Don Juan). Castaneda becomes acquainted with a sorcerer's family, and his apprenticeship into the religious cult comes to a conclusion in the book. As a climax, Castaneda and another man jump from the top of a mountain into an abyss. By doing this the author says he became "pure perception" and moved "back and forth between two inherent realms of creation." Further, he claims he burst into unity and was whole; his perception had coherence, and he had visions of order. He could not explain his feelings, but writes that "to say they were visions, vivid dreams or even hallucinations does not say anything to clarify their nature." In any case, no mention is made of any bodily harm resulting from the jump into the abyss. It is presumed that the author has survived to produce other sequels in which more disciples are initiated into the faith, and that the jump took place only in the mind.

609.   Castaneda, Carlos. **A Separate Reality: Further Conversations with Don Juan.** New York: Simon and Schuster, 1971. 317p. $6.95. LC 79-139617. ISBN 0-671-20897-7.

This book is a sequel to the author's first book, *The Teachings of Don Juan: A Yaqui Way of Knowledge* (*see* Andrews: *A Bibliography of Drug Abuse*, 1977, entry 561). According to the two books, Castaneda made the acquaintance of a Mexican Indian medicine man, Don Juan, and spent a great deal of time with him learning about the use of hallucinogenic plants (peyote, jimson weed, and mushrooms) and their part in the religious ritual of the Yaqui Indians. Detailed explanations of the meaning of the beliefs of the people are related. The hallucinogens were felt to be vehicles that would conduct an individual to certain impersonal forces or "powers," and the states they produced as being the meetings a sorcerer had to have with the "powers" in order to gain control over them. The states induced by the hallucinogens were believed to be reality, not distortion.

The book is in two parts: The preliminaries of "seeing," and The task of "seeing." At the end of the work Castaneda has his experience with "seeing."

The book is somewhat interesting to read, but as is revealed in de Mille's *Castaneda's Journey: The Power and the Allegory* (*see* Andrews: *A Bibliography of Drug Abuse*, 1977, entry 563), the material seems to be fiction rather than fact.

610.   Castaneda, Carlos. **Tales of Power.** New York: Simon and Schuster, 1974. 287p. $8.75. LC 74-10601. ISBN 0-671-21858-1.

This is the fourth book in a series about Don Juan, an Indian of Mexico who is a medicine man or sorcerer, and the use of hallucinogenic plants in the Yaqui Indian religion. The author related his religious experiences making use of the drug plants peyote, jimson weed, and hallucinogenic mushrooms, with the assistance of Don Juan and others.

The book is in three parts as follows: 1) A witness to acts of power, 2) The tonal (everything the world is perceived to be composed of) and the nagual (the part of the individual for which there is no description), and 3) The sorcerers' explanation.

(*See* the entries above and Andrews: *A Bibliography of Drug Abuse*, 1977, entries 561 and 563.)

611.   Church of the Tree of Life Staff. **The First Book of Sacraments of the Church of the Tree of Life: A Guide for the Religious Use of Legal Mind Alterants.** Edited by John Mann. San Francisco, CA: Tree of Life Press, (451 Columbus Ave., San Francisco, CA 94133), 1972. 32p. illus. bibliog.

The most fundamental belief of the Church of the Tree of Life is said to be that people have the right to do with themselves whatever they please as long as their actions do not interfere with the rights of others. Consequently, the members of this group believe that a person may treat ailments with any medicine and alter consciousness with any psychoactive agent that person wishes to use. Many of the "gifts of God" (herbs and psychedelic agents) have been outlawed in the United States and other places. The church has proclaimed for its sacraments all substances not illegal at the present time.

This publication, which deals primarily with the ritual use of legal mind-altering sacraments, imparts to the reader basic information necessary to use the sacraments successfully. It is of note that some of the substances listed are of doubtful legality.

There are short monographs on the following substances: areca (betel nut), calamus, calea, Canary Island broom, ginseng, goldenseal, kava, nutmeg, ololuique, peyote, pipilzintzintli, psilocybe mushrooms, San Pedro, sinicuichi, soma (*Amanita muscaria*), and yohimbe. Also provided are sections on the use of sacraments, the value of ritual, the use of mind alterants, suppliers of sacraments, the future of freedom, sacraments and magic, a good bibliography, and a "Table of Sympathetic Correspondences of Mind-Altering Sacraments."

In the monographs on the plants the following information is usually given: what the sacrament is for (e.g., divination and healing), scientific and other names, effects of the active constituents, historical use, habitat, description, preparation for use, and some toxicity information.

612.   Du Toit, Brian M., ed. **Drugs, Rituals, and Altered States of Consciousness.** Rotterdam, the Netherlands: A. A. Balkema, 1977. 272p. illus. bibliog. $16.50. ISBN 90-6191-014-5.

The work is an outgrowth of a symposium held during the 1975 Annual Meeting of the Society for Applied Anthropology in Amsterdam. The original papers have been expanded and a number of invited papers added. The editor is a professor of anthropology who has conducted field work among American Indians, in New Guinea, among urban Africans, and in a community of whites in South Africa.

The 15 chapters presented include a general theoretical introduction, a number of descriptive chapters, and discussion in the area of applied social sciences. There are studies of drug use in South Africa and South America and in modern American cities. The emphasis of most of the presentations is on ritual, sacred and secular. Hallucinogens, cannabis, alcohol, heroin, methaqualone, and polydrug complexities are dealt with. The contributions are on a high level, written by experts, but are not especially technical.

613.   Furst, Peter T. **Hallucinogens and Culture.** San Francisco, CA: Chandler & Sharp Publishers, Inc., 1976. 194p. illus. bibliog. index. (Chandler and Sharp Series in Cross-Cultural Themes.) $4.95pa. LC 75-25442. ISBN 0-88316-517-1.

Written by a professor of anthropology, this work serves as an introduction to some hallucinogenic drugs in a cultural and historical setting. It stresses their role in religious, healing, and magical ceremonies particularly. Various cultures about the world, both historical and modern, are explored.

The following chapters are presented: 1) "Idolatry," hallucinogens, and cultural survival, 2) Tobacco: "proper food of the gods," 3) Cannabis (spp.) and nutmeg derivatives, 4) Ibogaine and the vine of souls: from tropical forest ritual to psychotherapy, 5) Hallucinogens and "archetypes," 6) LSD and the sacred morning glories of Indian Mexico, 7) The sacred mushrooms: rediscovery in Mexico, 8) The fly-agaric: "mushroom of immortality," 9) R. Gordon Wasson and the identification of the divine Soma,.10) The "diabolic root," 11) "To find our life": peyote hunt of the Huichols of Mexico, 12) Datura: a hallucinogen that can kill, 13) Hallucinogenic snuffs and animal symbolism, 14) The toad as earth mother: a problem in symbolism and psychopharmacology, 15) Hallucinogens and the sacred deer.

The subject of this book is of growing interest because new or long forgotten naturally occurring psychoactive substances are now being discovered and scientifically described and tested. The identity of every species presently used by natives is not known.

614.   La Barre, Weston. **The Peyote Cult.** 4th ed. enl. S. 1.: Archon Books, 1975. 296p. illus. bibliog. index. $10.00. LC 75-19425. ISBN 0-208-01456-X.

The first 194 pages of this edition are identical to those of the 1st edition, which was issued as a Yale University Publication in Anthropology, Number 19, and which is perhaps the most important classic work available on the subject of hallucinogenic peyote and its use by Indians of the Southwest. The 4th edition, in addition, contains other material: "Twenty Years of Peyote Studies" (from Volume 1, number 1, 1960 of *Current Anthropology*), "The Last Five Years of Peyote Studies," and "Peyote Studies, 1963-1973." In effect, the subject has been brought up to date. It is a scholarly well-documented account.

The author is somewhat sympathetic to hallucinogenic drug use. At least he is convinced that there is no grave danger or evil in the Indian use of peyote in religious ceremonies. However, he deplores those "Caucasoid Americans" who pretend to follow their "religion" through the use of mescaline as a "sacrament." He believes the latter are hypocrites who use drugs under religious guise.

615.   Reichel-Dolmatoff, G. **Beyond the Milky Way: Hallucinatory Imagery of the Tukano Indians.** Los Angeles, CA: University of California, Los Angeles, UCLA Latin American Center Publications, 1978. 159p. illus. (part col.). bibliog. index. (UCLA Latin American Studies, v. 42.) $25.00. LC 78-620014. ISBN 0-87903-042-9.

The author of this work, an anthropologist, has collected a number of color pictures, made by the Tukano Indians of the Colombian Northwest Amazon, in which their hallucinatory experiences are depicted. The use of narcotic drugs of plant origin (especially the yajé plant) play a large part in the religion and symbolism of this group of aborigines. The pictures are accompanied by commentaries made by the Indians.

The main purpose of the book is to deal with ethnographic descriptions, mythology, and the ritual use of certain hallucinogenic plants. It also deals with some aspects of neurophysiological phenomena.

The contents of the book are as follows: 1) The myth, 2) The drug and its ritual, 3) The origins of decoration, 4) Subjective seeing and decorative patterns, 5) The color plates, 6) Some formal aspects of Tukano designs, and 7) Sign, meaning, and message.

616.   Schultes, Richard Evans, and Albert Hofmann. **Plants of the Gods: Origins of Hallucinogenic Use.** New York: McGraw-Hill Book Co., 1979. 192p. illus. (part col.). bibliog. index. $34.95. LC 79-13382. ISBN 0-07-056089-7.

The primary intent of this book seems to be to give its readers a better understanding of the role of hallucinogenic plants in the cultural development of man in various societies through the centuries. Some scientific information also is offered, however. The authors are noted authorities on the subject, and they have brought together a large number of illustrations, including photographs, drawings, and artistic reproductions from other works to illustrate the text. The book is quite attractive although perhaps lacking in organization. The information is scattered throughout the book with reference sections located in the center divided by text material.

Hallucinogenic drugs are of interest for several reasons. They have been used as media for attaining "the mystic experience" in religions, as aids in hedonistic adventure, and a more thorough understanding of their chemical composition may lead to new pharmaceutical products for psychiatric treatment and/or experimentation. The use of such drugs in psychoanalysis, the authors say, is based on effects that are opposite to those of tranquilizers. The latter suppress the patient's problems; hallucinogens bring conflicts to the surface making them more intense, and therefore more clearly recognizable and treatable. Hallucinogenic drug use was brought dramatically to the public eye in the 1960s. It has remained a controversial subject, and scientific research has been slowed. However, scientific interest has continued, and the authors feel the public should be informed about the drugs.

The main contents of the book in order of presentation are as follows: 1) What are plant hallucinogens?, 2) The plant kingdom (the extent and botanical relationship of hallucinogenic plants), 3) Phytochemical research on sacred plants, 4) Geography and usage and botanical range, 5) Plant lexicon (color illustrations and botanical description of 91 plants with psychoactive properties), 6) Users of hallucinogenic plants, 7) Overview of plant use (reference chart to the plants included in the lexicon), 8) Fourteen major hallucinogenic plants (detailed consideration of their cultural significance), 9) Mainstay of the heavens, Amanita (Fly Agaric), 10) The hexing herbs (henbane, deadly nightshade, mandrake), 11) The nectar of delight, Cannabis (hemp: marihuana, hashish), 12) St. Anthony's fire (ergot), 13) Holy flower of the north star, Datura (thorn apple, toloache, torna loco), 14) Guide to the ancestors (iboga), 15) Beans of the Hekula Spirit (Yopo), 16) Vine of the soul (ayahuasca), 17) Trees of the evil eagle (floripondio), 18) The tracks of the little deer (peyote), 19) Little flowers of the gods, Conocybe, Panaeolus, Psilocybe, Stropharia (Teonanacatl), 20) Cactus of the four winds, Trichocereus (San Pedro), 21) Vines of the serpent (morning glory: ololiuqui, badoh negro), 22) Semen of the sun, Virola (epená), 23) Chemical structures of hallucinogens, and 24) Uses of hallucinogens in medicine.

617. Steinmetz, E. F. **Piper Methysticum, Kava–Kawa–Yaqona; Famous Drug Plant of the South Sea Islands.** Amsterdam, the Netherlands: E. F. Steinmetz, 1960. 46p. illus. bibliog. (A 1973 reprinted edition entitled *Kava-Kava, Famous Drug Plant of the South Sea Islands* is available from High Times/Level Press, Box 386, Cooper Station, New York, NY 10003 for $2.00.)

This booklet contains information about the kava plant and the beverage made from it which is used primarily as a ceremonial drink in the South Pacific islands. The drink is habit forming, and it is occasionally abused, although it may have medicinal properties.

There are short chapters on the habitat of the plant, cultivation, description and varieties, structure of the root, harvesting the rootstock, history, preparing the beverage, effects, chemical composition, and use in therapy.

618. Wasson, R. Gordon. **The Wondrous Mushroom: Mycolatry in Mesoamerica.** New York: McGraw-Hill, 1980. 248p. illus. (part col.). bibliog. index. $525.00 deluxe

ed. (Ethnomycological Studies No. 7.) LC 79-26895. ISBN 0-07-068441-3; 0-07-068442-1 deluxe.

The deluxe edition of this work is a collector's item signed by the author and numbered. It is the report of several decades of research into the religious cult that has grown up around the hallucinogenic mushrooms of Mexico. The author is a noted authority in this field.

The book is in two parts. The first two chapters describe the present, the others the past. Chapter titles are: 1) A *velada* in Huautla, 2) Traits of the Mesoamerican *velada* and kindred topics, 3) Xochipilli, 'Prince of *Flowers*': a new interpretation, 4) The *flowers* in pre-conquest Nahuatl poetry, 5) The inebriating drinks of the Nahua, 6) *Códices, lienzos, mapas*, 7) Piltzintli, child god of the Nahua, and his Christian progeny, 8) Teotihuacán and the wondrous mushrooms, 9) The mushroom stones of the Maya highlands, 10) The historical record, and 11) The shaman and the mushroom: new perspectives.

The first chapter tells the story of a *velada* (an all-night shamanic vigil in which the divine mushrooms are 'consulted'). The second presents the traits of the night-time divination with hallucinogens. The purpose of the *velada* is to consult the mushrooms about a grave family worry.

The historical chapters explore literature, art, and various artifacts for folklore and information on rites and ceremonies involving the hallucinogens.

The book is handsome with fine illustrations that include photographs of present mushroom users and artistic works from the past.

619.   Wasson, R. Gordon, Albert Hofmann, and Carl A. P. Ruck. **The Road to Eleusis: Unveiling the Secret of the Mysteries.** New York: Harcourt Brace Jovanovich, 1978. A Helen and Kurt Wolf Book. 126p. illus. (part col.). bibliog. (Ethnomycological Studies No. 4.) $12.95; $4.95pa. LC 77-84399. ISBN 0-15-177872-8.

The title of this work refers to the religious rites the ancient Greeks held in honor of Demeter or Ceres, performed originally at Eleusis, Attica, and later at Athens as part of the state religion. Little is known about the details, and these rites have remained a puzzle for 4,000 years. The initiates taking part in the rites would come away wonderstruck by what they had lived through, and according to some they were never the same as before.

The authors of this book believe they have the solution to the mysteries—the Greeks prepared a hallucinogenic potion from the ergot fungus which was used in the rites, similar to the way Mexicans have used sacred hallucinogenic mushrooms.

The first three chapters of the book are presentations by each of the three authors who first read the papers before the Second International Conference on Hallucinogenic Mushrooms, held in October, 1977. The first chapter, by Wasson, who is a well-known ethnomycologist, is a review of the chief attributes of the Eleusinian Mysteries, showing parallels between them and the sacred mushroom cult of Mexico. The second chapter, by Hofmann, who discovered LSD, reviews the history and chemistry of ergot, and concludes that the herbalists of ancient Greece could have arrived at a hallucinogen from ergot. The third chapter, by Ruck, who is a professor of Greek, offers a novel interpretation of ancient Greek ethnobotany and spirituality and constructs a well-documented argument in support of the solution presented. Chapter 4 is ancillary data; Chapter 5 is a translation of "The Homeric Hymn to Demeter"; and Chapter 6 contains documentation.

As well as being a fascinating, scholarly book, the work is attractively printed and illustrated, and may, like Wasson's other contributions to ethnomycology, become a classic.

17

HALLUCINOGENS

Some of the works in the preceding section are similar to those listed here as material in section 16 also deals with hallucinogenic drug use. Aspects of the subject covered in this section include: general discussions; accounts of the hallucinogenic experience itself; research into uses; psychoses; and pharmacology, botany, and chemistry of the substances. Also included are a number of titles on growing hallucinogenic mushrooms and other hallucinogenic plants, an activity that seems to be important to the drug user and the scientific investigator alike.

The importance of continued research on the substances (particularly LSD) for their possible value in psychiatry is pointed out. Controlled use of the drugs may make it possible better to explore the unconscious mind. On the other side of the question, scientists are concerned about the non-logical thought sequences and disregard for reality produced by hallucinogens.

Serious concern is expressed about the increasing illicit use of phencyclidine (angel dust), considered a very dangerous drug.

620.   Blum, Richard, and associates. **Utopiates: the Use and Users of LSD-25.** New York: Atherton Press, 1964. 303p. bibliog. index. LC 64-23746.

Although the view of LSD use has changed considerably since this book was written in the mid-1960s, it is interesting because it reflects viewpoints and hopes for the drug prevalent at that time. Those who advocated the drug's use were not, for the most part, antisocial nor after "kicks." They included intellectuals, professionals, and scientists who believed that the drug offered great benefits to the individual and society. They thought that the users reaped rich inner experiences, could be free to be themselves, gained chances for further development of personality, and developed loving attitudes toward others. Some claimed that the drug could alter favorably neurosis and alcoholism.

While the contributors to the work acknowledge that there was in 1964 a group of young people who used LSD to get high, the contributions presented here accent culture. The following are the chapter headings: 1) Background considerations, 2) The research enterprise and its problems, 3) The natural history of LSD use, 4) LSD "regulars": continuing users compared with discontinuers, 5) Rejection and acceptance of LSD: users and controls compared, 6) Psychopharmacological considerations, 7) The institutionalization of LSD, 8) Zihuatanejo: an experiment in transpersonative living, 9) Rationale of the Mexican psychedelic training center, 10) Psychedelic experience and religious belief, 11) Social and legal response to pleasure-giving drugs, 12) Police views on drug use, 13) A police administrator comments on the drug movement, and 14) Conclusions and commentary.

The conclusion reached is that the beliefs voiced by those in the drug movement constitute a mythology and that such a movement is needed. It promises a return to paradise, a utopia of the inner life.

621.   Cashman, John. **The LSD Story**. Greenwich, CT: Fawcett Publications, Inc., 1966. 128p. $0.50pa.

Written by a reporter in the 1960s when LSD was not as well understood as it is now, this book reports on its effects in the sensational manner typical of that time. Many quotations selected from the literature have been included as have personal accounts on the effects of the chemical.

The book is interesting to read as representative of the attitudes toward the use of hallucinogenic drugs at the time it was written.

622.   **The Compleat Psilocybin Mushroom Cultivator's Bible**. 2nd ed. Miami, FL: Hongero Press, 1976. 71p. illus. (part col.). bibliog. $5.00pa.

This booklet offers complete growing directions for cultivating psilocybin mushrooms, a hallucinogenic type. In addition, it gives instructions on preserving and using the crop. Also included are a field guide section of all North American species and a color identification section of plates.

The following are the chapter headings: 1) Psilocybin and psilocin, 2) In the field, 3) Spore printing, 4) Growing mycelium, 5) Growing spawn, 6) Casing grain jars, 7) Cultivating in beds, 8) Pests of mushroom beds, 9) Preserving, and 10) Ingestion.

623.   Cooper, Richard. **A Guide to British Psilocybin Mushrooms**. rev. ed. London: Hassle Free Press (BCM Box 311, London WCIV 6XX, U.K.), 1979. 32p. illus. (part col.). bibliog. £1.25pa. ISBN 0-86166-004-8.

The purpose of this book is to assist the reader in finding and identifying psychoactive mushrooms of the British Isles. About a dozen are said to fall in this category when taken in the correct dosage. Other mushroom species that may be confused with the hallucinogenic ones, but which are dangerously poisonous, are pointed out, for instance, two members of the amanita family.

Following sections on history and identification, a short monograph on each species is presented with a line drawing of the plant. Then come sections on chemistry and dosage, collecting and preserving, effects, spore printing, spore details, legal position, and a glossary.

The information presented in the booklet seems to be reasonably correct, although it is dangerous to experiment in using these plants, as the author himself admits.

624.   Feldman, Harvey W., Michael H. Agar, and George M. Beschner, eds. **Angel Dust: An Ethnographic Study of PCP Users**. Lexington, MA: Lexington Books, D. C. Heath and Co., 1979. 226p. bibliog. index. $16.95. LC 79-8319. ISBN 0-669-03379-0.

This book presents an ethnographic study of phencyclidine (PCP), a synthetic hallucinogenic drug developed in the late 1950s. Its use is now a problem of national concern. Although it has received much negative publicity, PCP use continues to spread, particularly among the young. The book contains nine chapters, by various experts, which trace the street history of the drug from the 1960s, to its peak popularity in the mid-1970s, and to its current use in Chicago, Miami, Philadelphia, and the Seattle-Tacoma area.

The chapter titles are: 1) Introduction, 2) The study method, 3) PCP use in four cities: an overview, 4) A quantitative analysis of 100 PCP users, 5) "Buzzin": PCP use in Philadelphia, 6) Sea-Tac and PCP, 7) Burning out on the Northwest Side: PCP use in Chicago, 8) Freaks and cognoscenti: PCP use in Miami, and 9) The PCP study in context: some comments on policy and method.

The authors make much use of personal observations of PCP users. More than 300 were observed and interviewed. The investigators did not uncover the reasons young people take chances with the drug's use. The youths recognized it as a powerful drug. It appeared, however, that PCP loses its appeal as adolescents rid themselves of the need for group support and realize that it is a detriment to developing social and sexual relationships. The book does not answer many questions, but does suggest the complexity of them.

The study makes use of a new ethnographic methodology, which may serve as a model for further research of this kind. The simultaneous use of several ethnographers in different settings has not previously been tried in U.S. drug research.

625.   Grinspoon, Lester, and James B. Bakalar. **Psychedelic Drugs Reconsidered.** New York: Basic Books, Inc., 1979. 343p. bibliog. index. $16.95. LC 79-7336. ISBN 0-465-06450-7.

At the present time, say the authors of this work, "psychedelic drugs are very much out of fashion." Both researchers and illicit drug users have shown little interest in them in the last 15 years. In the case of illicit users, they are evidently fearful of bad effects; in the case of the researchers, psychiatrists and psychologists have not been allowed to use them either in research or practice because of restrictive laws.

Grinspoon, who is a psychoanalyst and Associate Professor of Psychiatry at Harvard Medical School, and Bakalar, who is a lawyer, believe good can come of reexamining this class of drug. In spite of the adverse attention psychedelics have received, the authors suggest that the drugs may be less harmful than tobacco or alcohol. They point out that these drugs were once believed to provide entry into a wider social and mental universe, and that truths and reality came with them. The hope is expressed that this book will heighten our consciousness of that influence.

The chemistry, psychoneurological effects, and the history of man's experience with psychedelic drugs from early time to the present (both medical and religious) are reviewed. The following are the chapter titles: 1) The major psychedelic drugs: sources and effects, 2) Psychedelic plants in preindustrial society, 3) Psychedelic drugs in the twentieth century, 4) The nature of psychedelic experience, 5) Adverse effects and their treatment, 6) Therapeutic uses, 7) Psychedelic drugs and the human mind, and 8) The future of psychedelic drug use and research. In addition there is an appendix on "The Legal Status of Psychedelic Drugs."

While many may not agree with all of the authors' views on this subject, some aspects of it are undoubtedly worth attention. A paradoxical situation exists in regard to research with the drugs. They are available on the street for consumption, but not for clinical investigation. Most will agree that serious human research into such areas as learning, dream states, and probing the unconscious is desirable and that research of this kind as well as investigation of therapeutic value of the drugs should be encouraged. However, the value of the psychedelic experience, the chemically induced transcendental state, for members of society generally is not so clear. The thought sequences during the experience are illogical, and reality is distorted, matters that concern scientists.

626.   Grof, Stanislav. **Realms of the Human Unconscious: Observations from LSD Research.** New York: E. P. Dutton, 1976. 257p. illus. bibliog. index. $4.95pa. LC 76-11863. ISBN 0-525-47438-2.

This volume is the first of a series planned by the author to report his observations and experiences during 17 years of research with LSD and other psychedelic drugs. Dr. Grof began his research on psychedelics in Czechoslovakia in 1956. LSD was a therapeutic agent as respected as any other in Czechoslovakia at that time. In contrast, when Grof came to the United States in 1967 he found that sensationalism surrounded the drug here, and that scientific research in the area was at a standstill.

The book summarizes basic information about LSD, outlines the various stages of the author's research, and focuses primarily on the phenomenological description of the various levels and types of experiences manifested in psychedelic drug sessions.

Chapter headings are: 1) General introduction, 2) Abstract and aesthetic experiences in LSD sessions, 3) Psychodynamic experiences in LSD sessions, 4) Perinatal experiences in LSD sessions, 5) Transpersonal experiences in LSD sessions, and 6) Multidimensional and multilevel nature of the LSD experience.

Grof feels that the use of psychedelics should be explored further and that they have potential for a number of uses, including the study of schizophrenia, for didactic purposes, for a deeper understanding of art and religion, for personality diagnostics, for the treatment of emotional disorders, and for altering the experience of dying. He says LSD has an affinity for emotionally highly charged dynamic structures. It will scan the unconscious, identifying the areas of tension, and bring them to the open. Thus it helps the patient and the therapist distinguish relevant material from the unimportant; the most urgent areas for therapeutic treatment are pointed out.

The author hopes his ideas will be accepted and that the use of LSD will be adopted as a tool in the professional community.

627.   Grubber, Hudson. **Growing the Hallucinogens: How to Cultivate and Harvest Legal Psychoactive Plants.** New York/Hermosa Beach, CA: High Times/Golden State Publishing, 1976. 32p. bibliog. $2.00pa.

This booklet presents general information on the cultivation and propagation of plants, then gives specific instructions on growing and harvesting a variety of psychoactive plants, all of them legal according to the author.

The following plants are discussed: belladonna, the brooms, betel nut, cabeza de angel, calamus, California poppy, catnip, chicalote (prickly poppy), coleus, colorines, damiana, daturas, doñana, fennel, Hawaiian baby woodrose, Hawaiian woodrose, heliotrope, henbane, hops, hydrangea, iochroma, kava kava, khat, lion's tail, lobelia, Madagascar periwinkle, mandragore (mandrake), maraba, maté, mescal beans, Mormon tea, morning glory, nutmeg, ololuique, passionflower, pipiltzintzintli, psilocybe mushrooms, rhynchosia, San Pedro, sassafras, shansi, silvervine, sinicuichi, so'ksi, Syrian rue, tobacco, wild lettuce, and wormwood.

In addition, a short list of suppliers of seeds, cuttings, and dried herbs is included as well as a glossary and a list of botanical names used, with pronunciation indicated.

628.   Harris, Bob. **Growing Wild Mushrooms: A Complete Guide to Cultivated Edible and Hallucinogenic Mushrooms.** Berkeley, CA: Wingbow Press, 1976. 82p. illus. (part col.). bibliog. $3.50pa. LC 76-6613. ISBN 0-914278-17-2.

The emphasis of this work is on cultivation of mushrooms, although there are some descriptions of species. There is a separate section on North American psilocybin mushrooms, a type that contains hallucinogenic agents. Some of the species discussed are currently restricted by law because of their chemical content.

Chapter titles are: 1) An introduction to the mushroom, 2) A note on cultivation, 3) Equipment for sterile culture work, 4) Media, 5) Starting cultures, 6) Incubation, 7) Sources of materials, and 8) North American psilocybin mushrooms.

The "Sources of Materials" chapter tells where one may get supplies and equipment necessary for mushroom cultivation. The last chapter contains descriptions and cautions that will help one distinguish lethal mushrooms from those sought.

629.   Hofmann, Albert. **LSD: My Problem Child.** Translated by Jonathan Ott. New York: McGraw-Hill Book Co., 1980. $9.95. LC 80-14536. ISBN 0-07-029325-2.

This is a translation of a work first published in Germany in 1979 as *LSD— Mein Sorgenkind*. The author is the research chemist who discovered LSD. The book, though, is not as much about the scientific discovery as it is about Hofmann's philosophy regarding the use of hallucinogens and the mystical experiences brought about by them. Hofmann's foreword says his intent is to give a comprehensive picture of LSD, its origin, effects, and dangers, in order to guard against abuse of the substance. He believes "that if people would learn to use LSD's vision-inducing capability more wisely, under suitable conditions, in medical practice and in conjunction with meditation, then in the future this problem child could become a wonder child."

The book begins with an account of how LSD originated. There are chapters about research results on the drug, chemical modifications, use in psychiatry, remedial uses, inebriant uses, and similar hallucinogens used in Mexico. The book also contains a number of accounts of encounters Hofmann has had with others interested in hallucinogenic substances: Ernst Jünger, Aldous Huxley, Walter Vogt, Timothy Leary, Rudolf Gelpke, and Gordon Wasson.

The last chapter is on the LSD experience and reality. Hofmann says he is often asked what has made the deepest impression upon him in LSD experiments, and whether he has arrived at new understanding through them. It seems that he has. His last paragraph states: "I see the true importance of LSD in the possibility of providing material aid to meditation aimed at the mystical experience of a deeper, comprehensive reality. Such a use accords entirely with the essence and working character of LSD as a sacred drug."

630.   Jenkins, David T. **A Taxonomic and Nomenclatural Study of the Genus** *Amanita* **Section** *Amanita* **for North America.** Vaduz: J. Cramer, 1977. 126p. illus. (part col.). bibliog. (Bibliotheca Mycologica, Bd. 57.) $20.00pa. ISBN 3-7682-1132-0.

This publication is of interest because it presents material on the genus *Amanita*, mushrooms of which many of the species are toxic and/or hallucinogenic. It is a scholarly, scientific treatment, suitable for those who are mushroom experts.

The presentation is introduced with historical background material; then general taxonomic characteristics are outlined. Next, each taxa is described, and lastly, there is a section of type studies. In the descriptions there is information on habitat and distribution, collections examined, and observational remarks.

631.   Johnson, Fred H. **The Anatomy of Hallucinations.** Chicago: Nelson-Hall, 1978. 239p. bibliog. index. $11.95. LC 77-22711. ISBN 0-88229-155-6.

Although this book does not deal with drug abuse directly, it should be of interest to specialists in the fields of psychology, psychiatry, and neurology who are interested in the field because a number of abused drugs produce hallucinations, very like those of the mentally ill. The emphasis of the work, however, is on hallucinations per se, particularly the auditory type connected with mental illness. The purpose of the publication is to set forth the available information about the true hallucinations of psychosis and their origins with the hope that the necessary therapeutic steps will be revealed. First, the historical aspects of hallucinations are sketched; then, the focus is on their origin in hallucinated inner speech, their pathology, their influence, their relation to delusions, complexes, and suggestibility, their disordering of inner speech, and their neuroanatomy. A bibliography of 40 pages has been included.

632.   Kimmens, Andrew C., ed. **Tales of Hashish.** New York: William Morrow and Co., 1977. 287p. index. $5.95. LC 77-1934. ISBN 0-688-03194-3; 0-688-08194-0 pa.

Called a literary look at the hashish experience, this work is a collection of papers, essays, and stories that focus on the use of the drug. Included are a number of well-known literary and historical accounts, including writings of Arnold of Lübeck, Marco Polo, Antoine Sylvestre de Sacy, Théophile Gautier, Charles Baudelaire, François Lallemand, Alexander Dumas Père, Bayard Taylor, Fitz Hugh Ludlow, Louisa May Alcott, Jules Giraud, Henry de Monfreid, Herodotus, Garcia da Orta, Jan Huyghen van Linschoten, Laurent d'Arvieux, Jean Chardin, Gerhard Rohlfs, and Henri A. Junod. In addition, three tales from *The Thousand and One Nights* are included. Most of the accounts are first-person narratives of drug-induced hallucinatory experiences.

Kimmens has edited and annotated the collection throughout. The introduction suggests there may be some connection between the use of hashish in nineteenth century America and the use of marijuana today.

633.   Lavender, Wayne. **LSD Psychosis and Acute Schizophrenia: A Follow-Up Study.** Oceanside, NY: Dabor Science Publications, 1977. 80p. bibliog. $15.00. LC 77-22127. ISBN 0-89561-002-7.

There was much concern in the late 1960s over the use of illicit hallucinogenic drugs, usually by the young. Since a good deal of time has passed and the use subsided, it is now possible to study the enduring problems, if any, it caused. Long-term as well as short-term use of the drug can be considered.

This book reports on a study of the personality and intellectual functioning of individuals hospitalized with LSD psychosis and contrasts them with similar individuals hospitalized for acute schizophrenia reactions. (There is similarity in a number of respects between LSD psychosis and acute schizophrenia.) The literature of the subject is explored, then the method, results, discussion, and summary of the research presented.

It was found that in almost all respects the two groups studied (21 LSD-using subjects and 21 control subjects) were identical in premorbid adjustment, cognitive function, psychological maturity, and the number of psychiatric rehospitalizations. This leads to the conclusion that the determining role of LSD in maladjustment may be less than was previously supposed.

634.   Ott, Jonathan, and Jeremy Bigwood, eds. **Teonanacatl: Hallucinogenic Mushrooms of North America.** Seattle, WA: Madrona Publishers, Inc., 1978. 175p. illus.

(part col.). bibliog. index. (Psycho-Mycological Studies, No. 2.) $14.50; $8.95pa. LC 78-14794. ISBN 0-914842-32-3; 0-914842-29-3 pa.

This book is based on the proceedings of the Second International Conference on Hallucinogenic Mushrooms, held in Port Townsend, Washington, in October 1977. Leading authorities in the field, such as R. Gordon Wasson, Albert Hofmann, Andrew Weil, and Richard Evans Schultes, presented papers. The history of the use of hallucinogenic mushrooms is traced; their use in religious ritual is discussed; and their botanical identification and cultivation outlined. In addition, an appeal for responsible use in modern society is made, doubtless a controversial matter.

The editors and contributors take the subject seriously. At least some of them believe that these mushrooms have had mystical power, although it may have been lost in modern times because of their use by a "profane and puerile, largely hedonistic cult which has succeeded its venerable ancestor." Wasson has observed that the superficial use by ignorant thrill-seekers is a desecration. It is hoped that there might be a resurgence in their use as sacraments.

635.   Radouco-Thomas, Simone, A. Villeneuve, and C. Radouco-Thomas. **Pharmacologie, Toxicologie, et Abus des Psychotomimétiques (Hallucinogènes). Pharmacology, Toxicology, and Abuse of Psychotomimetics (Hallucinogens).** Québec: Les Presses de l'Université Laval, 1974. 473p. bibliog. $20.00. ISBN 0-7746-6599-8.

This publication is based on material presented at the Laval University International Symposium on Psychodysleptics where about 30 experts met to discuss hallucinogenic drugs and their abuse. The book attempts to integrate multidisciplinary aspects of the field, including both the biomedical and the social.

There are 28 papers presented in five sections as follows: 1) Pharmacological effects of psychotomimetics, 2) Mechanism of action of psychotomimetics, 3) Complications and dangers of psychotomimetics, 4) Abuse of psychotomimetics, and 5) Legal aspects of psychotomimetics. A few of the papers are in the French language; the others in English.

636.   Schultes, Richard Evans, and Albert Hofmann. **The Botany and Chemistry of Hallucinogens.** With a Foreword by Heinrich Klüver. rev. and enl. 2nd ed. Springfield, IL: Charles C. Thomas, 1980. illus. bibliog. index. (American Lecture Series, Publication No. 1025.) $28.75. LC 78-27883. ISBN 0-398-03863-5.

Recent advances made since the publication of the original work in 1973 (*see* Andrews: *A Bibliography of Drug Abuse*, 1977, entry 596) have been encompassed in this 2nd edition. The botany and chemistry of this class of plants has progressed rapidly since 1973.

In the new edition historical material has been strengthened; a more thorough investigation of hallucinogenic plant chemistry has been made, making use of newer improved analytical methods; and more plants have been included of possible or suspected hallucinogenic properties. In addition, a new chapter has been provided that lists plants with alleged hallucinogenic effects. Ethnobotanical, pharmacological, and psychological aspects of hallucinogens are covered to some extent as well as the chemistry, botany, and history of the subject.

Chapter headings are: 1) Hallucinogenic or psychotomimetic agents: what are they?, 2) The botanical distribution of hallucinogens, 3) The structural types of the principal plant hallucinogens, 4) Plants of hallucinogenic use, 5) Plants of possible or suspected hallucinogenic use, and 6) Plants with alleged hallucinogenic effects.

The authors of the book are authorities on the subject. They have provided an extensive bibliography of more than 700 references, and the illustrations are outstanding. Most of the plants discussed are pictured, and views depicting the preparation and use of the drugs are included. Also included are photographs of scientists who have been involved with the development of the field.

The 1st edition of the book was quite well received.

637.   Stillman, Richard C., and Robert E. Willette, eds. **The Psychopharmacology of Hallucinogens.** New York: Pergamon Press, 1978. 338p. bibliog. index. $32.50. LC 78-14019. ISBN 0-08-021938-1.

This publication contains the papers of a conference held in Bethesda, Maryland on December 21-22, 1976 and sponsored by the National Institute on Drug Abuse. The experts who presented the papers discussed the state-of-the-art methodology for assessing hallucinogenic behavior, and correlated the molecular structure of these compounds with behavior. Also considered are the mystical aspects of the psychedelic experience.

The papers are in two groups, those on biochemistry and pharmacology, and those on animal and human behavior. The following are the titles: 1) Biosyntheses and action of hallucinogens in mammals, 2) Role of biogenic amines in the actions of monomethoxyamphetamines, 3) On the molecular mechanism of action of hallucinogens, 4) Molecular determinants for interaction with the LSD receptor: biological studies and quantum chemical analysis, 5) Progress toward the development of a receptor model for hallucinogenic amphetamines, 6) Characterization of three new psychotomimetics, 7) Pharmacological effects of ($+$)-, (S)-, and (R)-MDA, 8) Some aspects of the pharmacology of phencyclidine, 9) The mode of action of LSD-like hallucinogens and their identification, 10) Preclinical identification of hallucinogenic compounds, 11) Dual effects of LSD, mescaline and DMT, 12) Use of unconditioned and conditioned behaviors in evaluating possible hallucinogenic agents, 13) Analysis of hallucinogens by means of Pavlovian conditioning, 15) Behavioral measures of hallucinogen behavior, 16) Animal models of drug-induced hallucinations, 17) Hallucinogens and attentional dysfunction: a model for drug effects and reality testing, 18) A drug model of hallucinosis, 19) Euphorohallucinogens—toward a behavioral model, and 20) The chemical transcendental state: an experience in search of an explanation.

Hallucinogens are of interest and important because they do more than other drugs of abuse. They transform experience and often create states that mimic natural psychoses. Their controlled use may present research opportunities for learning about the psychotic process and possibly give insight into the mystical state.

638.   U.S. Congress. 95th, Second Session. Senate. **Phencyclidine (PCP or Angel Dust).** Joint Hearings before the Subcommittee on Alcoholism and Drug Abuse of the Committee on Human Resources and the Subcommittee to Investigate Juvenile Delinquency of the Committee on the Judiciary, on S. 2778, to provide for increased criminal penalties for the unauthorized manufacture or distribution of PCP and to provide for piperidine reporting. June 7 and 21, 1978. Washington: GPO, 1978. 382p.

These hearings were called to provide a clearer picture and understanding of the nature and extent of phencyclidine abuse. The substance, known as PCP, is a nonnarcotic, nonbarbiturate chemical that is relatively easy to make from readily available legal chemicals. It is very dangerous; users behave in bizarre fashion and are often responsible for strange, suicidal, or homicidal acts.

Testimony and prepared statements are given, which include accounts of effects of use by former users, history, incidence, chemical symptoms, treatment, and rehabilitation programs. Testimony also is given regarding production and trafficking of the drug and law enforcement aspect of the problem.

Some of the questions addressed are as follows: 1) Why is there so much of the drug available on the street?, 2) Why are present laws and penalties not more effective in deterring those who produce and sell it?, and 3) Is it possible to control the production by regulating the ingredient chemicals involved in PCP manufacture?

639.   U.S. National Institute on Drug Abuse. **Phencyclidine (PCP) Abuse: An Appraisal.** Edited by Robert C. Petersen, and Richard C. Stillman. Washington: GPO, 1978. 313p. bibliog. [DHEW Publication No. (ADM) 78-728; NIDA Research Monograph Series No. 21.] $11.75. S/N 017-024-00785-4. LC 78-600095.

Phencyclidine ("Angel Dust") abuse is a relatively recent problem as the drug originally had a poor street reputation and was rarely a drug of choice for abuse. A change in mode of use from oral ingestion to smoking or snorting has changed that picture. The drug is more frequently abused now since its effects can be better controlled. It is relatively easy to obtain as it is easily synthesized.

This volume represents an attempt to bring together present knowledge, which has been rather fragmentary. It presents conference papers presented by researchers and clinicians who have had experience with PCP. Seventeen papers, most with extensive bibliographies, have been included.

18

MARIJUANA

Books about marijuana are to some extent scattered throughout this bibliography, but this section contains titles dealing exclusively with the substance in a more general manner.

There is still interest in physiological effects and medical finding regarding the drug; "the truth" about marijuana is still being sought.

Other matters of concern include the therapeutic potential of marijuana, patterns of use, social implications of use, botany, and chemistry. There is even a title on how to use cannabis in cooking (entry 646) and one on the art of making marijuana products in the home laboratory (entry 650). Several titles on growing the marijuana plant are listed in section 3.

There have been efforts by certain groups to legalize marijuana. The popular press has published items on the use of the substance as a remedy for glaucoma and relief of cancer-related anxiety. Other suitable remedies for these conditions are available, though, and they do not have marijuana's intoxicating effects. The matter is still controversial.

640. Abel, Ernest L., ed. **The Scientific Study of Marihuana**. Chicago: Nelson-Hall Publishers, 1976. 299p. bibliog. $12.50. LC 76-4508. ISBN 0-88229-144-0.

The editor of this work is a noted research scientist active in the study of drugs. His view is that alleged "authorities" on the subject of cannabis have often based their arguments, pro and con, on anecdotal literature or on evidence that does not come up to modern scientific standards. He has collected into this volume scientific reports of some of the recent findings on the subject in order to make them available to those interested, both laymen and professionals. He feels they are representative of the more socially relevant approaches to cannabis research.

The contributions are grouped under the following headings: 1) Pharmacology of cannabis sativa, 2) Common experiences reported by users of marihuana, 3) Effects of marihuana on hunger, 4) Sensory and perceptual effects, 5) Marihuana and time distortion, 6) Marihuana and memory, 7) Effects of marihuana on psychomotor skills, 8) Physiological effects, 9) Adverse psychological effects, 10) Adverse social behavior: aggression and crime, and 11) Summary.

The last paper summarizes the evidence dealing with the effects of marijuana on humans. Much of the present work, it is pointed out, is a rediscovery of what has been known for some time. However, an explanation is given for the vastly different reports of behavioral effects of cannabis. It is because the potency of the material varies so much. This probably accounts for much of the controversy surrounding claims about the drug.

641.   Cohen, Sidney, and Richard G. Stillman, eds. **The Therapeutic Potential of Marihuana.** New York: Plenum Medical Book Co., 1976. 515p. bibliog. index. $25.00. LC 17106. ISBN 0-306-30955-6.

This book presents the proceedings of a conference held in Pacific Grove, California, in November 1975. It seemed advisable at that time to bring together investigators working on therapeutic aspects of the cannabinoid substances in marijuana and related synthetic compounds, because certain findings were pointing to therapeutic utility of the substances. Twenty-eight scientific papers are included, dealing with historical, preclinical, and clinical aspects of the subject. The contributors are distinguished experts in the field, and their discussions are also included, adding a good deal of interesting material.

The contributions are grouped under the following subjects: general papers, opthalmic effects, pulmonary and preanesthetic effects, mental functioning, tumor problems, anticonvulsant activity, and synthetic cannabinoid-like compounds.

The conclusion reached by the senior editor is that, although some promising leads have been developed, a considerable amount of work remains to be done before any cannabis compound can find its way to the marketplace. Indeed, at this writing it seems, marijuana propaganda to the contrary, that products already in use for the conditions under study are more satisfactory than those being developed from the plant.

This conference assembled many of those working on therapeutic aspects of the marijuana constituents, and focused attention on what has been done and what needs to be accomplished in this regard.

642.   Connell, P. H., and N. Dorn, eds. **Cannabis and Man: Psychological and Clinical Aspects and Patterns of Use.** Proceedings of the Third International Cannabis Conference organised by the Institute for the Study of Drug Dependence at the Ciba Foundation, London. Edinburgh: Churchill Livingstone, 1975. 236p. bibliog. index. $17.50. ISBN 0-443-01265-2.

This book contains 14 conference papers, prepared by 28 experts who attempt to present an overview of the state of knowledge regarding this particular drug. The editors hope that the findings will be of assistance to international groups whose duty it is to formulate international policy in this field, and be a valuable source of authentic information for inclusion in health education programs.

The material is divided into three sections: 1) Effects of use, 2) Patterns of use and social attitudes, and 3) Past and future research. A special feature is the reports of discussions held after each paper. One of the most important aspects of the book is the attempt made to point to fruitful areas of future research.

643.   Croes, Martin, and André McNicoll. **Marijuana Reappraised: Two Personal Accounts.** New York: Myrin Institute for Adult Education, 1977. 20p. $1.00pa. LC 77-015695. ISBN 0-913098-08-6.

The two essays in this pamphlet are personal accounts of marijuana use and its social implications. The first is called "Second Thoughts on Mary Jane," the second, "Let's Think Again About 'Soft' Drugs." The authors tell what drew them to the drug in the first place and describe the measures they now would take to spare others their experiences. They believe that marijuana use brings about personality changes.

644.   Dornbush, Rhea L., Alfred M. Freedman, and Max Fink, eds. **Chronic Cannabis Use.** New York: New York Academy of Science, 1976. 430p. bibliog. (New York Academy of Sciences. Annals. v. 282.) $36.00. LC 76-58481. ISBN 0-89072-028-2.

This book contains the papers of a conference held January 26-28, 1976, sponsored by the New York Academy of Sciences, National Institute on Drug Abuse, and New York Medical College. The conference was organized as a forum to review and evaluate the data from long-term cannabis users, to provide a body of knowledge about the drug's effects, and to attempt to extrapolate this data to casual use, and project the outcome for short-term users. There are five major areas of concern considered: central nervous system functioning, health implications, cannabis psychosis, the amotivational syndrome, and tolerance, dependence, and withdrawal. Some of the data presented had been reported previously.

In summary, the results of the studies did not show serious physiological effects resulting from cannabis use. There was evidence of tolerance but not for dependence or withdrawal. The studies, however, did not bear on the problem of interference with motor coordination or sensory perception associated with use of the drug.

645.   Goldman, Albert Harry. **Grass Roots: Marijuana in America Today.** New York: Harper and Row, 1979. 262p. illus. $12.95. LC 77-11806. ISBN 0-06-011554-8.

Written by a former English professor turned pop-culture historian, this work is a state-of-the-scene report on drug abuse in the United States today. It provides material on the botany, pharmacology, and what the author sees as political persecution and historic insights on marijuana. A plea is made for legalization of marijuana use.

646.   Gottlieb, Adam. **The Art and Science of Cooking with Cannabis: The Most Effective Methods of Preparing Food and Drink with Marijuana, Hashish and Hash Oil.** New York/San Francisco, CA: High Times/Level Press, 1974. 79p. $3.50pa.

The author of this booklet says this publication is not merely another cookbook. Instead, it serves as a guide to teach the reader the nature of cannabis, how it combines with different foods, how it is best assimilated in the human digestive tract, and how to get the most highs for the money.

The first section compares the results of ingesting cannabis to those from smoking it. (There is slower action from ingestion, but there are stronger, longer lasting effects.) The second section explains the physical and chemical nature of cannabis. The third section describes such basic materials as canna-butter (the Sacred Ghee of India) and cannabis tar, which is called for in some of the recipes that follow. The recipe section contains directions for about 30 different dishes and/or beverages. These include such concoctions as hash oil honey, cannabis chocolate icing, curried hash, creme de gras, and cannabis milk shake.

647.   Graham, J. D. F. **Cannabis Now.** Aylesbury, Buckinghamshire, England: H M + M Publishers Ltd., 1977. 122p. bibliog. index. £3.00. ISBN 0-85602-067-2.

The author says he wrote this book because most recent works on the subject have been technical, scientific, and fully documented. He felt that a book for the non-specialist was needed owing to the growing concern over possible changes in laws regarding marijuana. Graham, who is a professor of pharmacology, takes the view that the drug is not as harmful as the present law (in Great Britain) implies and that the people can handle it without disaster. He admits personal bias in his selection of literature upon which to base the book.

Chapter titles are as follows: 1) What is cannabis?, 2) The effect of cannabis on the mind, 3) On mind-altering plants, 4) On ways of using cannabis, 5) What are the active materials in cannabis?, 6) The good and bad in cannabis—physical effects, 7) Long-term consumption of cannabis and health, 8) Cannabis and the law, and 9) What shall we do about cannabis?

648.   Graham, J. D. P., ed. **Cannabis and Health**. London: Academic Press, 1976. 481p. bibliog. index. $30.00. LC 76-1082. ISBN 0-12-294650-2.

The editor of this book brought together a group of experts, most of them from the United Kingdom, to present information on the current state of research on all aspects of cannabis. The human or clinical aspects of the subject are emphasized, but animal experimentation is referred to when it fills gaps in knowledge.

The 12 chapters are grouped into three sections as follows: 1) The nature of cannabis and the cannabinoids, 2) The actions of cannabis and its effect on health, and 3) Cannabis and society. The material is on the research level, but has been written in as nontechnical language as possible.

Like a number of other books, the aim is to present a dispassionate account of the subject in the hope it will assist the reader in a decision on the desirability of more lenient laws and views on cannabis. And as with most other accounts, the conclusions are not clear cut. However, the last chapter takes the novel approach of treating cannabis as though it were a new drug awaiting clearance for safety and efficacy. The author concludes that "In view of the evidence reviewed in this book to permit these risks to occur widely would be difficult to justify in relation to herbal Cannabis or its resin."

The work is of particular value and interest ot pharmacologists, biochemists, medicinal chemists, pharmacists, and psychiatrists. The nontechnical aspects should interest sociologists, physicians, and members of the legal profession.

649.   Hart, Roy Hanu. **Bitter Grass: The Cruel Truth about Marijuana**. Shawnee Mission, KS: Psychoneurologia Press, in cooperation with the American Academy of Psychiatry and Neurology, 1980. 128p. illus. bibliog. index. $2.95pa. LC 79-91582. ISBN 0-935688-00-5.

Prepared by a clinical psychiatrist, this work is intended for high-school and college students and their parents, or anyone seeking a basic book on marijuana. An attempt has been made to keep technical language to a minimum without oversimplifying the subject.

The first chapter contains introductory material. The second explains the chemistry of delta-9-THC, the psychoactive component in cannabis. Chapter three, on cell-tissue-organ effect of marijuana, discusses effects on the reproductive, respiratory, immune, cardiovascular, and nervous-mental systems. Chapter four, "The Clinical Psychiatrist and Marijuana," contains a psychiatric classfication of cannabis intoxication. Twelve case studies are included as illustrations. Chapter 5 discusses treatment of marijuana problems and marijuana as treatment. Appended is an outline classification of the hallucinogens.

The author presents evidence from his own observations and scientific studies that show there are disruptive effects from marijuana on brain ultrastructure, particularly the areas controlling behavior and neuroendocrine regulation.

650.   Hoye, David. **Cannabis Alchemy: The Art of Modern Hashmaking: Methods for Preparation of Extremely Potent Cannabis Products**. New York/San Francisco,CA: High Times/Level Press, 1973. 35p. illus. $2.00pa.

Although the author notes that possession of cannabis products is illegal in many parts of the world, he presents detailed instruction with diagrams on how such products can be prepared in a homemade laboratory. The following are topic headings: 1) A safe method for extraction and purification of the oils of marijuana and hashish, 2) Conversion of cannabidiol, 3) Conversion of THC to the acetate, 4) Preparation of hashish from the intensified cannabis oil, 5) Removing the oil from intact marijuana flowers, 6) Preparation of oil capsules for oral consumption, 7) Preparation of translucent (honey) oil, 8) Preparation of "Reefers," 9) High-volume extraction method, and 10) Advanced refinement techniques.

651.   Joyce, C. R. B., and S. H. Curry, eds. **The Botany and Chemistry of Cannabis**. Proceedings of a Conference organized by The Institute for the Study of Drug Dependence at The Ciba Foundation, 9-10 April, 1969. London: J. & A. Churchill, 1970. 217p. illus. bibliog. index. $12.00. ISBN 0-7000-1479-9.

The primary purpose of this symposium was to establish botanical and chemical specifications of cannabinoid substances used pharmacological and medical study in order that comparisons of results from different research workers could be made. In addition, findings reported provided a basis for further study.

The 13 papers and discussions about them are grouped under one of three subject headings: botany, chemistry, or pharmacological aspects. In addition, an appendix on nomenclature has been included. The contributors are distinguished researchers in the field and represent a number of countries.

A good deal of valuable basic scientific information about cannabis is contained in the book.

652.   Mikuriya, Tod H. **Thinking About Using Pot**. Berkeley, CA: Medi Comp Press, 1969. 31p. $1.00pa.

The author claims that this booklet "presents facts about marijuana and practical suggestions for handling your own nonsmoking or responsible use of marijuana, whichever is your choice when the time comes to decide."

The material is addressed to the young person through the following chapters: 1) Looking at teenage marijuana use, 2) Quiz yourself, 3) Handling your own use or non-use of marijuana, and 4) More facts about marijuana.

653.   Nahas, Gabriel G. **Keep Off the Grass: A Scientific Enquiry into the Biological Effects of Marijuana**. Preface by Jacques Yves Cousteau; Foreword by Prof. Andre Cournand, Nobel Prize in Medicine and Physiology. Oxford; New York: Pergamon Press, 1979. 259p. illus. bibliog. index. $14.00; $9.95pa. LC 78-41170. ISBN 0-08-023779-7; 0-08-023780-0 pa.

The 1st edition of this work (with a different subtitle) was published in 1976 (*see* entry 654). The new edition also presents scientific and medical evidence that the layman can understand on the dangers of marijuana use. Since the 1st edition appeared, more evidence has accumulated from new studies that further suggests deleterious effects of the drug on the body.

Dr. Nahas is a crusader who makes powerful arguments for his stand against marijuana use. It is of note that his views are not so controversial any more.

The book reports on cannabis use in a number of other countries as well as in the United States, as the chapter titles show: 1) Englewood, 1969, 2) The history of marijuana, 3) A sabbatical leave, 4) An international problem, 5) Debate, 6) First scientific meetings on marijuana, 7) Marijuana and social reformers, 8) First investigations, 9) Journey to Morocco, 10) Journey to Egypt, 11) The Marijuana Commission

Report, 12) A working summer, 13) Return to Morocco, 14) Marijuana and the immunity system, 15) From Texas to Alaska to Washington, D.C., 16) Marijuana and DNA, 17) From Vancouver to Baalbek, 18) A press release, 19) The Senate hearings, 20) The quest continues, 21) The quest never ends, 22) The Helsinki Conference, 23) The abdication of the intellectuals, 24) Tinkering with the old brain, 25) The UN Commission on Narcotic Drugs, 26) For some addicts, some hope, and 27) The Reims Symposium: a biological indictment of marijuana. There are several appendices, including a glossary of cannabis terms, names and compositions of cannabis preparations, and details of some experiments and studies.

654.   Nahas, Gabriel G. **Keep Off the Grass: A Scientist's Documented Account of Marijuana's Destructive Effects.** New York: Reader's Digest Press; distr., Thomas Y. Crowell Co., 1976. 205p. bibliog. index. $7.95. LC 76-195. ISBN 0-88349-074-9.

This book was written for the general public by a physician scientist who has spent a number of years studying the effects of marijuana in many parts of the world. He presents documented medical, pharmacological, and other scientific evidence that reveals dangers of the drug. Dr. Nahas has been criticized for his crusading efforts against marijuana use and against lenience in laws prohibiting it. His critics say he lacks evidence for his views, or at least does not interpret the evidence properly. However, his work and ideas are accepted in at least some scientific circles.

The book is well-written and interesting, and to this reviewer it does not exaggerate the possible danger of the drug's use, nor is its plea for caution unwarranted. The following passage from the book makes a good point about attitudes toward drug use. A fellow physician remarked to the author: "If I ever prescribed a medicine made from weeds in my backyard and mixed on the kitchen counter, you'd hear the screaming from here to Washington! I'd lose my license. Yet I hear people . . . making judgments about marijuana on the basis of nothing more than rumor and fifth-hand observation. They don't know what they are talking about!" Pharmaceutical companies must subject their drugs to very rigid scrutiny before they can be released for public use. Marijuana or any of the other "recreational" drugs should be treated no differently.

A new edition of this work is reviewed above.

655.   Nahas, Gabriel G., and William D. M. Paton, eds. **Marihuana: Biological Effects—Analysis, Metabolism, Cellular Responses, Reproduction and Brain.** Proceedings of the Satellite Symposium of the 7th International Congress of Pharmacology, Paris, 22-23 July 1978. Co-editors: Monique Braude, Jean Claude Jardillier, David J. Harvey. New York: Pergamon Press, 1979. 777p. illus. bibliog. index. (Advances in the Biosciences, v. 22-23.) $80.00. LC 78-41169. ISBN 0-08-023759-2.

This substantial volume is a comprehensive review of the effects of cannabinoids on cellular metabolism, reproduction, and brain function. Fifty technical conference papers are included, written by chosen scientists, which update and extend the findings reported at a similar conference held in Helsinki three years before.

The papers are divided into four sections: 1) Quantification of cannabinoids and their metabolites in body fluids and tissues: pharmacokinetics, 2) Cannabinoids and cellular metabolism, 3) Cannabis and reproduction, and 4) Cannabis and the brain.

Evidence shows that all cannabinoids are highly lipid soluble, become sequestered in deep body compartments, and are released only slowly for clearance. There is a cumulative effect. This explains their potential for nonspecific toxicity which is the theme of the book. Much of the unavailable knowledge about the mechanism of action of the substances, however, is unclear at this time as well as confusing, and certain questions remain unanswered, according to the experts.

Some of the findings reported follow. Cannabinoids are anti-fertility drugs in both sexes. Structural changes in the central nervous system take place that outlast exposure to the drug. It is questionable whether the effects of long-term use, including that on memory, are reversible. Chronic use brings about damage to lungs, reproductive function, and the immune system. As to whether or not cannabis is addictive— tolerance occurs, characteristic withdrawal symptoms develop, and psychic dependence is shown. These are the usual criteria for an addictive drug. It is of note that the groups most susceptible to this drug are the very young, the old, the sick, and those who wish to have children.

A large amount of complex research is reported in this volume. Most of it has been known to specialists for several years, but the book brings it together for the first time.

An addendum to the volume touches on the dilemma of the rights of individuals versus the needs of society. It is not closer to being solved, perhaps, but the properties and effects of marijuana are now better understood than before. Perhaps the current efforts of scientists can eventually be translated into beneficial social action.

656.   Novak, William. **High Culture: Marijuana in the Lives of Americans.** New York: Alfred A. Knopf, 1980. 289p. bibliog. $12.95; $6.95pa. LC 79-2229. ISBN 0-394-50395-3; 0-394-73828-4 pa.

The author of this work, who is a journalist and reviewer, says he wrote the book to describe the "high" world in a way that makes sense to the "straight" one. He has drawn upon the experiences of about 300 cannabis users to accomplish this end. For himself, he says, marijuana has been an intellecutal stimulant, breaking down certain conceptual boundaries. In addition to learning what a marijuana high is like, the author hopes that users can benefit from the book by learning how others have found marijuana satisfying and about any problems experienced.

The author thinks that no one has previously written a book of this kind about the personal use of the drug. Those that are personal, such as the accounts by Baudelaire and Gautier, are more literary and elaborate.

Novak takes takes the view that marijuana use has been accepted into the mainstream of American life. Great numbers of users are no longer part of the younger generation, either. Little comment is made about the fact that use of the drug is illegal, although it is mentioned that some states in the U.S. have changed marijuana laws.

Most of the book is made up of personal accounts that describe the experience of the marijuana high. Chapter headings are: 1) An overview of marijuana, 2) The first time, 3) Marijuana activities I: food and music, 4) Marijuana activities II, 5) Sex and intimacy, 6) The social drug, 7) "I get paid for paranoia" a self-portrait of a marijuana dealer, 8) Marijuana and the mind, 9) The personal drug: heart, body, and soul, 10) Looking back: when grass was greener, 11) Varieties of marijuana, 12) Dangers and problems, real and alleged, 13) Using marijuana well—and using it badly, 14) Looking ahead: smokers speculate on the future. In addition there are two appendices: 1) Letters from smokers (and nonsmokers), 2) Studies on the effects of marijuana in users.

The book is well-written, and may be enlightening to readers. However, the accounts are a bit redundant and can be summed up rather simply by the statement that marijuana amplifies the senses; users become more sensitive to any sensual stimulation.

657. Rubin, Vera, and Lambros Comitas. **Ganja in Jamaica: A Medical Anthropological Study of Chronic Marihuana Use.** The Hague; Paris: Mouton, 1975. 205p. bibliog. (New Babylon Studies in the Social Sciences, 26.) ISBN 90-279-7731-3.

This book reports on a study sponsored by the Center for Studies of Narcotic and Drug Abuse of the National Institute of Mental Health. It was the first project in medical anthropology to be undertaken, and it is the first intensive, multidisciplinary study of marijuana use and users to be published.

The use of ganja (marijuana) was examined as part of the life style of the Jamaican working class; chronic long-term smokers were used as subjects.

The following are the chapter titles: 1) Introduction, 2) Notes on the ethnohistory of cannabis, 3) Ganja legislation, 4) The ganja complex, 5) Acute effects of ganja smoking in a natural setting, 6) The clinical studies, 7) Respiratory function and hematology, 8) Psychiatry and electroencephalography, 9) Psychological assessment, 10) Attitudes and reactions to ganja, 11) Cultural expectations and predisposition to ganja, and 12) Cannabis, society and culture.

In summary, there seems to be some physical risk in ganja use, similar to that of tobacco. Differences in lung function and hematology were found between users and nonusers. Psychiatric findings did not bear out any extreme deleterious effects of cannabis use on sanity, cerebral atrophy, brain damage, or personality deterioration. The "amotivational syndrome" feared in the U.S. was not borne out in life histories of Jamaican workers. Ganja use may provide an adaptive mechanism by which many Jamaicans cope with limited life chances in a harsh environment. In conclusion, the authors point out the importance of informal social controls in preventing drug abuse.

658. Russell, George K. **Marihuana Today: A Compilation of Medical Findings for the Layman.** rev. 3rd ed. New York: Myrin Institute for Adult Education, 1978. 75p. bibliog. $1.85pa. LC 77-79477. ISBN 0-913098-27-2.

This new edition of an earlier publication includes highlights of the Second International Symposium on Marihuana held in Reims, France, in July, 1978, and other new material. Some of the new findings include: the developing trend of evidence of cellular damage by cannabis; how tolerant and substantial abstinence effects are now established; and how actions on the reproductive system and on development become increasingly worrying. The author questions that the use of marijuana in *any* amount can be reconciled with the growing evidence of deleterious effects.

659. Small, Ernest. **The Species Problem in Cannabis: Science and Semantics.** Toronto: Corpus Information Services Ltd., 1979. 2 v. illus. bibliog. index. $28.00pa. ISBN 0-919217-10-9 (the set).

Cannabis is one of the oldest economic plants, and since it is a very complex one, controversy over identification of species exists. Further, it seems that a definition of "species" has never been generally agreed upon by biologists. Volume 1 of this work (subtitled "Science") presents a detailed, well-documented general discussion of the fundamental aspects of the species problem. This is an important matter where cannabis is concerned, because laws in most of the states of the U.S. and in many foreign countries have named only one species, *Cannabis sativa*, as a controlled substance.

The author takes the view that no matter what the scientific evidence, only one species of cannabis should be recognized. Society will be better served that way, he believes. Aside from the needs of society, scientists are not in agreement on the matter, and research on the matter is still in progress. It is possible that there are several species.

Volume 1 is in two parts: "Fundamental Aspects of the Species Problem in Biology" and "Scientific Studies on Cannabis." Volume 2, which is subtitled "Semantics," is presented in three parts: "Cannabis in Science," "Cannabis in Law," and "The Legal Debate." Volume 2 can be used independently of the first volume. Written in nontechnical language but containing essential scientific information, it will be of most interest to lawyers, whereas the first volume is addressed to scientists.

Whatever the feeling about the species problem in cannabis, and the legal implications, the work, particularly volume 1, contains a large amount of valuable information gleaned from meticulous scientific investigations.

660.   Stefanis, Costas, Rhea Dornbush, and Max Fink, eds. **Hashish: Studies of Long-Term Use.** New York: Raven Press, 1977. 181p. bibliog. index. $12.50. LC 76-19848. ISBN 0-89004-138-5.

Because of the anxiety in the late 1960s regarding the epidemic increase in marijuana use, the Center for Studies on Narcotics and Drug Abuse of the National Institute of Mental Health (the predecessor of the National Institute on Drug Abuse) initiated studies in foreign countries where cannabis use is more traditional and has had a longer history than in the United States. This volume is based on one of those studies which was made in Greece.

Over a three-year period a Greek population was defined by social, medical, neurologic, and psychologic characteristics and was compared with a matched nonuser population. Various aspects of cannabis use were assessed, such as the acute physiologic, psychologic, and behavioral consequences, as well as withdrawal effects on hashish users. The results of these studies were compared to the findings in young, American, occasional cannabis users.

There are 20 chapters by 11 contributors, divided into sections as follows: 1) Sample selection and methods, 2) Results: sample characteristics, 3) Results: acute experiments, and 4) Results: withdrawal studies.

The conclusions presented are reasonably reassuring in regard to the health consequences of long-term cannabis use. No evidence of brain damage was found, or of organic mental syndrome, or of amotivational syndrome. The users, however, did exhibit a higher incidence of psychopathology. Marijuana did not seem to be a "killer weed" as some had feared, but the report does not give hashish or marijuana a clean bill of health. The researchers realize that their sample was small and that they may have been studying the healthy and resistant survivors of the drug habit and may have missed victims who were not available. In spite of these limitations, however, the work provides scientific data that make the reader better informed as to the true nature of the drug.

661.   U.S. Drug Enforcement Administration. **Cannabis Sativa: A Lecture.** By John T. Maher. Rev. Washington: GPO, 1976. 35p. illus. bibliog.

This brief publication presents a very good overview of the subject. The marijuana plant is described, and the history of its use outlined, the effects noted, and chemical identification methods described. Also, a discussion of its present use is presented, and the social implications are pointed out. The author does not believe marijuana is as harmless as tobacco, because tobacco users show little or no emotional changes. In comparison with alcohol he says that "in the light of the tremendous costs of the permissive use of alcohol and to the people of this nature, one can only marvel at the seeming lack of social responsibility on the part of marihuana's proponents."

662.   U.S. National Institute on Drug Abuse. **Marihuana and Health: Seventh Annual Report to the U.S. Congress from the Secretary of Health, Education, and Welfare, 1977.** Washington: GPO, 1979. 52p. bibliog. index. $2.50pa. S/N 017-024-00890-7.

Several members of the scientific community provided technical reviews of research on marijuana which served in part as bases for this report. It is the seventh of an annual series, and again attempts were made to provide updated answers to the questions regarding health implications of marijuana use. Although the public has sought unequivocal answers, unfortunately such were still not available when this report was prepared. However, research developments have added to the understanding of the problem.

The publication contains digested information on the nature and extent of use, use detection, human effects, therapeutic aspects, and future directions. There were few new developments reported on human effects; use among younger users was up 25% from the year before; and no major therapeutic applications for the drug were reported.

663.   U.S. National Institute on Drug Abuse. **Marijuana and Health: Eighth Annual Report to the U.S. Congress from the Secretary of Health, Education, and Welfare, 1980.** Washington: GPO, 1980. 48p. bibliog.

As in previous publications of this series, noted researchers have provided the technical reviews on which this report is based. Material covering the entire year of 1979 has been included. Again, the attempt is made to provide an answer to the question: "What are the health implications of marijuana use for Americans?" It is acknowledged at the outset that the answers are not definitive because the American experience with the drug has been of short duration.

Sections are headed as follows: 1) Nature and extent of marijuana use in the United States, 2) Human effects, 3) Therapeutic aspects, 4) Effects in combination with alcohol and other drugs, 5) The hazards of marijuana versus other recreational drugs, and 6) Future directions.

In summary, it was found that marijuana may have deleterious effects on intellectual functioning, reproduction, memory, driving and related skills, heart rate, and lungs. Its use now begins at an earlier age, and it is likely to be used more frequently than formerly. "Street" marijuana has increased in potency. While the drug may have therapeutic uses, it has not been proven superior to other available medicines.

664.   U.S. National Institute on Drug Abuse. **Marihuana Research Findings: 1976.** Edited by Robert C. Petersen. Washington: GPO, 1977. 251p. bibliog. index. [DHEW Publication No. (ADM) 77-501; NIDA Research Monograph 14.] $3.00pa. LC 77-82238. S/N 017-024-00622-0.

Like its five predecessors, this report summarizes the growing, though still limited, knowledge of the health consequences of marijuana use. It is a rather complete reference report which provided the basis for the 1976 report on *Marihuana and Health* (*see* entries 662 and 663 for reviews of the 1979 and 1980 reports). The *Marihuana and Health* reports are intended for a general audience; the publication under review is a more detailed treatment of interest to the technically trained reader.

The following chapters, written by experts, are presented: 1) Epidemiology of marihuana use, 2) Chemistry and metabolism, 3) Toxicological and pharmacological effects, 4) Preclinical effects: unlearned behavior, 5) Preclinical effects: learned behavior, 6) Preclinical chronic effects: unlearned and learned behavior, 7) Human effects, 8) Effects of marihuana on the genetic and immune systems, and 9) Therapeutic aspects.

Findings of the report include the following: marijuana use continues to increase: the amount of research on chronic use remains modest; preliminary research evidence has been used to overdraw support for one or another side of the debate on social policy; there is good evidence that marijuana use is by no means harmless; to what extent, if any, chronic marijuana intoxication affects development is still unknown; the answer to the question, "Is marijuana harmful?" is complex; findings concerning possible adverse impact of marijuana on such areas as the body's immune responses, basic cell metabolism, and other areas of functioning have not yet been adequately explained; implications for marginal members of society may be quite different from those of the more competent advantaged student user.

A more recent report on *Marijuana Research Findings* is reviewed below.

665.   U.S. National Institute on Drug Abuse. **Marijuana Research Findings: 1980.** Edited by Robert C. Petersen. Washington: GPO, 1980. 225p. bibliog. [DHHS Publication No. (ADM) 80-1001; NIDA Research Monograph 31.] LC 80-600104.

This publication brings the record up to date for those with an interest in discovering the present extent and limits of knowledge about marijuana, its chemistry, metabolism, and effects on health. Extensive bibliographies of original sources are provided.

Results of recent research reports (through 1979) are reviewed by various scientists/authors in a balanced and unbiased manner. The following are the subjects covered and the authors: 1) Marijuana and health: 1980, Robert C. Petersen, 2) Human effects: an overview, Reese T. Jones, 3) Chemistry and metabolism, Carlton E. Turner, 4) Acute effects of marijuana on human memory and cognition, Douglas P. Ferraro, 5) Effects of marjuana on neuroendocrine function, Carol Grace Smith, 6) The effect of marijuana on reproduction and development, Jack Harclerode, 7) Effects of cannabis in combination with ethanol and other drugs, Albert J. Siemens, and 8) Therapeutic aspects, Sidney Cohen.

The findings presented are intended primarily for scientists, but others, such as legislators, health professionals, judges, educators, and parents, can benefit from the publication. There was a trend of public opinion in the early and mid-1970s to reduce penalties for possession and use of marijuana. That trend has now reversed. The first chapter of this volume is nearly identical to the text of the eighth *Marijuana and Health* report. (*See* entry 663 where findings are summarized.)

666.   U.S. National Institute on Drug Abuse. **Parents, Peers, and Pot.** By Marsha Manatt. Washington: GPO, 1979. 98p. bibliog. [DHEW Publication No. (ADM) 79-812.] S/N 017-024-00941-5.

This concise discussion of the marijuana problem is evidence of a change in official attitudes about the hazards of the use of the drug. Intended primarily for parents of children 9-14, it describes the strategy parents can use to prevent marijuana use by their children.

The author's position is that nonmedical drug use is not acceptable for children. Preadolescents and adolescents are in a period of intense growth and change, and regular use of marijuana can interfere with learning and development. Scientific studies are cited as evidence of this view. Among other effects, the drug accumulates in the body, causes problems in mental functioning and performance of psychomotor tasks such as driving, can be injurious to heart and lungs, contains more carcinogens than tobacco, may reduce the body's resistance to disease, can cause brain damage, has bad psychological effects, and can interfere with reproductive functions. The author feels that the campaign for decriminalization has conveyed the impression that the drug is harmless.

Chapter headings are: 1) Learning the hard way: parents, peers, and pot, 2) The family versus the drug culture, 3) What you may face if your child starts using drugs, 4) What you can do to prevent or stop your child from using drugs, and 5) How parents can work with the school and the community to create a healthier, nondrug-oriented environment for youngsters.

The approach suggested for dealing with the marijuana problem is based on one community's experience. Peer counseling, cross-age tutoring, career/life planning and decision making, and the development of alternatives to drug taking are all suggested as effective community and school-based prevention approaches.

667.   Walton, Robert P. **Marihuana: America's New Drug Problem**. New York: Arno Press, 1976. 223p. illus. bibliog. index. Reprint of the edition published by Lippincott in 1938. (Social Problems and Social Policy: The American Experience.) $14.00. LC 75-17248. ISBN 0-405-07474-3.

This book presents mainly a collection and summary of pre-existing literature. The following chapters are presented: 1) History of the hashish vice, 2) Distribution of the hashish vice, 3) Present status of the marihuana vice in the United States, 4) The plant source, 5) Technique of ingestion or administration, 6) Descriptions of the hashish experience, (literary and scientific), 7) Acute effects, 8) Chronic effects, 9) Therapeutic applications, 10) Pharmaceutical and chemical considerations relating to the drug, and 11) Nomenclature.

The book is of interest for its historical material and for the random observations on the subject. In addition, the bibliography is extensive.

19

STIMULANTS

Only a few titles are listed in this section. However, in view of the widely recognized danger of amphetamine use and the upsurge of cocaine use, particularly among fashionable affluent drug users, it seemed advisable to place the material in a separate section.

The use of amphetamines has declined since the mid-1960s, and concern about it has diminished. However, the increase in cocaine use has sparked renewed interest in studying the drug. Although cocaine is not addicting in the usual sense, it does produce psychic dependence. It is very expensive, and an exclusive subculture of cocaine lore has been developing. A few of the books listed (particularly the title by Gottlieb, entry 669) do little to discourage use of the drug.

668.   Ellinwood, Everett H., and M. Marlyne Kilbey, eds. **Cocaine and Other Stimulants.** Proceedings of a Conference on Contemporary Issues in Stimulant Research, held at Duke University Medical Center, Durham, NC, November 10-12, 1975. New York: Plenum Press, 1977. 721p. bibliog. index. (Advances in Behavioral Biology, v. 21.) $49.50. LC 76-47488. ISBN 0-306-37921-X.

This work provides a comprehensive view of the current research on stimulants such as cocaine and the amphetamines. Thirty-six papers, written by experts, cover a number of areas of neuropharmacological investigations in animals and man. Among the main concerns are: pharmacological studies, electrophysiological correlates of chronic administration of cocaine and amphetamine, and behavioral and physiological effects of cocaine and some other stimulants. The first paper is a historical outline, "Cocaine: 1884-1974."

The papers are highly technical, most suitable for research-level readers.

669.   Gottlieb, Adam. **If You Enjoy the Pleasures of Cocaine, this Book May Save Your Life.** Berekeley, CA: Golden State Publishing Co. (Available from And/Or Press, P. O. Box 2246, Berkeley, Calif. 94702), 1976. 127p. illus. bibliog. $4.25pa. ISBN 0-915904-33-0.

At the outset, the author of this booklet states his position on cocaine use. This is, briefly, that while possession and use of cocaine is illegal most places in the world, it has pleasures and usefulness as well as a potential for abuse and misuse. His purpose, he says, is to convey knowledge of both edges of the sword. There are chapters on how to get the most pleasure out of cocaine and others telling how to avoid its dangers. Actually, there is little in the book to discourage cocaine use.

The following sections and/or chapters are included: 1) Introductory statements, 2) What is cocaine—what is coca, 3) A concise history of coca and cocaine,

4) Cocaine and the Golden Age of Decadence, 5) Enjoying cocaine without abuse, 6) Methods of use, 7) Selection of quality, 8) Purification of cocaine, and 9) Cultivation of coca.

670.   Grinspoon, Lester, and James B. Bakalar. **Cocaine: A Drug and Its Social Evolution.** New York: Basic Books, Inc., 1976. 308p. bibliog. index. $15.00. LC 76-7675. ISBN 0-465-01189-5.

Written by a psychiatrist and a lawyer, this book is addressed mainly to the nonspecialist, although there is a little material on neurophysiology and pharmacology. The presentation is made up, for the most part, of accounts of the perceptions of users of cocaine (obtained from interviews) and material from novels and short stories that suggest the authors have had first-hand acquaintance with the drug or its users. The people interviewed were asked about such matters as the amount and frequency of cocaine use, price, quality, the nature of the high, long-term effects, adverse physiological reactions, sexual effects, tolerance, dependence, withdrawal reactions, comparisons with other drugs, and drug preference. The authors also tried to find out something about the drug's effect on the lives of its users. The authors do not suggest their subjects are a representative sample; they intend only to convey some of the flavor, atmosphere, and language of cocaine use in America today.

Generally, the tone of the book is favorable to cocaine use, at least in an abstract or ideal world. The view seems to be that the drug problem is not in the chemicals themselves but in the way society regards the use of them.

671.   Iversen, Leslie L., Susan D. Iversen, and Solomon H. Snyder, eds. **Stimulants.** New York: Plenum Press, 1978. 476p. bibliog. index. (Handbook of Psychopharmacology, v. 11.) $32.50. LC 75-6851. ISBN 0-306-38931-2.

Although it treats drugs of abuse, this volume does not emphasize drug abuse as such; rather, it presents recent research findings about the stimulant class of drugs, including nicotine, amphetamines, and a variety of psychotomimetics, the most valuable group of psychotropic drugs for examining the regulation of emotional behavior by neurotransmitters. In general, the stimulants are discussed in terms of their structure-activity relations, biochemical and behavioral actions in animals, and clinical uses.

The chapters, written by experts, are as follows: 1) Amphetamines: structure-activity relationships, 2) Amphetamines: biochemical and behavioral actions in animals, 3) Central nervous system stimulants: historical aspects and clinical effects, 4) Drug treatment in child psychiatry, 5) Plants and plant constituents as mind-altering agents throughout history, 6) Psychotomimetic drugs: structure-activity relationships, 7) Drug metabolism: review of principles and the fate of one-ring psychotomimetics, 8) Psychotomimetic drugs in man, and 9) Nicotine and smoking.

The editors hope that psychopharmacological research, because it contributes to an understanding of how the brain works, will offer help to the mentally ill with promises of escalating benefits in the future.

672.   Mulé, S. J., ed. **Cocaine: Chemical, Biological, Clinical, Social and Treatment Aspects.** Cleveland, OH: CRC Press, 1976. 267p. illus. bibliog. index. $53.95. LC 76-25486. ISBN 0-8493-5057-3.

The editor of this work writes that the need for more knowledge and information about this heavily abused drug is self-evident. It has been used for more than ten centuries, and once again it has become popular, especially among the affluent, creative, and innovative drug users. It is probably the best example of a substance that causes psychic dependence without the classical physical dependence.

The purpose of this highly technical work is to provide the chemical, pharmacological, physiological, psychological, clinical, behavioral, and social scientist with available information on cocaine's use in society. The sophisticated layman also may be interested in it. Most aspects of the subject are considered with some emphasis on detection.

The following topics are covered: 1) Historical aspects, 2) Chemical aspects, 3) Detection and identification, 4) Disposition and biotransformation, 5) Effect on biogenic amines, 6) Behavioral, psychic, neuropharmacologic, and physiologic aspects, 7) Clinical aspects, and 8) Sociological, treatment, and rehabilitation aspects.

673.   Smith, David E., ed. **Amphetamine Use, Misuse, and Abuse: Proceedings of the National Amphetamine Conference, 1978.** Boston: G. K. Hall and Co., 1979. 341p. bibliog. index. $24.95. LC 79-18583. ISBN 0-8161-2168-0.

The papers included in this volume were written by a panel of experts who provide a current and comprehensive overview of all aspects of the amphetamine problem. Amphetamine-related stimulants are also discussed for comparative purposes. In regard to terminology, amphetamine *use* means use of the drug for an appropriate medical indication; *misuse* means use for nonmedical indications without evidence of dysfunction; and *abuse* means use to the point where it interferes with the individual's physical, economic, or social functioning. Since amphetamines have a high potential for abuse, they are ordinarily prescribed sparingly and cautiously.

Twenty-seven chapters are presented arranged in 6 sections. Section 1 is a review of the pharmacology, history, and political policy issues under the Carter administration. Section 2 discusses the epidemiology of amphetamine and related substances. Since the med-1960s the abuse of the drug has declined somewhat. Possible reasons for the decline according to the authors are: the Federal Controlled Substances Act of 1970, which reduced diversion of the drug from legitimate sources to the drug culture; increase in the use of other stimulants such as cocaine; and deterioration of the quality of street amphetamine. Section 3 deals with therapeutic uses of amphetamine and reviews proper prescribing practices. At present, use of the drug is advised only for narcolepsy, hyperkinesis, and short-term treatment of obesity. Section 4 discusses the abuse of the substance and its relation to psychoses, violence, and sexual dysfunction. Crises and deaths in users are analyzed. Section 5 deals with the training techniques for physicians in the diagnosis and treatment of amphetamine abuse. The last section is concerned with regulatory issues, and interface between medicine and law. The authors of this section include representatives of the Food and Drug Administration, The Drug Enforcement Administration, the American Medical Association, and the legal community.

The volume is designed primarily to assist and inform physicians and other health care professionals who are involved or concerned with amphetamine treatment and usage. Others may be interested also, but much of the material presented is too technical for the average reader.

674.   Spotts, James V., and Franklin C. Shontz. **Cocaine Users: A Representative Case Approach.** New York: The Free Press, a Division of Macmillan Publishing Co., 1980. bibliog. index. $19.95. LC 79-7631. ISBN 0-02-930560-8.

The authors of this work felt there was a need for up-to-date research on cocaine, its effects, hazards, and sequelae in humans. They undertook this study of why people abuse the drug, but chose no specific position. The representative case method was used, advocating the intensive study of individuals. Four assumptions were formulated to guide the efforts of the research: 1) people who abuse drugs do so to produce a personal state they cannot achieve by their own efforts; 2) there is no typical personality for the drug user and no pathology typical of all addicts; 3) those who persist in heavy drug use gravitate to the regular use of the drug or a combination of drugs that helps them most closely approximate desired personal states; and 4) even though drug users develop preferences, different individuals may use the same drug to fulfill different needs.

The first part of the book presents background on cocaine and orientation to the research method. Part 2 contains the case studies of nine cocaine users, screened from more than 800 adult male abusers. Part 3, the interpretation, presents interpersonal comparisons and conclusions. It discusses physiological and psychological effects of cocaine and the toxic cocaine reaction.

The authors point out that some theorists have maintained that myths and illusions are necessary in human existence. They conclude that each of the cocaine users "lived by his myth," the way he sees himself. In a great many instances the myths of drug users have destroyed them.

Three months after the last formal assessment in the study, none of the nine cocaine users had suffered physical or psychological damage due to their participation in the research. Several seemed in better control of their lives. However, the epilogue of the book includes a paragraph on what happened to the men later. It is not an encouraging ending. One of the subjects was in prison; one was convicted of a felony involving cocaine; two were dead (drug-related slayings); two suffered accidents that left permanent physical disabilities; two were in school and doing fairly well; and one was a clerk in a large company and still using cocaine. The authors say, "These chilling statistics highlight the danger and volatile nature of the world of the cocaine user."

675.   U.S. National Institute on Drug Abuse. **Cocaine: 1977.** Edited by Robert C. Petersen, and Richard C. Stillman. Washington: GPO, 1977. 223p. bibliog. index. [DHEW Publication No. (ADM) 77-432; NIDA Research Monograph Series, No. 13.] $3.00. LC 77-77787. S/N 017-024-00592-4.

This volume summarizes the current limited knowledge of cocaine through a series of reports by leading workers in the field. In addition to an overview section, ten chapters as follows are presented: 1) History of cocaine, 2) Coca: the plant and its use, 3) Cocaine: the material, 4) Behavioral effects of cocaine in animals, 5) What are the effects of cocaine in man?, 6) Cocaine: recreational use and intoxication, 7) Cocaine: its use for central nervous system stimulation including recreational and medical uses, 8) The forensic toxicology of cocaine, 9) Cocaine in clinical medicine, and 10) Characteristics of clients admitted to treatment for cocaine abuse. While the evidence to date does not justify the claim that the public is suffering greatly as a consequence of illicit cocaine use, the view taken is that much more needs to be known about it before any actions should be taken that might result in a wider availability at lower cost.

The publication should be of value as a reference work for clinicians and scientists and for those interested in applying scientific knowledge to social policy questions associated with cocaine use.

676.   U.S. National Institute on Drug Abuse. **Use and Abuse of Amphetamine and Its Substitutes.** By James V. Spotts, and Carol A. Spotts. Washington: GPO, 1980. 560p. bibliog. index. [DHEW Publication No. (ADM) 80-941; NIDA Research Issues, No. 25.] S/N 017-024-00978-4.

The main part of this work is an annotated bibliography of 150 studies on the psychosocial factors associated with the use and abuse of amphetamine and similar drugs. In addition, there is a brief synopsis of some of the important legislation concerning the control of stimulant drugs and a supplemental reading list of 750 items.

The material is presented under the following headings: 1) Overview and theoretical issues, 2) Perceptual, cognitive and psychomotor effects, 3) Medically prescribed uses, 4) Misuse and abuse of amphetamines, 5) Misuse and abuse of amphetamine substitutes, 6) Adverse effects, toxicity and treatment, and 7) Future trends of abuse. Each section begins with an overview of the subject, and the annotations are rather complete.

This is an impressive publication, but no claims are made that it is definitive.

677.   Waldorf, Dan, Sheila Murphy, Craig Reinarman, and Bridget Joyce. **Doing Coke: An Ethnography of Cocaine Users and Sellers.** Washington: Drug Abuse Council, 1977. 76p. bibliog. LC 77-83763.

This brief work begins with a historical perspective about cocaine. The main section of the publication, however, is a report of a six-month study of 32 regular cocaine users from white, middle-class backgrounds. Their experiences with the drug are explored in detail. Throughout the presentation published literature on the subject is reviewed. Often the authors' observations on cocaine use do not agree with research findings.

The conclusion reached is that effects of cocaine, at least when snorted, are much more mild and subtle than its legal status would indicate. The authors do allow, however, that more research on cocaine use by all methods is needed. Perhaps results of such research will show that stringent legal controls are not necessary, they say.

It is pointed out that there is a subculture of cocaine lore prevalent, similar to the lore surrounding use of some other drugs of abuse. This phenomenon is of assistance to the user because "bad trips" tend to diminish.

20

ALCOHOL

Although alcoholism is not much different from other kinds of addiction or dependence, and works about it are found reviewed in other sections of this bibliography, there are recent titles that deal with it as a condition separate from other drug abuse. Some of these are listed below. The alcohol problem is different from problems involving most other drugs in that alcohol use is legal and widely accepted in society. It is, however, generally recognized as the number one abuse problem, and there has been serious thinking recently about the role alcohol plays in society.

Subject areas considered in works in this section include: the families of alcoholics, drinking habits, alcohol and its relation to health and disease, sociocultural aspects of alcohol use, diagnosis and treatment of alcoholism, alcohol in literature, alcohol and personality, alcohol effects on nutrition, heredity and alcoholism, alcohol and youth, and the nature of alcoholism.

In spite of recent extensive interest in the treatment of alcoholism, results have not been impressive. Experts feel that there is a long way to go before health care delivery in this area is successful and reaches all who are in need of it.

The section on Self-Help (section 8) of this bibliography lists materials of use to those attempting to help themselves deal with alcoholism. Section 7 contains works of treatment of alcoholism along with the treatment of other addictions, and some of the material reporting on alcohol research are found in section 14.

678.   Ackerman, Robert J. **Children of Alcoholics: A Guidebook for Educators, Therapists, and Parents.** Holmes Beach, FL: Learning Publications, 1978. 140p. bibliog. index. $7.95; $5.95pa. LC 78-55067. ISBN 0-918452-06-6; 0-918452-07-4 pa.

This work is presented in three parts: 1) The child of an alcoholic: what it's like, 2) Suggestions for educators, and 3) Suggestions for therapists and parents. Background information and practical advice is given on how to work with and help the unfortunate children of the alcoholic.

Appended materials include a list of pamphlets on the subject and a list of agencies that provide resources.

679.   Ahlström-Laakso, Salme. **Drinking Habits among Alcoholics.** Helsinki: Finnish Foundation for Alcohol Studies, 1975. 216p. bibliog. (Finnish Foundation for Alcohol Studies, v. 24.) $7.00pa.

This work reports on a study undertaken to measure the effects of a recent Finnish Alcohol Act that extended the availability of beer of medium strength on a group of alcoholics in three Finnish communities. The study has important implications because it shows to what degree alcoholics' drinking habits can be influenced by changes in the availability of alcohol. In addition, it contributes to an understanding of the drinking habits of alcoholics.

The following chapters are included: 1) The research problem and the background of the study, 2) Earlier studies on the drinking habits of alcoholics, 3) The execution of the study, 4) Drinking habits in 1968, 5) Earlier investigations of changes in drinking habits, 6) Changes in drinking habits, and 7) Alcoholics as a target of alcohol control measures.

Among other conclusions, it was found that the more the use of alcohol becomes part of everyday life and the wider the degree of its social acceptance, the more alcoholics increase their alcohol consumption without attracting attention. This increases health risks. Efforts to minimize the number of recruits to alcoholism by alcohol policy are incapable of achieving any far-reaching results. And lastly, the number of actual and potential alcoholics definitely cannot be cut down by making it easier to obtain liquor.

680.   **Alcohol and Cancer Workshop.** Sponsored by the Division of Cancer Control and Rehabilitation of the National Cancer Institute and the Division of Extramural Research of the National Institute of Alcohol Abuse and Alcoholism. Held at the National Institutes of Health, Bethesda, Md., October 23-24, 1978. Editors and Co-Chairmen, Vincent Groupé and Gian C. Salmoiraghi. Baltimore, MD: American Association for Cancer Research, Inc., 1979. 93p. bibliog. (*Cancer Research,* v. 39, No. 7, pt. 2, July, 1979.)

The workshop that produced the scientific papers in this publication was concerned with alcohol and cancer, particularly alcohol as a possible cause of the disease, i.e., its role as a carcinogen. Five sessions were held with the papers grouped under the following heads: 1) Introduction, 2) Drinking patterns, alcohol abuse, and alcoholism, 3) Alcohol as a factor in the incidence and development of cancer, 4) Alcohol use and abuse in the treatment, rehabilitation, and continuing care of cancer patients, and 5) Experimental approaches to studies on alcohol and cancer.

681.   Armor, David J., J. Michael Polich, Harriet B. Stambul. **Alcoholism and Treatment.** Prepared under a grant from the National Institute on Alcohol Abuse and Alcoholism. Santa Monica, CA: Rand Corporation, 1976. 216p. bibliog. (R-1739-NIAAA.)

This publication reports on data collected from alcoholism treatment centers about the United States. Among other findings, clients at these centers showed substantial improvement in drinking behavior after treatment. (However, only a relatively few became long-term abstainers.) One finding of the study has sparked a good deal of controversy. The widely-held view that abstention is the only method of recovery from alcoholism is questioned. Evidently some alcoholics could return to and maintain patterns of normal drinking.

The chapter titles are as follows: 1) Introduction, 2) Perspectives on alcoholism and treatment, 3) Social correlates of alcoholism and problem drinking, 4) Patterns of remission, 5) The effectiveness of treatment, and 6) Conclusions. Appended materials include a section on "Reliability and Validity of Self-Reported Drinking Behavior" and copies of "Data Collection Instruments."

This study was republished in 1978 by John Wiley and Sons. The two publications are virtually identical except for the addition of an appendix in the 1978 edition which documents some of the debate that followed the original publication of the report.

A later study (1980) by the Rand Corporation for the National Institute on Alcohol Abuse and Alcoholism reverses the conclusions of this report in its suggestion that many alcoholics could return to controlled social drinking.

682.   Bucky, Steven F., and others. **The Impact of Alcoholism.** Center City, MN: Hazelden, 1978. 120p. bibliog. $3.95pa. LC 78-52647. ISBN 0-89486-044-5.

The author of this work, who holds a Ph.D. degree in clinical psychology, and his associates present a thorough examination of alcoholism. The book describes first the signs and symptoms of the disease, then medical, emotional, legal, and inter-personal effects. Also, the effects of alcohol abuse on work performance are discussed. In addition, a chapter on treatment has been provided which emphasizes Alcoholics Anonymous but which also includes other approaches, such as biofeedback, psycho-drama, and power motivation training. The last chapter is on attitude and behavior changes.

The book is suitable for and recommended for a wide audience.

683.   Chafetz, Morris. **How Drinking Can Be Good for You.** New York: Stein and Day, 1978. 191p. index. (A Scarborough Book.) $3.95pa. LC 15934. ISBN 0-8128-2477-6.

The original hard-back edition of this work appeared in 1976 under the title *Why Drinking Can Be Good for You.* (*See* review below.)

684.   Chafetz, Morris. **Why Drinking Can Be Good for You.** New York: Stein and Day, 1976. 191p. index. $8.95. LC 76-15934. ISBN 0-8128-2108-7.

This book has appeared in reprinted edition under the title *How Drinking Can Be Good for You.* In spite of the two encouraging titles, the book contains a great deal of information showing that drinking all too often is not good for you.

The physician-author is well-known in the alcohol abuse field and is a pro-lific writer on the subject. His point of view is that alcohol used moderately, correctly, and with the proper frame of mind can do more good than harm. It answers a human need for one to be in communication with others, let go, and soar, he says.

The material is presented in question and answer format. Most aspects of alcohol use are covered. The reader is given much factual, practical, and authentic information, including what to eat before drinking, how to monitor drinking at home or when visiting, and much more. Chafetz even shows how to keep a personal drinking record. The reader is warned about physical conditions that preclude alcohol use.

There are several useful appendices, such as information about drugs that are affected by alcohol use, alcohol content of various drinks, effects of various blood alcohol concentrations, and a list of state alcohol authorities and program contacts.

685.   Cork, R. Margaret. **The Forgotten Children: A Study of Children with Alcoholic Parents.** Toronto: Addiction Research Foundation, 1969. 112p. bibliog. $1.50pa. ISBN 0-7737-7000-3.

The social worker who is the author of this book presents a study of 115 children who have an alcoholic parent or parents. She attempts to answer such ques-tions as: Is the alcoholic solely responsible for the breakdown of his family life?, Are his children more damaged than those in other troubled homes?, Is the harm more related to drinking or to the quality of the relationship between alcoholic and spouse?, Should the family as a whole be treated?, Would this assist recovery for the alcoholic?, Would it produce a lower rate of alcoholism in the children later on?, Can assistance be given to children if parents refuse it?

The book begins with a few case histories supplied through interviews. Then, tabulated data is presented showing the children's views and reactions. The book ends with recommendations concerning treatment of the alcoholics and their families. The material is presented in interesting fashion suitable for the general reader as well as health professionals and counsellors.

The author admits her recommendations are not new concepts, but believes they are important: 1) face the need for treatment of the families; 2) provide intensive treatment for the non-alcoholic spouse; 3) find a new approach to the alcoholic who is a family man; 4) give great attention to treatment of children; and 5) Give more serious consideration to the prevention of alcoholism and family breakdown.

686.   Deb, P. C. **Liquor in a Green Revolution Setting**. Delhi, India: Researchco Publications, 1977. 96p. bibliog. index.

This book reports on a research study conducted in Punjab where modernization in agriculture and rural life is taking place rapidly. The objectives of the study were to examine the prevalence of drinking practices in rural areas, the causal factors in alcoholism, and the effects of drink on socioeconomic life.

The chapter headings are as follows: 1) Introduction, 2) Nature of rural drinking, 3) Socio-cultural factors in drinking, 4) Economic aspects of drinking, 5) Socio-psychological aspects of drinking, 6) Consciousness of liquor effects, 7) Alcoholics and their behavior, and 8) Rural drinking: an overview. Statistical data has been provided in graphs and tables.

The author concludes that the causes for the increase in liquor consumption in rural Punjab are not economic in nature. It is the sociocultural environment, such as tradition, opportunity, and low level education that is responsible for the trend. Another conclusion reached is that drinking reduces work efficiency, leads to low level of living, crime, and pessimism.

687.   Edwards, G., M. M. Gross, M. Keller, J. Moser, and R. Room, eds. **Alcohol-Related Disabilities**. Geneva: World Health Organization, 1977. 154p. bibliog. (WHO Offset Publication No. 32.) $7.20pa.

The titles and authors of these seven papers relating to various important aspects of alcohol-related disabilities are as follows: 1) Report of a WHO group of investigators on criteria for identifying and classifying disabilities related to alcohol consumption, 2) A lexicon of disablements related to alcohol consumption, by Mark Keller, 3) Measurement and distribution of drinking patterns and problems in general populations, by Robin Room, 4) Screening and early detection instruments for disabilities related to alcohol consumption, by Robin M. Murray, 5) Psychobiological contributions to the alcohol syndrome: a selective review of recent research, by Milton M. Gross, 6) Legislation concerning alcohol-related disabilities, by Joy Moser, and 7) Social security programmes and alcohol-related disabilities, by Joy Moser.

688.   Edwards, Griffith, and Marcus Grant, eds. **Alcoholism: New Knowledge and New Responses**. Baltimore, MD: University Park Press, 1977. 359p. bibliog. index. $24.50. LC 77-24299. ISBN 0-8391-1155-X.

This work is based on papers presented at a conference held in September 1976 at the Institute of Psychiatry in London. The contributors are well-known in the field of alcoholism, particularly in the United Kingdom. The central purpose of the publication is to bridge the gap between clinical knowledge and research on alcoholism and the delivery of health care to those who need it.

The 31 papers are divided into three sections. The first, on scientific understanding, includes discussions of epidemiology, influencing factors, biological basis, genetics, psychology, and the role of licensing law in limiting the misuse of alcohol. The second section, on the varieties of harm caused by alcohol, covers liver diseases, blood disorders, nutritional deficiency, toxicity, hypoglycemia, head injuries, accidents, crime, suicide, and neurologic disorders. The third section is on treatment and education. It is more concerned with educating physicians and rehabilitation specialists than with educating drinkers.

The editors feel that there is a long way to go before the health care delivery system reaches the majority of alcoholics in need of effective treatment. The comment is made that a phrase like 'community based', or words like 'team', 'cooperation', and 'multidisciplinary' become modish slogans too easily, while the woman down the road still drinks three bottles of sherry a day behind closed curtains. The book should prove especially valuable to family physicians and other clinicians who may have the first opportunity to recognize alcoholic problems and initiate treatment early.

689.   Estes, Nada J., and M. Edith Heinemann, eds. **Alcoholism: Development, Consequences, and Interventions.** St. Louis, MO: C. V. Mosby Co., 1977. 332p. bibliog. index. $9.25. LC 77-1676. ISBN 0-8016-1529-1.

The nurses who edited this book hope it will contribute to the theoretical knowledge of alcoholism workers so that the needs of those with alcohol-related problems may be met with better understanding. It was written for all persons concerned with the care of those affected by alcoholism, but with emphasis on alcoholism nursing. It is the outgrowth of a course of study at a collegiate school of nursing (University of Washington).

Those who contributed to the book represent a variety of disciplines and are a well-qualified group. The editors take the view that alcoholism is a multifaceted condition, the effects of which are felt by others as well as by the victim.

The chapters are arranged under the following headings: 1) Developmental perspectives on alcoholism; 2) Pathophysiological effects of alcohol, 3) Alcohol problems in special groups, 4) Therapeutic approaches to alcoholism.

690.   Ewing, John A., and Beatrice A. Rouse, eds. **Drinking: Alcohol in American Society—Issues and Current Research.** Chicago: Nelson-Hall, 1978. 443p. bibliog. index. $19.95; $8.95pa. LC 76-47522. ISBN 0-88229-129-7; 0-88229-569-1 pa.

This publication is a well-documented collection of articles which cover a wide range of matters in the field of alcoholism, with emphasis on the sociocultural area. The contributors include many well-known in the field. An excellent survey of the subject is presented in 19 chapters, grouped under the following headings: Introduction and history, the complications of drinking, psychosocial aspects of drinking, social policy and drinking, and summing up.

Some of the studies synthesize present knowledge, others present new findings. In spite of the fact that the book is a collection of contributions by various authors, there is a good continuity.

The work will appeal to a large disparate audience, the general reader, health professionals, lawyers, psychologists, sociologists, and university teachers and students. The material is non-judgmental, technically sound, and interesting to read.

691.   Fairchild, Danial, Thomas N. Fairchild, David Starr, and Ed Woolmus. **Everything You Always Wanted to Know About Drinking Problems.* *And Then a Few Things You Didn't Want to Know.** Illustrated by Danial Fairchild; edited by Thomas N. Fairchild. Miami, FL: Health Communications, Inc., 1978. 119p. illus. $6.50pa. ISBN 0-932194-04-4.

This excellent book is able to convey an important message in a few words. It is almost entirely cartoons with short captions. The introduction succinctly points out that although alcoholism has in the recent past been considered by many to be a disease, many diseases illicit disapproval from the public, and classifying an alcohol problem as a disease does not necessarily eliminate any stigma. The basic message of the work is that an alcohol problem, although distasteful and no fun, is nothing more or less than a problem. It is all right to have problems, and all right to ask for assistance.

There are six chapters as follows: 1) Alcohol affects us all, 2) Who has alcohol problems?, 3) Symptoms of an alcohol problem, 4) Why people have alcohol problems, 5) What can they do?, and 6) What to do in a pinch. An appendix lists alcoholism program contacts by state.

In each chapter the cartoons and captions deliver a short, to the point, understandable message. The material is quite clever, even humorous, and will not offend. For example, in the chapter on "Symptoms of an Alcohol Problem," a caption asks "Do you always have a reason to drink? . . . such as, you're depressed, or you need to calm your nerves, or you've had an argument, it's Tuesday, and so on." The person in the cartoon is sitting at a bar saying, "Drinks are on me. It's Groundhog Day!"

The book covers our culture's drinking problem: the statistics; the magnitude and scope of the problem; who is affected; how to measure the seriousness of the problem; and the reasons—personal, social, etc.—for it. Several treatment methods are described in the cartoons in chapter 5. Chapter 6 is a brief general message to the alcoholics telling them the pain is their own responsibility, their own problem to solve.

This is an exceptionally fine book, which treats a complex problem in a simple, sensible, and sensitive manner.

692.   Fallding, Harold. **Drinking, Community and Civilization: the Account of a New Jersey Interview Study.** With the assistance of Carol Miles. New Brunswick, NJ: Rutgers Center of Alcohol Studies, 1974. 73p. bibliog. index. (Rutgers Center of Alcohol Studies. No. 9.) $6.00. LC 73-620137. ISBN 911290-41-9.

The author of this study reports on research into drinking practices conducted in two anonymous New Jersey communities. In addition, attitudes and abstinence patterns were also studied. The emphasis of the work is upon discerning to what extent alcohol serves positive, socially promotive functions. Four types of drinking are identified: ornamental, facilitation, assuagement, and retaliation. The message of the book is a plea for greater community cohesion in order to deal with problem drinking.

693.   Fisher, Benjamin Franklin IV. **The Very Spirit of Cordiality: The Literary Uses of Alcohol and Alcoholism in the Tales of Edgar Allan Poe.** Baltimore, MD: The Enoch Pratt Free Library, the Edgar Allan Poe Society, and the Library of the University of Baltimore, 1978. 32p. $2.75pa.

This publication contains a lecture delivered at the Fifty-fifth Annual Commemoration Program of the Edgar Allan Poe Society of Baltimore in 1977. In addition, the first version of a Poe short story "MS. Found in a Bottle" has been reproduced.

The author's view is that many of Poe's grotesque imaginative creations were linked to alcohol and alcoholism.

694.   Fisher, M. M., and J. G. Rankin, eds. **Alcohol and the Liver**. New York: Plenum Press, 1977. 405p. bibliog. index. (Hepatology: Research and Clinical Issues, v. 3.) $39.50. LC 77-8648. ISBN 0-306-34803-9.

The 15 papers in this volume constitute the Proceedings of the Third International Symposium of the Canadian Hepatic Foundation, held in Toronto in 1976. Current knowledge on the epidemiology, pathophysiology, and the natural history of the disease is reviewed. Also, therapy and preventive measures for controlling the increase in alcoholic liver disease are examined. The emphasis of the work is on the basic aspects of alcohol metabolism and metabolic effects. Some long-running controversies on certain questions are brought out in the discussions included, and some insights into the problems of research in the field can be gained.

695.   Freed, Earl X. **An Alcoholic Personality?** Thorofare, NJ: Charles B. Slack, Inc., 1979. 97p. bibliog. $6.50pa. LC 77-88389. ISBN 0-913590-51-7.

The view of the author of this work is that there is real merit in finding out why, after years of alcoholism research and millions of words, we still do not have an answer to the question, "is there an alcoholic personality." The book examines whether or not there is enough evidence to rule out the alcoholic personality or sufficient data to rule it in. The author has organized the chapters around provocative questions concerning the subject as follows: 1) Why should there be an alcoholic personality?, 2) Which came first—the alcoholism or the personality?, 3) What are the issues surrounding the alcoholic personality?, 4) Why blame alcoholism on personality?, 5) Do alcoholics drink to cope with their conflicts?, 6) Why doesn't everyone become an alcoholic?, 7) Are all alcoholics depressed?, and 8) Where do we go from here?

After examining a great deal of research literature on the subject, the author does not entirely reach a conclusion. He feels there could be an alcoholic personality even though it has not yet been well-defined. He suggests we need more research in the area of clinical judgment. Further, he hopes we may eventually find fundamental similarities in the personality of the alcoholic group.

696.   Gastineau, Clifford F., William J. Darby, and Thomas B. Turner, eds. **Fermented Food Beverages in Nutrition**. New York: Academic Press, 1979. 537p. illus. bibliog. index. (A Monograph Series—The Nutrition Foundation.) $45.00. LC 78-22526. ISBN 0-12-277050-1.

This presentation is based in part on papers prepared for the International Symposium on Fermented Food Beverages in Nutrition held in Rochester, Minnesota, at the Mayo Clinic, June 15-17, 1977. There are chapters on the clinical aspects of alcohol consumption and on the historical, cultural, social, and economic aspects of the subject. The intent of the book is to place the matter of mankind's long and diverse utilization of fermented food in perspective. The viewpoint taken is that many nutritionists and physicians have ignored the implications of moderate uses of alcoholic beverages.

The book begins with a view of the drinking habits in antiquity. The next section is on fermentation; the third on consumption of beer and wine; the fourth on the metabolism and therapeutic use of alcohol; the fifth on the effects of alcohol abuse; the sixth on an experimental model; and the last on socioeconomic considerations. The last paper covers socioeconomic and cultural attitudes toward drinking and is an analysis of the international literature. There is an appendix which identifies compounds in whiskey, wine, and beer.

The book is intended for physicians, nutritionists, health advisors, researchers, planners, producers, and regulators.

697.   Goldstein, Gerald, and Charles Neuringer, eds. **Empirical Studies of Alcoholism.** Cambridge, MA: Ballinger Publishing Co., a subsidiary of J. B. Lippincott Co., 1976. 270p. bibliog. index. $16.00. LC 76-17285. ISBN 0-88410-127-4.

The contributors to this book are scientists involved with innovative research in alcoholism-related areas. They share the general belief that the most promising opportunity for gaining an understanding of and assisting the alcoholic lies in scientific research. Objective methods are described. The question of possible causes of alcoholism is not dealt with except in distinguishing between cause and consequences. Neuropsychology is emphasized because many of the behavioral manifestations of alcoholism can be explained on the basis of alcohol-produced damage to the central nervous system. Another trend in the book is an attempt to bring concepts and techniques from the experimental psychology laboratory into alcoholism research, such as conditioning, reinforcement, the study of motor function, perception, concept learning, and the use of psychological tests in alcoholism diagnosis.

The following are the chapter headings: 1) Introduction, 2) The use of psychological tests for the study of the identification, prediction, and treatment of alcoholism, 3) Experimental investigations of tension-reduction models of alcoholism, 4) Behavioral approaches to the treatment of alcoholism, 5) Perceptual and cognitive deficit in alcoholics, 6) Neuropsychological studies of alcoholic Korsakoff patients, 7) An empirically derived typology of hospitalized alcoholics, and 8) Neuropsychological investigations of alcoholism.

698.   Goodwin, Donald. **Is Alcoholism Hereditary**? New York: Oxford University Press, 1978. 171p. bibliog. index. $2.95pa. LC 75-32346. ISBN 0-19-502432-X.

It is usually accepted as fact that alcoholism runs in families. It is not so clear, however, whether this can be explained on the basis of genes or on the basis of environment. The author of this concise, readable book presents both sides of the question. Dr. Goodwin describes research he has himself done on the subject, a study of adopted children, which provides evidence of genetic determination.

The book is suitable for physicians, medical students, and laymen.

699.   Grant, Marcus, and Paul Gwinner, eds. **Alcoholism in Perspective.** Baltimore, MD: University Park Press, 1979. 173p. bibliog. index. $14.50. LC 78-23556. ISBN 0-8391-1332-3.

In the introduction to this work, the editors call attention to the fundamental changes that have taken place in the past few years in concepts of alcoholism. Formerly, alcoholism was seen as a discrete condition affecting a distinct group of people who were presumed to suffer from an illness of uncertain biological origin. The change of emphasis has been to see the condition now as being at the extreme of the drinking continuum, emerging from normal drinking behavior. In addition, it is seen as a syndrome rather than a discrete condition. This book is an attempt to look at alcoholism from this fresh viewpoint. There is no attempt made to provide readers with a ready set of answers on how to deal with alcoholics, but alcoholism is put in a new light, and some practical guidelines have been provided to help alcoholism workers understand the theory and practices of their profession in a different framework.

The chapter titles are as follows, each contributed by an individual knowledgeable in the area discussed: 1) Introduction, 2) The physiology of alcohol, 3) Drinking behaviour, 4) Learning to drink, 5) Defining alcoholism, 6) Epidemiology, 7) The causes of alcoholism, 8) Alcohol and the family, 9) Prevention, 10) Services for alcoholics, 11) Treatment approaches, 12) Behavioural psychotherapy, 13) Social work theory and practice, and 14) Working with alcoholics.

700.   Hafen, Brent Q. **Alcohol: The Crutch that Cripples**. New York: West Publishing Co., 1977. 224p. illus. bibliog. index. $7.95. LC 75-43736. ISBN 0-8299-0083-7.

Although this work is intended primarily as a text for undergraduate courses in the social and health sciences, it can be recommended to anyone interested in the problem of alcoholism. A good deal of the material has been taken word-for-word or digested from publications of government agencies such as the National Institute of Mental Health and the National Institute of Alcohol Abuse and Alcoholism.

A rather wide range of topics involving drinking behavior and alcoholism is covered. Chapter headings are: 1) Introduction: alcohol and its uses, 2) Effects of alcoholic beverages on the body, 3) Alcohol-related behavior, 4) Problem drinking and alcoholism, 5) Social problems and excessive drinking, 6) Treatment of alcoholism, 7) Preventing alcohol problems and alcoholism, and 8) Laws, regulations, and drinking patterns. There is, in addition, an Appendix on "Acute Alcoholic Emergencies" reprinted from a work by experts on the subject. It is quite good.

The chapter on physiological effects of alcohol on the body is especially well done as it makes the subject clear to the layman. The treatment chapter is also quite successful. It describes a number of therapeutic approaches, and the author speaks for the use of a combination of these, a plan usually considered the most effective.

As is stated in the Preface, the book represents a gleaning from the research and writing of prominent experts in the field.

701.   Hoff, E. C. **Alcoholism: the Hidden Addiction**. Foreword by Frank A. Seixas. New York: Seabury Press, 1974. 170p. bibliog. $7.95. LC 74-13014. ISBN 0-8164-0248-5.

The author of this book has written extensively on alcoholism and its treatment. In general his attitude is one of concern for the victim of alcohol, and his belief, that treatment will help. The book begins with a discussion of social forces that may influence drinking patterns and attitudes toward alcohol abuse. Hoff thinks those who believe an alcoholic can through sheer will stop or control drinking are wrong, taking a view similar to that of Alcoholics Anonymous. He further believes that the alcoholic's "surrender" to therapy most often marks the turning point on the route to recovery. He warns that therapists, families, and friends should resist the temptation to cover for the alcoholic; in doing so they may be carrying the alcoholic "upright to his grave."

The book concludes with a description of treatment principles and ways to apply them.

702.   Hore, Brian D. **Alcohol Dependence**. London and Boston: Butterworths, 1976. 153p. bibliog. index. (Postgraduate Psychiatry Series.) $12.95. LC 76-23443. ISBN 0-407-00082-8.

This account of alcoholism was written for the specialist and particularly for the trainee in psychiatry. It is probably of most interest to the academically minded reader, but clinical aspects of the subject are included. The problem of alcoholism is first treated as a dependence disorder. Then methods of determining the condition are discussed, and medical and psychiatric consequences of misuse follow. The social difficulties of dependence are given attention, and the role of the sociologist mentioned. Traffic accidents, crime, and domestic problems are all discussed. Finally, the importance of community care of the alcoholic is highlighted.

The material presented adds up to an up-to-date, short, but reasonably comprehensive review of the subject.

703.   Hyde, Margaret O. **Know About Alcohol**. New York: McGraw-Hill, 1978. 80p. illus. bibliog. index. LC 78-7988. ISBN 0-07-031621-X.

Intended for young people, this short book discusses the effects of alcohol on the body, comments on making the decision whether or not to drink, emphasizes learning safe drinking habits if one does decide to drink, and advises seeking help from Alcoholics Anonymous, Al-Anon, or Alateen as is appropriate if problem drinking arises. A good presentation.

704.   Jacobson, George R. **The Alcoholisms: Detection, Assessment, and Diagnosis**. New York: Human Sciences Press, 1976. 414p. bibliog. $19.95. LC 76-6053. ISBN 0-87705-268-9.

The author of this work takes the view that the concept of alcoholism as a single disease that progresses along a predictable continuum, and that is measurable in terms of a single common symptom, is an oversimplification of the problem. He thinks it is more reasonable to assume there are several *alcoholisms*, which, once detected, may be amenable to different treatments. Therefore the book focuses on specialized techniques and materials for screening, measuring, and classifying the various forms of alcoholism. Each chapter presents a particular methodologic approach and contains information about the availability of instruments and tests designed to detect and diagnose the condition.

The following are the chapter titles: 1) Introduction, 2) Alcadd Test, 3) Alcohol History Form and Alcoholism Severity Scale, 4) Alcoholism assessment interview, 5) Alcohol use questionnaire, 6) Bell Alcoholism Scale of Adjustment, 7) Criteria for the diagnosis of alcoholism, 8) Drinking behavior interview, 9) Essential-reactive alcoholism dimension, 10) Iowa Alcoholic Intake Schedule, 11) MacAndrew Alcoholism Scale, 12) Manson Evaluation, 13) Michigan Alcoholism Screening Test, 14) Mortimer-Filkins Test, and 15) Summaries. In addition, an appendix of materials available for use in clinical and experimental settings and a glossary of technical terms have been provided.

705.   Kissin, Benjamin, and Henri Begleiter, eds. **Treatment and Rehabilitation of the Chronic Alcoholic**. New York: Plenum Press, 1977. 631p. bibliog. index. (The Biology of Alcoholism, v. 5.) $39.50. LC 74-131883. ISBN 0-306-37115-4.

This volume completes the five-volume series, *The Biology of Alcoholism*. The intention originally was to treat solely biological aspects of the syndrome, but a more comprehensive work was produced instead dealing with all aspects of the subject.

This volume presents a large variety of treatment approaches to the long-term rehabilitation of the alcoholic, including the biological, physiological, psychological, and social. Each of the therapies has its proponents, and the variety of them suggests that alcoholism is either a complex syndrome requiring a multipronged treatment approach or a very simple illness for which no remedy has been discovered. The conclusion reached is that probably a broad spectrum of treatment modalities is necessary.

The following are the chapter headings: 1) Theory and practice in the treatment of alcoholism, 2) Medical management of the alcoholic patient, 3) Psychotherapeutic approach, 4) Engaging the alcoholic in treatment and keeping him there, 5) Toward a social model: an assessment of social factors which influence problem drinking and its treatment, 6) Group psychotherapy in alcoholism, 7) Family therapy in alcoholism, 8) Behavioral assessment and treatment of alcoholism, 9) The role of the halfway house in the rehabilitation of alcoholics, 10) Evaluation of treatment methods in chronic alcoholism, 11) Factors in the development of Alcoholics Anonymous (A.A.), 12) Role of the recovered alcoholic in the treatment of alcoholism, 13) Training for professionals and nonprofessionals in alcoholism, and 14) Public health treatment programs in alcoholism.

The book should prove valuable to professionals and others seeking an effective treatment plan for the individual.

706.   Kricka, L. J., and P. M. S. Clark. **Biochemistry of Alcohol and Alcoholism.** Chichester, England: Ellis Horwood; distr., John Wiley and Sons, 1979. 285p. illus. bibliog. index. $57.95. (Ellis Horwood Series in Chemical Science.) ISBN 0-85312-31-1.

Diseases associated with alcohol abuse are very common, but are frequently not recognized by physicians because of their complexity and diversity and because patient history is often lacking. This book deals with the biochemical disturbances observed in long and short term alcohol abuse. Human studies only are cited; animal studies are omitted (although such books often include them).

The first half of the book includes such materials as the definition of alcoholism; incidence and diseases associated with it; and absorption, excretion, and metabolism of alcohol and its congeners.

Biochemcial complexities are cataloged in the second half of the book. Emphasis is given to biochemical tests for the detection and assessment of alcohol abuse. The last chapter deals with effects of alcohol intake on individual biochemical parameters.

The book includes an extensive bibliography. The work is intended for those involved in the diagnosis and management of alcohol abuse and addiction.

707.   Lee, Essie E. **Alcohol–Proof of What?** New York: Julian Messner, 1976. 191p. bibliog. index. $6.25. LC 75-45149. ISBN 0-671-32789-5.

Addressed primarily to young people, this book begins with personal narratives by teenagers who have had to cope with alcoholism in a member of the family or themselves. Next, there is a chapter on the history of alcohol use and one on drinking customs. The fourth chapter deals with medical treatment; the fifth with myths regarding alcohol. In addition, there is a chapter on alcohol and safety and one that contains personal testimonies by non-drinking youths. The last two chapters deal with Alcoholics Anonymous, Alateen, and other self-help groups.

The work is rather well done. It should help discourage youths from using alcohol and give them support if they wish to stop drinking.

708.   Lee, Essie E., and Elaine Israel. **Alcohol and You.** Illustrated by Jerry Smath. New York: Julian Messner, a division of Simon and Schuster, 1975. 64p. illus. index. $6.25. LC 75-29429. ISBN 0-671-32758-5.

Intended for juveniles, this this small book explores various matters pertaining to alcohol, its origins, its uses, its effect on the body, and the physical and social problems its use may bring about. The intent of the authors is to give information that will help young people decide whether or not to drink.

Chapter titles are as follows: 1) When two drinks are too many, 2) A long and stormy history, 3) What is alcohol?, 4) Drinking and getting drunk, 5) Other effects of alcohol on the body, 6) Alcoholics and alcoholism, and 7) Getting help. In addition, a glossary has been included.

709.   Mendelson, Jack H., and Nancy K. Mello, eds. **The Diagnosis and Treatment of Alcoholism.** New York: McGraw-Hill, 1979. 405p. bibliog. index. $17.50. LC 79-4128. ISBN 0-07-041476-9.

This text provides current and authoritative information on the alcoholic and problem drinker that is of particular value to the physician, psychologist, nurse, social worker, medical administrator, and others who are seeking an introduction to the subject above the beginner level.

Some of the material presented is on the clinical level for those who are practicing health professionals; other chapters are reviews or critiques with emphasis on problems as yet unsolved and additional research needed.

The following topics are covered: diagnostic criteria for early and advanced alcoholism; medical consequences of alcohol abuse; the genetics of alcoholism; problems peculiar to blacks and women; selection of treatments; treatment in outpatient and inpatient facilties; pharmacotherapy; behavior therapy; and therapy in various historical and social settings.

710.   Null, Gary, and Steve Null. **Alcohol and Nutrition.** New York: Pyramid Publications, 1976. 191p. bibliog. index. $1.75pa. LC 76-43188.

The intent of this book is to present a well-rounded, objective view of the effects of alcohol on the body. The relationship of alcohol and nutrition is stressed because malnutrition is involved in many alcohol-related illnesses. In addition, the effect of alcohol on the social environment and why it is used are also considered.

The following are the chapter headings: 1) Alcohol: what it is and why we drink it, 2) Two sides of the coin: nutrition and malnutrition, 3) The metabolism of alcohol, 4) Alcohol's effect on metabolism, 5) Alcohol: its effect on the vital systems, 6) Alcohol: related illnesses and diseases, 7) Alcohol and the liver, 8) Alcohol: use and misuse, and 9) Some answers to the problem.

The authors allow that alcohol in moderate amounts can be an excellent tranquilizer, but that it can also create havoc in the human body. In the last chapter methods of treatment of alcoholism are discussed. Physiological methods, such as the use of the drugs antabuse and lithium and the use of aversion therapy, are discussed. An adequate diet is considered. In addition, psychological methods such as bio-feedback and meditation are mentioned.

The book is written in a manner understandable to the general reader and is quite well done. There is adequate documentation, and many suggestions for additional reading are included. In spite of the fact that the authors of the work are also the authors of other nutrition books of questionable value, there is little to criticize about this one.

711.   Poulos, C. Jean, Donald Stoddard, and Kay Carron. **Alcoholism, Stress, Hypoglycemia, with Diets.** Santa Cruz, CA: Davis Publishing Co., 1976. 131p. illus. bibliog. $6.95pa. LC 76-24383. ISBN 0-89368-600-X.

This work summarizes a two-year research project conducted to determine the relationship of hypoglycemia and stress to alcoholism. It is not a typical research report in that it is written for the average reader in oversimplified fashion rather than for researchers in their language. In addition, the authors frequently take positions contrary to those held by most authorities.

The hypothesis is that hypoglycemia plays an important role in the causes of alcoholism, a resultant symptom that occurs from an unknown cause or causes. This interrelationship is examined in detail and is supported with references to selected research findings and the research carried out by the authors. Included at the end is a section on miscellaneous substances: protein, carbohydrates, fats, vitamins, minerals, sugar, tobacco, and caffeine. Diet suggestions are also included. There is a list of suggested readings, which are mostly popular "health food" and nutrition books. References to scientific literature have been included in the text, however.

It is presumed that the material on nutrition has been included so the reader can be advised on how to improve his or her diet and avoid various undesirable conditions such as alcoholism, stress, and hypoglycemia.

The publication is a curious mixture of the scientific and the popular. It suffers from poor organization and format; there is no table of contents or index, and no chapter titles have been used.

712.   Roe, Daphne A. **Alcohol and the Diet.** Westport, CT: Avi Publishing Co., 1979. 228p. illus. index. $15.00. LC 79-214. ISBN 0-87055-316-X.

The focus of this work is on the effects of alcoholic beverages and alcoholism on the diet, particularly the interrelationships between alcohol and nutrition.

Included are the following: A historical account of alcohol use with folklore recounted, The scientific findings on alcohol and the diet, Effects of alcohol abuse on nutrition, Fetal malnutrition induced by alcohol, Nutritional status of alcoholics, Nutritional rehabilitation, Food behavior modification, Components of alcoholic beverages, and Drug-alcohol-food interactions.

The book is intended for those concerned with the care of alcoholics, particularly nutritionists, physicians, nurses, and pharmacists.

713.   Rose, A. H., ed. **Alcoholic Beverages.** London; New York: Academic Press, 1977. 760p. illus. bibliog. index. (Economic Microbiology, v. 1.) $48.90. LC 77-77361. ISBN 0-12-596550-8.

This work covers an aspect of the subject seldom dealt with, beverage alcohol from the industrial and economic standpoint. History, the scientific and practical aspects of the brewing and distillation processes, microbiology, chemistry, technology, the industry, and consumer information are provided.

There are ten chapters as follows: 1) History and scientific basis of alcoholic beverage production, 2) Beer, 3) Cider and perry, 4) Table wines, 5) Fruit and honey wines, 6) Sake, 7) Fortified wines, 8) Gin and vodka, 9) Rum, and 10) Whiskey.

The book has been well-received. It is readable and authoritative.

714.   Silverstein, Alvin, and Virginia B. Silverstein. **Alcoholism.** With an Introduction by Gail Gleason Milgram, consulting editor. Philadelphia, PA: J. B. Lippincott Co., 1975. 128p. bibliog. index. $5.50; $2.95pa. LC 75-17938. ISBN 0-397-31648-8; 0-397-31649-6 pa.

Although this book is intended particularly for young people, it has a wider appeal because it is about alcoholism in general. The material is presented in an objective manner and is surprisingly pleasant to read. Major aspects of alcohol use and abuse are discussed dispassionately.

The following chapters are included: 1) The number one problem, 2) Alcoholic beverages, 3) What alcohol does in the body, 4) Alcohol in history, 5) Drinking today—social drinking and problem drinking, 6) Drinking and driving, 7) Teenage drinking, 8) What is alcoholism?, 9) Treating the alcoholic, 10) Living with an alcoholic parent, 11) A personal decision, and 12) For further information.

715.   Spahr, John Howard. **Sober Life**. Philadelphia and Ardmore, PA: Dorrance and Co., 1979. 105p. bibliog. index. $5.00. ISBN 0-8059-2626-7.

Written by a Protestant clergyman who has devoted a great deal of his professional career to counseling alcoholics and their families, this book addresses the question of the biblical stance on drinking. Many Protestant churches (at least in the past) have taken the view as part of their doctrine that drinking is morally wrong. This view is still prevalent to some extent in spite of widespread acceptance of the use of alcohol, and perhaps with considerable justification when one considers the societal problems that stem from problem drinking. However, Rev. Spahr points out that the biblical scriptures do not insist on abstinence, only responsible use and temperance. "The Bible offers unqualified acceptance of drinking but total rejection for *intoxication at any level*," according to the author.

The book is written in layman's terms and is well-documented. There is a scriptural index as well as a topical index.

716.   U.S. National Institute on Alcohol Abuse and Alcoholism. **Third Special Report to the U.S. Congress on Alcohol and Health**. From the Secretary of Health, Education and Welfare. Edited by Ernest P. Noble. Washington: GPO, 1978. 98p. [DHEW Publication No. (ADM) 78-569.] $3.00pa. S/N 017-024-00848-6.

The first special report was published in 1971; the second, in 1974. This one, the third, covers a wide range of matters associated with alcohol abuse. The recent most significant research findings on the prevalence, consequences, treatment, and prevention of alcoholism are presented.

Following are the chapter headings: 1) Alcohol use and alcohol related problems—prevalence and patterns, 2) Special population groups, 3) Biomedical consequences of alcohol use and abuse, 4) The fetal alcohol syndrome and other effects on offspring, 5) Interaction of alcohol and other drugs, 6) Psychological effects of alcohol, 7) Genetic and family factors relating to alcoholism, 8) Alcohol-related accidents, crime and violence, 9) Treatment of alcoholism and problem drinking, 10) Occupational alcoholism programming, 11) Financing alcoholism treatment services, and 12) The prevention of alcohol problems.

The editor sees a need to change the drinking attitudes and behavior of the nation, a difficult task, but one worth the commitment.

717.   Waddell, Jack O., and Michael W. Everett, eds. **Drinking Behavior Among Southwestern Indians: An Anthropological Perspective**. Tucson, AZ: University of Arizona Press, 1980. 248p. bibliog. index. $16.50; $9.50pa. LC 79-16379. ISBN 0-8165-0676-0; 0-8165-0615-9 pa.

The editors of this collection of ethnographic studies have been involved in academic work in the field of anthropology and have done field research in the area of alcohol use. Four contemporary American Indian cultures are examined:

Papagos, Taos Pueblos, Navajos, and White Mountain Apaches. The contributors discuss such matters as historical antecedents, aclohol and mental health programs, social drinking, and native perceptions of the problem.

It is pointed out that the consequences of alcohol abuse among Native Americans are very serious and are rapidly becoming worse. There is a prevailing view that "Indian drinking" is somehow different from drinking by other groups. Some studies, however, attribute some positive functions to Indian drinking, such as its value as an escape mechanism for coping with the problems of a changing society. The conclusion is reached that answers to the alcohol problem will come about when culturally meaningful plans of action can be established with a minimum of outside management, and Native American priorities and needs as they themselves see them are given formost attention.

718.   Ward, David. A. **Alcoholism: Introduction to Theory and Treatment.**
Dubuque, IA: Kendall/Hunt Publishing Co., 1980. 420p. illus. bibliog. index.
$15.95pa. LC 79-91055. ISBN 0-8403-2143-0.

This publication contains a collection of articles by noted authorities in the alcoholism field. The 37 contributions are arranged under the following chapter headings: 1) Conceptions of alcoholism, 2) Alcohol, the body, and alcohol-related illnesses, 3) The epidemiology of alcoholism, 4) Theories of etiology (Genetic theory, personality theory, sociological theory), 5) Alcohol education and prevention, 6) Diagnosis of alcoholism, 7) Motivation in treatment, 8) Certification, 9) Alcoholics Anonymous, 10) Behavioral treatment, 11) Family therapy, and 12) Transactional analysis. Each chapter is introduced by a brief overview of the topic under consideration and a short summary of the articles contained in the chapter, a technique that provides continuity throughout the book. A glossary has been provided.

Some chapters contain papers that give rise to contested issues, and when this is the case other papers are included which present other views of the matter.

The book is interdisciplinary in scope. It is hoped that the selections will provide understanding of the nature and treatment of alcoholism. The intent of the work is to provide teachers of such subjects as social work, nursing, psychology, sociology, education, and criminal justice with a text for course work. Practitioners in the field of alcoholism treatment should also find the book valuable. It is an impressive, comprehensive collection of materials.

21

TOBACCO

Although tobacco use does not cause social or other problems of the magnitude of the use of other drugs of abuse, it has become increasingly evident that it has deleterious effects on health and that dependence results from continued use. A recent report of the U.S. Surgeon General (*see* entry 741) indicates that smoking is even more dangerous than previously supposed. There have been attempts to produce a safer cigarette (*see* work by Gori, entry 727) for those who cannot break the smoking habit.

In addition to works that discuss health effects, these aspects of tobacco use have also received attention: how to stop smoking, history, behavior, public policy, chemistry, law, research, and teenage use.

719.   American Medical Association Education and Research Foundation. Committee for Research on Tobacco and Health. **Tobacco and Health.** Chicago: The Foundation, 1978. 369p. index. (Research Studies of the Relationship of Tobacco and Health.) $25.00. LC 78-52881.

In 1964 the American Medical Association Education and Research Foundation entered into a five-year agreement with six tobacco companies to conduct a program of research on tobacco and health. The research was to be devoted to the study of human ailments that may be caused or aggravated by smoking, the particular elements that may be the causal or aggravating agents, and the mechanisms of their action. The companies contributed a large amount of money to finance this effort. The agreement was renewed in 1969, although in 1972 it was altered to eliminate the industry's financial commitment and grants were curtailed. This publication contains summaries and abstracts of 795 research projects conducted between 1964 and 1975.

The material is arranged in seven sections as follows: 1) Absorption, distribution metabolism, excretion, toxicology, 2) Carcinogenesis, 3) Cardiovascular system, 4) Central and autonomic nervous system, 5) Gastrointestinal tract, 6) Reproduction, and 7) Respiratory system. There are two indexes, author and participating institutions. Each section is introduced with a general survey of the research findings reported in abstract form in that section.

720.   Bättig, K., ed. **Behavioral Effects of Nicotine.** International Workshop on Behavioral Effects of Nicotine, Zürich, September 15-17, 1976. Basel, S. Karger, 1978. 126p. bibliog. index. $32.00. LC 79-300595. ISBN 3-8055-2763-2.

This work presents nine scientific papers of a workshop organized by the Swiss Federal Institute of Technology, Zürich. It is an effort to approach the subject of nicotine from a behavioral point of view.

Earlier background studies have shown that small smoking doses of nicotine produce both peripheral autonomic effects and centrally transferred behavioral effects in laboratory animals. The effects seem to be somewhat unique in comparison to those of other psychotropic substances. They are subtle and vary from excitatory to inhibitory depending on the dose and some other factors. The properties of nicotine have been labelled 'normalizing' or 'harmonizing' in their actions. As a consequence of such findings in animals, there has been a growing interest in the effects of nicotine on human subjects. Although the effects of smoking may be attributed to other factors, nicotine may be the main one responsible for the widespread use of tobacco in human societies.

The book presents new results against the background of the earlier work. There are papers on psychological and physiological mechanisms of small nicotine doses. Effects on emotional, intellectual, and arousal functions are studied. Findings suggest that smoking behavior is directed by nicotine need in habitual smokers. Behavioral, physiological, and biochemical methods are all represented in the volume.

721.   Billingslea, Monroe L. **Smoking and How to Stop**. Los Angeles, CA: Brend House Publications, 1978. 110p. $13.95. LC 77-93634.
The author of this small book is a dentist who has devised a new method, called Conditioned Inhibition, to help those who want to stop smoking.

The first chapter is a short history of smoking. The following chapters explore the effects of smoking on the body and present in detail the steps to follow to break the smoking habit. Conditioned Inhibition involves giving oneself a series of negative thoughts concerning smokers and the use of tobacco.

A good deal of useful information has been provided, including statistical data and a table which lists brands and types of cigarettes with the tar and nicotine content and rank in tar content.

722.   Chute, Anthony. **Tabacco** (sic). Edited by F. P. Wilson. Oxford: published for the Luttrell Society by Basil Blackwell, 1961. 55p. (Luttrell Society Reprints No. 22.)
This publication is a reprint of what is said to be the first English work devoted to tobacco. It was written in the late 1500s in order to commend the medicinal properties of tobacco, which "may be taken for a variety of reasons, . . . health, conviviality, habit, fashion, bravado, or because it helps regulate thinking." The pamphlet is in two parts; first, it is concerned with dried tobacco applied to the patient by means of a pipe, and then, the plant itself is dealt with—its growth, and the presumed curative properties of the green leaf and of concoctions brewed from the leaf.

723.   Clark, Robert R. **Smoking: A Social Interaction Theory of Cigarette Smoking and Quitting**. Oceanside, NY: Dabor Science Publications, 1977. 104p. bibliog. index. $15.00. LC 77-10697. ISBN 0-89561-014-0.
Written by a clinical psychologist, this book explores smoking from a social behavioral point of view. The author applies this social interaction theory to understanding the experience of quitting smoking. In addition, new treatment techniques are presented.

The author studied more than 100 cases of smoking in the context of social interaction. He presents an analysis of a videotape of the interaction between a smoker and a nonsmoker. He has divided smoking into the following subprocesses: lighting up, dragging, exhaling, holding the cigarette, tapping ashes, and putting out the cigarette.

Clark concludes that smoking is an avenue for increased self-involvement and reduced situational involvement. In keeping with this theory, he develops a treatment program for quitting, giving attention to group treatment.

724.   Danaher, Brian G., and Edward Lichtenstein. **Become an Ex-Smoker**. Englewood Cliffs, NJ: Prentice-Hall, Inc., 1978. 226p. bibliog. index. (The Self-Management Psychology Series; A Spectrum Book.) $10.95; $4.95pa. LC 78-1679. ISBN 0-13-072249-9; 0-13-072231-6 pa.

This book was designed for self-help, presenting a step-by-step, week-by-week method for stopping the smoking habit. It is probably based on sound psychology.

The following are the section headings: 1) Preparing to become an ex-smoker, 2) Calling it quits, 3) Remaining an ex-smoker, 4) Decisions and information, and 5) Resource appendix. The chapter headings are as follows: 1) The psychology of cigarette smoking, 2) Finding out about your personal smoking habit, 3) Deep muscular relaxation, 4) Nonaversive methods, 5) Aversive smoking, 6) Changing the smoking signals, 7) Managing your thoughts, 8) Benefits of not smoking, 9) Successful weight management, 10) Planning ahead, and 11) If you can't stop smoking. The following appendices have been provided: 1) Common questions about smoking, 2) New arenas for smoking control, and 3) Behavioral treatment of smoking.

725.   Eckholm, Erik. **Cutting Tobacco's Toll**. Washington: Worldwatch Institute, 1978. 40p. bibliog. (Worldwatch paper 18.) $2.00pa. LC 78-53446. ISBN 0-916468-17-8.

Portions of this brief publication have been adapted from the author's book, *The Picture of Health: Environmental Sources of Disease*. The health consequences of the increase in tobacco use worldwide is described, and the hidden economic costs to nonsmokers and to society in general are pointed out. Strategies for curbing the spread of tobacco use and for a more equitable distribution of its social cost are presented. Government subsidies to tobacco interests are mentioned, and a section on the increased use of cigarettes in the Third World is included.

The following are the section headings: 1) The unnatural history of tobacco, 2) The broadening medical indictment, 3) World smoking trends, 4) Who profits?, 5) Public policy and public health, and 6) Notes.

The author remarks in conclusion that squelching the smoking habit in any country will be difficult. The social aura of it carries a strong force, and the huge consumer expenditure on cigarettes (equal to one-fourth the world military budget) shows that vested interests will struggle to keep sales on the rise.

726.   Friedman, Kenneth M. **Cigarette Smoking and Public Policy: The United States, Great Britain, and Canada**. Lafayette, IN: Midwest Center for the Study of Public Policy, Department of Political Science, Purdue University, 1973. (Discussion Paper No. 27.)

This footnoted document was prepared for discussion at the 1973 National Health Forum at Chicago, March 20-21, 1973. In it governmental response to the smoking-health controversy in the United States, Great Britain, and Canada is discussed. Similarities and differences are examined and explained. Theoretical notions concerning the formulation of public policies are also examined, although none of them provides a real explanation of the interacting forces involved. Implications for present and future public policy is evaluated.

The conclusion is reached that neither the role of science in government nor the role of government in the economy have yet been decided in any of the three countries. This may be because the priority of economic interests is being challenged as is the individual's freedom of choice. Smoking-health policy is unclear. It does appear, however, that corporate and governmental concern have led to less harmful cigarettes and a more informed public.

727.   Gori, Gio B., and Fred G. Bock, eds. **A Safe Cigarette**? Cold Spring Harbor, NY: Cold Spring Harbor Laboratory, 1980. 364p. illus. bibliog. (Banbury Report 3.) $45.00. LC 79-47999. ISBN 0-87969-202-2.

Presented in this publication are the edited proceedings of a meeting held at the Banbury Center, Cold Spring Harbor, on October 14-16, 1979. Scientific specialists discussed the recent drastic changes in cigarette components, the shift toward filter and low-tar cigarettes and what the implications of such trends are for the health of smokers.

The papers are arranged under the following session headings: 1) Introduction and epidemiological trends, 2) Toxicological dimensions, 3) Risk-reduction achievements and future directions, 4) Cigarette engineering, and 5) Behavioral and economic issues.

In summary, evidence was presented that could justify further promotion of less hazardous cigarettes as a public health measure. Consumption of cigarettes has not decreased the past 20 years, but has stabilized. Tar and nicotine content has been reduced by about one-half the past 15 years. For the future, it is speculated that we may look forward to further decreases in tar and nicotine along with flavor characteristics that may be satisfactory to the smoker.

728.   Robicsek, Francis. **The Smoking Gods: Tobacco in Maya Art, History, and Religion**. Forewords by Michael D. Coe, and Barbara A. Goodnight. Norman, OK: University of Oklahoma Press, 1978. 233p. illus. (col.). bibliog. index. $35.00. LC 78-64904. ISBN 0-8061-1511-4.

The author of this book is a physician, and, in addition, is an Adjunct Professor of Anthropology (at the University of North Carolina at Charlotte) with an interest in Maya history and culture. The aim of the work is to study the use of tobacco in Maya life in order to gain an understanding of certain scenes depicted in classic Maya art.

The presentation is in two parts. The first presents historical and ethnological background. Tobacco, according to the author, was used by the Mayas as a social pastime, but it also had religious and mythological implications. In addition, it penetrated folklore and influenced art.

Part 2 of the book is on archeological material. A great many materials where smoking scenes are depicted have been examined, such as pottery vessels, stone slabs, and monuments.

The book is lavishly illustrated. It is one of few publications on the subject.

729.   Rolfe, Burton Phillip. **How to Stop Smoking Before Smoking Stops You!** With illustrations by Steve Menteer. Chicago: Adams Press, 1978. 118p. illus. $6.75pa. LC 78-61906. ISBN 0-932636-00-4.

The author of this self-help book relates his plan to assist the reader to stop smoking forever. Cartoon illustrations accompany the text.

Many personal anecdotes are told to point out the unattractive and injurious aspect of tobacco use, and the reader is called upon to use will-power and to quit. Chapter headings are as follows: 1) Why I'm not a smoker, 2) The days I remember—

too well, 3) Sometimes once is not enough, 4) Smoking your way to the courthouse, 5) Seeing your habit as it really is, 6) What you always wanted to know about your habit, 7) Pssst! It's in the smoke, 8) Money vs time, 9) Is freedom of speech more important than health?, 10) The power of choice, 11) Power of imagination, 12) Power of observation, 13) Satisfying the urge, 14) Rearrange your eating habit, 15) The winner's blueprint, and 16) Get happy.

730.　Schmeltz, Irwin, ed. **The Chemistry of Tobacco and Tobacco Smoke**. Proceedings of the Symposium on the Chemcial Composition of Tobacco and Tobacco Smoke held during the 162nd National Meeting of the American Chemical Society in Washington, D.C., September 12-17, 1971. New York: Plenum Press, 1972. 186p. bibliog. index. $16.50. LC 72-76934. ISBN 0-306-30597-6.

This work presents papers that cover those aspects of tobacco research that are pertinent to the development of a less hazardous cigarette. The papers have been grouped under the following headings: 1) Introductory chapter, 2) Chemistry of tobacco leaf, 3) Chemistry of tobacco smoke, 4) Biological activity of tobacco smoke, and 5) Utilization of research findings.

Various aspects of the composition of the tobacco leaf are discussed and how that composition might be altered. Findings on the chemical composition of tobacco smoke, methods for fractionating the smoke, and resolving complex mixtures of smoke components by various analytical methods are described. The mode of origin of smoke components, including those considered biologically active is also taken up. And last, the matter of modifying the smoke and the use of various filter systems and additives are considered.

731.　Swedish Tobacco Company, Medical Advisory Board, ed. **Symposium on the Effects of Nicotine on Nervous Function**. Stockholm: Almqvist and Wiksell, 1980. 56p. bibliog. (Acta Physiologica Scandinavica, Supplementum 479.)

This publication presents the papers of a "mini-symposium" held in Stockholm on November 29, 1978. The participants were recipients of grants from the Swedish Tobacco Company engaged in research on the effects of nicotine on nervous functions, and, in addition, a few guest lecturers. Eleven scientific papers are included.

Some of the specific topics covered are: cholinergic neuronal activity, biosynthesis and metabolism of nicotine, muscarinic and nicotinic binding sites, neonatal effects, blockade of nicotine induced inhibition of gonadothrophin, blood pressure, smoking and blood temperature during exercise, effects on the formation of prostaglandins, and psychological effects.

732.　Thornton, Raymond E., ed. **Smoking Behaviour: Physiological and Psychological Influences**. New York: Churchill Livingstone; distr., Longman, 1978. 405p. bibliog. index. $45.00. LC 78-40889. ISBN 0-443-01815-4.

This book contains the papers and record of the International Smoking Behaviour Conference held at Chelwood Vachery, Sussex, England, in November 1977. It was originated and edited by the British American Tobacco Company.

A few of the participants were from such fields as psychology, psychiatry, and pharmacology, but most were from tobacco companies. Understandably, little mention was made of the hazards of tobacco use. It was spoken of as a proper phenomenon in the face of life's problems.

Several valuable papers on smoking behavior are included. Others give evidence that nicotine is the dominant cause of dependency and that smokers adjust their nicotine intake according to mental demands made on them so as to achieve the desired effect. There is a paper on the effects of carbon monoxide on driving performance.

The conclusion is reached that smoking is a very strong habit, easy to start and hard to stop, and that it is a source of much pleasure to many.

733.   U.S. Center for Disease Control. **State Legislation on Smoking and Health, 1978.** Washington: GPO, 1979. 84p. (HEW Publication No. CDC 79-8331.) $2.75pa. S/N 017-023-00131-1.

The fourth in a series on state legislative activity regarding smoking and health, this report was prepared by the Bureau of Health Education in response to widespread interest in the subject. The bureau was provided with copies of smoking and health bills and resolutions introduced in state legislatures in 1978. Some state legislatures did not meet in 1978, and some did not introduce legislation of this nature. However, 38 states did introduce such bills, and 26 were passed into law by 20 states.

The publication is made up primarily of tables as follows: 1) Summary of state legislation, 1978, 2) Laws by subject and state, 1978, 3) Legislation by subject for each state, 1978, and 4) Summary of laws enacted, 1975-1978.

The legislation is categorized as follows: 1) Limitations on smoking, 2) Commerce, 3) Smoking and schools, 4) Advertising, 5) Sales to or use by minors, 6) Insurance, and 7) Other.

734.   U.S. Department of Agriculture. **Nicotiana: Procedures for Experimental Use.** Edited by R. B. Durbin. Washington: U.S.D.A., 1979. 124p. illus. bibliog. index. (U.S. Department of Agriculture, Technical Bulletin 1586.)

The tobacco plant (*Nicotiana*) has been widely used in genetic research and in related botanical disciplines because of its special properties. This publication brings together the necessary background information and procedures for taking full advantage of its attributes. The hope is that experimenters in various disciplines will benefit from the information.

735.   U.S. National Cancer Institute. Office of Cancer Communications. **Clearing the Air: A Guide to Quitting Smoking.** Washington: GPO, 1979. 36p. illus. [DHEW Publication No. (NIH) 79-1647.]

This booklet contains a great many helpful hints on how to kick the smoking habit. It presents realistic approaches that have proved popular with ex-smokers. The victim can choose those that make sense to him or her. Helpful supplementary material has been included, such as a table showing caloric content of popular snacks, a list of formal programs for quitting smoking, and a list of other sources of information on the subject.

736.   U.S. National Heart and Lung Institute. Epidemiology Branch. **Smoking and General Mortality among U.S. Veterans, 1954-1969.** By Eugene Rogot. Washington: GPO, 1974. 65p. bibliog. [DHEW Publication No. (NIH) 74-544.] LC 74-602680.

This publication is the report of a long-term study of the general mortality experience as related to tobacco use of about 290,000 U.S. veterans who held Government Life Insurance Policies. The results of the study confirmed earlier work on the subject.

Cigarette smokers experienced much the highest mortality levels followed by cigar smokers and then pipe smokers. The age-adjusted probabilities of death in 16 years were .457 for pure cigarette smokers, .342 for pure cigar smokers, .316 for pure pipe smokers, and .294 for those who never smoked. Risk was related to amount smoked. Many groups of former cigarette smokers demonstrated annual risks at close to the nonsmoker levels, but for others some excess risk remained at the end of the study period. The publication contains detailed analysis with a great deal of tabular data.

737.   U.S. National Institute of Education. **Teenage Smoking: Immediate and Long Term Patterns**. Prepared by Dorothy E. Green. Washington: GPO, 1979. 259p. $6.00pa. S/N 017-080-02074-2.

It is hoped that this publication will be useful to those who are conducting research on teenage smokers and to those designing programs aimed at encouraging young people to avoid smoking. Presented are the results of two studies, conducted by the National Institute of Education in 1978 and 1979 on the prevalence of adolescent smoking and the variables related to it. In addition, the use of these variables in predicting later, more "habitual" smoking was studied.

The report is in two parts: 1) National patterns of cigarette smoking, 1979, and 2) Longitudinal study, 1974-1979.

Conclusions reached were that former smokers (in the 1979 sample) may not have been really committed to smoking, but were more like experimenters. They started smoking early and quit early. Current smokers, however, have tried to quit or would if they thought it possible. They are concerned about their health. Why these young adults became regular smokers when they are unsatisfied with this status is not clear. Educational aspirations and attainment is lower for this group. This finding probably is a reflection of lifestyle rather than a cause-effect relationship, however.

738.   U.S. National Institute on Drug Abuse. **The Behavioral Aspects of Smoking**. Edited by Norman A. Krasnegor. Washington: GPO, 1979. 192p. bibliog. [DHEW Publication (ADM) 79-882; NIDA Research Monograph 26.] LC 79-600141. S/N 017-024-00947-4.

This publication is a reprinting of Part II of the 1979 *Smoking and Health: Report of the Surgeon General* (*See* entry 741). The five papers provide for behavioral scientists and others who are interested a summary of current biological, behavioral, and psychosocial research on cigarette smoking behavior.

The titles of the papers are as follows: 1) Biological influence on cigarette smoking, 2) Behavioral factors in the establishment, maintenance, and cessation of smoking, 3) Smoking in children and adolescents: psychosocial determinants and prevention strategies, 4) Psychosocial influences on cigarette smoking, and 5) Modification of smoking behavior. Comprehensive bibliographies have been included with each paper.

739.   U.S. National Institute on Drug Abuse. **Cigarette Smoking as a Dependence Process**. Edited by Norman A. Krasnegor. Washington: GPO, 1979. 194p. bibliog. [DHEW Publication No. (ADM) 79-800; NIDA Research Monograph Series 23.]

The 14 papers in this publication explore such questions as why people persist in cigarette smoking in spite of the knowledge of the health consequences. Research results are presented that may throw light on the dependence process and offer help to cigarette users. The work points out that the nature of the dependency is not well-understood, and that more research into the matter is needed.

The papers are grouped under the following headings: 1) Psychosocial factors, 2) Behavioral factors, 3) Psychobiological factors, and 4) Implications and directions for future research.

740.   U.S. National Institute on Drug Abuse. **Research on Smoking Behavior.** Edited by Murray E. Jarvik, and others. Washington: GPO, 1977. 383p. bibliog. [DHEW Publication No. (ADM) 78-581; NIDA Research Monograph 17.] $4.50. LC 090890. S/N 017-024-00694-7.

The papers in this publication are from a symposium organized to focus on the dependence process associated with tobacco smoking. In order to understand the habit, it was analyzed from four different aspects: epidemiology, etiology, consequences, and treatment or behavioral change. The papers are grouped under these headings. They cover a wide range of topics.

The publication is timely because a consensus is growing that the national effort to cope with the tobacco habit has been defective even though there was a decrease in use after the 1964 Report to the Surgeon General on Smoking. However, children are now beginning to smoke at an earlier age, more people are dying prematurely from smoking damage, and cigarette smoking is often a precursor or gateway substance to use of stronger drugs.

741.   U.S. Office on Smoking and Health. **Smoking and Health: A Report of the Surgeon General.** Washington: GPO, 1979. 1 v. (various paging). bibliog. index. [DHEW Publication No. (PHS) 79-50066.] S/N 017-000-00218-0.

This is the second Surgeon General's Report on Smoking and Health; the first was published in 1964. No new conclusions about the effects of tobacco on health are contained in the voluminous, highly publicized report; rather, it intensifies the original findings. However, much new research is reviewed and the conclusion is reached that smoking is even more dangerous than was supposed in 1964. The new report was issued for three reasons primarily: 1) to bring together new information on the subject, 2) to extend the area of inquiry beyond medicine into the behavioral sciences, and 3) to provide a firm base of knowledge upon which to build public policy.

The work is in three main parts: The health consequences of smoking, Behavioral aspects of smoking, and Education and prevention. Some new findings about women smokers are included which were not available in 1964. Women, industrial workers, and teenagers are all felt to be high risk groups.

Significant findings are as follows: 1) life expectancy at any given age is shortened by cigarette smoking—the smoker's chance of dying from disease is approximately 70% greater than that of nonsmokers; 2) smoking is a major risk factor for cardiovascular and respiratory diseases, cancer, and peptic ulcer; 3) children of smokers are more likely to have bronchitis and pneumonia during the first year of life; 4) the lighted cigarette generates more than 2,000 chemicals, of which carbon monoxide, nicotine, and tar are the most likely contributors to the health hazards of smoking; 5) the longer one smokes and the older one gets, the more difficult it is to break this addictive-like pattern; and 6) cigarette smoking is the largest preventable cause of death in the United States.

It is hoped that further research in the next decade or so will reveal ways to help people stop smoking.

AUTHOR AND TITLE INDEX

SUBJECT INDEX

Addiction. *See* Alcohol abuse; Drug abuse.
Addictive mechanisms, 503, 510, 511
Aggression, 586
Agonists compounds, 532, 589
Alcohol
  forensic aspects, bibliographies, 9
  laws and regulations, 428, 433, 475
  See also Alcohol effects; Alcohol use
Alcohol abuse
  audiovisuals, bibliographies, 17, 63, 120
  bibliographies, 120, 123
  biochemistry, 706
  cartoons, 691
  community action programs, 80, 82, 83, 85, 692
  counseling, 81, 257, 274, 307
  detection, 704, 709
  economic aspects, 415, 431
  education, 61, 63, 82-84, 324, 328-37, 678
    bibliographies, 13
    medical, 347
    periodicals, 111
    training for, 100, 338-40
  emergency treatment, 51, 71
  epidemiology, 558, 560
  general works, 36, 62, 170, 178, 179, 201, 218, 220, 329, 544, 569, 678, 682-84, 691, 699-701, 703, 704, 708, 714, 716
  history, 173
  in business and industry, 594, 595, 597-601
    periodicals, 130
  incidence, 287, 288, 414
    Canada, 222
    Ireland, 361
    Micronesia, 413
    Punjab, 686
    Southwestern Indians, 717
  legal aspects, 435, 456, 457, 679
  periodicals, 107-112, 114-17, 119, 120, 122, 123, 125, 128, 130, 132-34, 137, 140, 142
  personal narratives, 145, 150, 163, 172, 176, 177, 181, 182, 187
  physiological effects, 422, 539
    bibliographies, 19
  prevention, audiovisuals (bibliography), 16
  psychological and psychiatric aspects, 310, 415, 422, 558, 560, 702
    bibliographies, 22

research, 281, 324, 496, 503, 512, 515, 516, 521, 524, 526, 527, 537, 539, 544, 547, 549, 557-60, 563, 569, 679, 680, 690, 697
  periodicals, 112, 140
self-help, 311-21
  See also Alcoholics Anonymous
sociological aspects, 352, 358, 361, 406, 407, 413-15, 422, 456, 558, 560, 690
  bibliographies, 23
statistics, 222, 287, 288, 443
theory, 269, 718
treatment, 67, 71, 218, 248, 253, 254, 256, 261, 269, 274, 544, 549, 557, 559, 681, 688, 701, 705, 709, 718
  behavior therapy, 267, 272, 282, 546, 547
  bibliographies, 4, 15, 18
  family therapy, 266, 315, 318
  See also Alcohol abuse–emergency treatment
treatment centers and programs, 74, 251, 252, 259, 260, 265, 275, 374, 598, 599, 681
  directories, 36
Alcohol beverage industry, 713
Alcohol effects, 687
  brain, 499, 553
  cancer, 680
  digestive, bibliographies, 12
  liver, 528, 694
  memory, 501
  metabolic, 498, 523, 536, 540, 543, 694
Alcohol use
  biblical stance, 715
  history, 157, 217
  positive aspects, 683, 684, 692
Alcoholics
  nursing care, 689
Alcoholics Anonymous, 144, 173, 311, 317
Alcoholism. *See* Alcohol abuse
Alternatives to drug abuse, 283, 284, 289, 299
Amphetamines, 207, 542, 673, 676
Analgesics, 532, 556, 580
Angel dust, 200, 624, 638, 639
Antagonists, narcotic, 529, 532, 545, 566, 580, 589
Aphrodisiacs, 162
Aviation and drug use, 77